Responsible Manufacturing
Issues Pertaining to Sustainability

T0382816

Responsible Manufacturing
Issues Pertaining to Sustainability

Edited by
Ammar Y. Alqahtani, Elif Kongar,
Kishore K. Pochampally and Surendra M. Gupta

CRC Press
Taylor & Francis Group
Boca Raton London New York

CRC Press is an imprint of the
Taylor & Francis Group, an **informa** business

CRC Press
Taylor & Francis Group
6000 Broken Sound Parkway NW, Suite 300
Boca Raton, FL 33487-2742

First issued in paperback 2020

© 2019 by Taylor & Francis Group, LLC
CRC Press is an imprint of Taylor & Francis Group, an Informa business

No claim to original U.S. Government works

ISBN-13: 978-0-8153-7507-4 (hbk)
ISBN-13: 978-0-367-78024-1 (pbk)

Visit the Taylor & Francis Web site at
http://www.taylorandfrancis.com

and the CRC Press Web site at
http://www.crcpress.com

Dedicated to our families:

Nojood Alqahtani, Yahya Alqahtani, Farah Alqahtani, and Lana Alqahtani

Ammar Y. Alqahtani

Mert Ozan Bahtiyar and Derin Ata Bahtiyar

Elif Kongar

Seema Dasgupta and Sai Pochampally

Kishore K. Pochampally

Sharda Gupta, Monica Gupta, and Neil M. Gupta

Surendra M. Gupta

Contents

Contents

Preface

Responsible manufacturing deals with developing strategies and methodologies for competitive and agile manufacturing technologies in response to evolving environmental sustainability and customer needs, as well as legislative and ethical standards, while maintaining profitability. Responsible manufacturing has become an obligation to the environment and to society itself, enforced primarily by the customer perspective and governmental regulations on environmental issues. This is mainly driven by the escalating deterioration of the environment: for example, diminishing raw material resources, overflowing waste sites, and increasing levels of pollution. Responsible manufacturing involves integrating environmental thinking into new product development, including design, material selection, manufacturing processes, and delivery of the product to the consumers, plus the end-of-life management of the product after its useful life. Responsible manufacturing-related issues have found a large following in industry and academia, who aim to find solutions to the problems that are arising in this newly emerged research area. Problems are widespread, including those related to the life cycle of products, disassembly, material recovery, remanufacturing, and pollution prevention. This book addresses several important issues faced by strategic, tactical, and operation planners of responsible manufacturing, using efficient models in a variety of decision-making situations and providing easy-to-use mathematical and/or simulation modeling–based solution methodologies for the majority of the issues.

The book is organized into 16 chapters. The first chapter, by Kalayci, Avinc, Yavas, and Coskun, presents information regarding responsible design and manufacturing in the textile industry. The information presented in the chapter is timely because the textile industry is considered to be one of the largest polluters of the environment due to the use of chemicals, harmful substances, dyes and pigments, and so on in all its stages of processing, from raw material to finished product. The second chapter, by Ilgin, proposes an integrated design for remanufacturing (DFR) approach, which considers the interactions among the various DFR criteria. First, interpretive structural modeling and analytical network process are employed to determine the weights of DFR criteria. Then, the design characteristics that best satisfy the DFR criteria are determined using House of Quality. The author also presents an application of the proposed approach in the automotive industry. In the third chapter, Joshi and Gupta use heuristic techniques to estimate the disassembly yields from end-of-life products to fulfill the demand for products, components, and materials. The purpose is to determine the best product design that will maximize the disassembly yields and minimize the costs.

The fourth chapter, by Polat, Ünal, Polat, and Güngör, integrates forward and reverse logistics networks for solving the hub location problem of an electrolytic wire company to eliminate wastes and optimize the logistical processes. The authors use a mixed integer linear programming model to find the solution. In the subsequent chapter (Chapter 5), Duman, Kongar, and Gupta apply Grey-analytical hierarchy process and Grey-technique for order preference by similarity to ideal solution to rank order the suppliers to a U.S.-based dispensing system manufacturing company.

Chapter 6, by McGovern and Gupta, compares assembly and disassembly lines qualitatively and quantitatively. In addition, the mathematical similarity between them is reviewed along with a single set of formulae that can be shared between both assembly and disassembly lines. Chapter 7, by Kinoshita, Yamada, and Gupta, proposes and compares two types of bi-objective environmentally friendly and economical disassembly parts selection by using goal programming to maximize the CO_2 savings or recycling rates while minimizing the recycling costs.

In Chapter 8, Korugan classifies the nature of uncertainties that arise in a remanufacturing process and discusses relevant methods for developing better design and control methods at an operational level. Chapter 9, by Aksoy and Gupta, examines the level of buffering and production capacity decisions to cope with uncertainties through the various stages of a remanufacturing system. The authors consider a hybrid system in which manufacturing and remanufacturing operations occur together. The hybrid system is modeled as an open queueing network to determine the system output rate, expected total cost, expected work-in-process inventory, and expected processing time. In Chapter 10, Ishigaki, Yamada, and Gupta present a manufacturing–remanufacturing model with cannibalization and its effect on market expansion. The authors determine the optimal discount rates and the starting period to sell the remanufactured products using numerical examples. Chapter 11, by Pandit and Gupta, describes some of the matters surrounding the issues of fraud and warranties around remanufacturing. The authors suggest an approach to mitigate fraud against the warranty provider.

In Chapter 12, Zhou and Gupta offer insights into pricing low-technology-level new products and high-technology-level remanufactured products using a pricing model that highlights product generation difference. The authors develop theoretical models using a basic single-channel demand diffusion function and then extend them by taking a separate sale-channel into account. This leads to optimal prices for the two types of products over time.

Chapter 13, by Alqahtani, Gupta, and Nakashima, studies and scrutinizes the impact of using the Internet of Things on offering warranties for remanufactured products. The authors suggest a methodology that simultaneously minimizes the cost incurred by the remanufacturers and maximizes the confidence of the consumers in buying remanufacturing products. In Chapter 14, Tozanli, Kongar, and Gupta analyze the integration of Industry 4.0 and the supplier selection problem using a numerical example. The example considers a disassembly-to-order system, which is modeled as a multi-criteria decision-making problem and is solved using a goal programming model.

Chapter 15, by Dulman and Gupta, proposes embedding sensors into washing machines and monitoring them through their life cycle as a means of accessing information about their condition. This information can be used to improve the efficiency of maintenance as well as the disassembly and inspection operations of end-of-life washing machines. The authors tested their assertion using a simulation study, in which the results demonstrated that sensor-embedded systems performed significantly better than regular systems in terms of maintenance cost, disassembly cost, inspection cost, and end-of-life profit.

In the final chapter (Chapter 16), Pochampally and Gupta show how to predict the efficiency of a collection center in a reverse supply chain using logistic regression. The authors present two examples. In the first example, a model is built to predict the probability of on-time delivery based on the number of trucks owned by the collection center. In the second example, the probability of a collecting center meeting specifications is estimated based on the age of the sorting equipment used by the collection center.

This work would not have been possible without the devotion and commitment of the contributing authors. They have been very patient in preparing their manuscripts. We would also like to express our appreciation to Taylor and Francis and its staff for providing seamless support in making it possible to complete this timely and important volume.

Ammar Y. Alqahtani, PhD
Jeddah, Saudi Arabia

Elif Kongar, PhD
Bridgeport, Connecticut

Kishore K. Pochampally, PhD
Manchester, New Hampshire

Surendra M. Gupta, PhD, PE
Boston, Massachusetts

Editors

Ammar Y. Alqahtani, PhD, is an Assistant Professor of Industrial Engineering at King Abdulaziz University in Jeddah, Saudi Arabia. He received his BS degree with first honors from the Industrial Engineering Department of King Abdulaziz University, Jeddah, Saudi Arabia, in May 2008. Being awarded a full scholarship by the King Abdulaziz University (KAU), he received his MS degree in Industrial Engineering from Cullen College of Engineering, University of Houston in 2012. He received his PhD degree in Industrial Engineering from Northeastern University, Boston, in 2017. He has been employed as a faculty member by King Abdulaziz University since December 2008. His research interests are in the areas of environmentally conscious manufacturing, product recovery, reverse logistics, closed-loop supply chains (CLSC), sustainable operations and sustainability, simulation and statistical analysis, and modeling with applications in CLSC and multiple lifecycle products. He has coauthored several technical papers published in edited books, journals, and international conference proceedings.

Elif Kongar, PhD, is a Professor of Technology Management and Mechanical Engineering and chair of the Technology Management Department at the School of Engineering, University of Bridgeport (UB). During her tenure at UB, she established research and graduate concentrations and coursework in several areas, including simulation and modeling, service management and engineering, and economic and environmental sustainability. Her main area of research is economically and environmentally sustainable waste recovery systems and operations. She also works on projects that aim at increasing female participation in engineering disciplines and at improving K–12 science, technology, engineering, and mathematics (STEM) and undergraduate and graduate engineering education programs. Prof. Kongar received her BS and MS degrees in Industrial Engineering from Yildiz Technical University and her PhD degree in Industrial Engineering from Northeastern University. Before joining the University of Bridgeport, Dr. Kongar was a visiting researcher in the Center for Industrial Ecology at Yale University. She also served as the coordinator and lecturer of the Logistics certificate program at Yildiz Technical University, where she held an assistant professor position.

Kishore K. Pochampally, PhD, is a Professor of Quantitative Studies, Operations and Project Management at Southern New Hampshire University (SNHU) in Manchester (NH). He also conducts corporate workshops in lean six sigma quality and project management. His prior academic experience is as a post-doctoral fellow at Massachusetts Institute of Technology (MIT) in Cambridge (MA). He holds graduate degrees (MS and PhD) in industrial engineering from Northeastern University in Boston (MA) and an undergraduate degree (BE) in mechanical engineering from the National Institute of Technology in India. His research interests are in the areas of six sigma quality management and quantitative decision-making. He has authored a number of technical papers for international journals and conference proceedings, and his research work has been cited by other researchers on six continents. He has published three books, titled *Strategic Planning Models for Reverse and Closed-Loop Supply Chains, Six Sigma Case Studies with Minitab®*, and *Reliability Analysis with Minitab®*. He has been nominated twice for the teaching excellence award at SNHU. He is also a Six Sigma Black Belt (American Society for Quality) and a Project Management Professional (PMP®).

Surendra M. Gupta, PhD, is a Professor of Mechanical and Industrial Engineering and the director of the Laboratory for Responsible Manufacturing at Northeastern University in Boston, Massachusetts. He received his BE in Electronics Engineering from Birla Institute of Technology and Science, an MBA from Bryant University, and MSIE and PhD in Industrial Engineering from Purdue University. He is a registered professional engineer in the state of Massachusetts. Dr. Gupta's research interests span the areas of production/manufacturing systems and operations research. He is mostly interested in environmentally conscious manufacturing, reverse and closed-loop supply chains, disassembly modeling, and remanufacturing. He has authored or coauthored 12 books and over 600 technical papers published in edited books, journals, and international conference proceedings. His publications have received over 12,250 citations (with an h-index of 56) from researchers all over the world in journals, proceedings, books, and dissertations. He has traveled to all seven continents and presented his work at international conferences on six continents. Dr. Gupta has taught over 150 courses in such areas as operations research, inventory theory, queuing theory, engineering economy, supply chain management, and production planning and control. Among the many recognitions received, he is the recipient of an outstanding research award and an outstanding industrial engineering professor award (in recognition of teaching excellence) from Northeastern University, as well as a national outstanding doctoral dissertation advisor award.

Contributors

H. Kıvanç Aksoy
Department of Statistics
Eskişehir Osmangazi University
Eskişehir, Turkey

Ammar Y. Alqahtani
Department of Industrial
  Engineering
Faculty of Engineering
King Abdulaziz University
Jeddah, Saudi Arabia

Ozan Avinc
Department of Textile
  Engineering
Faculty of Engineering
Pamukkale University
Denizli, Turkey

Semih Coskun
Department of Industrial
  Engineering
Faculty of Engineering
Pamukkale University
Denizli, Turkey

Mehmet Talha Dulman
Department of Mechanical and
  Industrial Engineering
Northeastern University
Boston, Massachusetts

Gazi Murat Duman
Department of Technology
  Management
University of Bridgeport
Bridgeport, Connecticut

Aşkıner Güngör
Department of Industrial Engineering
Faculty of Engineering
Pamukkale University
Denizli, Turkey

Surendra M. Gupta
Laboratory of Responsible
  Manufacturing
Department of Mechanical and
  Industrial Engineering
Northeastern University
Boston, Massachusetts

Mehmet Ali Ilgin
Department of Industrial
  Engineering
Manisa Celal Bayar University
Yunusemre, Manisa, Turkey

Aya Ishigaki
Department of Industrial
  Administration
Tokyo University of Science
Noda, Chiba, Japan

Aditi D. Joshi
Department of Mechanical and
  Industrial Engineering
Northeastern University
Boston, Massachusetts

Ece Kalayci
Department of Textile Engineering
Faculty of Engineering
Pamukkale University
Denizli, Turkey

Yuki Kinoshita
Department of Informatics
The University of
    Electro-Communications
Chofu, Tokyo, Japan

Elif Kongar
Departments of Mechanical
    Engineering and Technology
    Management
University of Bridgeport
Bridgeport, Connecticut

Aybek Korugan
Department of Industrial
    Engineering
Boğaziçi University
Bebek, Istanbul, Turkey

Seamus M. McGovern
Department of Mathematical Sciences
Bentley University
Waltham, Massachusetts

Kenichi Nakashima
School of Social Sciences
Waseda University
Shinjuku-ku, Tokyo, Japan

Aditya Pandit
Department of Mechanical and
    Industrial Engineering
Northeastern University
Boston, Massachusetts

Kishore K. Pochampally
Department of Management Science
Southern New Hampshire University
Manchester, New Hampshire

Leyla Özgür Polat
Department of Industrial Engineering,
    Faculty of Engineering
Pamukkale University
Denizli, Turkey

Olcay Polat
Department of Industrial
    Engineering
Faculty of Engineering
Pamukkale University
Denizli, Turkey

Ozden Tozanli
Department of Technology
    Management
School of Engineering
University of Bridgeport
Bridgeport, Connecticut

Ömer Faruk Ünal
Department of Industrial
    Engineering
Faculty of Engineering
Pamukkale University
Denizli, Turkey

Tetsuo Yamada
Department of Informatics
The University of
    Electro-Communications
Chofu, Tokyo, Japan

Arzu Yavas
Department of Textile Engineering
Faculty of Engineering
Pamukkale University
Denizli, Turkey

Liangchuan Zhou
Department of Mechanical and
    Industrial Engineering
Northeastern University
Boston, Massachusetts

1

Responsible Textile Design and Manufacturing: Environmentally Conscious Material Selection

Ece Kalayci, Ozan Avinc, Arzu Yavas, and Semih Coskun

CONTENTS

1.1 Introduction

The necessity and desire for clothing in ancient years has today turned into a huge textile industry that not only produces clothes but also has many different applications in our homes and in different fields such as construction, medical, agriculture, aviation, sports, and so on. The production rates of textile materials are increasing daily due to the growing world population, changes in consumption, and fashion trends. This rapid increase in production boosts the demand for raw materials and causes the consumption of tremendous amounts of clean water and energy resources. Chemical wastes and greenhouse gases resulting from chemical reactions harm the environment in many different ways, such as contributing to potential climate change and causing global warming (Fletcher, 2013; Muthu et al., 2012). Therefore, it cannot be denied that textile manufacturing processes and by-products may have harmful effects on the biophysical environment. For example, cotton and polyester, which are the most commonly used textile fibers, have critical problems in their life cycles (Waite, 2009; Shangnan Shui, 2013). Cotton cultivation needs a tremendous amount of clean water, leading to soil salinization. Moreover, many different chemicals, such as pesticides, insecticides, and so on, are required for cotton production to avoid various different pests and insects. Obviously, these kinds of negative effects result in some environmental issues. For instance, unsustainable and unrenewable petroleum is used to produce polyester (Sharma, 2013; Petry, 2008; Hayes, 2001). Synthetic fibers are oil-based materials, and the raw material of these fibers is unsustainable and on the verge of depletion due to limited petroleum reserves. Moreover, the waste accumulation problem of synthetic fibers is another important pollution problem. Therefore, to overcome all these possible negative effects of textile manufacturing on the environment and for a sustainable future, the responsible manufacturing of textile products is crucial.

Environmentally conscious design and manufacturing in textile production comprises the selection and use of sustainable, renewable, and biodegradable textile materials; reusability; recyclability; the use of new environmental textile production and finishing techniques leading to lower consumption of water, chemicals, and energy; and finally, using natural or natural-based auxiliary substances instead of synthetic chemicals, leading to a more environmentally friendly and sustainable world (Fletcher, 2013; Muthu et al., 2012; Maia et al., 2012).

Hence, important related issues such as environmentally conscious design, environmentally conscious material selection in textile production, assessment tools in environmentally conscious manufacturing (ECM), and innovative options in environmentally conscious textile manufacturing are discussed in detail in the following sections.

1.2 Environmentally Conscious Design

ECM is a system that involves various green approaches for addressing design (Desai and Mital, 2017), recycling (Lambert and Gupta, 2005; Igarashi et al., 2016), and other issues (Gungor and Gupta, 1999). Algorithms, models, and software (Kalayci and Gupta, 2013a; Kalayci and Gupta, 2013b) are required for efficient and responsible manufacturing. ECM has become an obligation for every industry as a result of increasing environmental awareness and imperative eco-friendly regulations. Ilgin and Gupta (2010) have classified ECM into four main issues: product design, reverse and closed-loop supply chains, remanufacturing, and disassembly.

It is necessary to carry out all operations, from the selection of materials to the final product, with environmental awareness to realize environmentally friendly textile production. It is also required to create a cycle in which the product can be recycled, reused, or remanufactured at the end of its lifetime. Conventional textile product design aims for a product with lower cost, higher functionality, and easier manufacturability. However, environmental concerns are forcing textile manufacturers and consumers to find greener ways to manufacture and to use textiles responsibly.

Traditional product development has the goal of achieving advancements in design in terms of cost, functionality, and efficiency. However, environmental issues are forcing designers to show special consideration for environmental aspects in various design processes. It is possible for product designers to make environment-friendly design choices, and a number of methodologies, such as Design for X (Veerakamolmal and Gupta, 2000), life cycle analysis (LCA) (Grote et al., 2007), and material selection (Isaacs and Gupta, 1997) have been developed (Ilgin and Gupta, 2010).

During the design of a textile product, designers should

- Consider the primary features that consumers may look for in the product
- Understand how consumers may use the product
- Follow developments in textile science and technology by collaborating with scientists
- Estimate the process steps required during the manufacturing of the product
- Question the applicability of alternative sources and methods

From cradle to grave, there are many negative social and environmental impacts arising at different stages of apparel production in the textile industry. High-volume production and low-price selling of apparel are strengthening these impacts with advancements in fast fashion (Steinberger et al., 2009).

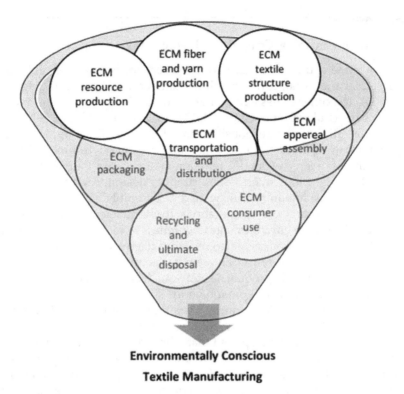

Environmentally Conscious

Textile Manufacturing

FIGURE 1.1
Environmentally conscious textile manufacturing. ECM: environmentally conscious manufacturing.

Apparel has a complicated production chain, including fiber, yarn, and textile production; assembly; packaging; transportation and distribution; retailing; and consumer use, recycling, and ultimate disposal (Lewis and Chen, 2006). A responsibly manufactured textile product should be environmentally conscious not only in terms of design, but also in material selection and manufacturing (Figure 1.1).

Material selection in textile production plays a critical role in environmentally conscious design and manufacturing.

1.3 Environmentally Conscious Material Selection in Textile Production

Mechanical properties, processability, and cost are the main parameters that affect material selection. In recent years, environmental factors such as recyclability, reusability, and biodegradability have started to affect material selection because of environmental awareness.

Material selection is the first step in product design and production. Environmentally conscious material selection is required for responsible textile design and manufacturing. Textile fiber is the smallest element of a textile structure. Yarn is produced by combining the fibers using various techniques called the *spinning process* and used to obtain two different types of textile structure by knitting and weaving. A nonwoven textile structure is obtained by entangling and bonding fibers mechanically, thermally, or chemically without the need for a yarn structure.

Textile fibers are mainly classified into natural fibers and man-made (chemical) fibers. Natural fibers are obtained from natural sources such as plants, animals, or minerals. The origin of the natural fibers affects the sub-classification of natural fibers. Plant fibers such as cotton, flax, jute, hemp, and so on are cellulosic natural fibers. Animal fibers (wool, mohair, silk, and so on) are protein fibers, which are obtained from different animals such as sheep, goats, camels, rabbits, caterpillars, and so on. Mineral fibers are another natural fiber class, which includes asbestos. Man-made fibers are subgrouped into regenerated fibers and synthetic fibers. Regenerated fibers are produced from a natural base material such as cellulose or protein. Viscose, modal, lyocell, casein, and soybean fibers are examples of regenerated fibers. Synthetic fibers are produced entirely from chemical substances, unlike regenerated fibers derived from natural substances. Synthetic fibers are mostly petroleum-derived fibers. Polyester, polyamide, polypropylene, and acrylic are examples of this fiber class.

Eco-friendly material selection plays an important role in the manufacturing of sustainable textile products (Islam and Khan, 2014). Environmentally conscious textile production studies showed that obtaining raw materials for textile products may potentially create environmental burdens for all classes of fibers. The magnitude of the environmental impact due to textile fiber use mainly relates to and depends on the fiber type. Therefore, natural fibers, regenerated fibers, synthetic fibers, recyclable/reusable fibers, biodegradable fibers, organic natural fiber production, and alternative cotton fiber programs (better cotton, cleaner cotton, and naturally colored cotton) are discussed in this respect in the following sections.

1.3.1 Natural Fibers

Natural fibers have an important role in responsible textile manufacturing, mainly due to their renewable, biodegradable, and carbon-neutral character. *Carbon-neutral* means that the amount of carbon dioxide produced is equal to the amount of carbon dioxide absorbed. Natural fibers are completely decomposed as a result of the biological activity of microorganisms such as bacteria, fungi, and other biological agents (100% biodegradable) at the end of their life cycle. Composted natural fibers enrich soil structure and can be incinerated with no harmful emissions. Natural fibers mainly produce organic waste during their processing, and these organic residues can be also used in alternative applications such as generating electricity or producing ecological materials. However, some natural fibers, such as cotton, require a huge amount of irrigation and pesticides during their agricultural production. Organic cotton, organic linen, bamboo fiber, jute fiber, hemp fiber, pineapple fiber, alpaca fiber, and many others can be considered to be more eco-friendly textile fibers.

Natural bamboo fiber is obtained from fast-growing bamboo trees without the use of water, pesticides, or fertilizers. Natural bamboo fiber, with its eco-friendly farming, has great potential to be used as a sustainable textile fiber source. Moreover, bamboo fibers naturally exhibit outstanding fiber properties; for example, they are antibacterial, hypoallergenic, UV resistant, breathable, and cool (Özdemir and Tekoğlu, 2014).

Hemp fiber is one of the sustainable textile material sources for environmentally conscious textile processes. The hemp plant grows quickly and does not need pesticides or insecticides when growing, it improves the condition of the soil that it is grown in, and it needs very little water, unlike cotton (Anon, 2018; Gedik and Avinc, 2018). Moreover, hemp is a drought-resistant plant, and it can be grown in most climates. Hemp fiber is suitable for yarn and fabric production without the use of toxic chemicals (Sharma, 2013; Anon, 2018). Hemp fibers are robust, durable, antibacterial, UV protective, and resistant to tearing. Hemp fibers are naturally long fibers, and this characteristic makes them processable, especially by spinning (Arık et al., 2018).

Nettle fiber is another natural fiber that does not need chemicals such as pesticides and herbicides during its agricultural production. The nettle (brennessel) plant is naturally resistant to vermin and parasites. Nettle fiber is stronger than cotton fiber and finer than linen fiber. It is an alternative option for sustainable material selection for responsible textile manufacturing (Sharma, 2013; Kurban et al., 2016; Yavaş et al., 2017).

Flax is one of the oldest agricultural plants in human history, and it is mostly farmed for its seeds. Linen (flax) fibers are obtained from the stalks of the flax plant (*Linum usitatissimum* L.), which remain as agricultural waste after seed cultivation. Linen fiber is stronger than cotton fiber. The tensile strength of wet linen fibers is 20% higher than that of dry linen fibers; therefore, linen fiber products are resistant to mechanical effects in wet processes (Özdemir and Tekoğlu, 2014).

The use of hemp, linen, and nettle fibers dates back to ancient times. Jute fiber is another historical fiber that has been used for thousands of years. The properties and structure of jute fiber are similar to those of hemp fiber, and it also has outstanding potential for the sustainable future of the textile industry. Ramie fiber, which is one of the strongest natural fibers, can be used as an alternative sustainable, eco-friendly textile material during environmentally conscious textile design and manufacturing.

Pineapple fibers are an alternative eco-friendly textile fiber source, which is also obtained from agricultural waste. Pineapple fibers, also called *pina fibers*, are extracted from the leaves of the pineapple plant by hand scraping, decortication, or retting (Kalayci et al., 2016a). Pineapple fiber production is an ecological solution for the tons of pineapple leaf residue produced by pineapple fruit farming. There are many other kinds of ecological fibers produced from agricultural waste; banana, abaca, sisal, and raffia fibers are just a few examples of these natural fibers.

1.3.2 Regenerated Fibers

Regenerated fibers are produced from natural polymers such as cellulose (from eucalyptus, pine, bamboo, etc.), proteins (from soy bean, corn, milk, peanut, etc.) (Waite, 2009), alginic acid, rubber, and so on. Viscose fiber is the most common cellulose-based regenerated fiber. It is mostly produced from the cellulose of farmed tree bark. Lyocell, modal, acetate, and triacetate fibers are the other cellulose-based regenerated fiber options. Regenerated bamboo fibers are also available. They are produced from the cellulose of bamboo trees.

Another regenerated fiber designated as sustainable is milk (casein) fiber obtained from milk protein (casein). A solution is obtained from the residual protein with the help of milk bioengineering techniques, which take in water and separate the slip. This solution is passed through a spinneret using a wet spinning method and converted into a textile fiber. Milk fibers exhibit antibacterial and antifungal properties as well as a hygroscopic character (Sharma, 2013; Sevgisunar, 2015; Sevgisunar et al., 2015).

Soybean protein fiber is another protein-based regenerated fiber. Soybean fibers, obtained from the waste materials of soybeans used in the food industry, are suitable for organic production and the manufacture of soft and comfortable products (Avinc and Yavas, 2017; Yıldırım et al., 2015; Yildirim et al., 2014). Soybean fibers, with their soft and attractive handle, are an alternative to cashmere fibers, which cause severe damage to grasslands during their production (Yildirim et al., 2014). Soybean protein fiber production is sustainable, soybean protein fibers are biodegradable, and non-toxic auxiliaries and additional agents are used in fiber production. Moreover, semi-finished soybean protein fibers can be recovered and reused (Yildirim et al., 2012a; Avinc et al., 2012b).

Most high-performance fibers are petroleum-based synthetic fibers, such as aramid fiber (Hearle, 2001), polybenzimidazole (PBI) fiber (Kalayci et al., 2014), polybenzobisoxole (PBO) fiber (Kalayci et al., 2015c; Hearle, 2001), polyether ether ketone (PEEK) fiber (Kalayci et al., 2017), polypyridobisimidazole (PIPD) fiber (Kalayci et al., 2015b), polyphenylene sulfide (PPS) fiber (Kalayci et al., 2016b), and ultra-high molecular weight polyethylene (UHMWPE) fiber

(Kalayci et al., 2015e; Kalayci et al., 2016c). These fibers are the predominantly used high-performance fibers in the textile industry.

However, these fibers may be harmful to the environment during their life cycle due to their petroleum-based structure. For that reason, researchers are investigating alternative natural or natural-based fibers with high-performance properties. Spider silk is the most commonly known natural protein-based high-performance fiber. Although natural spider silk exhibits extraordinary features, it is nearly impossible to farm and manufacture spider silk due to the cannibalistic characteristics of some kinds of spider (Eisoldt et al., 2011; Bunsell, 2009; Kalayci et al., 2015d). Therefore, spider silk is artificially produced using biotechnological spider silk recombinant protein production (Avinc et al., 2015; Chung et al., 2012). Hagfish slime fiber is another natural protein fiber that exhibits high-performance properties. The hagfish is a primitive sea animal that lives in burrows on the sea floor and releases a slime that contains thousands of fibers to defend itself when threatened (Kalayci et al., 2015d; Kalayci et al., 2015a). The production of hagfish slime fibers is also difficult, as with spider silk, due to the living conditions of the hagfish. Artificial hagfish slime fibers can be produced from regenerated proteins by biotechnological hagfish recombinant protein production (Fudge et al., 2010; Fudge et al., 2014).

Transgenic protein fiber production is not limited to spider silk and hagfish slime fibers. Honeybee silk protein fiber and mussel byssus fiber are alternative regenerated protein fibers produced using biotechnologically recombined proteins (Avinc et al., 2015; Reddy and Yang, 2014; Suhre et al., 2014).

1.3.3 Synthetic Fibers

When the annual consumption of textile fibers is examined, it is observed that the use of synthetic fibers is much more widespread than that of natural fibers. In particular, polyester fibers account for about 60% of the world's fiber production (Shangnan Shui, 2013). Most synthetic fibers are petroleum-based fibers produced from limited oil resources. These fibers are also threatening the environment with their waste accumulation due to their non-biodegradable structure. However, polyester fiber, which is a widely used synthetic fiber, has recyclable properties. Most synthetic fiber companies are now employing the recovery of garments, textiles, and post-consumer and post-industrial waste for recycling into new fibers, and some well-known companies around the world have begun using these processes to reduce the environmental impact of the garment industry (Hayes, 2001).

Polylactic acid (PLA) fiber is an aliphatic polyester based on lactic acid polyester that can be derived from 100% renewable resources, such as corn. PLA polymer is produced from agricultural resources, and it can be easily degraded (Avinc and Khoddami, 2010; Avinc and Khoddami, 2009; Hasani et al., 2017;

Khoddami et al., 2011; Avinc, 2011a). PLA fiber is like a bridge between natural and synthetic fibers; it incorporates many advantages of both natural and synthetic fibers. PLA fiber is renewable, non-polluting, and compostable, just like natural fibers; also, it is less environmentally costly than many of the recyclable polymers and biodegradable thermoplastics (Hasani et al., 2017; Avinc et al., 2011; Avinc, 2011b).

Poly trimethylene terephthalate (PTT) fiber is an aromatic polyester fiber, also known as *elastic polyester* due to its good elastic features (Yildirim et al., 2012b). In addition to its good resilience and elastic recovery properties, PTT fiber can be easily dyed at low temperatures. PTT fiber has great potential for use in sport textiles, carpets, garment textiles, and medical textiles (Yildirim et al., 2012c). PTT polymer is obtained by means of a polymerization reaction between DMT (dimethyl terephthalate) and PDO (1,3-propanediol). PDO can also be produced using a fermentation process (a biochemical method) as well as a synthetic chemical process. In the biochemical method, PDO is produced from bio-based corn glucose using biosynthesis. Thus, bio-based PTT fibers can be manufactured using PDO that is biologically derived from corn glucose (Yildirim et al., 2012b). Bio-based PTT fibers are commercially available, and these fibers can be categorized as sustainable textile fibers. It is reported that bio-based PTT fiber production consumes 30% less energy and produces 63% less greenhouse gas emissions compared with an equal amount of nylon 6, whereas the production of bio-based PTT fiber uses 40% less energy and reduces greenhouse gas emissions by 56% compared with an equal amount of nylon 6,6 (DuPont). Moreover, bio-based PTT fiber products have the potential to be recycled by manufacturers, and LCA of bio-based PTT fibers shows that no catalysts containing any heavy metals are used in the polymerization, and no additional chemical treatments for stain resistance are required (Sorona, 2016).

1.3.4 Recyclable/Reusable Fibers

Polyester fiber is a synthetic fiber that is widely used in the textile industry, and it has recyclable properties. For example, polyester yarns can be produced from 100% recycled plastic bottles by applying mechanical processes instead of chemical pathways. It has been reported that these yarns can be used in many different areas, such as fashion, sportswear, underwear, medical garments, and other clothes and furnishings, under the leadership of world-famous textile brands (Sharma, 2013; Hayes, 2001).

Another example of an eco-material is the so-called *Naoron* fabric, which is made of paper pulp yet has a soft, flexible, and robust structure. This fabric has been produced as an alternative ecological product for various use areas. It is animal friendly, and there is no need for chemicals to be used in artificial leather production. Made from recycled polyester and paper pulp, Naoron is a highly sustainable material thanks to its waterproof textile surface (Sharma, 2013).

Another fiber produced using waste materials is commercial Cocona fiber. These fibers, which are produced by the addition of natural ingredients to the polymer, are obtained using activated coconut shells (Anon, 2017). Woven, knitted, and nonwoven surfaces can be surface coated with different methods to produce light, comfortable, UV-resistant, breathable, and odor-adsorbing products. It has been described as an ideal fiber for underwear and sports textiles (Anon, 2017; Sharma, 2013).

1.3.5 Biodegradable Fibers

Biodegradation is the decomposition of a material as a result of the biological activity of microorganisms such as bacteria, fungi, and other biological agents. Biodegradable fibers can be broken down over time by microorganisms. All-natural fibers are biodegradable and sustainable, and therefore, they are commonly called *biofibers*. However, natural fiber production is not enough to meet the biodegradable and sustainable fiber requirements of the textile industry. Therefore, increasing the diversity of biodegradable synthetic fibers produced from renewable sources has become one of the primary goals of researchers to meet this demand.

Biodegradable fibers are mainly produced from biodegradable polymers, which can be generally classified into three basic categories: natural polysaccharides and biopolymers (cellulose, alginate, wool, silk, chitin, soybean protein), synthetic polymers (PLA, poly ε-caprolactone [PCL]), and polyesters produced by microorganisms (poly hydroxyalkanoate [PHB]) (Curteza, 2015; Hasani et al., 2013; Avinc, 2011b).

1.3.6 Organic Natural Fiber Production

Organic agriculture is an agricultural system that prohibits the application of agricultural medicines, artificial fertilizers, hormones, antibiotics, and harmful food additives. It controls every stage, from production to consumption, and produces healthy agricultural products in the best way using natural resources. Organic cotton fiber has been identified as a fiber that is grown using organic agriculture, processed with green methods, and certified according to organic standards. Organic cotton production is accepted as more sustainable than conventional cotton production, since there are some disadvantages, such as overuse of pesticides and similar crop protection products, during conventional cotton farming. Moreover, organic cotton farming also removes the risk of health problems caused by chemical residues in traditional cotton production (Islam and Khan, 2014; Palamutcu, 2017).

Organic fiber production is used not only for cellulosic fibers, such as cotton and linen, but also for protein fibers, such as wool and silk. Organic wool fiber is produced without chemicals and insecticides according to certified organic standards for animal needs. In organic silk production, the caterpillars eat green leaves (mostly mulberry leaves) that are free from pesticides.

1.3.7 Alternative Cotton Programs: Better Cotton, Cleaner Cotton, Naturally Colored Cotton

There are some commonly known alternative programs to organic cotton production. Better cotton, cleaner cotton, and naturally colored cotton fiber production are examples of these alternative approaches.

It is known that the coloration process is one of the most non-eco-friendly textile processes in textile manufacturing. For that reason, naturally colored natural textile material is valuable for responsible textile manufacturing (Figure 1.2). Organic cotton studies showed that it is possible to farm naturally colored cotton fiber without the necessity for wet textile processing (Kanık, 2008). In this way, much more ecological textile production can be achieved.

1.4 Sustainability Measurements and Assessment Tools in Environmentally Conscious Manufacturing

There are many different standards, tests, regulations, and tools aiming to measure and determine constraints for more sustainable and environmentally friendly textile products and production. In this section, some of the

FIGURE 1.2
Naturally colored organic cotton fiber, yarn, and knitted fabric samples.

important sustainability measurements and assessment tools in environmentally conscious textile manufacturing are summarized.

1.4.1 Life Cycle Analysis (LCA) of Textile Materials

LCA is a method for assessing the environmental impact of a product from "cradle to grave" (Ilgin and Gupta, 2010; Gupta and Lambert, 2007). LCA is also known as *eco-balance* and *cradle-to-grave analysis*. This technique is used to evaluate the environmental impact of a product by considering all the manufacturing stages, from raw material extraction through material processing, manufacturing, distribution, use, repair and maintenance, and disposal or recycling (Figure 1.3). Most researchers use LCA as a tool to evaluate the environmental impact of product design and production (Ilgin and Gupta, 2010). The procedures of LCA are part of the International Organization for Standardization (ISO) 14000 environmental management standards in ISO 14040:2006 and 14044:2006. (ISO 14044 replaced earlier versions of ISO 14041 to ISO 14043.)

Even though the textile industry is one of the largest consumer-intensive industries in the world, until recently, responsible manufacturing methodologies have not been given much importance. The application of ECM methodologies is required in the textile industry as much as in other industries. LCA has an important role in environmentally friendly textile manufacturing. It can help to avoid a narrow outlook on ECM by evaluating the potential impacts associated with identified material inputs and environmental releases. LCA can also help to provide interpretation of the results to make a more informed decision. Therefore, many researchers

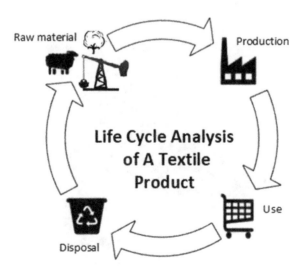

FIGURE 1.3
Life cycle analysis of a textile product.

and manufacturers focus on the LCA of various textile structures from raw material to the final product. Cotton and polyester are the most widely used fiber sources in the textile industry, and cotton is the most widely used natural fiber source. Hence, LCA of cotton fibers has been a primary research area for researchers and global cotton producers.

LCAs of organic cotton fibers were evaluated in a project that was funded by leading companies of the textile industry (International, 2014). Global warming potential, soil erosion potential, acidification potential, water consumption, and energy demand were evaluated using LCA methodology. In this study, potential impact savings of organic cotton were compared with conventionally grown cotton (per 1000 kg cotton fiber). It was determined that organic cotton reduced global warming potential, acidification potential, soil erosion potential, water consumption, and non-renewable energy demand by 46%, 70%, 26%, 91%, and 62%, respectively (International, 2014).

Numerous studies have examined the LCA of cotton fibers. LCA studies for the textile industry have been mainly focused on cotton and its end-uses due to the dominant role of cotton fiber in the textile industry. For instance, Gungor et al. (2009) analyzed the life cycle performance of a bathrobe using LCA (Gungor et al., 2009). Although life cycle assessment (LCA) of wool fibers have not been adequately studied as much as cotton fibers, life cycle of wool fiber is also another topic under research.

Cardoso (2013) investigated LCA of wool and cotton products. The life cycle stages were characterized as sheep farming, scouring of wool, and mechanical and chemical processes for dyed yarn production for wool, and as cotton farming, ginning, and mechanical and chemical processes during dyed cotton yarn production for cotton (Cardoso, 2013). Water and energy consumption, air and soil emissions, and solid waste production were evaluated using LCA in the production of wool and cotton textiles (Cardoso, 2013). It was indicated that cotton has greater impacts on freshwater eutrophication, marine eutrophication, freshwater ecotoxicity, and water resource depletion in the best-case scenario.

Van der Velden et al. (2014) investigated the environmental burdens of textile structures with cotton, polyester, nylon, acrylic, and elastane fiber, aiming to determine which fiber and which life cycle stage have the biggest impact on the environment (Van der Velden et al., 2014). It was stated in their study that a specified yarn thickness was required for an accurate LCA. Spinning and weaving processes had relatively higher burdens for textile structures with yarn thicknesses less than 100 dtex. It was also determined that knitting was better than weaving from the environmental point of view. LCA results showed that textile structures with acrylic and polyester fibers exhibited the lowest environmental burden, followed by elastane, nylon, and cotton fibers (Van der Velden et al., 2014).

The clothing production process may be the cleanest textile application step among all the textile manufacturing stages, especially when it is compared with wet processes. Altun (2012) studied the environmental burdens of the textile clothing production process (cutting, sewing, and packaging) using the cradle to grave methodology (LCA) (Altun, 2012). LCA showed that the sewing process makes the main contribution to nearly all impact categories considering energy consumption and environmental effects. It was also mentioned that dichloromethane-based chemicals used in the packaging step cause ozone layer depletion and photochemical oxidation (Altun, 2012).

Composite structures are increasingly becoming a new use area for textile fibers. Hence, some researchers have focused on LCA evaluations of fiber-reinforced composites to assess their environmental aspects. Song et al. (2009) evaluated LCA of fiber-reinforced composites manufactured using the pultrusion process, considering their energy consumption over their life cycle. In their study, economic input–output analysis and process analysis were combined in a hybrid model to determine the energy consumption of composite structures in automotive applications (Song et al., 2009).

Smart textiles and technical textiles are being developed daily, promising a bright future for the textile industry. Designers usually select engineering materials and advanced production methods to create functional products with enhanced properties. Even though technical textile applications are an emerging field within the textile industry, it is also starting to be affected by ECM approaches. Van der Velden et al. (2015) studied the LCA of a wearable smart textile device for ambulant medical therapy with the aim of creating a guide to empower designers in making sustainable design decisions. In this study, material selection was considered using the eco-cost approach and the LCA results of the original prototype design compared with several eco-redesign alternatives. Various alternatives were suggested for environmental improvement. Copper-based conductive yarns could be used in eco-designed prototypes instead of the silver-based conductive yarn used in the original prototype design. In addition, acrylic fiber could replace the wool fibers found in the original prototype design (Van der Velden et al., 2015).

1.4.2 Carbon Footprint in Textile Production

Carbon footprint, also named *carbon profile*, is a measure of the amount of carbon dioxide (CO_2) and other greenhouse gas emissions (methane, etc.) directly or indirectly resulting from all activities within a product's life cycle (Keskin et al., 2017; Rees and Wackernagel, 1996). Energy and raw material resources used during production are the main factors affecting carbon footprint. The textile industry meets its energy demands mostly in the form of natural gas, electricity, and fossil fuels, which cause emissions of atmospheric greenhouse gases (Thiry, 2011). Synthetic fibers, which are mainly obtained from oil, are necessary for the textile industry and release some gas emissions during their production. The reduction of energy consumption; the use of clean energy sources (wind, sun, water, etc.); and the choice of renewable, recyclable, or biodegradable raw materials are of utmost importance for production with a lower carbon footprint in the textile industry (Curteza, 2015).

1.4.3 Water Footprint in Textile Production

Water footprint is a measure of the total amount of water that is used directly and indirectly in the production and consumption processes of the products and services we use (Aldaya et al., 2012). The term *water footprint* was first introduced by Hoekstra in 2002 (Hoekstra and Hung, 2002). The water footprint can be calculated for an individual, a product, a country, or a business line (Curteza, 2015).

Careful consumption is essential in all areas where water resources are used, as the world population is constantly growing, and our natural resources are thought to be scanty. Water footprint has three components: blue, green, and gray water. The blue water footprint is the total amount of surface or underground freshwater resources used directly or indirectly in the production process of a good or service. These resources are particularly suitable for agricultural, industrial, and domestic purposes. The green water footprint refers to the consumption of green water sources such as rain water, and these sources are mainly used in agriculture, horticulture, and forestry activities. Moreover, the gray water footprint is the amount of fresh water needed to dilute the pollutant concentration in the waste water directly discharged or indirectly mixed into the water resources (e.g., lake, stream, sea water) to achieve a certain water quality criterion (Aldaya et al., 2012; Hoekstra et al., 2009).

The water footprint of a 300 gram t-shirt made of cotton is pretty high at about 2500 liters. It is reported that the annual water consumption of cotton products produced around the world is about 256 Gm^3, of which about 42% is blue water, 39% is green water, and 19% is gray water (Chapagain et al., 2006). The effect of this level of water consumption depends on the source of the water and when it is used. If the source of the water is a place with water scarcity, it can have very important consequences, and precautions may need to be taken.

1.4.4 Social Responsibility in Textile Production

Social factors are becoming more and more important in sustainability assessments, since the development, production, or sale of a product is virtually impossible without human beings. However, it is difficult to measure and quantify social factors, such as health and safety regulations for workers (Kokten and Avinc, 2014; Saiyed and Tiwari, 2004); labor conditions (Polat and Kalayci, 2016); employee rights and a living wage; avoiding forced labor and child workers (Nardinelli, 1980); non-discrimination; and training opportunities and freedom to be innovative (Curteza, 2015).

1.4.5 Sustainable Textile Production (STeP)

Sustainable textile production (STeP) by OEKO-TEX is a certification system from the International OEKO-TEX® Association to help brands and retailers evaluate and choose the sustainability of their suppliers (OEKO-TEX, 2018). The certification is available for enterprises operating in all stages of textile production, from fiber production, weaving mills, and knitting mills to finishing facilities and manufacturers of ready-made textile items. STeP certification provides a reliable and comprehensive analysis of the sustainable management system provided by a manufacturing facility through modular analysis of all relevant areas, such as chemical management, environmental performance and management, work safety, social responsibility, and quality management (OEKO-TEX, 2018; Curteza, 2015).

1.4.6 The Higg Index

The Higg Index is another sustainability tool, which focuses on measuring water and energy consumption, greenhouse gas emissions, waste, chemicals, and toxicity, aiming to assess the environmental and social impact of production (Radhakrishnan, 2015). The Higg Index was developed by the Sustainable Apparel Coalition (SAC), which aims to enhance the sustainable and social performance of the clothing and footwear industry. This tool is being used to identify risks and opportunities for sustainability and to get the best outcomes, to learn about sustainability impacts, to assess the company's position among companies of the same type, and to provide communication and business alliances and roadmap opportunities for possible improvements (Radhakrishnan, 2015; SAC, 2018).

1.4.7 Standards and Test Methods for Textile Sustainability

In recent years, increased environmental awareness has led to a significant enhancement in demand among consumers for environmentally friendly products and textile applications. Standards, regulations, and certificate programs have been defined both to meet consumer demand and to meet the requirements of responsible production. Especially, it is important for textile industry manufacturers to meet the requirements of eco parameters, aiming to be eco-friendly and sustainable during both the manufacturing and the consumption of the product.

1.4.7.1 Restricted Substance List (RSL) Testing

RSL testing is one of the tools that provide national and international regulations governing the levels of substances that are permitted in finished products in responsible home textile, apparel, and footwear manufacturing (AAFA, 2018). There are several substances that can be restricted during the production of textile products. The most prominent substances for RSL testing are formaldehyde, heavy metals, pesticide residues, polyaromatic hydrocarbons, polychlorinated biphenyls, carcinogenic dyes, allergenic disperse dyes, banned amines from azo dyes, chlorinated organic carriers, phthalates, flame retardants, chlorinated phenols, and orthophenylphenol (Fletcher, 2013; AAFA, 2018; Saranya and Amutha, 2018).

1.4.7.2 Consumer Product Safety Improvement Act (CPSIA)

The CPSIA requires independent testing of all the components of clothing for children under the age of 12 according to predetermined criteria. There are some requirements or limits for lead, flammability, and phthalates in CPSIA (Saranya and Amutha, 2018; US-CPSC, 2018).

1.4.7.3 Registration, Evaluation, Authorisation, and Restriction of Chemicals (REACH)

REACH is a European Community regulation, which applies to both chemicals and other substances that can be found in finished products (Curteza, 2015; Allwood et al., 2006).

1.4.7.4 Global Organic Textile Standard (GOTS)

GOTS defines specific environmental and social criteria for the complete manufacturing stages (spinning, weaving, knitting, pre-treatment, dyeing, printing, finishing, etc.) of textiles that are made from organic fibers, including the cultivation of cotton (Sangeetha et al., 2018). GOTS states specific requirements and limits for organic fiber production, product labeling, textile production stages, accessories, environmental management, waste water management, quality assurance system, end products, residues in accessories, textile dyes and pigments, textile auxiliaries, storage, packaging, transportation, and social compliance (GOTS, 2017; Curteza, 2015).

1.4.8 Eco Labels

Eco labeling is an evolving concept for commercial textile products. Especially in recent years, eco labels have been developed that vary according to the country and the product group, such as "The EU Ecolabel" (Maia et al., 2012), "Blue Angel," "Compostability Mark of European Bioplastics," "Coop Naturaline: Switzerland," "Global Organic Textile Standard (GOTS)" (Maia et al., 2012), "Green Mark," "GUT," "Made in Green," "Nordic Ecolabel"/"Swan," "NSF/ANSI 140 Sustainability Assessment for Carpet," "NSF Sustainability Certified Product," "Oeko-Tex Standard 100" (Maia et al., 2012), "Oeko-Tex Standard 1000" (Maia et al., 2012; Allwood et al., 2006), "Oeko-Tex Standard 1000plus," and "Soil Association Organic Standard" (Curteza, 2015).

1.5 Innovative Options in Environmentally Conscious Textile Manufacturing

Chemical textile finishing processes are generally the least ecological textile processes and result in a negative impact on sustainability. Both polluted water and harmful gases occur during these processes, which use abundant amounts of water, energy, and chemicals. For this reason, there are many eco-friendly technologies that minimize effluent, workload, processing time, and energy use as well as saving vital clean water during textile production.

For instance, it is possible to carry out the dyeing process using supercritical carbon dioxide ($scCO_2$) technology and without water, producing no effluent and using less energy (Odabaşoğlu et al., 2013). Further, bleaching and clearing using ozone (O_3) is a more eco-friendly method and requires less energy and chemical in comparison to conventional bleaching methods (Eren et al., 2011; Avinc et al., 2012a). Apart from these novel techniques, there are many more different methods, such as plasma (Khoddami et al., 2010), UV/ozone (Rahmatinejad et al., 2015; Rahmatinejad et al., 2016), laser, ultrasound (Yavaş et al., 2017; Davulcu et al., 2014), ultrasound/ozone (Eren et al., 2014; Aksel Eren et al., 2012), and so on, which contribute significant benefits for more sustainable and greener textile manufacturing.

In the wet processing stages, such as cleaning, scouring, bio-polishing, bleaching, dyeing, printing, washing, clearing, and finishing, the use of new, eco-friendly substances such as enzymes (Avinc et al., 2016), cyclodextrins (Setthayanond et al., 2017), chitins, chitosan (Arık et al., 2017), dendrimers, and liposomes as textile auxiliary materials in many textile processing applications is another sustainable textile production approach. Natural dyes from animals, plants, and bacteria can be used in textile dyeing processes for green production. This type of dye is not only sustainable but also renewable (Cireli et al., 2006; Bechtold and Mussak, 2009; Buschmann et al., 2001; Ravi Kumar, 2000; Burkinshaw et al., 2000; Altay and Sarıışık, 2012; Avinc et al., 2013; Gedik et al., 2013; Gedik et al., 2014).

What is more, new techniques to create novel textile fabrics, such as spray-on-fabric (Amato, 2011), bacterial cellulosic fabrics (fabrics created from sustainable bacteria) (Keshk, 2014; Yim et al., 2017), and fermented fabrics from wine (Fashion, 2013) are new futuristic ecological options.

1.6 Conclusion

The textile sector is known to be one of the most polluting industries, using many different chemicals, substances, dyes, and pigments during textile manufacturing from the raw material to the final textile product, which may result in hazardous effects on the environment and human health. Furthermore, the textile industry consumes high levels of energy and water during textile manufacturing and also releases greenhouse gases. Therefore, all the stages of textile production, from the material selection to the final textile product, should fulfill the requirements of environmentally conscious manufacturing (ECM).

For that reason, material selection plays a critical role in environmentally conscious design and manufacturing in the textile industry. Renewable and biodegradable textile materials have many advantages for responsible manufacturing. Also, the use of natural and natural-based textile fibers and the recyclability and reusability of all textile fibers should be considered for complete sustainable textile production.

Sustainable decisions and approaches for textile production can be summarized as the use of more environmental textile application techniques that require less water, fewer chemicals, and lower energy consumption as well as using improved versions of present textile application methods to create a more sustainable textile future. There are also standards, tests, regulations, and tools aiming to measure and determine constraints for more sustainable and environmentally friendly products and production.

Today, not only producers but also consumers are responsible for the application of all these sustainable methods and techniques in the textile industry. Consumers' sensitivity to and awareness of the environment will encourage producers to move to more sustainable production, and thus, natural resources will be preserved and passed on to the next generations.

References

AAFA, 2018. *Restricted Substance List (RSL)* [online]. Available from: www.aafaglobal. org/AAFA/Solutions_Pages/Restricted_Substance_List [Accessed June 2018].

Aksel Eren, H., Avinc, O. and Erismis, B. 2012. Comparison of different ultrasound support methods during colour and chemical oxygen demand removal of disperse and reactive dyebath solutions by ozonation. *Coloration Technology*, 128(6), 446–453.

Aldaya, M. M., Chapagain, A. K., Hoekstra, A. Y. and Mekonnen, M. M. 2012. *The Water Footprint Assessment Manual: Setting the Global Standard*. Routledge.

Allwood, J., Laursen, S., de Rodriguez, C., and Bocken, N. 2006. *Well Dressed! The Present and Future Sustainability of Clothing and Textiles in the United Kingdom*. Cambridge, UK: University of Cambridge Institute for Manufacturing. ISBN 1-902546-52-0.

Altay, P. and Sarışık, A. M. 2012. Tekstil Boyama İşlemlerinde Lipozomların Kullanımı. *Tekstil ve Mühendis*, 19, 86.

Altun, S. 2012. Life cycle assessment of clothing process. *Research Journal of Chemical Sciences*, 2(2), 87–89.

Amato, S. 2011. Fit to a T: Spray-on clothing, craft, commodity fetishism, and the agency of objects. *Utopian Studies*, 22(2), 285–302.

Anon., 2017. *Cocona: A Fabric Enhancer Derived From Coconuts* [online]. Available from: https://metaefficient.com/clothing/cocona-a-fabric-enhancer-derived-from-coconuts.html [Accessed November 2018].

Anon., 2018. *10 Sustainable textile innovations everyone should know* [online]. Available from: https://fashionunited.uk/news/business/10-sustainable-textile-innovations-everyone-should-know/2018090738711 [Accessed November 2018].

Arık, B., Avinc, O. and Yavas, A. 2018. Crease resistance improvement of hemp bio-fiber fabric via sol–gel and crosslinking methods. *Cellulose*, 25(8), 4841–4858.

Arık, B., Yavaş, A. and Avinc, O. 2017. Antibacterial and wrinkle resistance improvement of nettle biofibre using chitosan and BTCA. *Fibres & Textiles in Eastern Europe*.

Avinc, O. 2011a. Clearing of dyed poly (lactic acid) fabrics under acidic and alkaline conditions. *Textile Research Journal*, 81(10), 1049–1074.

Avinc, O. 2011b. Maximizing the wash fastness of dyed poly (lactic acid) fabrics by adjusting the amount of air during conventional reduction clearing. *Textile Research Journal*, 81(11), 1158–1170.

Avinc, O., et al. 2013. Natural dye extraction from waste barks of Turkish red pine (*Pinus brutia* Ten.) timber and eco-friendly natural dyeing of various textile fibers. *Fibers and Polymers*, 14(5), 866–873.

Avinc, O., Eren, H. A. and Uysal, P. 2012a. Ozone applications for after-clearing of disperse-dyed poly (lactic acid) fibres. *Coloration Technology*, 128(6), 479–487.

Avinc, O., et al. 2012b. The effects of ozone treatment on soybean fibers. *Ozone: Science & Engineering*, 34(3), 143–150.

Avinc, O., Erismis, B. and Eren, S. 2016. Treatment of cotton with a laccase enzyme and ultrasound/Tratamentul bumbacului cu enzima tip lacaza si ultrasunete. *Industria Textila*, 67(1), 55.

Avinc, O., et al., 2015. Biologically inspired some textile protein fibers. *International Conference on Life Science and Biological Engineering.* Tokyo, Japan.

Avinc, O. and Khoddami, A. 2009. Overview of poly (lactic acid)(PLA) fibre Part I: Production, properties, performance, environmental impact, and end-use applications of poly(lactic acid) fibres. *Fibre Chemistry*, 41(6), 391–401.

Avinc, O. and Khoddami, A. 2010. Overview of poly (lactic acid) (PLA) fibre. *Fibre Chemistry*, 42(1), 68–78.

Avinc, O., et al. 2011. A colorimetric quantification of softened polylactic acid and polyester filament knitted fabrics to 'Water-spotting'. *Fibers and Polymers*, 12(7), 893.

Avinc, O. and Yavas, A. 2017. Soybean: For textile applications and its printing. *Soybean—The Basis of Yield, Biomass and Productivity.* InTech.

Bechtold, T. and Mussak, R. 2009. *Handbook of Natural Colorants.* Wiley.

Bunsell, A. R. 2009. *Handbook of Tensile Properties of Textile and Technical Fibres.* Cambridge: Woodhead.

Burkinshaw, S., et al. 2000. The use of dendrimers to modify the dyeing behaviour of reactive dyes on cotton. *Dyes and Pigments*, 47(3), 259–267.

Buschmann, H.-J., Knittel, D. and Schollmeyer, E. 2001. New textile applications of cyclodextrins. *Journal of Inclusion Phenomena and Macrocyclic Chemistry*, 40(3), 169–172.

Cardoso, A. A. M. 2013. *Life Cycle Assessment of Two Textile Products Wool and Cotton.* (Master's thesis.) Porto University.

Chapagain, A. K., et al. 2006. The water footprint of cotton consumption: An assessment of the impact of worldwide consumption of cotton products on the water resources in the cotton producing countries. *Ecological Economics,* 60(1), 186–203.

Chung, H., Kim, T. Y. and Lee, S. Y. 2012. Recent advances in production of recombinant spider silk proteins. *Current Opinion in Biotechnology,* 23(6), 957–964.

Cireli, A., et al. 2006. *Advanced Technologies in Textiles,* (13), 61.

Curteza, A., 2015. *Sustainable Textiles* [online]. 2BFUNTEX, A project co-funded by the European Commission under the 7th Framework Programme within the NMP thematic area. Available from: http://www.2bfuntex.eu/sites/default/files/materials/Sustainable%20textiles_Antonela%20Curteza.pdf [Accessed April 2018].

Davulcu, A., et al. 2014. Ultrasound assisted biobleaching of cotton. *Cellulose,* 21(4), 2973–2981.

Desai, A. and Mital, A. 2017. An interactive system framework to enable design for disassembly. *Journal of Manufacturing Technology Management,* 28(6), 749–771.

DuPont. *Innovative, Sustainable Carpet that's Naturally Stain-Resistant* [online]. Available from: www.dupont.ae/products-and-services/fabrics-fibers-nonwovens/fibers/brands/dupont-sorona/products/dupont-sorona-for-sustainable-carpet.html [Accessed June 2018].

Eisoldt, L., Smith, A. and Scheibel, T. 2011. Decoding the secrets of spider silk. *Materials Today,* 14(3), 80–86.

Eren, H. A., et al. 2014. Ultrasound-assisted ozone bleaching of cotton. *Cellulose,* 21(6), 4643–4658.

Eren, H. A., et al. 2011. The effects of ozone treatment on polylactic acid (PLA) fibres. *Textile Research Journal,* 81(11), 1091–1099.

Startup Fashion. 2013. *Fermented Fashion: Fabric Made from Wine* [online]. Available from: https://startupfashion.com/fabric-made-from-wine/ [Accessed June 2018].

Fletcher, K. 2013. *Sustainable Fashion and Textiles: Design Journeys.* New York: Routledge.

Fudge, D. S., et al. 2010. Hagfish slime threads as a biomimetic model for high performance protein fibres. *Bioinspiration & Biomimetics,* 5(3), 350.

Fudge, D. S., Schorno, S. and Ferraro, S. 2014. Physiology, biomechanics, and biomimetics of hagfish slime. *Annual Review of Biochemistry,* 84, 6.1–6.21.

Gedik, G. and Avinc, O. 2018. Bleaching of hemp (*Cannabis sativa* L.) fibers with peracetic acid for textiles industry purposes. *Fibers and Polymers,* 19(1), 82–93.

Gedik, G., et al. 2014. A novel eco-friendly colorant and dyeing method for poly (ethylene terephthalate) substrate. *Fibers and Polymers,* 15(2), 261–272.

Gedik, G., Yavas, A. and Avinc, O. 2013. Cationized natural dyeing of cotton fabrics with corn poppy (*Papaver rhoeas*) and investigation of antibacterial activity. *Asian Journal of Chemistry,* 25(15), 8475.

GOTS, 2017. *Global Organic Textile Standard (GOTS) Version 5.0* [online]. Available from: https://www.global-standard.org/images/GOTS_Documents/GOTS_Standard_5.0_EN.pdf [Accessed November 2018].

Grote, C., et al. 2007. An approach to the EuP Directive and the application of the economic eco-design for complex products. *International Journal of Production Research,* 45(18–19), 4099–4117.

Gungor, A. and Gupta, S. M. 1999. Issues in environmentally conscious manufacturing and product recovery: A survey. *Computers & Industrial Engineering*, 36(4), 811–853.

Gungor, A., Palamutcu, S. and Ikiz, Y. 2009. Cotton textiles and the environment: Life cycle assessment of a bathrobe. *Tekstil & Konfeksiyon*, 19(3), 197–205.

Gupta, S. M. and Lambert, A. J. D. F., eds., 2007. *Environment Conscious Manufacturing*. CRC Press.

Hasani, H., Avinc, O. and Khoddami, A. 2013. Comparison of softened polylactic acid and polyethylene terephthalate fabrics using KES-FB. *Fibres & Textiles in Eastern Europe*, 3 (99), 81–88.

Hasani, H., Avinc, O. and Khoddami, A. 2017. Effects of different production processing stages on mechanical and surface characteristics of polylactic acid and PET fibre fabrics. *Indian Journal of Fibre & Textile Research (IJFTR)*, 42(1), 31–37.

Hayes, L. L. 2001. Synthetic textile innovations: Polyester fiber-to-fiber recycling for the advancement of sustainability. *AATCC Review*, 11(4), 37–41.

Hearle, J. W. 2001. *High-Performance Fibres*. Cambridge: CRC Press.

Hoekstra, A. Y., et al. 2009. Water footprint manual. *State of the Art*, 1–131.

Hoekstra, A. Y. and Hung, P. Q. 2002. *Virtual Water Trade. A Quantification of Virtual Water Flows between Nations in Relation to International Crop Trade*. Value of Water Research Report Series, 11, 166.

Igarashi, K., et al. 2016. Disassembly system modeling and design with parts selection for cost, recycling and CO_2 saving rates using multi criteria optimization. *Journal of Manufacturing Systems*, 38, 151–164.

Ilgin, M. A. and Gupta, S. M. 2010. Environmentally conscious manufacturing and product recovery (ECMPRO): A review of the state of the art. *Journal of Environmental Management*, 91(3), 563–591.

PE International. 2014. *The Life Cycle Assessment of Organic Cotton Fiber—A Global Average, Summary of Findings*. Textile Exchange, PE International.

Isaacs, J. A. and Gupta, S. M. 1997. Economic consequences of increasing polymer content for the US automobile recycling infrastructure. *Journal of Industrial Ecology*, 1(4), 19–33.

Islam, M. M. and Khan, M. M. R. 2014. Environmental sustainability evaluation of apparel product: A case study on knitted T-shirt. *Journal of Textiles*. 2014, 643080.

Kalayci, C. B. and Gupta, S. M. 2013a. River formation dynamics approach for sequence-dependent disassembly line balancing problem. *Reverse Supply Chains: Issues and Analysis*, 289–312.

Kalayci, C. B. and Gupta, S. M. 2013b. Simulated annealing algorithm for solving sequence-dependent disassembly line balancing problem. *IFAC Proceedings Volumes*, 46(9), 93–98.

Kalayci, E., Avinc, O. and Yavas, A. 2014. Polibenzimidazol (PBI) Lifleri. *Tekstil Ve Mühendis*, 21(96), 51–67.

Kalayci, E., Avinc, O. and Yavas, A. 2015a. Yarinin yüksek performansli liflerine doğal bir yaklaşim: balik asalaği salgisi lifleri. *Marmara Fen Bilimleri Dergisi*, 27(4), 135–142.

Kalayci, E., Avinc, O. and Yavas, A. 2017. Polieter eter keton (peek) lifleri. *Cumhuriyet Üniversitesi Fen-Edebiyat Fakültesi Fen Bilimleri Dergisi*, 38(2), 168–186.

Kalayci, E., et al. 2016a. Sustainable textile fibers obtained from agricultural wastes: Pineapple leaf fibers. *Sakarya University Journal of Science*, 20(2), 203–221.

Kalayci, E., Avinc, O. O. and Yavas, A. 2015b. Yüksek performansli lifler: PIPD, poli (piridobisimidazol) lifleri. *CBU Journal of Science*, 12(1), 93–101.
Kalayci, E., Avinc, O. O. and Yavas, A. 2015c. Yüksek performansli PBO (poli-p-fenilenbenzobisoksazol) lifleri. *Tekstil ve Mühendis*, 22(98).
Kalayci, E., Avinc, O. O. and Yavas, A. 2016b. Polifenilen sülfid (PPS) lifleri. *Düzce Üniversitesi Bilim ve Teknoloji Dergisi*, 4(1), 88.
Kalayci, E., Avinc, O. O. and Yavas, A. 2016c. Yüksek performanslı polietilen (HPPE) lifleri. *Marmara Fen Bilimleri Dergisi*, 1, 13–34.
Kalayci, E., et al. 2015d. From Seas and Oceans to the Textiles. ed. *Textile Science and Economy VII 7th International Scientific-Professional Conference May 25–31st, 2015*. Zrenjanin, Serbia, 166–175.
Kalayci, E., et al. 2015e. Textile Fibers Used in Products Floating on the Water. *Textile Science and Economy VII 7th International Scientific-Professional Conference May 25–31st, 2015*. Zrenjanin, Serbia, 85–90.
Kanık, M., 2008. Terbiye İşlemleri Sektöründe Yeni Teknolojiler - Kısa Bakış. Available from: http://aves.erciyes.edu.tr/ImageOfByte.aspx?Resim=8&SSNO=1&USER=2153 [Accessed November 2018].
Keshk, S. M. 2014. Bacterial cellulose production and its industrial applications. *Journal of Bioprocessing & Biotechniques*, 4(2), 1.
Keskin, S. S., Erdil, M. and Sennaroğlu, B. 2017. Bir Tekstil Fabrikasının Kumaş Üretiminde Enerji ve Karbon Ayak İzlerinin Belirlenmesi. ed. *VII. Ulusal Hava Kirliliği ve Kontrolü Sempozyumu Hava Kirlenmesi Araştırmaları ve Denetimi Türk Milli Komitesi*, November 1–3. Antalya, 95–105.
Khoddami, A., Avinc, O. and Ghahremanzadeh, F. 2011. Improvement in poly (lactic acid) fabric performance via hydrophilic coating. *Progress in Organic Coatings*, 72(3), 299–304.
Khoddami, A., Avinc, O. and Mallakpour, S. 2010. A novel durable hydrophobic surface coating of poly (lactic acid) fabric by pulsed plasma polymerization. *Progress in Organic Coatings*, 67(3), 311–316.
Kokten, M. and Avinc, O. 2014. 6331 Sayılı İş Sağlığı ve Güvenliği Kanunu'nda İşveren Yükümlülükleri ve Tekstil Sektörü Açısından Bir Bakış. *Tekstil ve Mühendis*, 21(93).
Kurban, M., Yavas, A. and Avinc, O. 2016. Nettle biofibre bleaching with ozonation/ Albirea biofibrei din urzica prin ozonizare. *Industria Textila*, 67(1), 46.
Lambert, A. F. and Gupta, S. M. 2005. *Disassembly Modeling for Assembly, Maintenance, Reuse and Recycling*. CRC Press.
Lewis, V. and Chen, C. 2006. The life of a piece of cloth: Developing garments into a sustainable service system. *International Journal of Environmental, Cultural, Economic and Social Sustainability*, 2(1), 197–207.
Maia, L. C., Alves, A. C. and Leão, C. P. 2012. Sustainable Work Environment with Lean Production in Textile and Garment Industry. ed. *Proceedings of International Conference on Industrial Engineering and Operations Management (ICIEOM2012)*, 9–11.
Muthu, S. S., et al. 2012. Quantification of environmental impact and ecological sustainability for textile fibres. *Ecological Indicators*, 13(1), 66–74.
Nardinelli, C. 1980. Child labor and the Factory Acts. *The Journal of Economic History*, 40(4), 739–755.
Odabaşoğlu, H. Y., Avinç, O. O. and Yavaş, A. 2013. Waterless Textile Dyeing. (20), 90.
OEKO-TEX. 2018. *STeP by OEKO-TEX* [online]. Available from: www.oeko-tex.com/ en/business/certifications_and_services/step_by_oeko_tex/step_start.xhtml [Accessed Jun 2018].

Özdemir, S. and Tekoğlu, O. 2014. Ekolojik Tekstil Ürünlerinde Kullanılan Hammaddeler. *Akdeniz Sanat Dergisi*, 4(8), 27–30.

Palamutcu, S., 2017. Sustainable Textile Technologies. *In:* Muthu, S. S. ed. *Textiles and Clothing Sustainability, Textile Science and Clothing Technology*. Hong Kong: Springer.

Petry, F. 2008. Environmental protection and sustainability in the textile industry. *Textile Finishing*, 7–8, 86–88.

Polat, O. and Kalayci, C. B. 2016. Ergonomic Risk Assessment of Workers in Garment Industry. ed. *Eighth International Conference on Textile Science & Economy VIII*. Zrenjanin, Serbia, 16–21.

Radhakrishnan, S., 2015. The Sustainable Apparel Coalition and the Higg Index. *In:* Muthu, S. S. ed. *Roadmap to Sustainable Textiles and Clothing: Regulatory Aspects and Sustainability Standards of Textiles and the Clothing Supply Chain*. Singapore: Springer Singapore, 23–57.

Rahmatinejad, J., Khoddami, A. and Avinc, O. 2015. Innovative hybrid fluorocarbon coating on UV/ozone surface modified wool substrate. *Fibers and Polymers*, 16(11), 2416–2425.

Rahmatinejad, J., et al. 2016. Polyester hydrophobicity enhancement via UV-ozone irradiation, chemical pre-treatment and fluorocarbon finishing combination. *Progress in Organic Coatings*, 101, 51–58.

Ravi Kumar, M. N. 2000. A review of chitin and chitosan applications. *Reactive and Functional Polymers*, 46(1), 1–27.

Reddy, N. and Yang, Y. 2014. *Innovative Biofibers from Renewable Resources*. Springer.

Rees, W. and Wackernagel, M. 1996. Urban ecological footprints: Why cities cannot be sustainable—and why they are a key to sustainability. *Environmental Impact Assessment Review*, 16(4–6), 223–248.

SAC, 2018. *The Higg Index* [online]. Available from: https://apparelcoalition.org/the-higg-index/ [Accessed June 2018].

Saiyed, H. N. and Tiwari, R. R. 2004. Occupational health research in India. *Industrial Health*, 42(2), 141–148.

Sangeetha, K., Abirami, T. and Keerthana Sri, A., 2018. Eco-friendly Technology Options Available for Textile Industry. *In:* Parthiban, M., Srikrishnan, M. R. and Kandhavadivu, P. eds. *Sustainability in Fashion and Apparels: Challenges and Solutions*. New Delhi: Woodhead.

Saranya, K. and Amutha, K. 2018. Eco-testing of textiles. *In:* Sangeetha, K., Abirami, T. and Keerthana Sri, A. eds. *Sustainability in Fashion and Apparels: Challenges and Solutions*. New Delhi: Woodhead, 12–21.

Setthayanond, J., et al. 2017. Influence of MCT-β-cyclodextrin treatment on strength, reactive dyeing and third-hand cigarette smoke odor release properties of cotton fabric. *Cellulose*, 24(11), 5233–5250.

Sevgisunar, H. G. 2015. Süt liflerinden üretilen kumaşların ön terbiye işlemlerinin araştırılması Master's Thesis. Pamukkale Üniversitesi.

Sevgisunar, H. G., Yavas, A. and Avinc, O. 2015. Regenerated Protein Fiber: Casein. ed. *Textile Science and Economy 7th International Scientific Professional Conference*, May 25–31. Zrenjanin, Serbia.

Shangnan Shui, A. P., 2013. *World Apparel Fibre Consumption Survey*. Washington: International Cotton Advisory Committee.

Sharma, A. 2013. Eco-friendly textiles: A boost to sustainability. *Asian Journal of Home Science*, 8(2), 768–771.

Song, Y. S., Youn, J. R. and Gutowski, T. G. 2009. Life cycle energy analysis of fiber-reinforced composites. *Composites Part A: Applied Science and Manufacturing*, 40(8), 1257–1265.

Sorona, D., 2016. *Life Cycle Assessment Validates Dupont Sorona Sustainability* [online]. Available from: http://sorona.com/article/life-cycle-assessment-validates-duponttm-soronar-sustainability/ [Accessed June 2018].

Steinberger, J. K., et al. 2009. A spatially explicit life cycle inventory of the global textile chain. *The International Journal of Life Cycle Assessment*, 14(5), 443–455.

Suhre, M. H., et al. 2014. Structural and functional features of a collagen-binding matrix protein from the mussel byssus. *Nature Communications*, 5.

Thiry, M. C. 2011. *Staying Alive: Making Textiles Sustainable*. AATCC review.

US-CPSC, 2018. *The Consumer Product Safety Improvement Act (CPSIA)* [online]. Available from: www.cpsc.gov/Regulations-Laws--Standards/Statutes/The-Consumer-Product-Safety-Improvement-Act [Accessed June 2018].

Van der Velden, N. M., Kuusk, K. and Köhler, A. R. 2015. Life cycle assessment and eco-design of smart textiles: The importance of material selection demonstrated through e-textile product redesign. *Materials & Design*, 84, 313–324.

Van der Velden, N. M., Patel, M. K. and Vogtländer, J. G. 2014. LCA benchmarking study on textiles made of cotton, polyester, nylon, acryl, or elastane. *The International Journal of Life Cycle Assessment*, 19(2), 331–356.

Veerakamolmal, P. and Gupta, S. M. 2000. Design for disassembly, reuse, and recycling. In: *Green Electronics/Green Bottom Line*. Elsevier, 69–82.

Waite, M. 2009. Sustainable textiles: The role of bamboo and a comparison of bamboo textile properties—part 1. *Journal of Textile and Apparel, Technology and Management*, 6(2).

Yavaş, A., Avinc, O. and Gedik, G. 2017. Ultrasound and microwave aided natural dyeing of nettle biofibre (*Urtica dioica* L.) with madder (*Rubia tinctorum* L.). *Fibres & Textiles in Eastern Europe*.

Yildirim, F. F., Avinc, O. and Yavas, A., 2012a. Eco-friendly Plant Based Regenerated Protein Fiber: Soybean. *19th International Conference Structure and Structural Mechanics of Textiles*. TU Liberec, Czech Republic.

Yildirim, F. F., Avinc, O. O. and Yavas, A. 2012b. Poli (trimetilen Tereftalat) Lifleri Bölüm 1: Üretimi, Özellikleri, Kullanım Alanları, Çevresel Etkisi. *Tekstil ve Mühendis*, 19(87).

Yildirim, F. F., Avinc, O. O. and Yavas, A. 2012c. Poli (Trimetilen Tereftalat) Lifleri Bölüm 2: Terbiye İşlemleri. *Tekstil ve Mühendis*, 19(88).

Yildirim, F. F., Avinc, O. O. and Yavas, A. 2014. Soybean protein fibres Part 1: Structure, production and environmental effects of soybean protein fibres. *Uludağ University Journal of The Faculty of Engineering*, 19(2), 29–50.

Yıldırım, F. F., Avinç, O. O. and Yavaş, A. 2015. Soybean protein fibres Part 2: Soybean fibres properties and application areas. *Uludağ University Journal of The Faculty of Engineering*, 20(1), 1–21.

Yim, S. M., Song, J. E. and Kim, H. R. 2017. Production and characterization of bacterial cellulose fabrics by nitrogen sources of tea and carbon sources of sugar. *Process Biochemistry*, 59, 26–36.

2

An Integrated Design for Remanufacturing Approach

Mehmet Ali Ilgin

CONTENTS

Overview

Remanufacturing is an industrial process involving the conversion of a used product to a like-new condition. Among other remanufacturing issues, design for remanufacturing (DFR) has received increased attention from researchers in recent years due to the vital importance of product design for the efficiency of the remanufacturing process. Although various criteria (e.g., durability, ease of disassembly, and use of appropriate materials) are used to evaluate the remanufacturability of design alternatives, the interactions among the criteria are ignored in the literature. This chapter fills this research gap by proposing an integrated DFR approach, which considers the interactions among DFR criteria. First, interpretive structural modeling (ISM) and analytical network process (ANP) are employed to determine the weights of DFR criteria. Then, the design characteristics that best satisfy the DFR criteria are determined using House of Quality (HoQ). An application of the proposed approach in the automotive industry is also presented.

2.1 Introduction

Depleted natural resources and landfill areas have forced many countries to examine the sustainability of their new product manufacturing and end of life (EOL) product disposal processes. As a result, the governments of these countries and various international organizations have issued many environmental protection regulations and guidelines, such as the WEEE (waste electrical and electronic equipment) and ROHS (restriction of hazardous substances) directives of the European Union, which require manufacturers to collect and properly dispose of their products. Besides these government regulations, manufacturers try to harvest the remaining value in EOL products by establishing specific facilities for product recovery, which involves the recovery of materials and components from returned products via recycling, refurbishment, repair, and remanufacturing.

Remanufacturing is the most environment-friendly and profitable product recovery option due to its many advantages over other product recovery options (recycling, refurbishment, and repair) (Shumon et al. [1]). A great deal of the labor, energy, and material values in an EOL product are recovered in remanufacturing, since the disassembled parts are used "as is" in the remanufacturing process. On the other hand, recycling, which simply involves the shredding of EOL products, can recover only the material content of an EOL product. Manufacturers usually give the same warranty provisions for remanufactured products as with new products, since worn-out parts are replaced, and some key parts are upgraded in remanufacturing.

However, the warranty conditions provided for refurbished and repaired products are inferior to those of new or remanufactured products, because there is no upgrading in repair or refurbishment except for the possible replacement of worn-out parts.

The first step in the remanufacturing process is the collection and transportation of EOL products to a remanufacturing plant, where they are disassembled into parts. After the cleaning and inspection of disassembled parts, repair and replacement operations are performed for defective and worn-out parts. The last step involves the reassembly of all parts into a remanufactured product.

Firms used not to consider these steps while designing a new product. That is why they have had various problems (e.g., high disassembly costs, difficult-to-disassemble and damaged parts) in remanufacturing their own products. Hence, these problems have forced their design teams to consider remanufacturing-related product characteristics in the design phase of the product. Academics have also developed various DFR models in recent years. In these models, the remanufacturability of design alternatives is evaluated considering various criteria, such as durability, ease of disassembly, and use of appropriate materials. The interactions among DFR criteria are ignored by just focusing on the individual impact of each criterion. Therefore, the importance weights calculated for DFR criteria are not realistic, since there are interactions among DFR criteria. This study fills this research gap by proposing an integrated DFR approach, which considers the interactions among DFR criteria. First, ISM is employed to analyze the interactions among DFR criteria through the presentation of a case study from the automotive industry. Then, ANP is used to determine the importance weights of DFR criteria based on the ISM results for the interactions of the factors. Finally, design characteristics that best satisfy the DFR criteria are determined using HoQ.

The rest of the chapter is organized as follows. In Section 2, a review of the issues considered in this chapter is presented. In Section 3, the characteristics of the remanufacturing system and DFR criteria are explained. Section 4 explains the steps of the proposed approach. Finally, some conclusions and future research directions are presented in Section 5.

2.2 Literature Review

Researchers have developed various tools, heuristics, and methodologies to deal with the unique characteristics of remanufacturing (e.g., the high level of uncertainty). They have applied these techniques to different domains in remanufacturing, including logistics (El korchi and Millet [2]; Mutha and Pokharel [3]; Jayant et al. [4]), disassembly planning (Tian et al. [5]; Kang et al. [6]), DFR (Shu and Flowers [7]), and design for disassembly (Desai and Mital [8];

Desai and Mital [9]; Mital and Desai [10]). A complete and up-to-date review of these issues can be found in the papers by Ilgin and Gupta [11] and Gungor and Gupta [12]. We also refer the reader to the recent book by Ilgin and Gupta [13] for a comprehensive overview of remanufacturing modeling and analysis techniques.

DFR has received increasing attention within remanufacturing in recent years. Shu and Flowers [7] consider alternative joint designs and compare remanufacturing costs against other life-cycle costs (e.g., manufacturing, maintenance). It is concluded that design features facilitating assembly and recycling may have negative impacts on the remanufacturability of a product. Ijomah et al. [14] develop DFR guidelines based on the findings from workshops carried out in the United Kingdom. Yuksel [15] investigates automobile engine characteristics that will ease remanufacturing using quality function deployment. Hatcher et al. [16] present the findings from a literature review and case study research carried out to understand the current state of DFR activities in China. Sakao and Mizuyama [17] approach DFR from a product/service system design perspective. Chakraborty et al. [18] integrate fuzzy analytical hierarchy process (AHP) and axiomatic design for the analysis of product design characteristics for remanufacturing. The interested reader is referred to reviews by Hatcher et al. [19] and Fegade et al. [20] on DFR.

Researchers have applied ISM to various problem domains, including manufacturing strategy selection (Abbasi et al. [21]), risk management (Alawamleh and Popplewell [22]), green supply chain management (Diabat and Govindan [23]; Govindan et al. [24]; Mathiyazhagan et al. [25]), and medical decision support (Kim and Watada [26]). The application of ISM in remanufacturing is limited to a study done by Mukherjee and Mondal [27]. In this study, the authors use ISM to analyze the relationships among key issues pertaining to the management of the remanufacturing process of an Indian photocopier remanufacturer.

ANP is a popular multi-criteria decision-making methodology. Energy management (Köne and Büke [28]), total quality management (Bayazit and Karpak [29]), and reverse logistics (Shaik and Abdul-Kader [30]; Ilgin et al. [31]; Gupta and Ilgin [32]) are some of the recent application areas of ANP. Although ANP has not been applied to a problem in the DFR area, there are several ANP applications in remanufacturing-related issues (disassembly and reverse logistics). Gungor [33] uses ANP to evaluate alternative connection types from a design for disassembly perspective. ANP is employed to analyze alternatives in reverse logistics for end-of-life computers in Ravi and Shankar [34]. Ravi et al. [35] integrate ANP and zero-one goal programming to select a reverse logistics project for end-of-life computers.

There are several papers integrating ANP and ISM. Chang et al. [36] employ this type of hybrid methodology to determine the critical agility factors when launching a new product into mass production. ISM is first used to identify the interactive causal relationships of the employed agility factors.

Then, an ANP model is applied to obtain the importance weights of the agility criteria. Shahbandarzadeh and Ghorbanpour [37] apply an ANP–ISM hybrid for the selection of health center locations. Thakkar et al. [38] integrate ANP and ISM to develop a balanced score card. ISM is integrated with ANP to identify the relationships among criteria and sub-criteria in both studies.

2.3 Description of Remanufacturing System and Design for Remanufacturing Criteria

2.3.1 Remanufacturing System

This section presents a case study to demonstrate the applicability of the proposed approach. The case company operates in the automotive sector and mainly deals with the remanufacture of truck engines. The remanufacturing process starts with the arrival of the returned engines to the remanufacturing plant. Severely damaged engines are sent to a recycling plant. Engines passing the inspection are cleaned and disassembled into their components and subassemblies. Severely damaged components and subassemblies are sent to recycling. Repairable components and subassemblies are repaired. Repaired and undamaged components and subassemblies are cleaned. If necessary, brand new components and subassemblies are ordered from suppliers. Finally, components and subassemblies are assembled into an engine. The steps of the engine remanufacturing process are summarized in Figure 2.1.

2.3.2 Design for Remanufacturing Criteria

The DFR criteria were determined by reviewing papers written on DFR (see the second column of Table 2.1) and discussion with the experts (four mechanical engineers and two industrial engineers) working in the company. Table 2.1 presents the identified DFR criteria together with the citations to the references using each criterion. The relationships among DFR criteria were determined based on the discussions with the previously mentioned six experts. The identified relationships are provided in Table 2.2, and the following paragraphs briefly explain those relationships.

- *Appropriate Surface Finish (ASF)* is an important DFR criterion, which positively affects *ease of cleaning, ease of identification, ease of sorting, durability,* and *ease of disassembly.* ASF is of the utmost importance in the cleaning process, since the cleaning materials may damage the surface of a product manufactured using inappropriate materials. The identification and sorting of products will be easier if

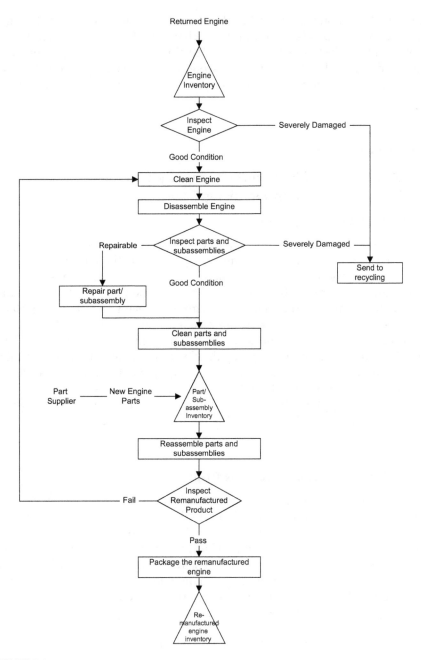

FIGURE 2.1
Engine remanufacturing process.

TABLE 2.1

Design for Remanufacturing Criteria

Design for Remanufacturing Criteria	References
Appropriate surface finish (ASF)	Shu and Flowers [7]; Ijomah et al. [14]; Ijomah et al. [42]; Ijomah [43]; Yuksel [15]; Chakraborty et al. [18]
Durability (D)	Shu and Flowers [7]; Ijomah et al. [14]; Ijomah et al. [42]; Charter and Gray [44]; Ijomah [43]; Yuksel [15]; Chakraborty et al. [18]
Ease of cleaning (EC)	Shu and Flowers [7]; Ijomah et al. [14]; Ijomah et al. [42]; Ijomah [43]; Yuksel [15]; Chakraborty et al. [18]
Ease of disassembly (ED)	Shu and Flowers [7]; Ijomah et al. [14]; Ijomah et al. [42]; Charter and Gray [44]; Ijomah [43]; Yuksel [15]; Chakraborty et al. [18]
Ease of identification (EI)	Shu and Flowers [7]; Ijomah et al. [14]; Ijomah et al. [42]; Ijomah [43]; Chakraborty et al. [18]
Ease of sorting (ES)	Ijomah [43]; Yuksel [15]
Ease of testing (ET)	Ijomah [43]; Yuksel [15]
Reduced number and type of joints (RNTJ)	Ijomah et al. [42]; Ijomah [43]; Yuksel [15]
Reduced number and type of fasteners (RNTF)	Yuksel [15]; Shu and Flowers [7]
Reduced number and type of parts (RNTP)	Yuksel [15]; Ijomah [43]; Chakraborty et al. [18]

TABLE 2.2

Relationships among DFR Criteria

DFR Criterion	DFR Criteria That Are Affected by the Criterion
ASF	EC, ES, EI, D, ED
D	ED, EC, ET
EC	ET, ES, EI
ED	ET, EC
EI	ES, ED, EC, ET
ES	ET
ET	EI
RNTJ	EC, ED, EI, ES, ET
RNTF	EC, ED, EI, ES, ET
RNTP	EC, ED, EI, ES, ET, RNTJ, RNTF

the surface finish has the appropriate color and texture. ASF also increases durability, since *it* protects the product, and the product can be disassembled with maximum ease and minimum damage.

- *Durability* guarantees that components and subassemblies will not be damaged during the disassembly operations. Durability positively affects *ease of disassembly, ease of cleaning,* and *ease of testing.* If the components and subassemblies of the product are not durable, they can be damaged during disassembly, cleaning, and testing processes. Heat (thermal cleaning), solvents (solvent-based cleaning), and aqueous emulsions (biological cleaning) are commonly used in the cleaning process (Ilgin and Gupta [13]). The product must be durable enough to resist these cleaning agents. Cleaning and testing processes also require disassembly and reorientation of the product. These operations may damage any non-durable component or subassembly. In addition, workers will need to put in extra time and effort while disassembling non-durable components and subassemblies.

- *Ease of cleaning* positively affects *ease of testing, ease of sorting,* and *ease of identification*. Identification, sorting, and testing operations require the product to be cleaned to a certain level. If the product can be cleaned with ease, these operations are completed with minimum effort.

- *Ease of disassembly* positively affects *ease of testing* and *ease of cleaning*, because the cleaning and testing of internal components require the disassembly of the product to a certain level.

- *Ease of identification* positively affects *ease of sorting, ease of disassembly, ease of cleaning,* and *ease of testing*. If the components are easily identifiable, then the workers will spend less time and effort distinguishing between different component types during disassembly, sorting, and testing processes. In addition, they can apply appropriate cleaning materials and methods if they can easily decide on the type and material of a component.

- *Ease of sorting* positively affects *ease of testing*. Prior to testing operations, products must be sorted into different groups depending on their condition. Different test methods and test equipment are used for each group. This is why, if the products can be sorted with minimum time and with minimum effort, testing operations can be completed quickly and effectively.

- *Ease of testing* positively affects *ease of identification*. The types and characteristics of some components in a product can only be identified by carrying out appropriate tests. If components and subassemblies can be tested with ease, the identification process will take less time.

- *Reduced number and type of fasteners (RNTF)* provide *ease of disassembly, ease of cleaning, ease of sorting, ease of testing,* and *ease of identification*. RNTF reduces the number of disassembly operations and associated tools. It also has positive effects on *cleaning, sorting, testing,* and *identification* operations due to its positive effect on disassembly.

- *Reduced number and type of joints (RNTJ)* provide *ease of disassembly, ease of cleaning, ease of sorting, ease of testing,* and *ease of identification* for the same reasons as RNTF.

- *Reduced number and type of parts (RNTP)* provide *ease of disassembly, ease of cleaning, ease of sorting, ease of testing,* and *ease of identification* for the same reasons as RNTF and RNTJ. In addition, a reduced number of parts will result in a reduced number and type of fasteners and joints. Hence RNTP positively affects RNTF and RNTJ.

2.4 Proposed Design for Remanufacturing Approach

The proposed DFR approach involves three main steps (see Figure 2.2). First, relationships among DFR criteria are analyzed using ISM. ANP is then employed to determine the importance weights of the DFR criteria. Finally, technical product characteristics satisfying the DFR criteria are determined using HoQ.

2.4.1 Analysis of Relationships among Criteria Using ISM

2.4.1.1 Structural Self-Interaction Matrix

The first step in ISM methodology is the construction of a structural self-interaction matrix (SSIM). This matrix is used to represent the contextual relationships among variables. In this study, the experiences of the engineers from the case company and research findings from the remanufacturing

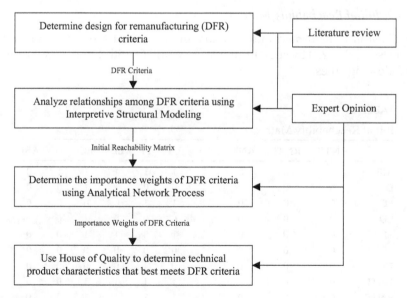

FIGURE 2.2
Flow chart of the proposed approach.

TABLE 2.3

Structural Self-Interaction Matrix

	RNTP	RNTF	RNTJ	ET	ES	EI	ED	EC	D	ASF
ASF	O	O	O	O	V	V	V	V	V	–
D	O	O	O	V	O	O	V	V	–	
EC	A	A	A	V	V	X	A	–		
ED	A	A	A	V	O	A	–			
EI	A	A	A	X	V	–				
ES	A	A	A	V	–					
ET	A	A	A	–						
RNTJ	A	O	–							
RNTF	A	–								
RNTP	–									

literature were used to identify the contextual relationships among DFR criteria. The following four symbols are used in SSIM, given in Table 2.3:

V: Driver *i* will help achieve driver *j*.

A: Driver *j* will help achieve driver *i*.

X: Drivers *i* and *j* will help achieve each other.

O: Drivers *i* and *j* are unrelated.

2.4.1.2 Initial Reachability Matrix

The SSIM is transformed into a binary matrix called the *initial reachability matrix* (see Table 2.4) by substituting V, A, X, and O with 1 and 0 according to the following rules.

TABLE 2.4

Initial Reachability Matrix

	RNTP	RNTF	RNTJ	ET	ES	EI	ED	EC	D	ASF
ASF	0	0	0	0	1	1	1	1	1	0
D	0	0	0	1	0	0	1	1	0	0
EC	0	0	0	1	1	1	0	0	0	0
ED	0	0	0	1	0	0	0	1	0	0
EI	0	0	0	1	1	0	1	1	0	0
ES	0	0	0	1	0	0	0	0	0	0
ET	0	0	0	0	0	1	0	0	0	0
RNTJ	0	0	0	1	1	1	1	1	0	0
RNTF	0	0	0	1	1	1	1	1	0	0
RNTP	0	1	1	1	1	1	1	1	0	0

(i) If the (i, j) entry in the SSIM is V, the (i, j) entry in the reachability matrix becomes 1, and the (j, i) entry becomes 0.

(ii) If the (i, j) entry in the SSIM is A, the (i, j) entry in the reachability matrix becomes 0, and the (j, i) entry becomes 1.

(iii) If the (i, j) entry in the SSIM is X, the (i, j) entry in the reachability matrix becomes 1, and the (j, i) entry becomes 1.

(iv) If the (i, j) entry in the SSIM is O, the (i, j) entry in the reachability matrix becomes 0, and the (j, i) entry becomes 0.

2.4.1.3 Final Reachability Matrix and Driving Power-Dependence Diagram

The final reachability matrix is constructed by incorporating transitivity, which states that if Driver 1 is related to Driver 2, and Driver 2 is related to Driver 3, then Driver 1 is necessarily related to Driver 3. Table 2.5 presents this matrix. The driving power and dependence of each driver can be determined using Table 2.5. The row total for each of the issues gives the driving power, while the column total represents the dependence power for the corresponding issues. A criterion with a high driving power controls and dictates other issues, while a criterion with a high dependence power is controlled by some other issues. Each criterion can be positioned in a two-dimensional plot based on its driver and dependence powers, as presented in Figure 2.3. There are four quadrants, representing the four classes of issues—autonomous, dependent, linkage, and driver/independent. RNTP, ASF, RNTF, RNTJ, and D are independent drivers, and EC, ED, EI, ET, and ES are dependent drivers. There are no linkage and autonomous drivers.

The final reachability matrix is partitioned into different levels by deriving the reachability and antecedent set for each driver. For a particular driver,

TABLE 2.5

Final Reachability Matrix

	RNTP	RNTF	RNTJ	ET	ES	EI	ED	EC	D	ASF	Driver Power
ASF	0	0	0	1*	1	1	1	1	1	1	7
D	0	0	0	1	1*	1*	1	1	1	0	6
EC	0	0	0	1	1	1	1*	1	0	0	5
ED	0	0	0	1	1*	1*	1	1	0	0	5
EI	0	0	0	1	1	1	1	1	0	0	5
ES	0	0	0	1	1	1*	0	0	0	0	3
ET	0	0	0	1	1*	1	1*	1*	0	0	5
RNTJ	0	0	1	1	1	1	1	1	0	0	6
RNTF	0	1	0	1	1	1	1	1	0	0	6
RNTP	1	1	1	1	1	1	1	1	0	0	8
Dependence Power	1	2	2	10	10	10	9	9	2	1	

*Relationships constructed by incorporating transitivity.

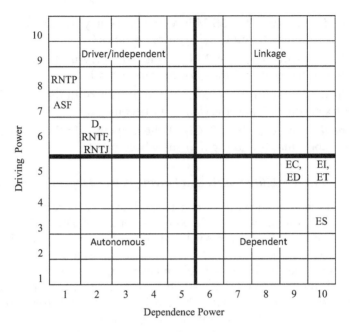

FIGURE 2.3
Driving power and dependence diagram.

the reachability set consists of the driver itself and those drivers it may help to achieve, whereas the antecedent set consists of the driver itself and those issues that may help in achieving it. The intersection set of a particular driver is the intersection of the corresponding reachability and antecedent sets. The drivers with the same reachability and intersection sets are placed in Level I of the ISM hierarchy. The rows and columns associated with these drivers are then removed from the final reachability matrix. Reachability, antecedent, and intersection sets are determined again for the remaining issues. The drivers with the same reachability and intersection sets are now placed in Level II of the ISM hierarchy. This process is repeated until the level of each driver has been determined (see Tables 2.6 through 2.8).

Using the levels determined earlier and the information from the driver-dependence diagram, an ISM-based model, presented in Figure 2.4, is developed. It must be noted that the arrows in Figure 2.4, move in the direction from Level IV toward Level I.

The ISM model indicates that reduced number and type of parts and appropriate surface finish are located at the bottom levels of the hierarchy (Level IV), implying higher driving power. Therefore, the firm should concentrate its product design efforts on these two design criteria, since they have the capability to influence other criteria. For instance, reduced number and type of parts will positively affect seven other design criteria (RNTF, RNTJ, ET, ES, EI, EC, and ED).

TABLE 2.6

Iteration 1

Element	Reachability Set	Antecedent Set	Intersection Set	Level
ASF	ET, ES, EI, ED, EC, D, ASF	ASF	ASF	
D	ET, ES, EI, ED, EC, D	ASF, D	D	
EC	ET, ES, EI, ED, EC	ASF, D, EC, ED, EI, RNTJ, RNTF, RNTP	EC, ED, EI	
ED	ET, ES, EI, ED, EC	ASF, D, EC, ED, EI, RNTJ, RNTF, RNTP	EC, ED, EI	
EI	ET, ES, EI, ED, EC	ASF, D, EC, ED, EI, ES, ET, RNTJ, RNTF, RNTP	ET, ES, EI, ED, EC	I
ES	ET, ES, EI	ASF, D, EC, ED, EI, ES, ET, RNTJ, RNTF, RNTP	ET, ES, EI	I
ET	ET, ES, EI, ED, EC	ASF, D, EC, ED, EI, ES, ET, RNTJ, RNTF, RNTP	ET, ES, EI, ED, EC	I
RNTJ	RNTJ, ET, ES, EI, ED, EC	RNTJ, RNTP	RNTJ	
RNTF	RNTF, ET, ES, EI, ED, EC	RNTF, RNTP	RNTF	
RNTP	D, EC, ED, ES, ET, RNTJ, RNTF, RNTP	RNTP	RNTP	

TABLE 2.7

Iteration 2

Element	Reachability Set	Antecedent Set	Intersection Set	Level
ASF	ED, EC, D, ASF	ASF	ASF	
D	ED, EC, D	ASF, D	D	
EC	ED, EC	ASF, D, EC, ED, RNTJ, RNTF, RNTP	EC, ED	II
ED	ED, EC	ASF, D, EC, ED, RNTJ, RNTF, RNTP	EC, ED	II
RNTJ	RNTJ, ED, EC	RNTJ, RNTP	RNTJ	
RNTF	RNTF, ED, EC	RNTF, RNTP	RNTF	
RNTP	D, EC, ED, RNTJ, RNTF, RNTP	RNTP	RNTP	

TABLE 2.8

Iteration 3

Element	Reachability Set	Antecedent Set	Intersection Set	Level
ASF	D, ASF	ASF	ASF	
D	D	ASF, D	D	III
RNTJ	RNTJ	RNTJ, RNTP	RNTJ	III
RNTF	RNTF	RNTF, RNTP	RNTF	III
RNTP	D, RNTJ, RNTF, RNTP	RNTP	RNTP	

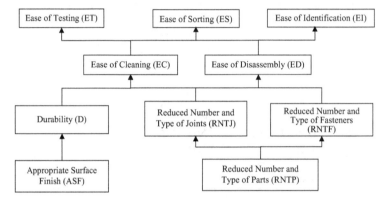

FIGURE 2.4

ISM model for DFR criteria.

2.4.2 Determination of the Importance Weights of Criteria Using ANP

Interrelationships among DFR criteria have been analyzed using ISM in the previous section. However, ISM does not provide any information on the importance weights of DFR criteria. That is why we employ ANP to determine the weights of DFR criteria.

ANP (Saaty [39]) is a more general form of AHP (Saaty [40]). In AHP, it is assumed that there is independence among criteria and sub-criteria. This assumption contradicts real-life situations. ANP resolves this contradiction by allowing for dependence within a set of criteria as well as between sets of criteria. Contrary to the hierarchical structure of AHP, a looser network structure is used in ANP. This allows the modeling of complex relationships among decision levels and attributes.

Figure 2.5 presents the ANP model. Curved arcs in this figure represent the relationships among DFR criteria. These relationships were determined based on ISM analysis carried out in the previous section. A questionnaire based on Saaty's nine-point scale (see Table 2.9) was given to the previously mentioned six experts to allow them to evaluate the relationships among DFR criteria numerically. In this questionnaire, experts compare pairs of DFR criteria considering the goal (remanufacturability of the product). One question from this questionnaire is given in Table 2.10 to present the structure of

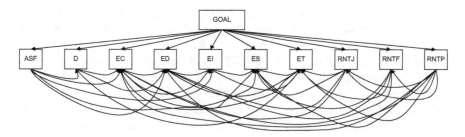

FIGURE 2.5
ANP model.

TABLE 2.9

Scale of Pairwise Judgements

Intensity of Importance	Definition
1	Equally important
3	Moderately more important
5	Strongly important
7	Very strongly more important
9	Extremely more important
2, 4, 6, 8	Intermediate judgment values

TABLE 2.10

Example Question from the ANP Questionnaire

Please mark or circle the impact levels of the following DFR criteria on EI based on the pairwise comparisons given below																	
ASF	9	8	7	6	5	4	3	2	1	2	3	4	5	6	7	8	9	EC
ASF	9	8	7	6	5	4	3	2	1	2	3	4	5	6	7	8	9	ET
ASF	9	8	7	6	5	4	3	2	1	2	3	4	5	6	7	8	9	RNTF
ASF	9	8	7	6	5	4	3	2	1	2	3	4	5	6	7	8	9	RNTJ
ASF	9	8	7	6	5	4	3	2	1	2	3	4	5	6	7	8	9	RNTP
EC	9	8	7	6	5	4	3	2	1	2	3	4	5	6	7	8	9	ET
EC	9	8	7	6	5	4	3	2	1	2	3	4	5	6	7	8	9	RNTF
EC	9	8	7	6	5	4	3	2	1	2	3	4	5	6	7	8	9	RNTJ
EC	9	8	7	6	5	4	3	2	1	2	3	4	5	6	7	8	9	RNTP
EC	9	8	7	6	5	4	3	2	1	2	3	4	5	6	7	8	9	RNTF
EC	9	8	7	6	5	4	3	2	1	2	3	4	5	6	7	8	9	RNTJ
EC	9	8	7	6	5	4	3	2	1	2	3	4	5	6	7	8	9	RNTP
RNTF	9	8	7	6	5	4	3	2	1	2	3	4	5	6	7	8	9	RNTJ
RNTF	9	8	7	6	5	4	3	2	1	2	3	4	5	6	7	8	9	RNTP
RNTJ	9	8	7	6	5	4	3	2	1	2	3	4	5	6	7	8	9	RNTP

the questions involved in the questionnaire. This question involves the pair-wise comparisons of the DFR criteria that affect the criterion EI. According to the seventh column of the initial reachability matrix presented in Table 2.4, there are six criteria (ASF, EC, ET, RNTJ, RNTF, and RNTP) affecting EI. That is why there are 15 pairwise comparisons in Table 2.10. The other questions in the questionnaire involve similar pairwise comparisons.

If an expert fills out the first line of the example question given in Table 2.10 as follows, this means that ASF has moderately more impact than EC on EI for that expert.

ASF	9	8	7	6	5	4	③	2	1	2	3	4	5	6	7	8	9	EC

Experts may circle different importance levels for the same pairwise comparison. That is why the geometric average of the importance levels circled by different experts is calculated for a pairwise comparison to give a single value.

After the pairwise comparisons of criteria have been completed and the interrelationships among criteria have been determined, an unweighted super matrix is formed (see Table 2.11). The unweighted super matrix is a partitioned matrix, in which each submatrix is composed of a set of relationships between and within the levels as represented by the ANP model. Then, the weighted super matrix is formed by normalizing the unweighted super matrix. Finally, the limiting super matrix is obtained by raising the weighted super matrix to limiting powers. Table 2.12 presents the priority of each criterion based on the limiting super matrix. According to Table 2.12, the criteria with the highest priority values are ASF, RNTP, RNTF, and RNTJ. In other words, a product highly satisfying these criteria will have a high level of remanufacturability. HoQ can be used to determine the technical product characteristics that will best satisfy the DFR criteria. The following section presents the details of the HoQ study.

TABLE 2.11

Unweighted Super Matrix

	ASF	D	EC	ED	EI	ES	ET	RNTF	RNTJ	RNTP	Goal
ASF	0	0	0.18079	0.27388	0.24080	0.15490	0	0	0	0	0.11616
D	0	0	0.20685	0.07597	0	0	0.10242	0	0	0	0.07859
EC	0	0	0	0	0.27073	0.11243	0.11492	0	0	0	0.04811
ED	0	0	0.21453	0	0	0	0.28076	0	0	0	0.16594
EI	0	0	0.05873	0.11191	0	0.07947	0.15461	0	0	0	0.07155
ES	0	0	0	0	0	0	0.22288	0	0	0	0.06570
ET	0	0	0	0	0.18501	0	0	0	0	0	0.06848
RNTF	0	0	0.08543	0.14744	0.08708	0.15590	0.03621	0	0	0	0.10054
RNTJ	0	0	0.08543	0.14744	0.08708	0.15590	0.03621	0	0	0	0.10054
RNTP	0	0	0.16824	0.24335	0.12930	0.34141	0.05200	0	0	0	0.18440
Goal	0	0	0	0	0	0	0	0	0	0	0

TABLE 2.12

Priority of each DFR Criterion

Criterion	Priority
ASF	0.19544
D	0.09010
EC	0.08689
ED	0.09353
EI	0.07479
ES	0.02893
ET	0.04238
RNTF	0.10343
RNTJ	0.10343
RNTP	0.18109

2.4.3 Use of House of Quality to Determine Technical Product Characteristics Satisfying DFR Criteria

HoQ is commonly used for the development of new products (Besterfield et al. [41]). However, in this chapter, we use it to evaluate the remanufacturability potential of an existing product design. In the first case, the customer is the end user who will use the new product. In the second case, the customer is the original equipment manufacturer (OEM) that remanufactures its own product or the independent remanufacturer. The completed HoQ is presented in Figure 2.6. The steps followed while constructing the HoQ are presented in the following sections.

2.4.3.1 Determination of Customer Requirements

At this stage, the expectations of customers from the product being analyzed are collected through the use of different tools (e.g., surveys, interviews). In Section 3.2, we have already determined the expectations of the company as DFR criteria by interviewing the company personnel. Hence, the DFR criteria presented in Table 2.1 are taken as customer requirements.

2.4.3.2 Determination of Technical Descriptors

Technical descriptors or engineering characteristics that will have an effect on at least one of the customer requirements are decided by a team of experts at this stage. Technical descriptors involve the design tips that can be used to satisfy the customer requirements listed in the customer requirements section. In this chapter, technical descriptors that will meet the DFR criteria are determined by a team of engineers and workers who have expertise in engine remanufacturing. They are presented in the "Technical Descriptors" section of the HoQ.

FIGURE 2.6
House of Quality.

2.4.3.3 Construction of a Relationship Matrix between Customer Requirements and Technical Descriptors

Relationships between customer requirements and technical descriptors are defined in this stage. The symbols in the center of the house represent the relationships between customer requirements and design tips.

2.4.3.4 Construction of an Interrelationship Matrix between Technical Descriptors

This stage involves the development of an interrelationship matrix between technical descriptors. This matrix is called the *correlation matrix* and forms the roof of the HoQ.

2.4.3.5 Competitive Assessments

In the competitive assessments sections of the HoQ, the competitors' products are compared with the product being analyzed. There are two sections for competitive assessments: customer assessment and technical assessment.

The section associated with customer competitive assessment is placed on the right side of the relationship matrix developed in Stage 3. It shows the position of the company compared with its competitors regarding each customer requirement. In this section, the numbers 1 through 5 are used for rating the company and its competitors (1: worst, 5: best).

The technical competitive assessment section is placed under the relationship matrix. It is used to evaluate the company and its competitors for each technical descriptor. As for the customer competitive assessment, the numbers 1 through 5 are used for rating the company and its competitors (1: worst, 5: best).

2.4.3.6 Development of Prioritized Customer Requirements

The prioritized customer requirements section is placed on the right side of the customer competitive assessment section. This section involves blocks devoted to "importance to customer," "target value," "scale-up factor," and "absolute weight."

- *Importance to Customer* is the evaluation of each customer requirement based on its importance to customers. Numbers 1 through 10 are used to rate each customer requirement (1: the least important, 10: the most important). "Importance to customer" values of the DFR criteria are determined by converting "criteria weights" presented in Table 2.9 into a 10-point scale using the following formula:

$$c_i = \frac{\text{Priority of customer requirement } i}{\text{Maximum priority value}} \cdot 10 \qquad (2.1)$$

  For instance, the importance to customer value of the second customer requirement (durability) is calculated as follows:

$$c_2 = \frac{0.09010}{0.19544} \cdot 10 = 4.6$$

- *Target Value* shows the rating value targeted by the company for each customer requirement. It is on the same scale as customer competitive assessment.

- *Scale-up Factor* is calculated by dividing the target value by the rating given in the customer competitive assessment section for the company's product.

- *Absolute Weight* of customer requirement i is calculated as follows:

$$d_i = c_i \cdot sf_i \qquad (2.2)$$

For instance, the absolute weight for the second customer requirement (durability) can be calculated as follows:

$$d_2 = 4.6 \cdot 1.3 = 6.0$$

2.4.3.7 Development of Prioritized Technical Descriptors

The prioritized technical descriptors section is placed under the technical competitive assessment section. This section involves blocks devoted to "degree of difficulty," "target value," "absolute weight," and "relative weight."

- *Degree of Difficulty* shows the technical difficulty associated with the implementation of a technical descriptor. Numbers 1 (the least difficult) through 10 (the most difficult) are used to rate each technical descriptor.
- *Target Value* shows the rating value targeted by the company for each technical descriptor. It is on the same scale as technical competitive assessment.
- *Absolute Weight* for the *j*th technical descriptor is calculated as follows:

$$a_j = \sum_{i=1}^{n} w_{ij} c_i \tag{2.3}$$

where

a_j is the row vector of absolute weights for the technical descriptors $(j = 1,\ldots,m)$

w_{ij} is the weights in the relationship matrix $(i = 1,\ldots,n, j = 1,\ldots,m)$

c_i is the column vector of importance to customer values $(i = 1,\ldots,n)$

m is the number of technical descriptors

n is the number of customer requirements

- *Relative Weight* for the *j*th technical descriptor is calculated as follows:

$$b_j = \sum_{i=1}^{n} w_{ij} d_i \tag{2.4}$$

where

b_j is the row vector of relative weights for the technical descriptors $(j = 1,\ldots,m)$

d_i is the column vector of absolute weights for the customer requirements $(i = 1,\ldots,n)$

Engineering efforts must be concentrated on the technical descriptors with high absolute and relative weights. For each technical descriptor, a competitive assessment is made by comparing the product being evaluated for redesign with the other two products produced by the competitors. Based on this assessment, *target value* is determined for each technical descriptor. The *absolute weight* is calculated using Equation 2.3 for each technical descriptor. For instance, the absolute weight for the fourth technical descriptor can be calculated as follows:

$$a_4 = 10 \cdot 3 + 4.6 \cdot 9 + 4.4 \cdot 3 + 4.8 \cdot 3 + 2.2 \cdot 3 = 106$$

The relative weight for each technical descriptor is calculated using Equation 2.4. For instance, the relative weight for the fourth technical descriptor can be calculated as follows:

$$b_4 = 3 \cdot 13 + 9 \cdot 6 + 3 \cdot 5.8 + 3 \cdot 6.2 + 3 \cdot 2.8 = 137$$

We can state that the most important technical descriptor is "use standard parts" according to the absolute and relative weight values presented in Figure 2.6. This descriptor is followed by "use appropriate material, texture and color" and so on. The remanufacturability of the product design can be improved by concentrating engineering efforts on one or more of these technical descriptors. When decisions are being made, the degree of technical difficulty associated with a technical descriptor should also be considered besides its absolute and relative weight values.

2.5 Conclusions and Future Research

Potential economic gains as well as strict government regulations have forced manufacturers to deal with product recovery operations. Being the most environment-friendly product recovery option, remanufacturing has received increased attention during the past decade. The success of remanufacturing operations is largely dependent on the design of the product being remanufactured. Thus, the design of products considering the remanufacturing operations (DFR) is an active research area. Researchers have proposed various DFR approaches. However, there is no study analyzing the relationships among DFR criteria. In this chapter, a DFR approach that considers the interactions among DFR criteria is proposed, and the proposed approach is implemented in an engine remanufacturing company. The following managerial insights can be gained from this study:

- The case company is owned by a large industrial group. This group has other companies that manufacture brand new engines. Hence, the results obtained at the end of this study can be shared with those companies. They may consider the proposed technical characteristics while designing/manufacturing brand new engines.

- It must be noted that designers do not apply the proposed approach. That is why they do not need to determine DFR criteria or learn the details of ISM, ANP, and HoQ. The proposed approach is applied in remanufacturing companies by research groups involving scientists and/or engineers. The results are shared with designers, and they consider those results while designing brand new engines.

- Conventional criteria such as cost and quality can be considered together with DFR criteria in the proposed approach. However, new interviews and questionnaires must be conducted with the experts, and ISM, ANP, and HoQ matrices must be reconstructed in that case.

The proposed approach can be improved by considering the following future research directions:

- The ISM technique used in the proposed approach presents an initial model for the interactions of DFR criteria. Hence, this model has not been statistically validated. Statistical validation of the presented ISM model using structural equation modeling (SEM) could be an interesting future research topic.

- The proposed approach requires the integrated use of three techniques (ISM, ANP, and HoQ). The implementation of those techniques in an integrated way may be difficult. Excel and Visual Basic for Applications (VBA) can be used together to automate ISM, ANP, and HoQ calculations.

References

1. Shumon RH, Arif-Uz-Zaman K, Rahman A (2011) Prospects of Remanufacturing, Bangladesh perspective. *International Journal of Industrial Engineering: Theory, Applications and Practice* 18: 254–259.
2. El korchi A, Millet D (2011) Designing a sustainable reverse logistics channel: The 18 generic structures framework. *Journal of Cleaner Production* 19: 588–597.
3. Mutha A, Pokharel S (2009) Strategic network design for reverse logistics and remanufacturing using new and old product modules. *Computers & Industrial Engineering* 56: 334–346.
4. Jayant A, Gupta P, Garg SK (2012) Reverse logistics: Perspectives, empirical studies and research directions. *International Journal of Industrial Engineering: Theory, Applications and Practice* 19: 369–388.

5. Tian G, Liu Y, Ke H, Chu J (2012) Energy evaluation method and its optimization models for process planning with stochastic characteristics: A case study in disassembly decision-making. *Computers & Industrial Engineering* 63: 553–563.
6. Kang JG, Lee DH, Xirouchakis P (2003) Disassembly sequencing with imprecise data: A case study. *International Journal of Industrial Engineering: Theory, Applications and Practice* 10: 407–412.
7. Shu LH, Flowers WC (1999) Application of a design-for-remanufacture framework to the selection of product life-cycle fastening and joining methods. *Robotics and Computer-Integrated Manufacturing* 15: 179–190.
8. Desai A, Mital A (2003) Evaluation of disassemblability to enable design for disassembly in mass production. *International Journal of Industrial Ergonomics* 32: 265–281.
9. Desai A, Mital A (2003) Review of literature on disassembly algorithms and design for disassembly guidelines for product design. *International Journal of Industrial Engineering: Theory, Applications and Practice* 10: 244–255.
10. Mital A, Desai A (2007) A structured approach to new product design, development and manufacture part II: Putting the product together (assembly) and disposal (disassembly). *International Journal of Industrial Engineering: Theory, Applications and Practice* 14: 23–32.
11. Ilgin MA, Gupta SM (2010) Environmentally conscious manufacturing and product recovery (ECMPRO): A review of the state of the art. *Journal of Environmental Management* 91: 563–591.
12. Gungor A, Gupta SM (1999) Issues in environmentally conscious manufacturing and product recovery: A survey. *Computers and Industrial Engineering* 36: 811–853.
13. Ilgin MA, Gupta SM (2012) *Remanufacturing Modeling and Analysis*. CRC Press, Boca Raton, FL.
14. Ijomah WL, McMahon CA, Hammond GP, Newman ST (2007) Development of design for remanufacturing guidelines to support sustainable manufacturing. *Robotics and Computer-Integrated Manufacturing* 23: 712–719.
15. Yuksel H (2010) Design of automobile engines for remanufacture with quality function deployment. *International Journal of Sustainable Engineering* 3: 170–180.
16. Hatcher G, Ijomah W, Windmill J (2013) Design for remanufacturing in China: A case study of electrical and electronic equipment. *Journal of Remanufacturing* 3: 3.
17. Sakao T, Mizuyama H (2014) Understanding of a product/service system design: A holistic approach to support design for remanufacturing. *Journal of Remanufacturing* 4: 1.
18. Chakraborty K, Mondal S, Mukherjee K (2017) Analysis of product design characteristics for remanufacturing using Fuzzy AHP and Axiomatic Design. *Journal of Engineering Design* 28: 338–368.
19. Hatcher GD, Ijomah WL, Windmill JFC (2011) Design for remanufacture: A literature review and future research needs. *Journal of Cleaner Production* 19: 2004–2014.
20. Fegade V, Shrivatsava RL, Kale AV (2015) Design for remanufacturing: Methods and their approaches. *Materials Today: Proceedings* 2: 1849–1858.
21. Abbasi M, Shirazi MA, Aryanezjad MB (2012) Determination of manufacturing strategy using interpretive structural modeling. *African Journal of Business Management* 6: 881–887.

22. Alawamleh M, Popplewell K (2011) Interpretive structural modelling of risk sources in a virtual organisation. *International Journal of Production Research* 49: 6041–6063.
23. Diabat A, Govindan K (2011) An analysis of the drivers affecting the implementation of green supply chain management. *Resources, Conservation and Recycling* 55: 659–667.
24. Govindan K, Pokharel S, Sasi Kumar P (2009) A hybrid approach using ISM and fuzzy TOPSIS for the selection of reverse logistics provider. *Resources, Conservation and Recycling* 54: 28–36.
25. Mathiyazhagan K, Govindan K, NoorulHaq A, Geng Y (2013) An ISM approach for the barrier analysis in implementing green supply chain management. *Journal of Cleaner Production* 47: 283–297.
26. Kim I, Watada J (2009) Towards a New Medical Decision Support System with Bio-inspired Interpretive Structural Modelling. In: K Nakamatsu, G Phillips-Wren, LC Jain and RJ Howlett (eds) *New Advances in Intelligent Decision Technologies*. Springer, Heidelberg, pp 459–466.
27. Mukherjee K, Mondal S (2009) Analysis of issues relating to remanufacturing technology—A case of an Indian company. *Technology Analysis & Strategic Management* 21: 639–652.
28. Köne AÇ, Büke T (2007) An Analytical Network Process (ANP) evaluation of alternative fuels for electricity generation in Turkey. *Energy Policy* 35: 5220–5228.
29. Bayazit O, Karpak B (2007) An analytical network process-based framework for successful total quality management (TQM): An assessment of Turkish manufacturing industry readiness. *International Journal of Production Economics* 105: 79–96.
30. Shaik M, Abdul-Kader W (2012) Performance measurement of reverse logistics enterprise: A comprehensive and integrated approach. *Measuring Business Excellence* 16: 23–24.
31. Ilgin MA, Gupta SM, Battaia O (2015) Use of MCDM techniques in environmentally conscious manufacturing and product recovery: State of the art. *Journal of Manufacturing Systems* 37: 746–758.
32. Gupta SM, Ilgin MA (2018) *Multiple Criteria Decision Making Applications in Environmentally Conscious Manufacturing and Product Recovery*. CRC Press, Boca Raton.
33. Gungor A (2006) Evaluation of connection types in design for disassembly (DFD) using analytic network process. *Computers & Industrial Engineering* 50: 35–54.
34. Ravi V, Shankar R (2005) Analysis of interactions among the barriers of reverse logistics. *Technological Forecasting and Social Change* 72: 1011–1029.
35. Ravi V, Shankar R, Tiwari MK (2008) Selection of a reverse logistics project for end-of-life computers: ANP and goal programming approach. *International Journal of Production Research* 46: 4849–4870.
36. Chang A-Y, Hu K-J, Hong Y-L (2013) An ISM-ANP approach to identifying key agile factors in launching a new product into mass production. *International Journal of Production Research* 51: 582–597.
37. Shahbandarzadeh H, Ghorbanpour A (2011) The Applying ISM/FANP approach for appropriate location selection of health centers. *Iranian Journal of Management Science* 4: 5–28.

38. Thakkar J, Deshmukh SG, Gupta AD, Shankar R (2007) Development of a Balanced Scorecard: An integrated approach of Interpretive Structural Modeling (ISM) and Analytic Network Process (ANP). *International Journal of Productivity and Performance Management* 56: 25–59.
39. Saaty TL (1996) *Decision Making with Dependence and Feedback: The Analytic Network Process.* RWS Publications, Pittsburgh, PA.
40. Saaty TL (1980) *The Analytic Hierarchy Process.* McGraw-Hill, New York.
41. Besterfield DH, Besterfield-Michna C, Besterfield GH, Besterfield-Sacre M (2003) *Total Quality Management.* Prentice Hall, Upper Saddle River, NJ.
42. Ijomah WL, McMahon CA, Hammond GP, Newman ST (2007) Development of robust design-for-remanufacturing guidelines to further the aims of sustainable development. *International Journal of Production Research* 45: 4513–4536.
43. Ijomah WL (2009) Addressing decision making for remanufacturing operations and design-for-remanufacture. *International Journal of Sustainable Engineering* 2: 91–102.
44. Charter M, Gray C (2008) Remanufacturing and product design. *International Journal of Product Development* 6: 375–392.

3

Effects of Product Designs on End-of-Life Product Recovery under Uncertainty

Aditi D. Joshi and Surendra M. Gupta

CONTENTS

3.1 Introduction

Lately, the use of consumer products has increased tremendously. A variety of new products and existing products with updated technologies are being continuously introduced into the market; consequently, consumers constantly upgrade their products to keep up with the new technology. This forces the products to reach their end of life (EOL) sooner. Therefore, even though a product is in good condition, its disposal is inevitable. Most products are eventually disposed of in landfills, and due to the increasing rate of waste production, the available landfills are quickly filling up, reducing the number of landfills at an alarming rate.

To protect the environment from such hazardous waste, governments have enforced strict rules and regulations. Original equipment manufacturers (OEMs) or product recovery facilities are responsible for products beyond their useful lives. To comply with government rules and regulations and to earn profits, OEMs implement product recovery techniques such as recycling, remanufacturing, and disposal. Disassembly is also an important technique and is normally carried out as a first operation in the product recovery process.

The efficiency of the product recovery processes can have a significant impact on the management of EOL products. A key factor affecting the efficiency of product recovery processes is the products' design. Therefore, OEMs are considering EOL strategies at an early stage of product design. Various methodologies to ease the work of designers have been developed, including Design for X (DfX), life cycle assessment, and material selection. DfX involves different design specialties such as Design for environment (DfE), Design for disassembly (DfD), Design for recycling (DfR), and Design for remanufacturing (DfRem) (Veerakamolmal and Gupta, 2000).

This chapter proposes an Advanced-Remanufacturing-To-Order-Disassembly-To-Order (ARTODTO) system, which receives a variety of EOL products with design alternatives to satisfy the demand for products, components, and materials by implementing disassembly and remanufacturing processes. However, there are numerous uncertainties, including the quantity and conditions of the received EOL products, which complicate the process and make it difficult to identify the exact number of EOL products needed for disassembly to fulfill all the demands. The uncertainties are eliminated using heuristic techniques, which predict the disassembly yields to form a deterministic problem. The deterministic problem is solved using a multi-criteria decision making (MCDM) technique known as *linear physical programming* (LPP). The multiple criteria considered are total profit, procurement cost, purchase cost, and disposal cost. The main objective here is to determine how many EOL products need to be acquired to satisfy all the demands, criteria, and constraints.

3.2 Literature Review

The literature related to this study is divided into five categories: environmentally conscious manufacturing and product recovery, disassembly, remanufacturing, product design, and heuristic techniques.

3.2.1 Environmentally Conscious Manufacturing and Product Recovery

There are two important review papers that are available in the literature and are directly related to the subject area of this research. The first one is the state-of-the-art survey paper by Gungor and Gupta (1999) covering papers in environmentally conscious manufacturing and product recovery (ECMPRO) published through 1998. The second one is another state-of-the-art survey paper in the same area covering papers published between 1998 and 2010 by Ilgin and Gupta (2010). Together, they classified more than 870 papers (330 and 540, respectively) under four main categories: environmentally conscious product design, reverse and closed-loop supply chains, remanufacturing, and disassembly.

There are additional review papers that are available in the literature and are of some interest for the subject matter of this research. Gupta (2013) in his book gave an overview on reverse supply chain and various issues involved in its implementation. The first chapter of the book by Ilgin and Gupta elucidated forward and reverse supply chains and their differences and provided a detailed literature review on various aspects of reverse supply chains: for example, network design (deterministic models and stochastic models), transportation issues, selection of used products, and facility layout. Ma et al. (2018) proposed an integrated method based on Decision-Making Trial and Evaluation Laboratory (DEMATEL) and rough set theory, which considers the enablers of environmentally conscious manufacturing (ECM) strategy and interrelationships between them. The authors also applied the method to analyze the enablers of ECM strategy in an equipment manufacturing company to illustrate the feasibility and effectiveness of the proposed method. Gupta and Ilgin (2018) in their book presented various applications and techniques of MCDM in ECM and product recovery. The techniques presented in this book can be used to solve problems concerning product design, logistics, disassembly, and remanufacturing.

3.2.2 Disassembly

Scholars have categorized the disassembly processes as scheduling, sequencing, disassembly line balancing, disassembly-to-order, and automated disassembly. Disassembly-to-order (DTOs) is the most relevant category here. DTOs determine the optimal lot sizes of EOL products to disassemble to satisfy the component demands from a mix of different product types that have a number of components/modules in common (Lambert and Gupta, 2002). Kongar and Gupta (2002) proposed a multi-criteria optimization model of a DTO system to determine which and how many of the EOL products are to be disassembled to meet the demands for products, components, and materials to achieve the goals of maximum total profit, maximum material sales revenue, minimum number of disposed items, minimum number of stored items, minimum cost of disposal, and minimum cost of preparation. Kongar and Gupta (2006) extended 14Kongar and Gupta's (2002) method by using fuzzy goal programming (GP) to model the fuzzy aspirations of numerous goals. Kongar and Gupta (2009b) proposed an LPP model for solving the DTO problem, which can satisfy tangible or intangible financial and environmental performance measures. Kongar and Gupta (2009a) also developed a multi-objective tabu search algorithm for EOL product disassembly considering the multiple objectives of maximizing the total profit, maximizing the resale and recycling percentage, and minimizing the disposal percentage.

Lambert and Gupta (2005) in their book *Disassembly Modeling for Assembly, Maintenance, Reuse and Recycling* discussed the different aspects of disassembly. Özceylan et al. (2018) presented a review of the state of the art of disassembly line balancing. The authors reviewed 116 publications, including proceedings and journals since 1999, and identified trends and gaps in the literature to clarify and provide future research directions. Kim et al. (2018), with the objective of minimizing the sum of disassembly and penalty costs, proposed a stochastic integer programming model, which considers a problem with random operation times in a parallel disassembly environment where one or more components can be removed at the same time by a single disassembly operation. The authors proposed a sample average approximation-based solution algorithm to solve a problem under a given set of scenarios for disassembly operation times.

3.2.3 Remanufacturing

Remanufacturing is an industrial process that restores worn-out products to like-new conditions (Aksoy and Gupta, 2005; Kim et al., 2006). Yang et al. (2014) proposed a decision support tool for evaluating the remanufacturability of components to facilitate component EOL strategy planning. The authors performed qualitative and quantitative analyses to maximize the expected savings under quality uncertainty. They also proposed a new approach to quantify and integrate environmental considerations into the decision-making process. Andrew-Munot et al. (2015) examined the key motivating factors for companies to engage in remanufacturing programs, the major sources for acquiring used products, and subsequent markets for selling remanufactured products. The authors also presented four examples of remanufacturing processes of different products to demonstrate that the exact number and sequence of remanufacturing processes are dependent on the type of product being remanufactured. The various remanufacturing issues include forecasting, production planning, production scheduling, capacity planning, and uncertainty in remanufacturing.

3.2.4 Heuristic Procedures

Few researchers have considered the uncertainty related to disassembly yields. To manage the stochastic disassembly yields, Inderfurth and Langella (2007), and Langella (2007) developed two heuristic procedures (one-to-one and one-to-many) to accurately predict the disassembly yields in a DTO problem. The authors managed the stochastic disassembly yields by converting them into their deterministic equivalents and then solving the deterministic problem. They concluded that the one-to-many approach is better than the one-to-one approach, as it produced more accurate results. Imtanavanich and Gupta (2006) used the heuristics developed by Inderfurth and Langella (2007) to handle the stochastic elements of a DTO system. They also proposed a GP model to determine the number of returned products that satisfy the goals. The authors also generated a DTO plan to satisfy the demand of components while maximizing profit and minimizing the cost of the system. They used three techniques to solve the problem: a genetic algorithm, LPP, and a refining algorithm.

3.2.5 Environmentally Conscious Product Design

The primary aim of traditional product development is to achieve improvements in design with respect to cost, functionality, and manufacturability. However, product designers are now considering environmental factors in the design process. A number of methodologies have been developed to help designers make environmentally friendly design choices. For example, Cheung et al. (2015) proposed and developed a roadmap to facilitate the prediction of disposal costs, which will be used to determine whether the EOL parts are viable to be remanufactured, refurbished, or recycled at an early design concept phase. The authors illustrated the proposed roadmap with a defense electronic system case study. Li et al. (2015) presented a state-of-the-art review paper on environmentally conscious product design. They reviewed 120 references on theories, methods, and software tools for environmentally conscious product design published during 2005 to 2015. The references were divided into five categories: product eco-design, DfD, DfR, material selection, and eco-design software tools. DfD includes the methodologies directly related to this research study. Kim and Moon (2016) introduced a design methodology to develop eco-modular product architecture and assess its modularity for product recovery. They proposed modularity assessment metrics to identify independent interactions between modules and the degrees of similarity within each module. de Aguiar et al. (2017) proposed a diagnostic tool to evaluate product recyclability to be applied during the product design phase for designer decision making. The procedure allows the product redesign to be simulated to improve its EOL performance. Li et al. (2018) proposed a time-series forecasting procedure for evaluating a product's recyclability at the product design phase. The authors considered several economic and environmental factors of different phases of the product's life cycle and predicted the cost of recycled material at the product's EOL. The authors also provided a case study of a cylinder engine design, which concluded that the methodology was fully capable of providing decision support to designers by assessing the recyclability of the product at the design phase.

3.3 Problem Statement

The ARTODTO system acquires a wide variety of EOL products to fulfill various demands. Figure 3.1 illustrates an ARTODTO system. The acquired EOL products are first inspected, sorted, and cleaned and are then prepared for disassembly. Depending on the final use and condition of the products and components, the type of disassembly process is determined. Components that are demanded for remanufacturing and reuse (i.e., functional components) are disassembled using non-destructive disassembly, while components that are demanded for recycling and/or disposal (i.e., non-functional components), are disassembled using destructive disassembly.

The component yields from destructive and non-destructive disassembly processes are stochastic due to the uncertainty regarding the condition of the received EOL products. Components from the non-destructive disassembly are inspected for good and bad components. Good non-destructive components are used to satisfy the demand for remanufactured products and reused components, while bad non-destructive components are sent to the recycling process. If the demands cannot be met using the disassembled components, additional components are procured from outside suppliers, as demand shortage is not allowed. Components from destructive disassembly are also inspected for good and bad destructive components. Good components from destructive disassembly, along with the bad components from non-destructive disassembly, are sent to the

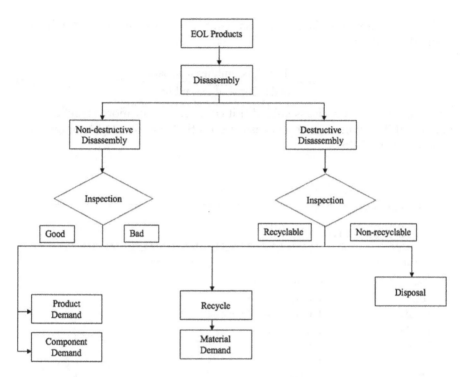

FIGURE 3.1
Advanced-remanufacturing-to-order-disassembly-to-order system under stochastic yields.

recycling facility. Finally, the bad components from destructive disassembly are disposed of.

The received EOL products are available in various design alternatives depending on customer demand, manufacturer, model, version, use, and so on. Some of the factors affected by the different product designs are

1. Size and shape of the product—the size and shape of the alternatives can be different.
2. Location of use—an alternative can be specific to the location or function of the use.
3. Ease of disassembly—the assembly or arrangement of components in different alternatives can be different, affecting the retrieval of components from the products.
4. Time for disassembly—the time for disassembly can differ depending on the design alternative.
5. Labor skills and costs—An alternative that is difficult to disassemble may require more skilled labor than an alternative that is easy to disassemble, in which case the labor cost will also be different.

To account for these factors, a disassembly factor is introduced, which is defined as follows:

$$f = \frac{\text{number of assemblies to separate}}{\text{total number of assemblies}}$$ (3.1)

An assembly will be disassembled if it contains one or more target components or if it contains lower-level assemblies that contain target components (Cheung et al., 2015).

3.4 Nomenclature

Variable/Parameter	Description
RSR	Resale revenue
TDISPC	Total disposal cost
TDISSC	Total disassembly cost
THOLC	Total holding cost;
TOPC	Total outside procurement cost;
TP	Total profit;
TPURC	Total purchase cost;
TRECC	Total recycling cost;
TREMC	Total remanufacturing cost;
ca_j	Assembly cost per unit of component j;
cdc_j	Disposal cost for component j;
cdm_j	Disposal cost for material of component j;
cdp_i	Disposal cost for product i;
chc_j	Holding cost per unit of component j;
chm	Holding cost per unit of material of component j;
cpc_j	Outside procurement cost per unit of component j;
cpp_i	Purchase cost per unit of product i;
crc_j	Recycling cost per unit of material of component j;
$drec_j$	Demand for reuse component j;
f	Disassembly factor;
$lcdd_j$	Labor cost for destructive disassembly of component j;
$lcndd_j$	Labor cost for non-destructive disassembly of component j;
mv_j	Value of material of component j;
$qbrc_j$	Quantity of bad non-destructively disassembled component j;
$qddc_j$	Quantity of destructively disassembled component j;
$qdispc_j$	Quantity of component j disposed of;
$qdispm_j$	Quantity of material of component j disposed of;
$qdispp_i$	Quantity of product i disposed of
$qdissc_j$	Quantity of disassembled component j

Variable/Parameter	Description
$qdissp_i$	Quantity of product i disassembled
$qgrc_j$	Quantity of good non-destructively disassembled component j
$qnddc_j$	Quantity of non-destructively disassembled component j
$qopc_j$	Quantity of component j procured from outside
$qpurp_i$	Quantity of product i purchased
qrc_j	Quantity of reused component j
$qrecc_j$	Quantity of recycled material of component j
$qrecm_j$	Quantity of recycled material of component j
$qredc_j$	Quantity of recycled component j that is disposed of
$qremp_i$	Quantity of remanufactured product i
$qrmc_j$	Quantity of component j used for remanufacturing
qsc_j	Quantity of stored component j
qsm_j	Quantity of stored material of component j
rv_j	Resale value of component j
scv_j	Stored value of component j
sdy_{ij}	Stochastic disassembly yield of component j in product i
sgp_i	Stochastic good condition percentage of product i
smv_j	Stored value of material of component j
$srcp_j$	Stochastic recyclable percentage of component j
srp_j	Stochastic reusable percentage of component j
tdd_j	Time for destructive disassembly of component j
$tndd_j$	Time for non-destructive disassembly of component j
wc_j	Weight of component j
$wrecm_j$	Weight of recycled material of component j

3.5 Heuristic Technique

The purchased EOL products are received in a variety of conditions. Since the conditions of the purchased products are unknown, it is impossible to know the exact yield from the disassembly. However, it is possible to estimate the probable yield. The fulfillment of demands depends on how accurately the disassembly yield is predicted. If the actual yield is lower than the prediction, we may have to supplement the components by buying them from an outside supplier to satisfy the demand. If the actual yield is higher than the prediction, we may incur a disposal cost due to excess components. Therefore, predicting accurate yield value is very important in the disassembly process.

This section explains the heuristic procedures first introduced by Inderfurth and Langella (Inderfurth and Langella, 2007). These procedures are used to predict the stochastic disassembly yields and convert them into their deterministic equivalents. Once the stochastic part is converted into deterministic, the problem can be solved using deterministic techniques.

3.5.1 Mathematical Formulation for Heuristic Procedures

The following equations are used to identify the number of procured components and the number of disposed components. The basic concept to identify the number of procured components (l_j) and disposed components (fd_j) is to compare the component demands (drc_j) with the number of components from the disassembly process (which is a multiplication of the number of purchased products (TPC_i), component multiplicity (CM_{ij}), and the stochastic disassembly yields (SDY_j). If the demand is greater than the number of components, the demand is fulfilled by outside procurement, and if the demand is less than the number of components, excess components are disposed of.

$$l_j = \max\left[drc_j - \sum_i \left(TPC_i * CM_j * SDY_j\right); 0 \right] \tag{3.2}$$

$$fd_j = \max\left[\sum_i TPC_i * CM_{ij} * SDY_j - drc_j; 0 \right] \tag{3.3}$$

In the next step, a basic deterministic model is considered, whose objective is to minimize the total cost function (TC_D). It comprises total purchase cost (number of purchased products [TPC_i] multiplied by its corresponding unit purchase cost [cpr_i], total procurement cost (number of procured components [pc_j] multiplied by its corresponding unit procurement cost [cpc_i]), and total disposal cost (the number of disposed components [fd_j] multiplied by its corresponding unit disposing cost [cdc_j]).

$$\min TC_D = \sum_i \left(TPC_i * cpr_i\right) + \sum_j (pc_j * l_j) + \sum_j \left(fd_j * cds_j\right) \tag{3.4}$$

subject to

$$\sum_i \left(TPC_i * CM_{ij} * SDY_j\right) + l_j - fd_j = drc_j \tag{3.5}$$

$TTB_j, OPC_j, TDIC_j \geq 0$ and are integer.

In the next step, stochastic l_j and fd_j from Equations 3.2 and 3.3 are applied into the deterministic problem from Equations 3.4 and 3.5. Therefore, the stochastic problem is formulated as follows:

$$TC_s = \underset{SDY_j}{E} \left\{ \sum_i TPC_i * cpr_i \right)$$

$$+ \sum_j (pc_j * \max[drc_j - \sum_i (SDY_j * TPC_i * CM_{ij}); 0] \qquad (3.6)$$

$$+ \sum_j \left(cds_j * \max\left[\sum_i (SDY_j * TPC_i * CM_{ij}) - drc_j; 0 \right] \right) \right\}$$

subject to $TPC_i \geq 0$ and integer.

This stochastic problem can be solved heuristically by replacing the stochastic yields by deterministic equivalents and then solving the deterministic problem. Two heuristic procedures, one-to-one and one-to-many, which help calculate the deterministic equivalents, are presented in the following sections.

3.5.2 One-to-One Heuristic Approach

For this approach, a product with single core and a single component is considered. So if a product has multiple components, the product is split into one-to-one relationships. To achieve this, the core cost (which is purchase cost plus separation cost) is split and attributed to each component. The cost is split proportionally to the procurement costs of the components. Split core cost, for each component of each product, can be calculated as follows:

$$c_{ij}^S = (cpr_i + cse_i) * (rv_j / \sum_j rv_j) \qquad (3.7)$$

For example, in Figure 3.2, if the core cost is $9, and procurement costs of components A, B, and C are $2, $3, and $4, respectively, the split core costs of component A, B, and C will be $2, $3, and $4, respectively.

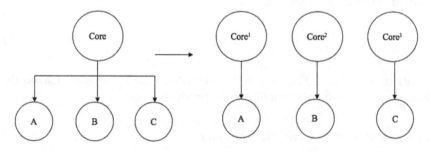

FIGURE 3.2
One-to-one heuristic.

It is assumed that each stochastic yield rate SDY_{ij} has a continuous density function $g_{ik}(SDY_{ij})$. The stochastic objective function TC_s for one-to-one heuristic is as follows:

$$TC_S = TPC * CM * SDY + pc$$

$$* \int_{SDY^-}^{drc/TPC} (drc - TPC * SDY) * g(SDY).d(SDY) + cds$$

$$* \int_{drc/TPC}^{SDY^+} (TPC * SDY - drc) * g(SDY).d(SDY)$$

(3.8)

As TC_s is convex in TPC, simple differential calculus gives the optimal number of purchased products TPC to be processed by disassembly. The TPC turns out to be

$$TPC = drc / \gamma \qquad (3.9)$$

where γ is given by

$$\gamma = \sqrt{\frac{rv.(SDY^-)^2 + cds * (SDY^+)^2 + 2 * c^s * (SDY^+ - SDY^-)}{rv + cds}} \qquad (3.10)$$

In the corresponding deterministic problem from Equations 3.4 and 3.5, for a system of single core and single component, the optimal number of purchased products would be

$$TPC = drc / SDY \qquad (3.11)$$

Comparing Equations 3.9 and 3.11,

$$S\hat{D}Y = \gamma \qquad (3.12)$$

Equations 3.7, 3.9, and 3.11 are used to calculate the deterministic yield equivalent factor for each component of each product.

3.5.3 One-to-Many Heuristic Approach

In this approach, many-to-many problem structure is broken down into a one-to-many problem structure. For illustration, consider a product with two

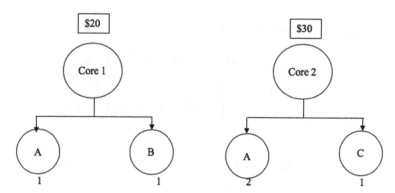

FIGURE 3.3
One-to-many heuristic.

components, A and B, as shown in Figure 3.3. The core cost of the product is the sum of take-back product cost (*ctb*) and product separation cost (*cse*). We assume that each stochastic yield rate has a continuous density function $g(SDY)$. Therefore, each yield is bounded from above and below as $SDY^- \le SDY \le SDY^+$ ($g(SDY)=0$ for $SDY \le SDY^-$ and $SDY \ge SDY^+$. Then, the stochastic objective function TC_s (derived from Equation 4.5) can be formulated as follows:

$$TC_s = TTB*(ctb+cse)+cpc_A$$

$$*\int_{SDY^-}^{DRC/TTB} (DRC_A - TTB_A * SDY_A)* g_A(SDY_A)* d(SDY_A)+cdc_A$$

$$*\int_{DRC/TTB}^{SDY^+} (TTB_A * SDY_A - DRC_A)* g_A(SDY_A)* d(SDY_A)+cpc_B$$

$$*\int_{SDY^-}^{DRC/TTB} (DRC_B - TTB_B * SDY_B)* g_B(SDY_B)* d(SDY_B)+cdc_B \qquad (3.13)$$

$$*\int_{DRC/TTB}^{SDY^+} (TTB_B * SDY_B - DRC_B)* g_B(SDY_B)* d(SDY_B)$$

The cost function TC_s is convex in TTB. We assume that the yield rates of the different components are independently distributed to avoid incorporating joint density functions with SDY_A and SDY_B. From taking the first-order derivative and setting equal to zero, we have

$$\frac{dTC_s}{dTTB} = 0 = (ctb + cse) + cpc_A$$

$$* \int_{SDY_{\bar{A}}}^{DRC_A/TTB} \frac{(-SDY_A)g(SDY_A)d(SDY_A) + cdc_A}{\ast \int_{DRC_A/TTB}^{SDY_A^+} (SDY_A)g(SDY_A)d(SDY_A)}$$

$$+ cpc_B * \int_{SDY_{\bar{B}}}^{DRC_B/TTB} (-SDY_B)g(SDY_B)d(SDY_B) + cdc_B$$

$$* \int_{DRC_B/TTB}^{SDY_B^+} (SDY_B)g(SDY_B)d(SDY_B)$$

(3.14)

Therefore,

$$(cpc_A + cdc_A) * \int_{DRC_A/TTB}^{SDY_A^+} SDY_A * g_A(SDY_A)d(SDY_A) + (cpc_B + cdc_B) *$$

$$\int_{DRC_B/TTB}^{SDY_B^+} SDY_B * g_B(SDY_B)d(SDY_B)$$

(3.15)

$$= cpc_A * S\bar{D}Y_A + cpc_B * S\bar{D}Y_B - (ctb + cse)$$

If the yield rates are uniformly distributed, we can solve for the integration terms:

$$(cpc_A + cdc_A) * \int_{DRC_A/TTB}^{SDY_A^+} SDY_A * \frac{1}{SDY_A^+ - SDY_A^-} d(SDY_A) + (cpc_B + cdc_B) *$$

$$\int_{DRC_B/TTB}^{SDY_B^+} SDY_B * \frac{1}{SDY_B^+ - SDY_B^-} d(SDY_B)$$

(3.16)

$$= cpc_A * S\bar{D}Y_A + cpc_B * S\bar{D}Y_B - (ctb + cse)$$

Then,

$$\frac{(cpc_A + cdc_A)}{2(SDY_A^+ - SDY_A^-)} * (SDY_A^{+2} - (\frac{DRC_A}{TTB})^2) + \frac{(cpc_B + cdc_B)}{2(SDY_B^+ - SDY_B^-)} *$$

$$(SDY_B^{+2} - (\frac{DRC_B}{TTB})^2)$$

(3.17)

$$= cpc_A * S\bar{D}Y_A + cpc_B * S\bar{D}Y_B - (ctb + cse)$$

After that,

$$(cpc_A + cdc_A) * (SDY_A^+ - SDY_A^-) * \left(SDY_A^{+2} - \left(\frac{DRC_A}{TTB} \right)^2 \right) +$$

$$(cpc_B + cdc_B) * (SDY_B^+ - SDY_B^-) * \left(SDY_B^{+2} - \left(\frac{DRC_B}{TTB} \right)^2 \right) \qquad (3.18)$$

$$= 2(cpc_A * \bar{SDY}_A + cpc_B * \bar{SDY}_B - (ctb + cse)) * (SDY_A^+ - SDY_A^-)$$

Thus,

$$(cpc_A + cdc_A) * (SDY_B^+ - SDY_B^-) * (\frac{DRC_A}{TTB})^2 + (cpc_B + cdc_B) *$$

$$(SDY_A^+ - SDY_A^-) * (\frac{DRC_B}{TTB})^2 = (cpc_A + cdc_A) * (SDY_B^+ - SDY_B^-) * SDY_A^{+2} + \qquad (3.19)$$

$$(cpc_B + cdc_B) * (SDY_A^+ - SDY_A^-) * SDY_B^{+2}$$

$$-2 * (cpc_A * \bar{SDY}_A + cpc_B * \bar{SDY}_B - (ctb + cse)) * (SDY_A^+ - SDY_A^-)$$

Finally, we have a closed form formula for the optimal number of take-back products (*TTB*):

$$TTB = \sqrt{ \frac{c_{AB} * DRC_A^2 + c_{BA} * DRC_B^2}{\begin{array}{c} c_{AB} * (SDY_A^+)^2 + c_{BA} * (SDY_B^+)^2 - 2 * (cpc_A * \bar{SDY}_A + cpc_B * \\ \bar{SDY}_B - (ctb + cse)) * (SDY_A^+ - SDY_A^-) * (SDY_B^+ - SDY_B^-) \end{array}} } \qquad (3.20)$$

where

$$c_{AB} = (cpc_A + cdc_A) * (SDY_B^+ - SDY_B^-) \qquad (3.21)$$

$$c_{BA} = (cpc_B + cdc_B) * (SDY_A^+ - SDY_A^-) \qquad (3.22)$$

Therefore, deterministic yield equivalent factors can be calculated by

$$S\hat{D}Y_A = DRC_A / TTB \qquad (3.23)$$

and

$$S\hat{D}Y_B = DRC_B / TTB \qquad (3.24)$$

If there are component commonalities in a general many-to-many problem structure, the demands have to be split up for any components that have component commonalities for each of their own cores. One way to split and balance the demand for each component is to do it corresponding to the core cost and its component multiplicity for each core.

Consider the example shown in Figure 3.3 for illustration purposes. The demand for Component A is 500, and core costs for Products 1 and 2 are \$20 and \$30, respectively. Product 1 contains 1 unit of Component A and 1 unit of Component B, while Product 2 contains 2 units of Component A and 1 unit of Component C.

The split demands for Component A for Product 1 (DRC_{1A}) and Product 2 (DRC_{2A}) can be calculated by using the following formula:

$$DRC_{1A} = DRC_A * \frac{(CM_{1A} / C_1^s)}{\sum_i CM_{iA} / C_i^s)} \tag{3.25}$$

and

$$DRC_{2A} = DRC_A * \frac{(CM_{2A} / C_2^s)}{\sum_i (CM_{iA} / C_i^s)} \tag{3.26}$$

Therefore, using this formula, $DRC_{1A} = 214$ and $DRC_{2A} = 286$.

Equations 3.23 through 3.26 can be used to calculate the split demands and deterministic yield equivalent for each component of each product.

3.6 Linear Physical Programming

Messac, Gupta, and Akbulut (Messac et al., 1996) proposed a new optimization technique known as *linear physical programming*. It addresses issues related to multiple objective optimization, such as problem formulation, the nature of the obtainable solutions, and the algorithm. Most real-world decision-making problems are characteristically multi-objective, and there are various tools to solve them. One such popular tool is goal programming. It treats each objective as a goal and attempts to achieve preset target values for these goals. The goals are weighed according to the decision maker's (DM's) preferences. But the greater challenge here is to accurately determine the weights that reflect the DM's true preferences.

LPP avoids this task of choosing weights. In physical programming (PP), the DM has some concrete idea about the objectives, which can be represented in physically meaningful objectives or constraints or decision variables. Many models have been developed using PP (Messac 2015).

In LPP, the DM expresses his/her preferences with respect to each criterion using four different classes. Each class has two cases, soft and hard, related to the details of the preferences.

Therefore, there are four hard classes: "Must be smaller" (Class 1-H), "Must be larger" (Class 2-H), "Must be equal" (Class 3-H), and "Must be in the range" (Class 4-H), and four soft classes: "Smaller is better" (Class 1-S), "Larger is better" (Class 2-S), "Value is better" (Class 3-S), and "Range is better" (Class 4-S).

In this chapter, only soft classes are implemented, which are illustrated in Figure 3.4. The decision variable vector is denoted as x and the kth generic criterion as $g_k(x)$. The horizontal axis represents the value of the criterion g_k, and the vertical axis represents the class function that will be minimized for the criterion z_k. The ideal value for the class function is zero. The class function allows the DM to give the desired range of preference for each criterion.

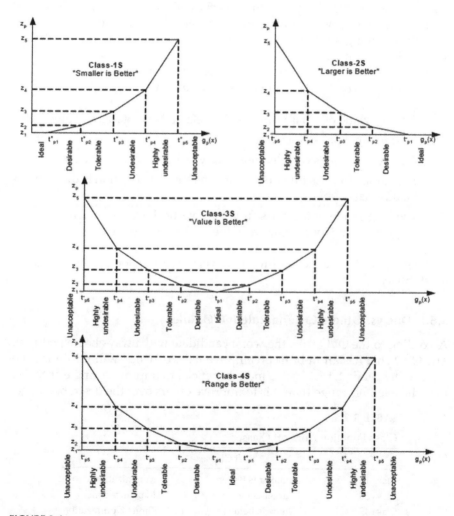

FIGURE 3.4
LPP soft class function.

TABLE 3.1

Preference Levels and Constraints for Class 1

Preference Levels	Constraints
Ideal	$g_k \leq t_{k1}^+$
Desirable	$t_{k1}^+ \leq g_k \leq t_{k2}^+$
Tolerable	$t_{k2}^+ \leq g_k \leq t_{k3}^+$
Undesirable	$t_{k3}^+ \leq g_k \leq t_{k4}^+$
Highly undesirable	$t_{k4}^+ \leq g_k \leq t_{k5}^+$
Unacceptable	$g_k \geq t_{k5}^+$

Table 3.1 represents the preference levels and constraints for Class 1-S: Smaller is better. Any two points in any range are of the equal value to the DM. Thus, having a lower value within the same range will not result in a lower objective function.

Table 3.2 represents the four different soft class functions.

The properties of the class functions are as follows:

1. A lower value of a class function is preferred over a higher value.
2. A class function is strictly positive.
3. A class function is continuous, piecewise linear, and convex.
4. The value of a class function at a given range intersection is the same for any class-type.
5. The magnitude of the class function's vertical excursion across any range must satisfy the One vs. Others (OVO) criteria rule.

The magnitude of the class function's vertical excursion across any range must satisfy.

3.6.1 One vs. Others Criteria Rule (OVO Rule)

According to the OVO rule, the worst candidate will always be helped first. The OVO rule has an in-built preemptive nature, which will minimize the worst criterion first; that is, it is more beneficial to improve a single criterion over the tolerable range than it is to improve others over the desirable range.

TABLE 3.2

Class Functions for Soft Classes

Soft Classes		
Class 1S	Smaller Is Better	Minimization
Class 2S	Larger Is Better	Maximization
Class 3S	Value Is Better	Target Optimization
Class 4S	Range Is Better	Range Optimization

To maintain the convexity of the class functions, the length of the sth range of the kth criterion is defined as

$$\tilde{t}_{ks}^{+} = t_{ks}^{+} - t_{k(s-1)}^{+}; \quad \tilde{t}_{ks}^{-} = t_{ks}^{-} - t_{k(s-1)}^{-}; \; (2 \leq s \leq 5) \tag{3.27}$$

The magnitude of the slopes of the class function of the generic kth criterion can be calculated as

$$w_{ks}^{+} = \tilde{z}^{s} / \tilde{t}_{ks}^{+}; \quad w_{ks}^{-} = \tilde{z}^{s} / \tilde{t}_{ks}^{-}; \; (2 \leq s \leq 5) \tag{3.28}$$

Once the slopes are calculated, the convexity requirement can be verified by the following relationship:

$$\tilde{w}_{\min} = \underset{k,s}{Min}\{\tilde{w}_{ks}^{+}, \tilde{w}_{ks}^{-}\} > 0; \; (2 \leq s \leq 5) \tag{3.29}$$

The weight values $\tilde{w}_{ks}^{+}$ and $\tilde{w}_{ks}^{-}$ are used in the LPP model of the class functions. Kongar and Gupta (2009b) proposed that the weights should be normalized before their use in the LPP model. The weights are normalized as follows:

$$\tilde{w}_{ks}^{+} = (w_{ks}^{+} - w_{k(s-1)}^{+}) / \sum_{s=2}^{5} w_{ks}^{+} - w_{k(s-1)}^{+}) \tag{3.30}$$

$$\tilde{w}_{ks}^{-} = (w_{ks}^{-} - w_{k(s-1)}^{-}) / \sum_{s=2}^{5} (w_{ks}^{-} - w_{k(s-1)}^{-}) \tag{3.31}$$

$$w_{k1}^{+} = w_{k1}^{-} = 0 \tag{3.32}$$

The weights must be positive for the class function to be piecewise linear and convex. The above relationship is used to derive an algorithm known as the *linear physical programming weight* (LPPW) algorithm, which determines the weights that are going to be used in the LP model of the class function. The weights obtained from the LPPW algorithm are used to write the mathematical expressions for the piecewise linear class function for each criterion.

3.6.2 The Algorithm

There are four steps to form a PP model:

1. DM determines the soft and hard classes to apply for each criterion.
2. For each criterion, the DM defines the limits of ranges of differing degrees of desirability.

3. The LPPW algorithm is used to generate the weights from the input range boundaries.
4. The following LP problem is then solved:

$$\min \phi = \sum_{k \in K} \sum_{s \in \{2,3,4,5\}} (\tilde{w}_{ks}^+ d_{ks}^+ + \tilde{w}_{ks}^- d_{ks}^-) \qquad (3.33)$$

Subject to:

$$g_k - d_{ks}^+ \le t_{k(s-1)}^+; \ d_{ks}^+ \ge 0; \ g_k \le t_{k5}^+ \qquad (3.34)$$

These equations complete the development of the LPP model.

3.7 Mathematical Model Using Linear Physical Programming Model

The system criteria for LPP are divided into two different classes: 1-S and 2-S. The first criterion is to maximize the total profit for the ARTODTO system. As this objective function is being maximized, it belongs to Class 2-S. The mathematical expression is written as follows:

$$TP - d_{1,s}^- \ge t_{1,s}^- \qquad (3.35)$$

$$TP \ge t_{1,5}^- \qquad (3.36)$$

The second criterion is to minimize the outside procurement cost. As the objective function is being minimized, it belongs to Class 1-S. The mathematical expression is written as follows:

$$TOPC - d_{2,s}^+ \le t_{2,s}^+ \qquad (3.37)$$

$$TOPC \le t_{2,5}^+ \qquad (3.38)$$

The third criterion is to minimize the purchase cost. As the objective function is being minimized, it belongs to Class 1-S. The mathematical expression is written as follows:

$$TPRC - d_{3,s}^+ \le t_{3,s}^+ \qquad (3.39)$$

$$TPRC \le t_{3,5}^+ \qquad (3.40)$$

The fourth criterion is to minimize the disposal cost. As the objective function is being minimized, it belongs to Class 1-S. The mathematical expression is written as follows:

$$TDIC - d_{4,s}^+ \leq t_{4,s}^+ \tag{3.41}$$

$$TDIC \leq t_{4,5}^+ \tag{3.42}$$

The different product designs are evaluated based on four criteria: total profit, outside procurement cost, purchase cost, and disposal cost. They are defined as follows:

3.7.1 Total Profit

Total profit consists of resale revenue, total disassembly cost, total disposal cost, total holding cost, total outside procurement cost, total recycling cost, total remanufacturing cost, and total purchase cost. It is represented as follows:

$$TP = RSR - TDISSC - TDISPC - THOLC$$
$$-TOPC - TRECC - TREMC - TPURC \tag{3.43}$$

3.7.1.1 Resale Revenue

Resale revenue is gained by reusing the good non-destructively disassembled components. It is the multiplication of the amount of reused components, that is, the demand for reuse components, and the component resale value.

$$RSR = drec_j * rv_j \tag{3.44}$$

3.7.1.2 Total Disassembly Cost

Total disassembly cost is divided into two parts; destructive disassembly cost and non-destructive disassembly cost. The first part of destructive disassembly is the multiplication of the disassembly factor, labor cost, and disassembly time for destructive disassembly. The second part of non-destructive disassembly is the multiplication of the disassembly factor, labor cost, and disassembly time for non-destructive disassembly.

$$TDISSC = (f * lcdd_j * tdd_j) + (f * lcndd_j * tndd_j) \tag{3.45}$$

3.7.1.3 Total Disposal Cost

Total disposal cost is divided into three parts: disposal cost of products, disposal cost of components, and disposal cost of materials. The first part is the multiplication of the total amount of disposed products and the disposal cost of products. The second part is the multiplication of the disposed components and the disposal cost of components. The third part is the multiplication of the disposed materials and the disposal cost of materials.

$$TDISPC = qdispp_i * cdp_i + qdisc_j * cdc_j + qdispm_j * cdmj \qquad (3.46)$$

3.7.1.4 Total Holding Cost

Total holding cost is divided into two parts: the holding cost of components and the holding cost of products. The first part is the multiplication of the amount of stored components and the holding cost of components. The second part is the multiplication of the amount of stored materials and the holding cost of materials.

$$THOLC = qsc_j * chc_j + qsm_j * chm_j \qquad (3.47)$$

3.7.1.5 Total Outside Procurement Cost

Total outside procurement cost is the multiplication of the amount of components procured from outside and the outside procurement cost of the components.

$$TOPC = qopc_j * cpc_j \qquad (3.48)$$

3.7.1.6 Total Recycling Cost

Total recycling cost is the multiplication of the amount of materials recycled and the recycling cost of the materials.

$$TRECC = qrecm_j * crc_j \qquad (3.49)$$

3.7.1.7 Total Remanufacturing Cost

Total remanufacturing cost consists of two processes: the disassembly of broken or lifetime deficit components and the assembly of the required components. Therefore, it is the multiplication of the amount of products remanufactured and the sum of non-destructive disassembly and assembly costs.

$$TREMC = qremp_i * ((f * lcndd_j * tndd_j) + ca_j) \qquad (3.50)$$

3.7.1.8 Total Product Purchase Cost

Total product purchase cost is the multiplication of the amount of EOL products taken back from suppliers and the cost of the purchased products.

$$TPURC = qpurp_i * cpp_i \qquad (3.51)$$

3.7.2 Constraints

3.7.2.1 Disassembly Process

The total number of products i to be disassembled has to be equal to the total number of EOL products i purchased, multiplied by the stochastic good condition percentage of products i. Therefore,

$$qdissp_i = qpurp_i * sgp_i \tag{3.52}$$

The total number of disassembled components should be equal to the number of disassembled products multiplied by the multiplicity of that component in the product.

$$qdissc_j = qdissp_i * m_{ij} \tag{3.53}$$

The total number of non-destructively disassembled components should be less than or equal to the total number of disassembled products multiplied by the multiplicity and disassembly yields of the component in that product.

$$qnddc_j \leq qdissp_i * m_{ij} * sdy_{ij} \tag{3.54}$$

The total number of destructively disassembled components is equal to the subtraction of the total number of non-destructively disassembled components from the total number of disassembled components.

$$qddc_j = qdissc_j - qnddc_j \tag{3.55}$$

3.7.2.2 Reuse Process

The total number of components disassembled for reuse cannot exceed the total number of non-destructively disassembled components.

$$qrc_j \leq qnddc_j \tag{3.56}$$

The quantity of functional components that can be reused is equal to the multiplication of the number of components j sent for reuse and its stochastic reusable percentage.

$$qgrc_j = qrc_j * srp_j \tag{3.57}$$

The quantity of non-functional components j that cannot be reused and will eventually be recycled is equal to the subtraction of functional components from the quantity of components disassembled for reuse.

$$qbrc_j = qrc_j - qgrc_j \tag{3.58}$$

The demand for reusable components is fulfilled by good reusable components obtained from non-destructively disassembled components and components procured from outside.

$$drc_j = qgrc_j + qopc_j \tag{3.59}$$

The components are procured from outside when the demand cannot be met using the good reuse components. Hence, the number of procured components is the subtraction of the number of reusable components from the demand for reusable components, or zero, whichever is greater.

$$qopc_j = Max\{(drc_j - qgrc_j), 0\} \tag{3.60}$$

3.7.2.3 Recycling Process

The recycling process does not usually recover all the materials from components. Therefore, the total number of recycled components is equal to the demand of recycled components divided by the recyclable percentage.

$$qrecc_j = drecc_j / srec_j \tag{3.61}$$

The total number of recycled components cannot exceed the sum of the bad reuse components and the total number of destructively disassembled components.

$$qrecc_j \le qbrc_j + qddc_j \tag{3.62}$$

The quantity of recycled components that exceeds the recycling demands is sent to disposal. Therefore, the quantity of recycled components sent to recycling is the subtraction of the quantity of components recycled from the sum of non-functional components that cannot be reused and the quantity of destructively disassembled components, or zero, whichever is greater.

$$qredc_j = Max\{[(qbrc_j + qddc_j) - qrecc_j], 0\} \tag{3.63}$$

The total weight of recycled material is equal to the multiplication of the number of recycled components, the weight of the component, and its stochastic recyclable percentage.

$$wrecm_j = qrecc_j * wc_j * srec_j \tag{3.64}$$

3.7.2.4 Disposal Process

The total number of disposed products is the subtraction of the total number of disassembled products from the total number of purchased products.

$$qdispp_i = qpurp_i - qdissp_i \qquad (3.65)$$

The total number of disposed components is equal to the subtraction of the number of recycled components from the sum of the bad reuse components and destructively disassembled components.

$$qdispc_j = qbrc_j + qddc_j - qrecc_j \qquad (3.66)$$

The total number of disposed materials is the multiplication of the amount of recycled components, the weight of the components, and the non-recyclable percentage.

$$qdispm_j = qdispc_j * wc_j * (1 - srec_j) \qquad (3.67)$$

3.8 Numerical Example

To illustrate the formulated model, an example is presented in this section. The ARTODTO system receives three different models of EOL cell phones: Nokia 6300, iPhone 4, and Samsung Galaxy S5. Some of the important common components between these cell phone models are the back cover, battery, camera, circuit board, front cover, microphone, screen, and speaker. The disassembly precedence relationships for the three cell phone models are displayed in Figures 3.5 through 3.7.

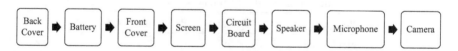

FIGURE 3.5
Disassembly precedence relationship for Nokia 6300.

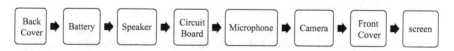

FIGURE 3.6
Disassembly precedence relationship for iPhone 4.

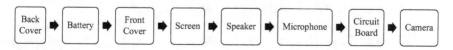

FIGURE 3.7
Disassembly precedence relationship for Samsung Galaxy S5.

Tables 3.3 through 3.9 display the input data required to solve the formulated model.

It was observed that the one-to-many technique provides more accurate results than the one-to-one technique. Therefore, the component disassembly yields were calculated using the one-to-many heuristic technique.

The disassembly factor is an indication of the relative difficulty of separating a component from a product. For example, separating the circuit board from the Nokia 6300 would involve five separations: back cover, battery, front cover, screen, and then, circuit board. Therefore, the disassembly factor of the circuit board in the Nokia 6300 = 5/8 = 0.625. In the case of the iPhone 4, separating the

TABLE 3.3

Reuse Demand and Recycling Demand for Components

Component	Reuse Demand	Recycling Demand
Back cover	300	100
Battery	350	80
Camera	200	0
Circuit board	350	200
Front cover	300	100
Microphone	100	0
Screen	250	100
Speaker	100	0

TABLE 3.4

Product Demand and Purchase Cost

Product	Demands	Purchase Cost ($)
Nokia 6300	10	200
iPhone 4	30	300
Samsung Galaxy S5	25	250

TABLE 3.5

Component Yields

Component	Nokia 6300	iPhone 4	Samsung Galaxy S5
Back cover	0.47	0.28	0.78
Battery	0.84	0.23	0.00
Camera	0.34	0.50	0.26
Circuit board	0.17	0.00	0.28
Front cover	0.52	0.62	0.21
Microphone	0.59	0.74	0.51
Screen	0.00	0.72	0.65
Speaker	0.68	0.63	0.82

TABLE 3.6

Disassembly Factors

Component	Nokia 6300	iPhone 4	Samsung Galaxy S5
Back cover	0.125	0.125	0.125
Battery	0.250	0.250	0.250
Camera	1.000	0.750	1.000
Circuit board	0.625	0.500	0.875
Front cover	0.375	0.875	0.375
Microphone	0.875	0.625	0.750
Screen	0.500	1.000	0.500
Speaker	0.750	0.375	0.625

TABLE 3.7

Resale Component Price, Material Price, Stored Component Value, and Holding Cost

Component	Resale Component Price ($)	Material Price ($)	Holding Cost ($)
Back cover	15.00	4.00	0.20
Battery	8.00	8.00	1.00
Camera	4.00	0.00	0.50
Circuit board	25.00	10.00	1.00
Front cover	15.00	4.00	0.20
Microphone	2.00	0.00	0.20
Screen	5.00	4.00	0.50
Speaker	2.00	0.00	0.20

TABLE 3.8

Component Disposal Cost, Outside Procurement Cost, and Material Disposal Cost

Component	Component Disposal Cost ($)	Outside Procurement Cost ($)	Material Disposal Cost ($)
Back cover	0.60	10.00	0.40
Battery	0.40	30.00	0.20
Camera	0.70	20.00	0.50
Circuit board	0.40	35.00	0.30
Front cover	0.60	10.00	0.40
Microphone	0.70	15.00	0.40
Screen	0.60	20.00	0.40
Speaker	0.70	15.00	0.50

circuit board would involve four separations: back cover, battery, speaker, and then, circuit board. Therefore, the disassembly factor of the circuit board in the iPhone $4 = 4/8 = 0.500$. In the case of the Samsung Galaxy S5, separating the circuit board would involve seven separations: back cover, battery, front cover, screen, speaker, microphone, and then, circuit board. Therefore, the disassembly factor of the circuit board in the Samsung Galaxy S5 $= 7/8 = 0.875$.

TABLE 3.9

Desirability Ranges

	Total Profit ($)	Procurement Cost ($)	Purchase Cost ($)	Disposal Cost ($)
Ideal	≥200,000	≤60,000	≤100,000	≤2,000
Desirable	[170,000, 200,000)	(60,000, 65,000]	(100.000, 110.000]	(2,000, 2,050]
Tolerable	[140,000, 170,000)	(65,000, 70,000]	(110.000, 120.000]	(2,050, 3,000]
Undesirable	[110,000, 140,000)	(70,000, 75,000]	(120.000, 130.000]	(3,000, 3,050]
Highly Undesirable	[80,000, 110,000)	(80,000, 85,000]	(130.000, 140.000]	(3,050, 3,100]
Unacceptable	<80,000	>85,000	>140.000	>3,100

TABLE 3.10

Weights Calculated by LPPW Algorithm

Target	Weights							
$k=1$	$\tilde{w}_{12}^-$	0.00008	$\tilde{w}_{13}^-$	0.00053	$\tilde{w}_{14}^-$	0.001587	$\tilde{w}_{15}^-$	0.00049
$k=2$	$\tilde{w}_{22}^+$	0.0004	$\tilde{w}_{23}^+$	0.00027	$\tilde{w}_{24}^+$	0.002463	$\tilde{w}_{25}^+$	0.00028
$k=3$	$\tilde{w}_{32}^+$	0.0001	$\tilde{w}_{33}^+$	0.00098	$\tilde{w}_{34}^+$	0.006471	$\tilde{w}_{35}^+$	0.00079
$k=4$	$\tilde{w}_{42}^+$	0.001	$\tilde{w}_{43}^+$	0.0076	$\tilde{w}_{44}^+$	0.01526	$\tilde{w}_{45}^+$	0.0051

TABLE 3.11

Aspiration Levels and Values for Each Criterion

	Description	Aspiration Level	Value
Objectives	Total profit ($)	Desirable	185,000
	Procurement cost ($)	Tolerable	66,000
	Purchase cost ($)	Tolerable	115,000
	Disposal cost ($)	Undesirable	3,010

TABLE 3.12

Number of Purchased EOL Products

Purchased products for Nokia 6300	250
Purchased products for iPhone 4	150
Purchased products for Samsung Galaxy S5	80

3.9 Results

In LPP, the worst candidate will always be helped first; that is, it will try to improve a single criterion over the tolerable range versus improving others over the desirable range. Once the input data were gathered, the model was formulated and solved using LINDO Systems' LINGO 16.0. The results are displayed in Tables 3.10 through 3.12.

The results show that total profit is in the desirable range, procurement cost and purchase cost are in the desirable range, and disposal cost is in the undesirable range.

3.10 Conclusion

ECM and product recovery are gaining importance with the depletion of virgin resources and landfills. OEMs are encouraged to implement product recovery techniques to reduce the harmful effects of product disposal on the environment. Product design is an important aspect of the management of EOL products. To manage EOL products efficiently, reduce disposal waste, and earn profits, it is important to improve the efficiency of the disassembly process. One of the key ways of achieving this is by designing the products in a way that aids disassembly or product recovery at the product's EOL. One of the main obstacles in EOL product recovery is the uncertainty related to the condition of the returned EOL products. This uncertainty leads to stochastic disassembly yields. To solve the problem of stochastic yields, heuristic methods can be used to convert the stochastic yields into their deterministic equivalents, and then, the deterministic problem can be solved.

In this chapter, an ARTODTO system was proposed, which purchased EOL cell phones to satisfy all the demands for products, components, and materials. The cell phones were available in three different design alternatives: Nokia 6300, iPhone 4, and Samsung Galaxy S5. The model evaluated these design alternatives to determine how many EOL products of which design alternative should be purchased. To meet all the demands, 250 Nokia 6300, 150 iPhone 4, and 80 Samsung Galaxy S5 were purchased, which indicates that the Nokia 6300 has a favorable design for disassembly.

References

Aksoy, H. K., and Gupta, S. M. (2005). Buffer allocation plan for a remanufacturing cell. *Computers & Industrial Engineering*, 48(3), 657–677.
Andrew-Munot, M., Ibrahim, R. N., and Junaidi, E. (2015). An overview of used-products remanufacturing. *Mechanical Engineering Research*, 5(1), 12.
Cheung, W. M., Marsh, R., Griffin, P. W., Newnes, L. B., Mileham, A. R., and Lanham, J. D. (2015). Towards cleaner production: A roadmap for predicting product end-of-life costs at early design concept. *Journal of Cleaner Production*, 87, 431–441.

de Aguiar, J., de Oliveira, L., da Silva, J. O., Bond, D., Scalice, R. K., and Becker, D. (2017). A design tool to diagnose product recyclability during product design phase. *Journal of Cleaner Production*, 141, 219–229.

Gungor, A., and Gupta, S. M. (1999). Issues in environmentally conscious manufacturing and product recovery: A survey. *Computers & Industrial Engineering*, 36(4), 811–853.

Gupta, S. M. (Ed.). (2013). *Reverse Supply Chains: Issues and Analysis*. CRC Press.

Gupta, S. M., and Ilgin, M. A. (2018). *Multiple Criteria Decision Making Applications in Environmentally Conscious Manufacturing and Product Recovery*. CRC Press.

Ilgin, M. A., and Gupta, S. M. (2010). Environmentally conscious manufacturing and product recovery (ECMPRO): A review of the state of the art. *Journal of Environmental Management*, 91(3), 563–591.

Imtanavanich, P., and Gupta, S. M. (2006). Calculating disassembly yields in a multi-criteria decision making environment for a disassembly-to-order system. In Kenneth Lawrence, Ronald K. Klimberg (eds.), Applications of Management Science: In Productivity, Finance, and Operations. Elsevier, 109–125.

Inderfurth, K., and Langella, I. M. (2007). Heuristics for solving disassemble-to-order problems with stochastic yields. *OR Spectrum*, 28(1), 73–99.

Kim, H. W., Park, C., and Lee, D. H. (2018). Selective disassembly sequencing with random operation times in parallel disassembly environment. *International Journal of Production Research*, 1–15. doi:10.1080/00207543.2018.1432911

Kim, K., Song, I., Kim, J., and Jeong, B. (2006). Supply planning model for remanufacturing system in reverse logistics environment. *Computers & Industrial Engineering*, 51(2), 279–287.

Kim, S., and Moon, S. K. (2016). Eco-modular product architecture identification and assessment for product recovery. *Journal of Intelligent Manufacturing*, 1–21. doi:10.1007/s10845-016-1253-7

Kongar, E., and Gupta, S. M. (2002). A multi-criteria decision making approach for disassembly-to-order systems. *Journal of Electronics Manufacturing*, 11(02), 171–183.

Kongar, E., and Gupta, S. M. (2006). Disassembly to order system under uncertainty. *Omega*, 34(6), 550–561.

Kongar, E., and Gupta, S. M. (2009a). A multiple objective tabu search approach for end-of-life product disassembly. *International Journal of Advanced Operations Management*, 1(2–3), 177–202.

Kongar, E., and Gupta, S. M. (2009b). Solving the disassembly-to-order problem using linear physical programming. *International Journal of Mathematics in Operational Research*, 1(4), 504–531.

Lambert, A. F., and Gupta, S. M. (2005). *Disassembly Modeling for Assembly, Maintenance, Reuse and Recycling*. CRC Press.

Lambert, A. J. D., and Gupta, S. M. (2002). Demand-driven disassembly optimization for electronic products package reliability. *Journal of Electronics Manufacturing*, 11(02), 121–135.

Langella, I. M. (2007). Heuristics for demand-driven disassembly planning. *Computers & Operations Research*, 34(2), 552–577.

Li, Z., Gómez, J. M., and Pehlken, A. (2015). A systematic review of environmentally conscious product design. *Enviroinfo ICT for Sustainability*, 22, 197–206.

Li, Z., He, J., Lai, X., Huang, Y., Zhou, T., Vatankhah Barenji, A., and Wang, W. M. (2018). Evaluation of product recyclability at the product design phase: A time-series forecasting methodology. *International Journal of Computer Integrated Manufacturing*, 31(4–5), 457–468.

Ma, L., Song, W., and Zhou, Y. (2018). Modeling enablers of environmentally conscious manufacturing strategy: An integrated method. *Sustainability*, 10(7), 2284.

Messac, A. (2015). *Optimization in Practice with Matlab®: For Engineering Students and Professionals*. Cambridge University Press.

Messac, A., Gupta, S. M., and Akbulut, B. (1996). Linear physical programming: A new approach to multiple objective optimization. *Transactions on Operational Research*, 8(2), 39–59.

Özceylan, E., Kalayci, C. B., Güngör, A., and Gupta, S. M. (2018). Disassembly line balancing problem: A review of the state of the art and future directions. *International Journal of Production Research*, 1–23. doi:10.1080/00207543.2018.1428775

Veerakamolmal, P., and Gupta, S. M. (2000) Design for Disassembly, Reuse and Recycling. In: *Green Electronics/Green Bottom Line: Environmentally Responsible Engineering*, edited by L. Goldberg, Newnes, Chapter 5, 69–82.

Yang, S. S., Ong, S. K., and Nee, A. Y. C. (2014). EOL strategy planning for components of returned products. *The International Journal of Advanced Manufacturing Technology*, 77(5–8), 991–1003.

4

Integrated Forward-Reverse Logistics Network Design: An Application for Electrolytic Copper Conductor Reel Distribution

Olcay Polat, Ömer Faruk Ünal, Leyla Özgür Polat, and Aşkıner Güngör

CONTENTS

4.1 Introduction

Supply chain network design requires the determination of a model specific to the problem considered and its targets. It is also important to define the problem environment clearly and to determine from whose perspective the problem should be solved. Therefore, network decision makers are at a key position in network design (Coskun et al., 2016). The objectives of the problem are achieved through the implementation of strategic and tactical decisions (Pochampally, Nukala, and Gupta, 2008). Accordingly, decision makers seek a single objective or multiple objectives such as cost minimization, customer satisfaction, environmental benefit, revenue or profit maximization, determination of locations or the number and the capacities of facilities, etc. (Liao, 2018). In the next stage, determination of the constraints and decision variables is needed to formulate mathematically under assumptions that reflect real-life situations. Model constraints are general constraints such as the capacity related to transportation, production, storage, etc.; customer expectations such as quality and delivery time, etc.; and demand- and model-specific constraints such as collection amounts, ratio of recycling, CO_2 emission, or environmental impacts (Gungor and Gupta, 1999; Ilgin and Gupta, 2010). Decision variables consist of decisions such as the facility location, the number of facilities, the structure of the network, the schedule of processes, transportation routes, stock levels, prices of products, etc.

The model is designed based on various supply chain approaches such as forward, reverse, closed-loop, or integrated supply chain networks.

In the forward supply chain network design, there is a direct flow from the manufacturers to the customers. The aim is to minimize the total cost of the network to satisfy customer demand by production and product delivery without exceeding the production capacity. Figure 4.1 depicts the general view of a forward supply chain network.

Reverse logistics is defined as the movement of the product from the customer to the producer, contrary to forward logistics (Rogers and Tibben-Lembke, 2001; Gupta, 2016). Dowlatshahi (2000) defines reverse logistics as "the systematic recall of the products or parts from the consumption point for recycling, remanufacturing or disposal by the manufacturer." As a result, the reverse supply chain is related to the flows between collection, control, sorting, disassembly, remanufacturing/recycling, and disposal centers (Kalayci and Gupta, 2013; Kalayci, Polat, and Gupta, 2015, 2016). The most important topics in the reverse supply chain are "which channels will be used for product collection" (Shaharudin et al., 2017), "how much returned product will be collected" (Pochampally, Gupta, and Kamarthi, 2004) and "which returned product type and quality will be collected" (Chen et al., 2017), and "where returned products will be recycled" (Polat, Capraz, and Gungor, 2018; Capraz, Polat, and Gungor, 2017, 2015).

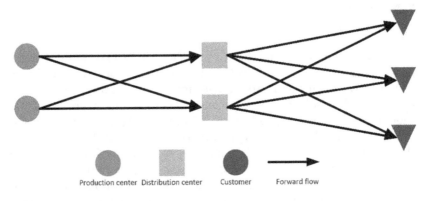

Production center   Distribution center   Customer   Forward flow

FIGURE 4.1
Forward supply chain network.

Figure 4.2 depicts the general view of a reverse supply chain network.

The forward supply chain is influenced mainly by the product demand, standard product packaging and structure, traditional marketing techniques, and speed. On the other hand, the reverse supply chain is interested in product returns, variable packaging, and modified product structure (Pochampally and Gupta, 2012). Compared with the forward supply chain, the reverse supply chain is more environmentally oriented and more complex and includes fuzziness (Pochampally and Gupta, 2005; Pochampally and Gupta, 2003).

Closed supply chains include both forward and reverse supply flow activities. The raw materials are delivered by the producers as new products to meet customer demands in the closed supply chain network (Figure 4.3). The products that are delivered to the customer return as used products to the manufacturer for reasons such as expiration of lifespan or malfunction (Nakashima and Gupta, 2012). The producers recover or dispose of returning products in a way that meets the requirements set out in the regulations (Nukala and Gupta, 2007). Therefore, reverse and closed-loop supply chain network design include similar decisions at all levels, including which plants (collection centers, remanufacturing centers, disassembly centers, etc.) will be in the network, depending on the product type and other factors; which recycling transactions (refurbishing, repair, disassembly, reproduction, etc.) will be implemented; how many returned products will be recovered (estimation); and determination of the market plan for the recycled products or parts (Das and Chowdhury, 2012; Pochampally, Gupta, and Govindan, 2009).

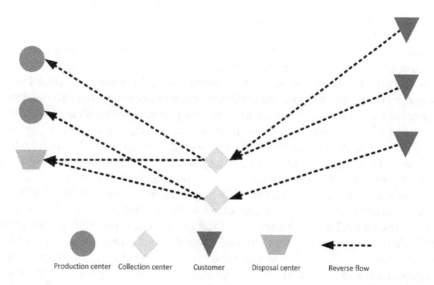

Production center   Collection center   Customer   Disposal center   Reverse flow

FIGURE 4.2
Reverse supply chain network.

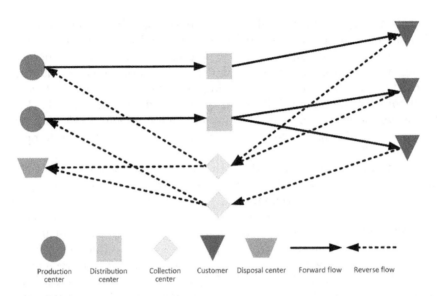

FIGURE 4.3
Closed-loop supply chain network.

The reverse logistics network design has a critical impact on the performance of the forward logistics network design, and vice versa, since they share a number of resources, such as transport and warehouse capacity (Pishvaee, Farahani, and Dullaert, 2010). Designing the forward and reverse networks separately provides sub-optimal results in terms of costs, service levels, and responsiveness. Therefore, forward and reverse logistics networks should be designed in an integrated way (Fleischmann et al., 2001).

An example integrated forward-reverse logistics network is represented in Figure 4.4. In this structure, new products are also transported from production centers to customers through a hybrid distribution-collection facility, whereby both distribution and collection centers are established to meet the demand in the forward flow, and returned products are collected in these centers in the reverse flow. In such an integrated logistics network, hybrid processing centers provide possible cost savings compared with separate distribution or collection centers (Lee and Dong, 2008). These savings are due to the tradeoff of fixed opening costs of warehouses, transportation costs, and the responsiveness of the network (Pishvaee, Farahani, and Dullaert, 2010).

This study includes the integration of forward and reverse logistics network design and an allocation hub location selection problem for an electrolytic wire company. It aims to make logistics processes more efficient by eliminating waste. For this aim, a mixed integer linear programming model is proposed and solved. Having proposed an efficient approach in the economic sense, this study is intended to reduce transportation costs, improve the efficiency of transportation activities, increase customer satisfaction by

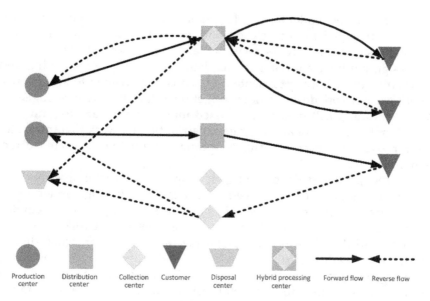

FIGURE 4.4
Integrated forward-reverse logistics network.

delivering in a short time, expand the customer portfolio, and therefore maintain the competitive advantage of the company.

This chapter enables the efficient use of elements in the system by dealing with the concept and process of logistics with a broad perspective. The rest of the chapter is organized as follows. Section 2 presents recent literature on integrated forward-reverse logistics network design. In Section 3, the problem environment is defined. Section 4 presents the environment of the case study and numerical results. Finally, conclusions are drawn, and suggestions for further research are given in the last section.

4.2 Literature Review

When the scientific literature of the last 20 years is examined, it can be seen that there are various studies integrating forward and reverse logistics networks. Salema, Póvoa, and Novais (2006) proposed a mixed integer linear programming (MILP) formulation for the design of a reverse logistics network based on a depot location model that simultaneously optimizes forward and reverse networks. The proposed model is compared with the published work in the field, where different model assumptions are proposed. Two phenomena are explained to enable understanding the model better and making a comparative analysis. Listeş (2007) presented a general stochastic model for the design of nets with both feed and return channels arranged in both closed and closed-loop systems. The model explains a set of alternative scenarios that can be generated based on critical design parameter levels such as demand or profit. A modeling and solution methodology is presented, which can contribute to an effective solution of network design models under uncertainty for reverse logistics. Ko and Evans (2007) presented a mixed integer nonlinear programming model for the design of an integrated distribution network that integrates the forward and reverse network optimally with the integrated directional account.

Pishvaee, Jolai, and Razmi (2009) developed a stochastic programming model for integrated forward-reverse logistics network design under uncertainty. First, a deterministic MILP model was developed for integrated logistic network design models for forward and reverse networks. Then, the proposed MILP model was developed using a stochastic approach. Pishvaee, Farahani, and Dullaert (2010) proposed a model to avoid the sub-optimality caused by the separate design of the forward and reverse networks. The first two objectives are to reduce the total cost of a mixed integer programming formulation and to maximize a logistical network response. For the solution, a non-multiple memetic algorithm was developed. El-Sayed, Afia, and El-Kharbotly (2010) developed a multi-term, multi-layer forward-reverse logistics network design model at risk. The proposed network structure consists of three stages (suppliers, facilities, and distribution centers) in the forward direction and two stages (disassembly and redistribution centers) in the reverse direction. The problem was formulated using stochastic mixed integer linear programming (SIP). The aim is to maximize the total expected profit.

Demirel et al. (2011) have developed a capacity-constrained, multi-stage, multi-product MILP model for the design of an integrated logistics network. The problem involves determining the number and location of facilities in the forward and reverse networks and designing the distribution network to meet customer demands with the minimum cost. Because of the complicated structure of the model, a hybrid solution method based on a genetic algorithm, using heuristic and linear programming together, has been developed. The results of various test problems were obtained from GAMS-CPLEX. Khajavi, Seyed-Hosseini, and Makui (2011) presented a mixed integer programming model (MIP) for multi-stage logistics network design for a generalized logistics network problem involving an integrated forward-reverse logistics network. The aim was to achieve simultaneous optimization of the total cost and the response of the closed-loop supply chain network. Keyvanshokooh et al. (2013) proposed integrated applications of forward-reverse logistics networks to solve multi-layer, multi-term, and multi-product planning problems. They were categorized taking into account the quality levels of returned items and the different purchase price offered for each returned product type. In addition, the customer's booking discount, the expected price, and the customer return request were considered in the model. Forward-reverse logistics network configuration and inventory decisions, taking into account the dynamic pricing approach for products, were considered in the proposed MILP-based model. The model was solved with CPLEX.

Ramezani, Bashiri, and Tavakkoli-Moghaddam (2013) presented a multi-objective stochastic reverse logistics network design model under uncertainty. The aim of the logistics network was to maximize profit, customer sensitivity, and quality. Hatefi and Jolai (2014) proposed a reliable and strong model for forward-reverse logistics network design with uncertain parameters and facility hitches. The proposed model was formulated based on a strong optimization approach to protect against uncertainty. Hatefi et al. (2015) presented a constrained programming model for the reliable design of forward-reverse logistics networks and hybrid facilities under uncertainty and random facility interactions. They proposed a new mathematical model to solve this problem. Later, the parameters were developed based on reliable constrained programming to deal with uncertainties.

Soleimani and Zohal (2017) offered a model for integrated forward-reverse logistics network design. This model contains seven levels; four in the forward direction and three in the reverse direction. They proposed an efficient algorithm based on ant colony optimization to maximize the benefits. The proposed metaheuristic algorithm is new in the field of closed-loop supply chain network design. In addition, the objective function includes revenues, costs, and CO_2 emissions. The performance of the proposed algorithm was tested using solutions drawn from LINGO software. Fattahi and Govindan (2017) proposed a multi-term integrated forward-reverse logistics network design model for used and new products. Numerical experiments were carried out for the model, including sensitivity analysis of the main parameters of the problem.

Considering the studies in the literature, to the best of the authors' knowledge, no study has been conducted that is relevant to integrated logistics network design in the electrolytic copper conductor industry. This study, unlike other theoretical studies, contains the implementation of an electrolytic copper reel allocation problem with industry-specific constraints. Furthermore, in this study, it is possible to decide the type of loading method to be used. The network is designed to provide service to the customers from both the production center and the distribution center, if is open. The decision on where the customer receives service is made based on the economic evaluation. In this study, considering partial loading (less than container load [LCL]) and complete loading approach (full container load [FCL]) together, only a full container load is delivered to the distribution center—if it is open—to benefit from economy of scale. When providing both forward and reverse-direction service to customers, either LCL or FCL is preferred, whichever is more economical. It is not obligatory for the delivering vehicle to be fully loaded to its maximum capacity. Depending on the sales amount, flow cost in the case of FCL and flow cost in the case of LCL are compared.

4.3 The Problem Environment

Copper is used mainly as an electrical conductor in industry. Electrical conductivity, the most distinctive property of copper, is improved to the required level by electrolytic refining. After several operations, including melting, refining, casting, wire drawing, plating, and bunching, the electrolytic copper wires are made ready in accordance with the customers' requests and standards. After being wrapped and packed, the electrolytic copper conductor reels are distributed to the customers. After use of the full reels by customers, the empty reels are usually stored by customers and returned to the factory at certain intervals.

The growing number of customers all around the world is significantly increasing logistics costs as a proportion of total costs for electrolytic wire companies. This change is leading companies with a large customer portfolio to concentrate more on service networks. Generally, the supply chain network design problem involves the transfer system, suppliers, and warehouses to fulfill the demands of customers in a distribution network. The common goal is to decide the least costly system without exceeding the demand, warehouse, and plant capacity and to satisfy industry-specific constraints such as temperature and duration.

This study is based on converting LCL into FCL by benefiting from economy of scale in forward and reverse logistics integration to reduce logistics costs. Third party logistics sources are used during logistics activities. This enables enterprises to decrease the number of partial loads while increasing complete loads through logistics network design and optimization, which will result in a marked reduction in logistics costs. LCL is perceived and implemented as a loading method used according to customer orders. LCL makes it possible to combine flows even though it is hard to estimate the flow time. The enterprise is able to provide service to customers through the most economical route by means of forward and reverse logistics thanks to two way distribution network design. In the process of deciding how a customer is to be served, efficient solution options will be provided at the operational level depending on orders on a periodic (weekly, monthly) basis.

There is a minimum number of empty reels to be returned by customers. The empty reels remaining with a customer will be either sold to this customer or returned to the distribution center. Through reverse logistics network design, backward logistics costs will be reduced. Figure 4.5 shows the proposed integrated forward-reverse network design. There are three options for transportation from the factory to the customer. In the first option (represented by 1 in Figure 4.5), the demand of the customer is delivered to a third party logistics company as FCL, which means that containers are only loaded with a single customer's goods and transported to customers without

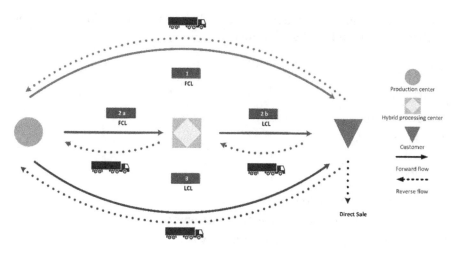

FIGURE 4.5
Integrated forward-reverse service network design.

visiting a distribution center for transfer purposes. In the second option (represented by 2 in Figure 4.5), the demands of various customers are merged in a single container in the factory, delivered to a third party logistics company as FCL, and sent to a distribution center, in which consolidation costs are paid by the factory (represented by 2a in Figure 4.5). The reels come in a single container, are transferred to different containers according to their final destination area in distribution centers, and are sent to customers as LCL with goods of different companies (represented by 2b in Figure 4.5). In the last option (represented by 3 in Figure 4.5), the demands of customers are delivered to a third party logistics company as LCL, and the logistics company is responsible for all transportation and transfer operations until the goods arrive at the customer. In the model, if a customer's demand is more than the capacity of a container, the model could select a combination of two different options. All loads could be sent using the first option without fully loading the container, or some part of the demand could be sent by fully loading containers as in the first option, and the remaining goods could be sent using the second or third option. Moreover, if a customer or distribution center is served by FCL, the reverse transportation costs for empty reels as FCL from this customer to the factory are usually much lower than for forward transportation. This situation is usually defined by agreements, but logistics companies generally offer lower prices for backward transportation after sending a truck to that location. The distribution centers are usually limited to a minimum number of handling operations in the total of forward and reverse operations. The handling cost of a full reel is usually lower than for an empty reel.

The indices, parameters, decision variables, and objective function of the mathematical model are listed as follows:

Indices

f: factories

m: customers

d: depots

Parameters

D_m: Demand of customer m

TD_m: Total number of empty reels at customer m

S_f: Unit (kg) production cost at factory f

C^1_{fm}:   Unit (container) FCL sending cost from factory f to customer m

C^2_{fd}:   Unit (container) FCL sending cost from factory f to depot d

B^1_{fm}:   Unit (kg) LCL sending cost from factory f to customer m

B^2_{dm}:   Unit (kg) LCL sending cost from depot d to customer m

TC^1_{mf}:   Unit (container) empty reel FCL sending cost from customer m to factory f

TC^2_{df}:   Unit (container) empty reel FCL sending cost from depot d to factory f

TB^1_{mf}:   Unit (kg) empty reel LCL sending cost from customer m to factory f

TB^2_{md}: Unit (kg) empty reel LCL sending cost from customer m to depot d

O_d: Opening/settlement cost of depot d

H_d: Unit (container) handling cost of depot d

K_d: Capacity of depot d

M: Maximum number of available depots

Q: Vehicle capacity

QF_f: Production capacity of factory f

L: Minimum required handling amount (container) for opening a depot

α: Discount ratio when the same vehicle transports forward and reverse loads

Decision Variables

A_d: 1, if depot d is open; 0, otherwise

X_{fm}:   FCL amount from factory f to customer m

XX_{fm}:   Number of FCL traveling from factory f to customer m

Y_{fm}:   LCL amount from factory f to customer m

Z_{fdm}:   LCL amount from factory f to customer m via depot d

N_{fd}:   Number of FCL traveling from factory f to depot d

R_m: Number of empty reel direct sales at customer m

TX_{mf}:   Empty reel FCL amount from customer m to factory f

TXX_{mf}:   Total number of FCL for empty reel travel from customer m to factory f

TXX^1_{mf}:   Number of FCL with regular tariff for empty reel travel from customer m to factory f

TXX^2_{mf}:   Number of FCL with discounted tariff for empty reel travel from customer m to factory f

TY_{mf}:   Empty reel LCL amount from customer m to factory f

TZ_{mdf}:   Empty reel LCL amount from customer m to factory f via depot d

TN_{df}:   Total number of FCL for empty reel travel from depot d to factory f

TXX^1_{mf}:   Number of FCL with regular tariff for empty reel travel from depot d to factory f

TXX^2_{mf}:   Number of FCL with discounted tariff for empty reel travel from depot d to factory f

Objective Function

Depot opening and handling cost

$$Min \sum_d O_d \cdot A_d + \sum_f \sum_d \sum_m H_d \cdot Z_{fdm} + \sum_f \sum_d \sum_m H_d \cdot TZ_{mdf}$$

Forward logistics transportation cost

$$+ \sum_f \sum_m C^1_{fm} \cdot XX_{fm} + \sum_f \sum_d C^2_{fd} \cdot N_{fd} + \sum_f \sum_m B^1_{fm} \cdot Y_{fm} + \sum_f \sum_d \sum_m B^2_{dm} \cdot Z_{fdm}$$

Reverse logistics transportation cost

$$+ \sum_f \sum_m TC^1_{fm} \cdot TXX^1_{mf} + \sum_f \sum_m TC^1_{fm} \cdot (1-\alpha) \cdot TXX^2_{mf} + \sum_f \sum_d TC^2_{fd} \cdot TN^1_{df}$$

$$+ \sum_f \sum_d TC^2_{fd} \cdot (1-\alpha) \cdot TN^2_{df} + \sum_f \sum_m TB^1_{fm} \cdot TY_{mf} + \sum_f \sum_d \sum_m TB^2_{dm} \cdot TZ_{mdf}$$

Production cost

$$+ \sum_f \sum_m S_f \cdot X_{fm} + \sum_f \sum_m S_f \cdot Y_{fm} + \sum_f \sum_d \sum_m S_f \cdot Z_{fdm} \tag{4.1}$$

The objective function (Equation 4.1) aims to minimize total cost regarding depot opening and handling cost, forward and reverse logistics transportation cost, and production cost. The income from empty reel direct sales to customers and the marginal revenue regarding the return of a reel to the factory and using it again are additional terms for decreasing the total cost to the company.

Constraints

$$\sum_f X_{fm} + \sum_f Y_{fm} + \sum_f \sum_d Z_{fdm} \geq D_m \qquad \forall m \qquad (4.2)$$

$$\sum_m Z_{fdm} \leq Q \cdot N_{fd} \qquad \forall f, d \qquad (4.3)$$

$$X_{fm} \leq Q \cdot XX_{fm} \qquad \forall f, m \qquad (4.4)$$

$$\sum_f TX_{mf} + \sum_f TY_{mf} + \sum_f \sum_d TZ_{mdf} = TD_m \qquad \forall m \qquad (4.5)$$

$$\sum_m TZ_{mdf} \leq Q \cdot TN_{df} \qquad \forall f, d \qquad (4.6)$$

$$TX_{mf} \leq Q \cdot TXX_{mf} \qquad \forall f, m \qquad (4.7)$$

$$TXX_{mf} = TXX_{mf}^1 + TXX_{mf}^2 \qquad \forall f, m \qquad (4.8)$$

$$XX_{fm} \geq TXX_{mf}^2 \qquad \forall f, m \qquad (4.9)$$

$$TN_{df} = TN_{df}^1 + TN_{df}^2 \qquad \forall f, d \qquad (4.10)$$

$$N_{fd} \geq TN_{df}^2 \qquad \forall f, d \qquad (4.11)$$

$$\sum_f \sum_m Z_{fdm} + \sum_f \sum_m TZ_{mdf} \leq K_d \cdot A_d \qquad \forall d \qquad (4.12)$$

$$\sum_f TN_{df} + \sum_f N_{fd} \geq A_d \cdot L \qquad \forall d \qquad (4.13)$$

$$\sum_m X_{fm} + \sum_m Y_{fm} + \sum_d \sum_m Z_{fdm} \leq QF_f \qquad \forall f \qquad (4.14)$$

$$\sum_d A_d \leq M \qquad (4.15)$$

$$A_d \in \{0,1\} \quad \forall d \tag{4.16}$$

$$X_{fm}, XX_{fm}, TX_{mf}, TXX_{mf}, Y_{fm}, TY_{mf}, Z_{fdm},$$
$$TZ_{mdf}, N_{fd}, TN_{df}, TXX^1_{mf}, TXX^2_{mf}, TN^1_{df}, TN^2_{df} \geq 0 \qquad \forall f,d,m \tag{4.17}$$

Equation 4.2 explains that each customer's demand has to be satisfied using only one of the three different transportation alternatives. Equation 4.3 means that the amount of product going to customers from depots cannot be greater than the amount of product going to depots from factories. Equation 4.4 means that the product can go if a transfer occurs from factories to customers, and the amount of product cannot exceed the vehicle capacity. Equation 4.5 shows that the empty reels with the customer have to be returned using only one of the three different transportation alternatives. Equation 4.6 means that the amount of the product returned to depots from customers cannot be greater than the amount of the product returned to factories from depots. Equation 4.7 means that the product can be returned if a transfer is traveling to factories from customers, and the amount of product to be returned cannot exceed the vehicle capacity. Equation 4.8) balances the amount of total FCL reverse flow from customers to factories with the total number of flow. Equation 4.9 shows that the discount ratio will be available only if the same vehicle transports forward and reverse FCL loads from the factory to the customer. Equation 4.10 balances total FCL reverse flow from depot to factory. Equation 4.11 allows the discount ratio, which will be available only if the same vehicle transports forward and reverse FCL loads from a depot to a customer. Equation 4.12 is the depot capacity constraint. Equation 4.13 is the minimum handling amount constraint. Equation 4.14 is the production capacity of the factory. Equation 4.15 indicates that the number of depots to be opened cannot be greater than the maximum allowed number. Equations 4.16 and 4.17 define variable domains.

4.4 Case Study

In the content of this study, only customers located in the European region, where 78% of total export sales are made, are considered for a single factory. In the region, there are 90 customers located in 18 countries. There are also eight different distribution center alternatives in this region. The problem is solved for a one-term demand period for the company.

The solution of the problem depends on the number of distribution centers. Since the decision on the maximum number of distribution centers to be opened has been made previously, and the decision on the economically optimum number of distribution centers to be opened is given by the mathematical model, this mathematical model shows both exogenous and endogenous characteristics. The MILP model contains 2205 variables and 7795 constraints. All experiments were performed using the IBM ILOG CPLEX SOLVER 12.7.1. Tables 4.1 through 4.4 present problem-specific parameter values used in this case study.

First, we solved the current case, in which no distribution center is allowed to be open, to validate the mathematical model with realistic values of the factory (*Scenario 1*). In this case, the objective value of the mathematical model is found to be around $346,964. This is the best solution for customer service when goods are distributed directly from the current facility using the first or the third option. Note that in this case, no discount ratio is applied when the same vehicle transports forward and reverse loads, since there is

TABLE 4.1

The Problem Data for Related Parameters

f	M	d	S_1	QF_f	M	Q	L	α
1	90	8	0	50,000	3	20	50	0.5

TABLE 4.2

Parameter Values Related to the Customers

						m					
	1	2	3	4	5	6	7	8	9	. . .	90
D_m	77.87	0.68	61.65	50.41	41.66	41.66	4.64	33.33	3.82		67.22
TD_m	18.69	0.16	14.80	12.10	10.00	10.00	1.12	8.00	0.92		16.13
C^1_{1m}	2,923	2,335	2,365	1,873	1,963	1,953	2,273	2,055	2,371		2,333
B^1_{1m}	175	253	169	184	174	172	211	173	251		144
TC^1_{m1}	2,923	2,335	2,365	1,873	1,963	1,953	2,273	2,055	2,371		2,333
TB^1_{m1}	175	253	169	184	174	172	211	173	251		144

TABLE 4.3

Parameter Values Related to the Alternative Depot Locations

					d			
	1	2	3	4	5	6	7	8
C^2_{1d}	1,896	1,547	1,043	1,842	2,114	1,871	1,865	1,693
TC^2_{d1}	1,896	1,547	1,043	1,842	2,114	1,871	1,865	1,693
O_d	8,00	2,000	1,300	850	850	850	1,000	2,000
H_d	5.11	13.22	8.29	5.34	5.34	5.34	6.73	13.22
K_d	20,000	20,000	20,000	20,000	20,000	20,000	20,000	20,000

TABLE 4.4

B_{dm}^2 and TB_{md}^2 Parameter Values between Depot d and Customer m

						m					
d	1	2	3	4	5	6	7	8	9	. . .	90
1	41.65	57.64	56.52	33.16	27.24	27.93	43.98	30.87	49.85		42.16
2	56.61	40.18	41.19	51.01	26.99	26.36	44.00	31.84	49.87		57.38
3	56.82	59.52	61.33	58.02	45.17	44.54	63.73	50.03	69.60		57.05
4	43.68	80.38	79.27	43.52	50.84	51.52	67.57	54.47	73.44		33.15
5	47.28	83.35	82.23	47.12	54.44	55.12	71.17	58.07	77.04		31.99
6	36.78	72.86	71.74	36.62	43.94	44.62	60.67	47.57	66.54		32.02
7	37.61	75.13	74.01	37.45	46.21	46.89	62.95	49.84	68.82		24.23
8	32.14	66.41	65.29	33.34	37.50	38.18	54.23	41.13	60.10		32.37

no integration in designing the networks. This value is consistent with the current logistics costs of the company.

Then, the model was applied again, setting the maximum number of distribution centers to three without integration (*Scenario 2*). The most efficient solution for the problem was obtained in each case when only one distribution center was open. Of 90 customers, 61 were provided with service through the distribution center in forward flow, and 61 were provided with service through the distribution center in reverse flow. The objective value of the model was reduced to $318,838.

Finally, the model solved the integrated forward-reverse logistics network design problem by setting the maximum number of distribution centers to three and the discount ratio to 0.5 (*Scenario 3*). In this case, only one distribution center was open. Of 90 customers, 65 were provided with service through the distribution center in forward flow, and 71 were provided with service through the distribution center in reverse flow. The objective value of the model was reduced to $304,169.

Table 4.5 summarizes the monetary results of these three scenarios. Note that since there is only one production facility in the scenarios, the production cost is not considered.

The results in Table 4.5 show that Scenario 2 improves the total cost of the network by 8.10%, from $346,964 to $318,838. When Scenarios 2 and 3 are

TABLE 4.5

Monetary Terms for Alternative Scenarios

	Scenario 1	Scenario 2	Scenario 3
Depot opening and handling cost	0	9,590	9,590
Forward logistics transportation cost	274,388	248,958	249,157
Reverse logistics transportation cost	72,576	60,290	45,422
Production cost	0	0	0
Total cost	346,964	318,838	304,169

compared, the integration of the network decreases the total cost of the network by around 4.61% to $304,169. Finally, when the current case of the network of the company is compared with the integrated forward-reverse logistics network design, the total improvement is around 12.33% in terms of total cost.

4.5 Conclusion

In this study, a MILP model enabling the network design and optimization of enterprises having a forward and reverse logistics network for an electrolytic wire company was presented. The results of the study suggest that enterprises that desire to reduce their costs by reusing materials that have been used in the forward flow from company to customer could do so efficiently using a reverse logistics network design. Enterprises can choose what type of loading to use in the operational level according to customer demands.

This study may be beneficial to enterprises that have production centers, distribution centers, logistics processes including customers, and other similar factors presented in the proposed study. Particularly, it helps enterprises with high export rates to make decisions on operational-level network design and to make investment decisions at strategic level. In future studies, the logistics cost terms may be used as fuzzy numbers, because the pricing of third party logistics companies is very hard to estimate in advance.

References

Capraz, Ozan, Olcay Polat, and Askiner Gungor. 2015. "Planning of waste electrical and electronic equipment (WEEE) recycling facilities: MILP modelling and case study investigation". *Flexible Services and Manufacturing Journal* 27 (4):479–508. doi:10.1007/s10696-015-9217-3.

Capraz, Ozan, Olcay Polat, and Askiner Gungor. 2017. "Performance evaluation of waste electrical and electronic equipment disassembly layout configurations using simulation". *Frontiers of Environmental Science & Engineering* 11 (5):5. doi:10.1007/s11783-017-0992-9.

Chen, Y. T., F. T. Chan, S. H. Chung, and W. Y. Park. 2018. Optimization of product refurbishment in closed-loop supply chain using multi-period model integrated with fuzzy controller under uncertainties. *Robotics and Computer-Integrated Manufacturing* 50, 1–12.

Coskun, Semih, Leyla Ozgur, Olcay Polat, and Askiner Gungor. 2016. "A model proposal for green supply chain network design based on consumer segmentation". *Journal of Cleaner Production* 110:149–157. doi:http://dx.doi.org/10.1016/j.jclepro.2015.02.063.

Das, Kanchan, and Abdul H. Chowdhury. 2012. "Designing a reverse logistics network for optimal collection, recovery and quality-based product-mix planning". *International Journal of Production Economics* 135 (1):209–221. doi:10.1016/j.ijpe.2011.07.010.

Demirel, Neslihan, Hadi Gokcen, M. Ali Akcayol, and Eray Demirel. 2011. "Çok aşamalı bütünleşik lojistik ağı optimizasyonu probleminin melez genetik algoritma ile çözümü". *Gazi Üniversitesi Mühendislik-Mimarlık Fakültesi Dergisi* 26 (4):929–936. doi:10.17341/gummfd.89525.

Dowlatshahi, Shad. 2000. "Developing a theory of reverse logistics". *Interfaces* 30 (3):143–155.

El-Sayed, M., N. Afia, and A. El-Kharbotly. 2010. "A stochastic model for forward–reverse logistics network design under risk". *Computers & Industrial Engineering* 58 (3):423–431. doi:10.1016/j.cie.2008.09.040.

Fattahi, Mohammad, and Kannan Govindan. 2017. "Integrated forward/reverse logistics network design under uncertainty with pricing for collection of used products". *Annals of Operations Research* 253 (1):193–225. doi:10.1007/s10479-016-2347-5.

Fleischmann, M., P. Beullens, J.M. Bloemhof-Ruwaard, and L. Wassenhove. 2001. "The impact of product recovery on logistics network design". *Production and Operations Management* 10 (2):156–173. doi:10.1111/j.1937-5956.2001.tb00076.x.

Gungor, Askiner, and Surendra M. Gupta. 1999. "Issues in environmentally conscious manufacturing and product recovery: A survey". *Computers & Industrial Engineering* 36 (4):811–853.

Gupta, Surendra M. 2016. *Reverse Supply Chains: Issues and Analysis*: CRC Press.

Hatefi, S. M., and F. Jolai. 2014. "Robust and reliable forward–reverse logistics network design under demand uncertainty and facility disruptions". *Applied Mathematical Modelling* 38 (9):2630–2647. doi:10.1016/j.apm.2013.11.002.

Hatefi, S. M., F. Jolai, S. A. Torabi, and R. Tavakkoli-Moghaddam. 2015. A credibility-constrained programming for reliable forward–reverse logistics network design under uncertainty and facility disruptions. *International Journal of Computer Integrated Manufacturing* 28 (6):664–678.

Ilgin, Mehmet Ali, and Surendra M. Gupta. 2010. "Environmentally conscious manufacturing and product recovery (ECMPRO): A review of the state of the art". *Journal of Environmental Management* 91 (3):563–591. doi:10.1016/j.jenvman.2009.09.037.

Kalayci, Can B., and Surendra M. Gupta. 2013. "Simulated annealing algorithm for solving sequence-dependent disassembly line balancing problem". *IFAC Proceedings Volumes* 46 (9):93–98. doi:https://doi.org/10.3182/20130619-3-RU-3018.00064.

Kalayci, Can B., Olcay Polat, and Surendra M. Gupta. 2015. "A variable neighbourhood search algorithm for disassembly lines". *Journal of Manufacturing Technology Management* 26 (2):182–194. doi:10.1108/JMTM-11-2013-0168.

Kalayci, Can B., Olcay Polat, and Surendra M. Gupta. 2016. "A hybrid genetic algorithm for sequence-dependent disassembly line balancing problem". *Annals of Operations Research* 242 (2):321–354. doi:10.1007/s10479-014-1641-3.

Keyvanshokooh, E., M. Fattahi, S. M. Seyed-Hosseini, and R. Tavakkoli-Moghaddam. 2013. "A dynamic pricing approach for returned products in integrated forward/reverse logistics network design". *Applied Mathematical Modelling* 37 (24):10182–10202. doi:10.1016/j.apm.2013.05.042.

Khajavi, L., S. Seyed-Hosseini, and A. Makui. 2011. "An integrated forward/reverse logistics network optimization model for multi-stage capacitated supply chain". *iBusiness* 3 (2):229–235. doi:10.4236/ib.2011.32030.

Ko, Hyun Jeung, and Gerald W. Evans. 2007. "A genetic algorithm-based heuristic for the dynamic integrated forward/reverse logistics network for 3PLs". *Computers & Operations Research* 34 (2):346–366. doi:10.1016/j.cor.2005.03.004.

Lee, Der-Horng, and Meng Dong. 2008. "A heuristic approach to logistics network design for end-of-lease computer products recovery". *Transportation Research Part E: Logistics and Transportation Review* 44 (3):455–474. doi:https://doi.org/10.1016/j.tre.2006.11.003.

Liao, Tsai-Yun. 2018. "Reverse logistics network design for product recovery and remanufacturing". *Applied Mathematical Modelling* 60, 145–163.

Listeş, Ovidiu. 2007. "A generic stochastic model for supply-and-return network design". *Computers & Operations Research* 34 (2):417–442. doi:10.1016/j.cor.2005.03.007.

Nakashima, Kenichi, and Surendra M. Gupta. 2012. "A study on the risk management of multi Kanban system in a closed loop supply chain". *International Journal of Production Economics* 139 (1):65–68. doi:https://doi.org/10.1016/j.ijpe.2012.03.016.

Nukala, Satish, and Surendra M Gupta. 2007. A fuzzy mathematical programming approach for supplier selection in a closed-loop supply chain network. *Paper presented at the Proceedings of the 2007 POMS-Dallas meeting.*

Pishvaee, Mir Saman, Reza Zanjirani Farahani, and Wout Dullaert. 2010. "A memetic algorithm for bi-objective integrated forward/reverse logistics network design". *Computers & Operations Research* 37 (6):1100–1112. doi:https://doi.org/10.1016/j.cor.2009.09.018.

Pishvaee, Mir Saman, Fariborz Jolai, and Jafar Razmi. 2009. "A stochastic optimization model for integrated forward/reverse logistics network design". *Journal of Manufacturing Systems* 28 (4):107–114. doi:10.1016/j.jmsy.2010.05.001.

Pochampally, K. K., and S. M. Gupta. 2003. A multi-phase mathematical programming approach to strategic planning of an efficient reverse supply chain network. *Paper presented at the IEEE International Symposium on Electronics and the Environment*: Boston MA, 19–22 May.

Pochampally, Kishore K, Satish Nukala, and Surendra M Gupta. 2008. *Strategic planning models for reverse and closed-loop supply chains*: CRC Press.

Pochampally, Kishore K., and Surendra M. Gupta. 2005. "Strategic planning of a reverse supply chain network". *International Journal of Integrated Supply Management* 1 (4):421–441. doi:10.1504/ijism.2005.006304.

Pochampally, Kishore K., and Surendra M. Gupta. 2012. "Use of linear physical programming and Bayesian updating for design issues in reverse logistics". *International Journal of Production Research* 50 (5):1349–1359. doi:10.1080/00207543.2011.571933.

Pochampally, Kishore K., Surendra M. Gupta, and Kannan Govindan. 2009. "Metrics for performance measurement of a reverse/closed-loop supply chain". *International Journal of Business Performance and Supply Chain Modelling* 1 (1):8–32. doi:10.1504/ijbpscm.2009.026263.

Pochampally, Kishore K., Surendra M. Gupta, and Sagar V. Kamarthi. 2004. Identification of potential recovery facilities for designing a reverse supply chain network using physical programming. *Paper presented at the Photonics Technologies for Robotics, Automation, and Manufacturing. International Society for Optics and Photonics* 5262, 139–147.

Polat, Olcay, Ozan Capraz, and Askiner Gungor. 2018. "Modelling of WEEE recycling operation planning under uncertainty". *Journal of Cleaner Production* 180:769–779. doi:10.1016/j.jclepro.2018.01.187.

Ramezani, Majid, Mahdi Bashiri, and Reza Tavakkoli-Moghaddam. 2013. "A new multi-objective stochastic model for a forward/reverse logistic network design with responsiveness and quality level". *Applied Mathematical Modelling* 37 (1):328–344. doi:http://dx.doi.org/10.1016/j.apm.2012.02.032.

Rogers, Dale S., and Ronald Tibben-Lembke. 2001. "An examination of reverse logistics practices". *Journal of Business Logistics* 22 (2):129–148.

Salema, M. I., A. P. B. Póvoa, and A. Q. Novais. 2006. "A warehouse-based design model for reverse logistics". *Journal of the Operational Research Society* 57 (6):615–629. doi:10.1057/palgrave.jors.2602035.

Shaharudin, Mohd Rizaimy, Kannan Govindan, Suhaiza Zailani, Keah Choon Tan, and Mohammad Iranmanesh. 2017. "Product return management: Linking product returns, closed-loop supply chain activities and the effectiveness of the reverse supply chains". *Journal of Cleaner Production* 149:1144–1156.

Soleimani, Hamed, and Mostafa Zohal. 2017. "An ant colony approach to forward-reverse logistics network design under demand certainty". *Journal of Optimization in Industrial Engineering* 10 (22):103–114. doi:10.22094/joie.2017.281.

5

A Holistic Grey-MCDM Approach for Green Supplier Elicitation in Responsible Manufacturing

Gazi Murat Duman, Elif Kongar, and Surendra M. Gupta

CONTENTS

5.1 Introduction

Increasing awareness regarding environmental pollution and prevention and accompanying governmental legislation has resulted in businesses measuring and analyzing the environmental impacts of their operations. Therefore, responsible manufacturing has attracted growing attention from both researchers and industry professionals [1]. Regarding the responsible manufacturing concept, comprehensive reviews on the issues have been provided by Gungor and Gupta [2], Ilgin and Gupta [3], Gupta [4], and Wang and Gupta [5].

Responsible manufacturing processes begin with selecting the appropriate supplier. Hence, green supplier selection and evaluation has become one of the major topics that have gained attention in responsible manufacturing. Maintaining long-term relationships with reliable suppliers is the primary focus of current supply chain management [6, 7]. Lower cost, higher quality, and shorter lead times have been the three main criteria in traditional supplier selection and evaluation activities. In recent practice, an additional factor, environmental responsibility [8], has been added to this list, since suppliers today are being prioritized with a stronger emphasis on environmental sustainability.

Green supplier selection and evaluation (GSES) has been well studied in the literature. In their literature survey, Ilgin, Gupta and Battaia [9] stated that the multi-criteria decision-making (MCDM) techniques appeared to be the appropriate tools to use in GSES. In another literature survey, Tozanli et al. [10] reviewed recent studies with MCDM approaches for green supplier selection and evaluation in a fuzzy environment. According to Tozanli et al. [10], studies with the grey system, a theory derived from grey sets, which copes with both known and unknown information, are relatively limited.

Li et al. [11] applied a grey-based decision-making approach to the supplier selection problem. Golmohammadi et al. [12] developed a two-phased grey decision-making approach to supplier selection. Bai and Sarkis [13] used grey system and rough set theory for sustainable supplier selection. Bali et al. [14] studied a green supplier selection problem for an automobile company integrating intuitionistic fuzzy set (IFS) and grey relational analysis (GRA). Hashemi et al. [15] developed a grey-based carbon management model for green supplier selection. Furthermore, Hashemi et al. [6] used and combined analytic network process (ANP) and GRA for green supplier selection. Dou et al. [16] applied a grey ANP-based methodology to evaluate the selection of green supplier development programs. Sahu et al. [17] developed a green supplier appraisal platform using grey concepts.

Analytical hierarchy process (AHP) and technique for order preference by similarity (TOPSIS) are two frequently used methods in supplier selection problems. Several studies have been published with different variations and combinations of these two methods [10]. However, to the best of our knowledge, there is no other study that aims at combining grey systems, AHP, and TOPSIS for green supplier evaluation and selection. With this motivation, this chapter proposes a hybrid multi-criteria decision-making framework using Grey-AHP and Grey-TOPSIS methods. The theoretical background, the problem statement, and the proposed methodology are detailed in the following sections. A case study in a U.S.-based manufacturing company is provided along with the conclusions and discussion regarding future research.

5.2 Methodology

This study proposes a combined hierarchical approach that combines Grey-AHP and Grey-TOPSIS methods, forming a holistic solution methodology for the green supplier selection problem. Grey-AHP is used to determine the importance weights of the customer requirements (CRs). Following this, Grey-TOPSIS is applied to rank the provided suppliers. Detailed steps of the proposed method are provided in Figure 5.1.

5.2.1 Grey-Systems Theory

Grey systems theory was first introduced by Deng [18] to deal with insufficient and incomplete information. In grey systems theory, if the system

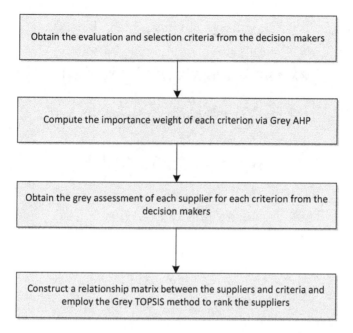

FIGURE 5.1
The steps of the proposed methodology.

information is fully known, the system is called a *white system*. Similarly, if the information is not known at all, it is called a *black system*. A system with partially known information is called a *grey system*. Hence, a grey number is a number with uncertain/incomplete information. A grey number is defined as $\otimes X = \left[\underline{X}, \overline{X}\right] = \left\{X| \underline{X} \leq X \leq \overline{X}, \underline{X} \text{ and } \overline{X} \in R\right\}$. Thus, $\otimes X$ contains two real numbers: $\underline{X}$ (the lower limit of $\otimes X$) and $\overline{X}$ (the upper limit of $\otimes X$), defined as follows:

- If $\underline{X} \to -\infty$ and $\overline{X} \to \infty$, then $\otimes X$ is called the *black number* with no meaningful information.
- If $\underline{X} = \overline{X}$, then $\otimes X$ is called the *white number* with complete information.
- Otherwise, if $\otimes X = \left[\underline{X}, \overline{X}\right]$, $\otimes X$ is called the *grey number* with insufficient and uncertain information.

Let there be two sets of grey numbers denoted by $\otimes X_1 = \left[\underline{X_1}, \overline{X_1}\right]$ and $\otimes X_2 = \left[\underline{X_2}, \overline{X_2}\right]$. The basic mathematical operations for these two sets of grey numbers are listed as follows.

$$\otimes X_1 + \otimes X_2 = \left[\underline{X_1} + \underline{X_2}, \overline{X_1} + \overline{X_2}\right] \tag{5.1}$$

$$\otimes X_1 - \otimes X_2 = \left[\underline{X_1} - \underline{X_2}, \overline{X_1} - \overline{X_2} \right] \tag{5.2}$$

$$\otimes X_1 * \otimes X_2 = \Big[\min \left(\underline{X_1}\underline{X_2}, \overline{X_1}\overline{X_2}, \underline{X_1}\overline{X_2}, \overline{X_1}\underline{X_2} \right),$$
$$\max \left(\underline{X_1}\underline{X_2}, \overline{X_1}\overline{X_2}, \underline{X_1}\overline{X_2}, \overline{X_1}\underline{X_2} \right) \Big] \tag{5.3}$$

$$\otimes X_1 : \otimes X_2 = \left[\underline{X_1}, \overline{X_1} \right] * \left[\frac{1}{\overline{X_2}}, \frac{1}{\underline{X_2}} \right] \tag{5.4}$$

$$k * \otimes X_1 = \left[k\underline{X_1}, k\overline{X_1} \right], k\epsilon\ R \tag{5.5}$$

$$\otimes X_1^{-1} = \left[\frac{1}{\overline{X_1}}, \frac{1}{\underline{X_1}} \right] \tag{5.6}$$

5.2.2 Grey-AHP

To determine the importance weights of the CRs, a grey-AHP approach is applied. The detailed steps of this approach are provided in the following.

(i) Create a grey decision matrix D where $\otimes X_{ij}$ are linguistic variables. This stage includes the pairwise comparison of the CRs from the decision makers.

$$D = \begin{bmatrix} \otimes X_{11} \otimes X_{12} \ldots \otimes X_{1n} \\ \otimes X_{21} \otimes X_{22} \ldots \otimes X_{2n} \\ \vdots \\ \vdots \\ \otimes X_{m1} \otimes X_{m2} \ldots \otimes X_{mn} \end{bmatrix} \tag{5.7}$$

(ii) Normalize the paired comparisons matrix.

$$D^* = \begin{bmatrix} \otimes X_{11}{}^* \otimes X_{12}{}^* \ldots \otimes X_{1n}{}^* \\ \vdots \\ \vdots \\ \vdots \\ \otimes X_{m1}{}^* \otimes X_{m2}{}^* \ldots \otimes X_{mn}{}^* \end{bmatrix}$$

$$= \begin{bmatrix} \left[\underline{X_{11}}^*, \overline{X_{11}}^*\right]\left[\underline{X_{12}}^*, \overline{X_{12}}^*\right]......\left[\underline{X_{1n}}^*, \overline{X_{1n}}^*\right] \\ \vdots \\ \vdots \\ \vdots \\ \left[\underline{X_{m1}}^*, \overline{X_{m1}}^*\right]\left[\underline{X_{m2}}^*, \overline{X_{m2}}^*\right]......\left[\underline{X_{mn}}^*, \overline{X_{mn}}^*\right] \end{bmatrix}$$

$$\underline{X_{ij}}^* = \left[\frac{2\underline{X_{ij}}}{\sum\limits_{i=1}^{m} \underline{X_{ij}} + \sum\limits_{i=1}^{m} \overline{X_{ij}}} \right] \tag{5.8}$$

$$\overline{X_{ij}}^* = \left[\frac{2\overline{X_{ij}}}{\sum\limits_{i=1}^{m} \underline{X_{ij}} + \sum\limits_{i=1}^{m} \overline{X_{ij}}} \right] \tag{5.9}$$

3. Calculate the relative weights of CRs. The relative weights of factors in each level are calculated using normalized paired comparisons matrix according to Equation 5.10. The calculated weight is (W_i), a grey number.

$$W_i = \frac{1}{n}\sum\limits_{i=1}^{m}\left[\underline{X_{ij}}^*, \overline{X_{ij}}^*\right] \tag{5.10}$$

5.2.3 Grey-TOPSIS

To determine the best alternative, the Grey-TOPSIS method is used. The detailed steps of this method are provided in the following.

(i) Construct a decision matrix R where $\otimes R_{ij}$ are linguistic variables. This stage includes the linguistic assessments of each alternative with respect to each CR from the decision makers.

$$R = \begin{bmatrix} \otimes R_{11} \otimes R_{12}......\otimes R_{1n} \\ \otimes R_{21} \otimes R_{22}......\otimes R_{2n} \\ \vdots \\ \vdots \\ \otimes R_{m1} \otimes R_{m2}......\otimes R_{mn} \end{bmatrix} \tag{5.11}$$

(ii) Normalize the decision matrix. For the benefit type of criteria, Equation 5.12 is used for the normalization, and for the cost type of criteria, Equation 5.13 is used [19, 20].

$$\otimes r_{ij} = \frac{\otimes R_{ij}}{max_i\left(\overline{R_{ij}}\right)} = \left(\frac{\underline{R_{ij}}}{max_i\left(\overline{R_{ij}}\right)}, \frac{\overline{R_{ij}}}{max_i\left(\overline{R_{ij}}\right)}\right) \tag{5.12}$$

$$\otimes r_{ij} = 1 - \frac{\otimes R_{ij}}{max_i\left(\overline{R_{ij}}\right)} = \left(1 - \frac{\overline{R_{ij}}}{max_i\left(\overline{R_{ij}}\right)}, 1 - \frac{\underline{R_{ij}}}{max_i\left(\overline{R_{ij}}\right)}\right) \tag{5.13}$$

(iii) Determine the positive ideal alternative (A^+) and the negative ideal alternative (A^-)

$$A^+ = \left\{(\max_i \overline{r_{ij}} \mid j \in J'), (\min_i \underline{r_{ij}} \mid j \in J'')\right\} = \left\{r_1^+, \dots, r_m^+\right\} \tag{5.14}$$

$$A^- = \left\{(\min_i \underline{r_{ij}} \mid j \in J', (\max_j \overline{r_{ij}} \mid j \in J'')\right\} = \left\{r_1^-, \dots, r_m^m\right\} \tag{5.15}$$

where J' is associated with benefit criteria and J'' is associated with cost criteria. Using Equation 5.13 as the normalization operator, a cost type of criterion is converted to a benefit type of criterion. Hence, the cost criteria could be handled as benefit criteria [19].

(iv) Compute the distance of each alternative from A^+ and A^- using Equations 5.16 and 5.17. In these equations, W_i represents the weight of each criterion calculated in Grey-AHP.

$$d_i^+ = \sqrt{\frac{1}{2}\sum_{j=1}^{m} W_i\left(\left|r_j^+ - \underline{r_{ij}}\right|^2 + \left|r_j^+ - \overline{r_{ij}}\right|^2\right)} \tag{5.16}$$

$$d_i^- = \sqrt{\frac{1}{2}\sum_{j=1}^{m} W_i\left(\left|r_j^- - \underline{r_{ij}}\right|^2 + \left|r_j^- - \overline{r_{ij}}\right|^2\right)} \tag{5.17}$$

(v) Compute the closeness coefficient (CC_i) of each alternative:

$$CC_i = \frac{d_i^-}{d_i^- + d_i^+} \tag{5.18}$$

(vi) Rank the alternatives according to the closeness coefficient, CC_i, in decreasing order.

5.3 Case Study in Dispensing Systems Industry

The case study is conducted in a leading global manufacturer and distributor of dispensing systems for beauty and personal care in addition to home and consumer healthcare needs. The U.S.-based manufacturing company uses plastics as one of its major raw materials. The study focused on evaluating and selecting supplier(s) of plastics used in the plastic injection molding of innovative dispensing pumps. To select the best alternative, 13 potential suppliers were evaluated according to their performance using eight decision criteria. The evaluation was conducted based on the linguistic judgements of decision makers in the company. The criteria defined by these experts are given in Table 5.1.

Given this set of criteria, the decision makers are asked to rank their preference levels for each criterion. Following this, to prioritize the green image in the supplier evaluation process, a Grey-AHP approach is employed. The evaluation scale used in Grey-AHP is provided in Table 5.2.

The data obtained from the decision makers for pairwise comparison are provided in Table 5.3.

The weights of the main criteria are obtained by applying Equation 5.7 to Equation 5.10, and the results are presented in Table 5.4.

The weights of the criteria are used as an input in the Grey-TOPSIS method to evaluate the suppliers. Additional inputs are the grey evaluations of the suppliers with respect to each criterion. These are obtained from the decision makers in the company using linguistic terms (Table 5.5).

The evaluation data of each supplier with respect to each criterion obtained from the decision makers are provided in Table 5.6.

The normalized grey decision matrix is obtained using Equations 5.11 and 5.12 and presented in Table 5.7. In our study, the first criterion is defined as the cost criterion, and the others are defined as the benefit criteria.

The positive ideal alternative (A^+) and the negative ideal alternative (A^-) are calculated using Equations 5.14 and 5.15. In our study, the first criterion is defined as the cost criterion, and the others are defined as the benefit criteria. For instance, for the criterion Quality, the maximum value of the upper limit is 1, and the lowest value at the lower limit is equal to 0, so that the positive ideal value is set to 1, and the negative ideal value is determined as 0. The distances d^+ and d^- of each supplier's evaluation ratings from A^+ to A^- are calculated via Equations 5.16 and 5.17. The closeness coefficient, CC_i, is computed via Equation 5.18, and the supplier ranking summary is provided in Table 5.8. The highest closeness coefficient determines the highest rank, implying that Supplier 2 is the best alternative, followed by Suppliers 5, 1, 12, 9, 11, 8, 3, 4, 6, 7, 10, and finally, Supplier 13.

TABLE 5.1

Criteria and Their Definitions

Criterion	Definition
Cost	A measure related to the order and purchasing cost of the raw material for manufacturing.
Quality	A measure related to the quality of the raw material obtained from the suppliers and its performance in molding and injection processes.
Logistics operations	A measure related to the service level of transportation and warehousing, on time and full delivery performance operations of the suppliers.
Service level	A measure related to the response time to customer requests, flexibility, and past customer service performance of each supplier.
Financial position	A measure related to the financial strengths of each supplier for continuous business.
Organization	A measure related to the company size of the supplier, business existence, and continuity in industry.
Continuous improvement	A measure related to the continuous improvement in product capability of suppliers, research and development activities, and operational efficiencies.
Green image	A measure related to the energy, waste, and natural resources reduction performance of suppliers and environmental policies.

TABLE 5.2

Comparative Linguistic Scale for Ratings of Alternatives and Weights of Criteria

Linguistic Terms	Grey Numbers
Just equal [EQ]	[1,1]
Weak importance of one over another [WI]	[1,3]
Fairly preferable [FP]	[3,5]
Strongly preferable [SP]	[5,7]
Absolutely preferable [AP]	[7,9]

In the pairwise comparison matrix, the value of each criterion j compared with criterion i is calculated as the reciprocal of the value of criterion i compared with criterion j.

TABLE 5.3

Pairwise Comparison of Criteria Collected from Decision Makers via Linguistic Terms

Criterion	Cost	Quality	Service Level	Logistics	Financial Position	Organization	Continuous Improvement	Green Image
Cost	EQ	1/WI	FP	FP	WI	AP	SP	1/FP
Quality	WI	EQ	WI	FP	FP	FP	WI	1/WI
Service level	1/FP	1/WI	EQ	WI	WI	WI	EQ	1/FP
Logistics	1/FP	1/FP	1/WI	EQ	WI	WI	EQ	1/FP
Financial position	1/WI	1/FP	1/WI	1/WI	EQ	WI	WI	1/SP
Organization	1/AP	1/FP	1/WI	1/WI	1/WI	EQ	1/WI	1/AP
Continuous improvement	1/SP	1/WI	EQ	EQ	1/WI	WI	EQ	1/FP
Green image	FP	WI	FP	FP	SP	AP	FP	EQ

TABLE 5.4

Weights of the Main Criteria

Criterion	Weights
Cost	[0.151,0.240]
Quality	[0.122,0.246]
Service level	[0.050,0.097]
Logistics	[0.044,0.083]
Financial position	[0.039,0.087]
Organization	[0.025,0.050]
Continuous improvement	[0.050,0.094]
Green image	[0.240,0.383]

TABLE 5.5

Linguistic Scale to Evaluate Ratings of Suppliers

Linguistic Terms for TOPSIS	Grey Numbers
Very low [VL]	[0,1]
Low [L]	[1,3]
Medium [M]	[3,5]
High [H]	[5,7]
Very high [VH]	[7,9]

TABLE 5.6

Linguistic Ratings of Each Supplier with Respect to Each Criterion

	Cost	Quality	Service Level	Logistics
Supplier 1	M	VH	L	M
Supplier 2	L	H	L	H
Supplier 3	H	VL	M	H
Supplier 4	VH	H	L	L
Supplier 5	L	M	H	VL
Supplier 6	H	M	M	M
Supplier 7	M	H	VH	VH
Supplier 8	L	M	M	H
Supplier 9	M	VH	H	VL
Supplier 10	L	VL	H	M
Supplier 11	M	M	VL	M
Supplier 12	H	L	VH	L
Supplier 13	M	L	L	VH

	Financial Position	Organization	Continuous Improvement	Green Image
Supplier 1	H	VH	H	H
Supplier 2	L	H	VL	VH
Supplier 3	H	VL	L	H
Supplier 4	L	M	H	M
Supplier 5	VL	VH	H	VH
Supplier 6	H	VL	H	M
Supplier 7	L	H	M	L
Supplier 8	M	L	H	M
Supplier 9	VH	VH	M	M
Supplier 10	H	L	H	M
Supplier 11	L	H	L	H
Supplier 12	VL	VH	M	VH
Supplier 13	M	L	M	L

TABLE 5.7

Normalized Grey Decision Matrix

	Cost	Quality	Service Level	Logistics
Supplier 1	[0.444,0.667]	[0.778,1]	[0.111,0.333]	[0.333,0.556]
Supplier 2	[0.667,0.889]	[0.556,0.778]	[0.111,0.333]	[0.556,0.778]
Supplier 3	[0.222,0.444]	[0,0.111]	[0.333,0.556]	[0.556,0.778]
Supplier 4	[0,0.222]	[0.556,0.778]	[0.111,0.333]	[0.111,0.333]
Supplier 5	[0.667,0.889]	[0.333,0.556]	[0.556,0.778]	[0,0.111]
Supplier 6	[0.222,0.444]	[0.333,0.556]	[0.333,0.556]	[0.333,0.556]
Supplier 7	[0.444,0.667]	[0.556,0.778]	[0.778,1]	[0.778,1]
Supplier 8	[0.667,0.889]	[0.333,0.556]	[0.333,0.556]	[0.556,0.778]
Supplier 9	[0.444,0.667]	[0.778,1]	[0.556,0.778]	[0,0.111]
Supplier 10	[0.667,0.889]	[0,0.111]	[0.556,0.778]	[0.333,0.556]
Supplier 11	[0.444,0.667]	[0.333,0.556]	[0,0.111]	[0.333,0.556]
Supplier 12	[0.222,0.444]	[0.111,0.333]	[0.778,1]	[0.111,0.333]
Supplier 13	[0.444,0.667]	[0.111,0.333]	[0.111,0.333]	[0.778,1]

	Financial Position	Organization	Continuous Improvement	Green Image
Supplier 1	[0.556,0.778]	[0.778,1]	[0.556,0.778]	[0.556,0.778]
Supplier 2	[0.111,0.333]	[0.556,0.778]	[0,0.111]	[0.778,1]
Supplier 3	[0.556,0.778]	[0,0.111]	[0.111,0.333]	[0.556,0.778]
Supplier 4	[0.111,0.333]	[0.333,0.556]	[0.556,0.778]	[0.333,0.556]
Supplier 5	[0,0.111]	[0.778,1]	[0.556,0.778]	[0.778,1]
Supplier 6	[0.556,0.778]	[0,0.111]	[0.556,0.778]	[0.333,0.556]
Supplier 7	[0.111,0.333]	[0.556,0.778]	[0.333,0.556]	[0.111,0.333]
Supplier 8	[0.333,0.556]	[0.111,0.333]	[0.556,0.778]	[0.333,0.556]
Supplier 9	[0.778,1]	[0.778,1]	[0.333,0.556]	[0.333,0.556]
Supplier 10	[0.556,0.778]	[0.111,0.333]	[0.556,0.778]	[0.333,0.556]
Supplier 11	[0.111,0.333]	[0.556,0.778]	[0.111,0.333]	[0.556,0.778]
Supplier 12	[0,0.111]	[0.778,1]	[0.333,0.556]	[0.778,1]
Supplier 13	[0.333,0.556]	[0.111,0.333]	[0.333,0.556]	[0.111,0.333]

TABLE 5.8

Ranking of Suppliers

Supplier	d^+	d^-	CC	Rank
Supplier 1	0.361	0.432	0.545	3
Supplier 2	0.342	0.479	0.584	1
Supplier 3	0.476	0.325	0.406	8
Supplier 4	0.477	0.299	0.386	9
Supplier 5	0.365	0.465	0.561	2
Supplier 6	0.471	0.284	0.376	10
Supplier 7	0.510	0.301	0.372	11
Supplier 8	0.453	0.320	0.414	7
Supplier 9	0.425	0.378	0.470	5
Supplier 10	0.506	0.294	0.367	12
Supplier 11	0.420	0.355	0.458	6
Supplier 12	0.414	0.428	0.508	4
Supplier 13	0.560	0.217	0.279	13

5.4 Conclusions and Discussion

The AHP and TOPSIS methods are both well known and well studied in multi-criteria decision-making problems. However, these methods are not applied jointly to solve the green supplier evaluation and selection problem using grey numbers.

In this chapter, Grey-AHP is applied to determine the weights of the decision criteria, and Grey-TOPSIS is applied to rank the alternatives. To demonstrate the effectiveness of the proposed approach, the method is then applied to a U.S.-based dispensing systems manufacturing company. Eight criteria are determined by the experts along with the linguistic assessments of the potential suppliers with respect to each criterion. Eventually, based on this information, the rankings of the suppliers are obtained via the proposed approach.

Grey theory is an effective method when dealing with systems with uncertain information. In grey theory, a system is called *white* if the related information is fully known and available and *black* if the information is unknown and/or not available. Similarly, a system with partial information is called a *grey* system [11].

Grey sets are sometimes perceived as an extension of interval valued fuzzy sets [21–23] with additional advantages over fuzzy systems [6, 23]. Similarly to fuzzy theory, grey theory is appropriate for problems with some levels of uncertainty and indetermination. This multidisciplinary and generic theory deals with systems characterized by poor information and/or systems where information is lacking [24]. One of the main factors that make grey theory more advantageous is its ability to consider the condition of the fuzziness and its flexibility when dealing with a fuzziness situation [11]. Daisuke et al. [21] argue that even though the grey sets are based on the mapping of fuzzy sets, grey theory allows the introduction of strict values for upper and lower limits, whereas fuzzy theory considers those boundaries as fuzzy values. Furthermore, Baskaran et al. [25] stated that in the fuzzy approach, the initial representation of criteria would be in fuzzy linguistic values later to be converted into known exact values, while in the grey approach, the uncertainty represented in criteria using linguistic values would continue until the estimation of weights and evaluation of alternatives. Supplier selection problems often require methodologies that are able to handle multiple selection criteria and uncertainty in the model environment, making grey theory a very suitable methodology for such problems. As a result, several approaches using fuzzy and grey sets have been proposed to deal with supplier selection problems. A comparative analysis of fuzzy and grey sets in addition to conventional methods and rough sets is provided in Table 5.9. For additional criteria and further information, please see Daisuke et al. [21].

Grey systems are gaining popularity in the literature due to their ability to cope with uncertainty. In their literature survey, Tozanli et al. [10] stated that

TABLE 5.9

Comparison of Classic, Fuzzy, Grey, and Rough Sets

	Classic	Fuzzy	Grey	Rough
Objective	Elucidate property of population	Knowledge expression	Automatic systems control	Knowledge discovery in databases
Uncertainty	Probabilistic events	Degree of cognition	Lack information situation	Conflict between certainty and possibility
Data-type	Observed real values	Real values of membership	Observed real values and interval values	Observed real values and nominal values
Data distribution	Typical distribution—required in advance	Membershipfunction—experience	Any distribution—non-parametric	Any distribution—non-parametric
Operation	Set or Boolean algebra	Max/min selection	Interval algebra	Set algebra
Crisp-conversation	Unnecessary	α-cuts: collection of high membership elements	Whitening function: Compute one point from interval	$Apr*(X)=Apr(X)$ No boundary region state

Source: Partially adopted from Daisuke, Y. et al., *Reviewing Crisp, Fuzzy, Grey and Rough Mathematical Models*, 2007.

the total number of fuzzy articles incorporating grey theory has increased significantly over the past 5 years. In this study, the decision makers found grey system theory to be a better fit, considering its various advantages, and used grey numbers for the ratings of attributes that were initially expressed using linguistic variables.

References

1. Gupta, S.M.: 'Lean manufacturing, green manufacturing and sustainability', *Journal of Japan Industrial Management Association*, 2016, 67, (2E), pp. 102–105.
2. Gungor, A., and Gupta, S.M.: 'Issues in environmentally conscious manufacturing and product recovery: A survey', *Computers & Industrial Engineering*, 1999, 36, (4), pp. 811–853.
3. Ilgin, M.A., and Gupta, S.M.: 'Environmentally conscious manufacturing and product recovery (ECMPRO): A review of the state of the art', *Journal of Environmental Management*, 2010, 91, (3), pp. 563–591.
4. Gupta, S.M.: *Reverse Supply Chains: Issues and Analysis* (CRC Press, Boca Raton, FL, 2013).
5. Wang, H.-F., and Gupta, S. M.: *Green Supply Chain Management: Product Life Cycle Approach*, (McGraw Hill, New York, 2011).
6. Hashemi, S.H., Karimi, A., and Tavana, M.: 'An integrated green supplier selection approach with analytic network process and improved Grey relational analysis', *International Journal of Production Economics*, 2015, 159, pp. 178–191.
7. Ho, W., Xu, X., and Dey, P.K.: 'Multi-criteria decision making approaches for supplier evaluation and selection: A literature review', *European Journal of Operational Research*, 2010, 202, (1), pp. 16–24.
8. Lee, A.H.I., Kang, H.Y., Hsu, C.F., and Hung, H.C.: 'A green supplier selection model for high-tech industry', *Expert Systems with Applications*, 2009, 36, (4), pp. 7917–7927.
9. Ilgin, M.A., Gupta, S.M., and Battaïa, O.: 'Use of MCDM techniques in environmentally conscious manufacturing and product recovery: State of the art', *Journal of Manufacturing Systems*, 2015, 37, pp. 746–758.
10. Tozanli, O., Duman, G., Kongar, E., and Gupta, S.M.: 'Environmentally concerned logistics operations in fuzzy environment: A literature survey', *Logistics*, 2017, 1, (1), p. 4.
11. Li, G.D., Yamaguchi, D., and Nagai, M.: 'A grey-based decision-making approach to the supplier selection problem', *Mathematical and Computer Modelling*, 2007, 46, (3), pp. 573–581.
12. Golmohammadi, D., and Mellat-Parast, M.: 'Developing a grey-based decision-making model for supplier selection', *International Journal of Production Economics*, 2012, 137, (2), pp. 191–200.
13. Bai, C., and Sarkis, J.: 'Integrating sustainability into supplier selection with grey system and rough set methodologies', *International Journal of Production Economics*, 2010, 124, (1), pp. 252–264.

14. Ozkan, B., Erkan, K., and Serkan, G.: 'Green supplier selection based on IFS and GRA', *Grey Systems: Theory and Application*, 2013, 3, (2), pp. 158–176.
15. Hashemi, S.H., Karimi, A., Aghakhani, N., and Kalantar, P.: 'A grey-based carbon management model for green supplier selection', in (Eds.): *A Grey-Based Carbon Management Model for Green Supplier Selection* (2013, edn.), pp. 402–405.
16. Dou, Y., Zhu, Q., and Sarkis, J.: 'Evaluating green supplier development programs with a grey-analytical network process-based methodology', *European Journal of Operational Research*, 2014, 233, (2), pp. 420–431.
17. Nitin Kumar, S., Saurav, D., and Siba Sankar, M.: 'Establishing green supplier appraisement platform using grey concepts', *Grey Systems: Theory and Application*, 2012, 2, (3), pp. 395–418.
18. Ju-Long, D.: 'Control problems of grey systems', *Systems & Control Letters*, 1982, 1, (5), pp. 288–294.
19. Oztaysi, B.: 'A decision model for information technology selection using AHP integrated TOPSIS-Grey: The case of content management systems', *Knowledge-Based Systems*, 2014, 70, pp. 44–54.
20. Zavadskas, E.K., Vilutiene, T., Turskis, Z., and Tamosaitiene, J.: 'Contractor selection for construction works by applying SAW-G and TOPSIS grey techniques', *Journal of Business Economics and Management*, 2010, 11, (1), pp. 34–55.
21. Daisuke, Y., Guo-Dong, L., Li-Chen, C., and Masatake, N.: 'Reviewing crisp, fuzzy, grey and rough mathematical models', in (Eds.): *Reviewing Crisp, Fuzzy, Grey and Rough Mathematical Models* (2007, edn.), pp. 547–552.
22. Deschrijver, G., and Kerre, E.E.: 'On the relationship between some extensions of fuzzy set theory', *Fuzzy Sets and Systems*, 2003, 133, (2), pp. 227–235.
23. Khuman, A.S., Yang, Y., and John, R.: 'A commentary on some of the intrinsic differences between grey systems and fuzzy systems', in (Eds.): *A Commentary on Some of the Intrinsic Differences between Grey Systems and Fuzzy Systems* (2014, edn.), pp. 2032–2037.
24. Hsu, C.I., and Wen, Y.H.: 'Application of Grey theory and multiobjective programming towards airline network design', *European Journal of Operational Research*, 2000, 127, (1), pp. 44–68.
25. Baskaran, V., Nachiappan, S., and Rahman, S.: 'Indian textile suppliers' sustainability evaluation using the grey approach', *International Journal of Production Economics*, 2012, 135, (2), pp. 647–658.

6

Categorical and Mathematical Comparisons of Assembly and Disassembly Lines

Seamus M. McGovern and Surendra M. Gupta

CONTENTS

6.1 Overview

Just as the assembly line is considered the most efficient way to manufacture large numbers of products, the disassembly line has been successfully used in the reverse manufacturing of products at their end of life. A significant amount of research has addressed the challenges associated with sequencing assembly on a paced line to minimize the number of workstations needed and in some studies, to ensure that idle times at each workstation are similar. As reverse supply chains grow in importance, research into the contemporary area of sequencing and balancing disassembly on a paced line has begun to increase.

Assembly and disassembly have many obvious similarities. Alternatively, while sequencing on a paced disassembly line has often been seen as simply the reverse of assembly sequencing, current research has revealed a wide range of, sometimes subtle, differences. Disassembly possesses considerations that add to its line's complexity when compared with an assembly line, including the need to consider treatment of hazardous parts as well as a used-part demand that typically varies between components in a product. As research into disassembly has grown, there can be value in considering what is similar between the two—ideally in a way that allows flexibility in also addressing what is unique about each—and in identifying the unique differences.

In this chapter, the assembly line and the disassembly line are introduced and then compared qualitatively and quantitatively for both similarities and differences. Quantitative similarities include the presentation of a single set of unified metrics for mathematically evaluating assembly and disassembly sequences for application to a paced line. The unified metrics include two line-balance metrics (Line Balance [Strict] B and Line Balance [Conventional] I), three general-purpose metrics that allow the development of additional evaluation criteria (General Binary Identifying H, General Ordinal Ranking D, and General Adjacency Grouping R), and a generalized metric (Efficacy Index EI) for use with any of the other measures in providing a statistical comparison of any achieved line performance with either theoretical or actual best- and worst-case results. Quantitative differences include a complexity theory analysis addressing the maximum search-space-size formulations for assembly and then for disassembly. In addition, in using a range of the previously introduced unified metrics, differing assembly and disassembly solution priorities are demonstrated, and then, a five-part case study of a notional product is analyzed to illustrate the application of the metrics as well as to provide an example of measurable differences between assembly sequencing and disassembly sequencing even when applied to the same product.

6.2 Literature Review

Gutjahr and Nemhauser [1] first described a solution to the assembly-line-balancing problem with an algorithm developed to minimize the delay times at each workstation. Elsayed and Boucher [2] include an overview of assembly-line balancing in their text. Scholl [3] visits the balancing and sequencing of assembly lines. Ponnambalam et al. [4] compare line-balancing heuristics with a quantitative evaluation of six assembly-line-balancing techniques. Boysen et al. [5] provide guidance on which assembly-line-balancing model to use for different situations.

Remanufacturing models are reviewed by Ilgin and Gupta [6]. Johnson and Wang [7] use a disassembly tree in designing products to enhance material-recovery opportunities. Vujosevic et al. [8] study the design of products that can be easily disassembled for maintenance. Brennan et al. [9] and Gupta and Taleb [10] investigate the problems associated with disassembly planning and scheduling. Disassembly-line heuristics and metaheuristics are detailed by McGovern and Gupta [11], while a range of researchers [12–16] continue to extend the state of the art in disassembly-specific search algorithms.

The literature also includes several thorough surveys of existing research [17–22] as well as comprehensive reviews of green supply chains [23] and reverse supply chains [24, 25].

6.3 Assembly-Line and Disassembly-Line Backgrounds and Qualitative Similarities

Assembly lines and disassembly lines have similar sequential processes and a similar end-state intent—the only difference being that one ends with the final product, while the other starts with that end product—which makes it easy to see that one can often be seen as just a reverse of the other. A detailed overview of assembly lines and of disassembly lines is summarized by McGovern and Gupta [11].

6.3.1 Assembly Lines

The assembly line is often considered to be the most efficient way to produce many identical or near-identical products. One definition of an assembly line is that it is a manufacturing process where parts are sequentially added together by workers (including robots) until a final product is attained at the end of the line. The most familiar of these processes is a flow shop, where the product being assembled moves at a constant rate on a paced line, possibly on a conveyor belt. While often attributed to the Ford Motor Company's assembly-line efforts from 1908 to 1915, the history of sequential mass production can be traced much further back.

The first evidence of an assembly line is attributed to the commissioning by Chinese Emperor Qin Shi Huangdi of the Terracotta Army in approximately 215 BCE. The 8000 life-sized figures each had separate body parts, which were manufactured at different locations/facilities (and individually labeled as such), collected, and then assembled into the final product.

In the 1500s, the Venetian Arsenal (an Italian shipyard, key to Venice's expansion at the time) employed almost 20,000 workers and reportedly delivered a ship each day. This was accomplished through the use of standardized parts and an assembly-line type of manufacturing process.

Prior to the early 1800s, pulley-block (four-part sail-rigging pulley mechanisms for wooden ships) production had been performed by a variety of contractors. This was expensive, made intensive use of manual labor, and provided inconsistent quality. Portsmouth Block Mills then began producing pulley blocks for the British Royal Navy using what is considered to be one of the first linear, continuous assembly lines. These—now standardized—pulleys were mass produced using all-metal machine tools.

While not creating any of these assembly-line concepts, Eli Whitney is credited with introducing interchangeable parts and machine (as opposed to hand) tools and jigs (i.e., fixtures for holding parts in position during assembly), moving the skills from the worker to the machine, and making use of unskilled or semiskilled workers. This all took place in his manufacturing of firearms in the early 1800s.

The Chicago meatpacking industry of the 1860s is often considered the first assembly line in the United States (and, obviously, the first disassembly line). In these facilities, workers would be assigned to fixed workstations, and the product would come to them. The line was an overhead trolley system that followed a given path at a relatively constant rate. Each worker on the line performed one task and repeated that task for each product that passed their workstation on the line.

The Industrial Revolution (1860s to 1890s) saw extensive improvements in mass-production technologies and concepts throughout Western Europe and the United States (primarily New England). In 1901, the assembly-line concept was patented in the United States by Ransom Olds and used to mass produce automobiles at his Olds Motor Vehicle Company. Inspired by the idea of one person performing one job over and over again in the Chicago slaughterhouses, the assembly line was applied and refined by the Ford Motor Company, moving from a concept in 1908 to a finalized system by 1915 that increased production of a vehicle from taking almost 13 hours to just over 1.5 hours, used fewer workers, and increased worker safety (since assignment at one workstation prevented them from roaming about the facility). From this time, assembly-line use expanded rapidly; companies that did not adopt them could be expected to disappear.

Dating back to the mid-1950s and early 1960s, assembly-line-balancing research has enjoyed a great deal of significant study. While commonly treated as being from the field of manufacturing and production (more precisely, the field of scheduling), assembly lines are also regularly studied in the field of facility layout (e.g., Finch [26] considers four types of facility layouts: process-oriented layouts, product-oriented layouts, cellular layouts, and service layouts).

Process-oriented layouts are characterized by functional departments and have the primary objective of locating the departments that have the greatest interaction physically near to each other.

Product-oriented layouts consist of production or assembly lines, where products flow through a large number of workstations, each adding components and labor, until a final product is achieved. While providing low costs at high volumes per unit, they typically have minimal flexibility.

Cellular layouts offer a compromise between the two, requiring that a family of products be produced in a cell containing all of the resources necessary to produce all of the products in the family.

Finally, service layouts may be similar in design to either a product-oriented layout (but having a service, rather than a product, flowing through the system) or a process-oriented layout. An example of a service layout would be the floor plan and product placement (e.g., placing high-frequency purchase items at the rear, requiring customer traffic through low-frequency areas) in a retail store.

Other authors consider additional configurations, such as fixed-position layouts and layouts based on group technology [27].

Assembly-line balancing is also considered a component of contemporary lean manufacturing. A concise definition and example tailored toward end users and line managers can be gleaned from Tapping [28]. Here, line balancing is described as a six-step process with goals of evenly loading all workers, defining the order in which work elements should be performed, and defining the number of line workers required. It is implied that the last step (i.e., evenly distributing work elements) in the process is performed either exhaustively or by trial and error. Either way, it is also implied that this step can be readily accomplished using either of these methods. In fact, for all but the simplest cases, this seemingly innocuous sequencing portion of the process is exceptionally difficult, necessitating many of the heuristics and metaheuristics that have been proposed for and used in assembly-line balancing.

The recent flexibility of plants and of plant layouts has moved assembly-line balancing more toward the dynamic-scheduling problem area. While various scheduling algorithms exist that address the challenge of sequencing, in general, these attempt to minimize the number of workstations while often not addressing the balance of the workload between workstations.

6.3.2 Disassembly Lines

The disassembly line has existed for over a century, attributed to the Chicago slaughterhouses of the nineteenth century. The practices at these slaughterhouses are recognized as being the first production lines, and they certainly provided the impetus that led to the first true assembly lines, attributed to the Ford Motor Company in the early 1900s. Assembly lines improved dramatically over the next 100 years, yielding improvements in speed, precision, flexibility, and product cost. Manufacturing improvements resulting from assembly lines motivated the creation or evolution of the fields of industrial engineering, human factors, operations research, and later, computer-processor task scheduling. Assembly-line-specific research flourished as well, with many significant and fundamental technical problems being addressed in the literature of the 1960s. The success of assembly lines would ultimately lead to a need to remove the multitude of low-cost products (no longer justifiable to repair when new replacements could be acquired at a lower cost) with the environmental movement of the 1960s and 1970s (and often dated to the 1962 publication of the Rachael Carson book *Silent Spring*). This, and the revolutionary idea that assembly problems could be most efficiently studied by considering them as reverse disassembly problems, led to the study of disassembly in the 1980s by Bourjault [29]. The subsequent stream of disassembly research has steadily increased with continued motivation from government regulation, corporate profit, and consumer desires. By the 2000s, the disassembly line had received its first disassembly-unique description as having features that separate it from treatment as an assembly line [30], and balancing the disassembly line was then mathematically modeled [31] and formally defined [32].

The success of assembly lines—inspired by the first disassembly line—has led full circle to the need for disassembly lines and associated disassembly-line-specific research (see Lambert and Gupta [21] for additional historical perspectives), and the historical linkage and commonalities of assembly and disassembly lines can be seen to be significant. Ironically, disassembly lines—which are only becoming a topic of rigorous research and analysis at the beginning of the twenty-first century—led to the creation of assembly lines at the beginning of the twentieth century: The disassembly lines of the Chicago slaughterhouses inspired Henry Ford to legitimize the assembly line, spurring manufacturing and the Industrial Revolution.

6.4 Assembly-Line and Disassembly-Line Qualitative Differences

Qualitative differences between assembly lines and disassembly lines are primarily seen in the uncertainty of the end-product components and issues associated with this. Güngör and Gupta [30] were the first to formally define the disassembly line. The following is a summary of some of the various considerations in a disassembly-line setting due to the observation of a disassembly line as being fraught with a variety of disassembly-unique complications that serve to qualitatively distinguish it from assembly [11, 30].

6.4.1 Product Considerations

The number of different products disassembled on the same line is an important characteristic of a disassembly line. The line may deal with only one type of product, whose original configuration is the same for every product received. The line may also be used to disassemble products belonging to the same family; that is, whose original configurations are only slightly different from each other. The line may receive several types of products, partially disassembled products, and subassemblies whose configurations are significantly or completely different from one another.

Changing the characteristics of the products complicates the disassembly operations on the line. Intuitively, balancing a disassembly line that is used for the disassembly of several types of products can become very complex; such a line may be balanced for a group of products, yet its status may become unbalanced when a new type of product is received.

6.4.2 Line Considerations

Various disassembly-line configurations may be possible. Some layouts are inspired by assembly-line layouts. For example, layouts such as serial, parallel, circular, U-shaped, cellular, and two-sided lines [26] also find their way onto disassembly lines. Even so, new layout configurations may still be required to enable more efficient disassembly lines.

One of the most important considerations of a disassembly line is the line speed. Disassembly lines can be either paced or unpaced. Paced lines may be used to regulate the flow of parts on disassembly lines. However, if there is too much variability in the task times (which depends on the conditions of the products being disassembled and the variety of the products processed on the line), it might be preferable to have an unpaced line. In such lines, each station works at its own pace and advances the product to the next workstation after it completes the assigned tasks. The advantages of paced lines over unpaced lines include less work in process (WIP), less space requirements, more predictable and higher throughput, and—if properly handled—a lower chance of bottlenecks. To take advantage of the positive aspects of a paced line, its speed can be dynamically modified throughout the entire disassembly process to minimize the negative effects of variability (including variability in demand).

6.4.3 Part Considerations

6.4.3.1 Quality of Incoming Products

When a disassembly system receives the returned products, their condition is usually unknown. Sometimes they are in good condition and relatively new, while at other times they are obsolete, nonfunctioning items. Therefore, there is a high level of uncertainty in the quality of the products and their constituent parts. There is a trade-off between the level of uncertainty and the efficiency of the disassembly line. When the level of uncertainty increases, the disassembly efficiency worsens, especially if the disassembly line has not been designed to cope with the uncertainty in product/part quality.

A part is considered to be defective if the part has a different structure and/or different operational specifications from its original structure and/or specifications. A part can become defective in various ways, such as suffering physical damage or being exposed to extreme operating environments. There are primarily two types of defects:

- Physical defect: the geometric specifications (i.e., dimensions and shape) of the part are different from its original design.
- Functional defect: the part does not function as it was originally designed to.

There are three considerations with these two types of defects:

- Removable defective parts (Type A defect): some of the physically defective parts in the product can be disassembled even though they have sustained some level of damage. This type of physical defect is referred to as a *Type A defect*. When a part is physically defective and yet removable, it might take longer to remove that part. However, it does not affect the removal of other parts, since the precedence relationship is not affected by the longer disassembly time.

- Non-removable defective parts (Type B defect): sometimes a physically defective part in a product cannot be disassembled because it is either badly damaged (and thus gets stuck in position) or its connection is of the type that must be physically broken. This is a Type B defect, and it has a tremendous impact on the efficiency of the disassembly line. For example, even if the non-removable part does not have a demand, it may still precede other demanded parts. Also, a part with a Type B defect may result in what is known as the *disappearing workpieces* phenomenon.

- Parts with functional defects: assume that part k does not have a physical defect (Type A or B) but rather, sustains a functional defect. If this fact is known in advance, then the disassembler may or may not have an incentive to remove the part (unless, of course, it precedes other demanded parts). Therefore, in addition to concerns related to physical defects, the possibility of functional defects in parts on incoming products should also be incorporated into operating and balancing a disassembly line.

6.4.3.2 Quantity of Parts in Incoming Products

Another complication is related to the quantity of parts in the incoming products. Due to upgrading, downgrading, or cannibalization of the product during its useful life, the number of parts in the product may not match its original configuration. The actual number of parts may be higher or lower than expected when the product is received. The following should be considered:

- The demanded part of the product may be absent, or its quantity may be less than expected. This may require a provision in the calculation to ensure that the demand for the missing part is met. Another approach would be to carry out a preliminary evaluation of the product to make sure that all the parts of interest exist in the product before it is pushed down the disassembly line. This evaluation may be used to determine the route of the product on the disassembly line.

- The number of demanded parts may be higher than expected.

6.4.4 Operational Considerations

6.4.4.1 Variability of Disassembly Task Times

Similarly to the assembly-line case, the disassembly task times may vary depending on several factors that are related to the condition of the product and the state of the disassembly workstation (or worker). Task times may be considered as deterministic, stochastic, or dynamic (dynamic task times are possible due to learning effects, which allow a systematic reduction in disassembly times).

6.4.4.2 Early Leaving Workpieces

If one or more, but not all, tasks of a workpiece that has been assigned to the current workstation cannot be completed due to some defect, the workpiece could leave the workstation early. This phenomenon is termed the *early leaving workpiece*.

Due to an early leaving workpiece, the workstation experiences an unscheduled idle time. Note that the cost of unscheduled idle time is high, because even though the demand for parts associated with failed tasks is unfulfilled, the disassembly cost of failed tasks has been incurred.

6.4.4.3 Self-skipping Workpieces

If none of the tasks of a workpiece that have been assigned to the current workstation are performed due to some defect and/or precedence relationships, the workpiece leaves the workstation early without being worked on. This is known as a *self-skipping workpiece*.

6.4.4.4 Skipping Workpieces

At workstation j, if one or more defective tasks of a workpiece directly or indirectly precede all the tasks of workstation $j + 1$ (i.e., the workstation immediately succeeding workstation j), the workpiece skips workstation $j + 1$ and moves on to workstation $j + 2$. This is known as a *skipping workpiece*.

A workpiece can skip one workstation, two workstations, and so on. In addition to unscheduled idle time, both the self-skipping workpiece and the skipping workpiece contribute added complexities in material handling (e.g., how to transfer the out-of-turn workpiece to the downstream workstation) and the status of the downstream workstation (e.g., it may be busy working on other workpieces and therefore, may require some sort of buffer-allocation procedure to hold the skipped workpiece until the machine becomes available).

6.4.4.5 Disappearing Workpieces

If a defective task disables the completion of all the remaining tasks on a workpiece, the workpiece may simply be taken off the disassembly line before it reaches any downstream workstation. In other words, the workpiece effectively disappears, which is referred to as a *disappearing workpiece*.

A disappearing workpiece may result in starvation of subsequent workstations, leading to a higher overall idle time, highly undesirable in a disassembly line. It is, in a way, a special case of a skipping workpiece where the workpiece skips all succeeding workstations. The consequences of the disappearing workpiece are similar to those of the skipping workpiece, but to a greater extent.

6.4.4.6 Revisiting Workpieces

A workpiece currently at workstation j may revisit a preceding workstation $j - p$ (where $j - p \geq 1$ and $p \geq 1$ and integer) to perform task x if the completion of current task y enables work on task x, which was originally assigned to workstation $j - p$ and was disabled due to the failure of another preceding task. These are termed *revisiting workpieces*.

A revisiting workpiece results in the overloading one of the previous workstations. As a consequence, it may lead to complications in the material-handling system because of reverse flow, decoupling from the revisited workstation, or the introduction of a buffer to hold the revisiting workpiece until the workstation becomes available. This would obviously have a financial impact as well. Complicated revisiting workpieces that could make the material handling and flow control more difficult may simply exit the line.

6.4.4.7 Exploding Workpieces

A workpiece may split into two or more workpieces (subassemblies) as it moves on the disassembly line. Each of these subassemblies acts as an individual workpiece on the disassembly line. This phenomenon is known as *exploding workpieces*.

An exploding workpiece complicates the flow mechanism of the disassembly line; however, it can be planned for in advance, since it is known which part will result in the exploding workpiece when removed. In a disassembly line, a complication occurs when the part that would normally result in an exploding workpiece cannot be removed due to some defect.

6.4.5 Demand Considerations

Demand is one of the most crucial issues in disassembly-line design and optimization, since it is desirable to maximize the use of the disassembly line while meeting the demand for parts in associated planning periods. In disassembly, the following demand scenarios are possible: demand for one part only, demand for multiple parts, and demand for all parts.

Parts with physical or functional defects may influence the performance of the disassembly line. If part x is not demanded, and it directly or indirectly precedes a demanded part y, then part x must be disassembled before the removal of part y. (Note that when part a precedes part b, which precedes part c, then part a is said to be a direct precedent of part b and an indirect precedent of part c.) The removal of part x may require additional time due to the presence of a defect. This may cause the processing time to exceed the cycle time, which could result in the starvation of subsequent workstations and blockage at these previous workstations. Placing buffers at the workstations may be necessary to avoid starvation, blockage, and incomplete disassembly.

If part x has a demand, then the various types of demand affect the number of products to be disassembled and eventually, the disassembly line's balance. There are three types of demand.

In the first type, the demand source may accept part x as is. This is possible, for example, when part x is demanded for its material content (in which case, the defect in a part may not be important).

In the second type of demand, the demand source may not accept parts with any type of defect. This occurs when a part is used as is (e.g., in remanufacturing or in the repair of other products). Thus, if a demanded part has a defect, its disassembly does not satisfy the requirement. Since an objective of a disassembly line may be to meet the demand, the objective function and demand constraints must cope with this type of complication. If the part has this second type of demand, and it does not directly or indirectly precede another demanded part, the disassembly of the part is redundant. This can have an effect on the efficiency of the disassembly line, since the workstation responsible for removing the defective part will remain idle for an extended time.

In the third type of demand, the demand source may accept certain defective parts depending on the seriousness of the defect. This type of demand may be received from a refurbishing environment, where the parts undergo several correction processes (e.g., cleaning and repair) before reuse. This type of demand introduces a further complication: the requirement for some sort of tracing mechanism to identify the type of defect and the associated demand constraint(s).

6.4.6 Assignment Considerations

In addition to precedence relationships, several other restrictions limit the assignment of tasks to workstations. While similar restrictions are also present in assembly lines, the following are some restrictions related specifically to disassembly.

Certain tasks must be grouped and assigned to a specific workstation (e.g., if the removed parts are to be sorted and packaged together for shipment to the demand source). Thus, assigning the disassembly of these components (parts or joining elements) to the same workstation minimizes the distance that the components travel in the disassembly system. Moreover, the tasks requiring similar operating conditions (e.g., temperature and lighting) can be restricted to certain workstations as well.

The availability of special machining and tooling at certain workstations or at a limited number of workstations may necessitate the assignment of certain tasks to these workstations.

Tasks may be assigned to workstations so that the amount of repositioning of the workpieces on the disassembly line (e.g., the product orientation changes) is minimized. Similarly, tasks may need to be assigned to minimize the number of tool changes in the disassembly process.

6.4.7 Other Disassembly Considerations

There are additional uncertainty factors associated with the reliability of the workstations themselves. Some parts may cause pollution or nuisance due to the nature of their contents (e.g., oil and fuel), which may increase the chance of breakdowns or workstation downtime. Furthermore, hazardous parts may require special handling, which can also influence the use of the workstations. In addition, assembly may have differing priorities and differing objectives (e.g., minimizing the objective function versus maximizing it) from disassembly. Other items that further distinguish disassembly from assembly include: there is a differing number of priorities to consider; part-removal times in disassembly are potentially different from part-installation times in assembly; there is less certainty (i.e., more variability) in the disassembly times (i.e., the removal of identical parts on end-of-life products could be expected to be less predictable and less consistent due to age-related corrosion, wear, damage, etc.); disassembly uniquely may need to be destructive (e.g., breaking connections and bonds); disassembly may require multiple tools or tool sequences if parts are not able to be removed as they were installed when new; and disassembly may be incomplete if only certain items are needed from the product or if the product is only to be broken down to sub-components having similar material make-up, resulting in an increase in the number of possible solution sequences beyond that of assembly [33].

6.5 Assembly-Line and Disassembly-Line Quantitative Similarities

Although not precisely the same as for disassembly lines, the quantitative study of assembly lines provides a sound basis for the description and mathematical study of the disassembly line, and vice versa. While some solution-generating algorithms that are made available to the practitioner are too simplistic for all but the smallest of lines, much of the breadth and depth of the half century of work in sequencing assembly lines can be leveraged in the study and analysis of disassembly lines. In many cases, assembly-line mathematics, algorithms, and techniques can be directly applied or applied with slight modification to disassembly lines; McGovern and Gupta [33] first unified the mathematical formulae that are, or can be, common to both assembly lines and disassembly lines, as seen here.

6.5.1 Line-Model Introduction

Measuring differing solutions to line-sequencing problems necessitates describing wide-ranging multi-criteria objectives. While not every criterion is of interest for every problem—and considering that assembly-line problems may have objectives that are not relevant to disassembly-line problems or, if relevant, may have different priorities—unifying assembly- and disassembly-line modeling formulae suggests the use of general equations to allow flexibility.

With the establishment of common line-balance formulae that seek to minimize the number of workstations and the idle time (and potentially, to equalize idle time between stations), three additional structures can be used to form basic prototypes of any additional line-processing evaluation criteria.

These three different models therefore become the basis for developing differing or additional metrics in the future.

The first, a general prototype for any binary criteria, is used to rank the installation or removal of a part in an assembly or disassembly sequence based on its falling into one of only two categories. For example, a part could be listed according to the categories "hazardous" or "not hazardous," or "valuable" and "not valuable."

The second general formulation can be used as the prototype for any known-value criteria, where the part's position in the assembly/disassembly sequence would vary depending on some part-unique numerical assignment. For example, a version of this type of metric could be used to assign a part's actual dollar value (note that this example is primarily a disassembly application).

The final general metric can be used as the prototype for any adjacency or grouping criteria. For example, a part could be categorized as "glass," "metal," or "plastic" if it were desirable to install or remove parts together in this form of grouping; by tool-type required for assembly or disassembly to minimize the number of tools or the number of tool changes on a line; or by product orientation to minimize the number of times a product is re-oriented on a line in the interest of time or practicality (e.g., for large or heavy objects such as automobiles or aircraft).

Each of these metrics can provide a further statistical performance evaluation of any chosen sequence by use of the Efficacy Index metric.

In any assembly or disassembly sequence, a major constraint is the requirement to provide a feasible (i.e., precedence-preserving) sequence for the product. The result is modeled as an integer, deterministic, n-dimensional, multiple-criteria decision-making problem with an exponentially growing search space. Solutions consist of an ordered sequence (i.e., n-tuple, where n represents the number of parts—including virtual parts; i.e., tasks—for installation or removal) of elements. For example, if an assembly solution consisted of the eight-tuple ⟨5, 2, 8, 1, 4, 7, 6, 3⟩, then component 5 would be installed first, followed by component 2, then component 8, and so on. Testing a found solution against the precedence constraints fulfills the major constraint of precedence preservation.

Also, while different researchers use a variety of definitions for the term "balanced" in reference to assembly [2] and disassembly lines, the following definition [34, 35] is adopted here for Line Balance (Strict) that considers the total number of workstations *NWS* and the station times ST_j (i.e., the total processing-time requirement in workstation *j*) on a paced line:

Definition: A paced line is optimally balanced when the fewest possible number of workstations is needed, and the variation in idle times between all workstations is minimized, while observing all constraints. This is mathematically described by

$$\text{Minimize } NWS$$

then

$$\text{Minimize} \left[\max(ST_x) - \min(ST_y) \right] \forall x, y \in \{1, 2, \ldots, NWS\}$$

where the first item is used alone in defining the Line Balance (Conventional) metric.

6.5.2 Formulae

Along with the metrics themselves, various upper and lower bounds are considered here as well. For example, while the total number of workstations *NWS* (a count that is obtained by observation once a proposed part sequence is generated) is not considered as a metric, as it is encompassed in the metric that minimizes the total idle time (i.e., Line Balance [Conventional]), it is used here to provide an example of how upper and lower bounds are proved.

Theorem: Let PT_k be the part-installation/removal time for the *k*th of *n* parts, where *CT* is the maximum amount of time available to complete all tasks assigned to each workstation. Then, for the most efficient distribution of tasks, the optimal minimum number of workstations NWS^* satisfies

$$NWS^* \geq \left\lceil \frac{\sum_{k=1}^{n} PT_k}{CT} \right\rceil = NWS_{lower} \tag{6.1}$$

where NWS_{lower} indicates the theoretical lower bound on the number of workstations.

Proof: If the above inequality is not satisfied, then there must be at least one workstation completing tasks requiring more than CT of time, which is a contradiction.   □

Additional bounds are seen to be true in a similar fashion and are presented without proof. The theoretical upper bound for the number of workstations NWS_{upper} is given by

$$NWS_{upper} = n \tag{6.2}$$

The first metric demonstrated, the balancing metric Line Balance (Strict), seeks to simultaneously recognize a minimum number of workstations while measuring whether or not idle times at each workstation are similar [34, 35]. A resulting minimal numerical value is indicative of a more desirable solution, providing both a minimum number of workstations and similar idle times across all workstations.

6.5.2.1 Line Balance (Strict) Metric, B

The Line Balance (Strict) metric is a variation on the line-balancing metric F [11] from disassembly-line balancing. The Smoothness Index (Section 6.5.2.4) rewards similar idle times at each workstation but at the expense of allowing for a large (i.e., sub-optimal) number of workstations. This is because the Smoothness Index compares workstation elapsed times with the largest ST_j instead of with CT. (This Smoothness Index is very similar in format to the sample standard deviation from the field of statistics, but using $MAX\{ST_j\} \mid j \in \{1, 2, ..., NWS\}$ rather than the mean of the station times.) Line Efficiency (Section 6.5.2.3) rewards the minimum number of workstations but allows unlimited variance in idle times between workstations, because no comparison is made between ST_js. The original measure of balance F seeks to combine the two and simultaneously minimize the number of workstations while ensuring that idle times at each workstation are similar, though at the expense of the generation of a nonlinear objective function. The method is computed based on the minimum number of workstations required as well as the sum of the square of the idle times for each of the workstations. This penalizes solutions in which even though the number of workstations may be minimized, one or more have an excessive amount of idle time when compared with the other workstations. It also provides for leveling the workload between different workstations on the disassembly line. Similarly to the calculation of variance in the field of statistics, the disassembly-line balancing metric F [35] is given by

$$F = \sum_{j=1}^{NWS} (CT - ST_j)^2 \tag{6.3}$$

where each station time ST_j is given by

$$ST_j = \sum_{k=1}^{n} PT_k \cdot X_{k,j} \text{ where } 1 \le j \le NWS \tag{6.4}$$

and

$$X_{k,j} = \begin{cases} 1 & \text{if part } k \text{ is assigned to workstation } j \\ 0 & \text{otherwise.} \end{cases} \tag{6.5}$$

Just as the variance provides insight into what is being calculated, while the standard deviation provides a numerical value that is more intuitive for interpretation, the square root of the disassembly-line balancing metric F provides a more easily interpreted value [11]. For example, an instance having two solutions consisting of an equal number of workstations, such as $NWS = 3$, and hence, equal total idle times (e.g., 6 time units), but differing idle times at each workstation—for example (1, 1, 4) and (2, 2, 2)—resulting in differing balance (the latter's idle times are more evenly distributed and therefore, better balanced; in fact, optimally in this example) would have balance values of 18 and 12, respectively, while the normalized values would stand at 4.24 and 3.46, still indicating better balance with the latter solution but also giving a sense of the relative improvement that this solution provides in terms of time units (versus time units squared), which the metric generated by Equation 6.3 lacks. The square root of F becomes the Line Balance (Strict) metric B, given by

$$B = \sqrt{\sum_{j=1}^{NWS} (CT - ST_j)^2} \tag{6.6}$$

with the objective being its minimization. The lower bound on B is given by B_{lower} (i.e., simply the square of the total idle time at the theoretical lower number of workstations divided by the number of workstations; this squared idle time at each workstation is then multiplied by the total number of workstations) and is related to the optimal balance B^* by

$$B^* \ge B_{lower} = \sqrt{\left(\frac{(NWS_{lower} \cdot CT) - \sum_{k=1}^{n} PT_k}{NWS_{lower}}\right)^2 \cdot NWS_{lower}}$$

which reduces to

$$B^* \ge B_{lower} = \sqrt{\frac{\left(NWS_{lower} \cdot CT - \sum_{k=1}^{n} PT_k\right)^2}{NWS_{lower}}}. \tag{6.7}$$

The upper bound is described by the worst-case balance B_{upper} as

$$B_{upper} = \sqrt{\sum_{k=1}^{n}(CT - PT_k)^2}$$ (6.8)

which represents having only one part in each workstation.

6.5.2.2 Line Balance (Conventional) Metric, I

Minimizing the number of workstations, rather than equalizing idle times, is often referred to in the assembly-line and disassembly-line literature as *balancing*. To distinguish between the two, separate metrics are referred to here as Line Balancing (Strict), where workstations are minimized and idle times are equalized, and Line Balancing (Conventional), where workstations (and hence, total idle time) are minimized. Minimizing the sum of the workstation idle times, which will also minimize the total number of workstations, is described by [11]

$$I = (NWS \cdot CT) - \sum_{k=1}^{n} PT_k$$ (6.9)

or

$$I = \sum_{j=1}^{NWS}(CT - ST_j)$$ (6.10)

with the objective being the minimization of *I*.

6.5.2.3 Line Efficiency Metric, LE

The assembly-line literature [2] provides the measure Line Efficiency as

$$LE = \frac{\sum_{j=1}^{NWS} ST_j}{NWS \cdot CT}$$ (6.11)

This metric can equally be applied to disassembly-line problems.

6.5.2.4 Smoothness Index Metric, SI

The Smoothness Index [2] is given as

$$SI = \sqrt{\sum_{j=1}^{NWS}[MAX\{ST\} - ST_j]^2}.$$ (6.12)

An assembly-line metric, this too can readily be applied to disassembly-line problems.

6.5.2.5 Utilization Metric, U

While Utilization [26] is often used as a metric, it should be noted that it will always give the same result as Line Efficiency. However, in the interest of completeness, Utilization is included here and is given as

$$U = \frac{\sum_{k=1}^{n} PT_k}{NWS \cdot CT} \tag{6.13}$$

6.5.2.6 General Binary Identifying Metric, H

A General Binary Identifying metric H has been developed as a metric prototype from the disassembly line's original hazard metric. This metric prototype is based on binary variables that indicate whether a part is categorized as being of interest or not—for example, a part could be listed according to the two categories "valuable" and "not valuable"—and then assigned a value of 1 if it is in one of the categories and 0 if it is not. In its original use for identifying hazardous parts (which needed to be removed early in a part-removal sequence to avoid damaging any remaining parts), parts containing hazardous materials are identified as being in the category of interest and therefore, have a binary variable equal to 1.

A given solution-sequence's H metric is defined as the sum of binary flags multiplied by their position in the solution sequence (rewarding, in the original application, the removal of hazardous parts early in the part-removal sequence by minimizing H).

The General Binary Identifying metric is determined using

$$H = \sum_{k=1}^{n} (k \times h_{PS_k}), \quad h_{PS_k} = \begin{cases} 1, & \text{within category} \\ 0, & \text{otherwise} \end{cases} \tag{6.14}$$

where PS_k identifies the kth part in the solution sequence PS; i.e., for solution $\langle 3, 1, 2 \rangle$, $PS_2 = 1$. The lower bound on H is given by H_{lower} and is related to the optimal General Binary Identifying metric H^* by

$$H^* \geq H_{lower} = \sum_{p=1}^{|HP|} p, \quad |HP| = \sum_{k=1}^{n} h_k \tag{6.15}$$

where the set of parts in the category of interest $HP = \{k : h_k \neq 0 \ \forall \ k \in P\}$ and where P is the set of n part-installation/removal tasks. For example, a product with three hazardous parts would give an H_{lower} value of $1 + 2 + 3 = 6$. The upper bound on the General Binary Identifying metric is given by

$$H_{upper} = \sum_{p=n-|HP|+1}^{n} p \qquad (6.16)$$

For example, three hazardous parts in a product consisting of 20 parts would give an H_{upper} value of $18 + 19 + 20 = 57$.

6.5.2.7 General Ordinal Ranking Metric, D

A General Ordinal Ranking metric D has been developed as a metric prototype from the disassembly line's original demanded-part metric. This metric is based on positive integer values d that indicate, for example, the quantity required of a part after it is removed—or zero if it is not desired—and its position in the sequence. Any given solution-sequence's D metric is defined as the sum of each d value multiplied by its position in the sequence, rewarding, in the case of the original disassembly example, the removal of high-demand parts early in the part-removal sequence.

The General Ordinal Ranking metric is calculated using

$$D = \sum_{k=1}^{n} (k \cdot d_{PS_k}), \quad d_{PS_k} \in N, \forall PS_k \qquad (6.17)$$

where **N** represents the set of natural numbers, that is $\{0, 1, 2, ...\}$ (note that if d is used to represent, for example, a part's inventory cost in the case of assembly, the d value can later be divided by 100 to comply with the natural-number structure as well as with the ordinal description and intent, while also being able to represent a monetary value; e.g., $d_1 = 1237$ could indicate that part-number-one's inventory cost is \$12.37). The lower bound on the metric $(D_{lower} \leq D^*)$ is given by Equation 6.17, where

$$d_{PS_1} \geq d_{PS_2} \geq ... \geq d_{PS_n} \qquad (6.18)$$

For example, a three-part product with the three parts having d values of 4, 5, and 6 would give a best-case D metric of $(1 \cdot 6) + (2 \cdot 5) + (3 \cdot 4) = 28$. The upper bound on the General Ordinal Ranking metric (D_{upper}) is given by Equation 6.17, where

$$d_{PS_1} \leq d_{PS_2} \leq ... \leq d_{PS_n} \qquad (6.19)$$

For example, the three-part product with parts having d values of 4, 5, and 6 would give a worst-case D metric of $(1 \cdot 4) + (2 \cdot 5) + (3 \cdot 6) = 32$.

6.5.2.8 General Adjacency Grouping Metric, R

Finally, a General Adjacency Grouping metric R has been developed. Originally formulated for disassembly, where a lower calculated value would indicate minimal direction changes in the product's (or subassembly's) orientation during disassembly and therefore, a more desirable solution, the metric can be used as a prototype for assembly and disassembly where it is of interest to keep similar items together in the sequence. This is a prototype for any adjacency or grouping criteria; for example, a part could be categorized as "glass," "metal," or "plastic" if it were desirable to remove parts together in this form of grouping. These groupings have a hazardous material application as well. That is, it may be desired that certain hazardous materials all be removed at the same or at nearby workstations. Alternatively, certain materials or processes might be incompatible with each other and could be hazardous, damaging, or dangerous if combined or adjacent. Using the example of the metric representing the count of the direction changes, integer values of r could represent each possible direction (e.g., $r \in \{+x, -x, +y, -y, +z, -z\}$—in this case $|r| = 6$—these directions are easily expanded to other or different directions in a similar manner).

The General Adjacency Grouping metric is formulated as

$$R = \sum_{k=1}^{n-1} R_k, \quad R_k = \begin{cases} 1, & r_{PS_k} \neq r_{PS_{k+1}} \\ 0, & \text{otherwise} \end{cases} \tag{6.20}$$

The lower bound on the metric R is given by R_{lower} and is related to the optimal General Adjacency Grouping metric R^* by

$$R^* \geq R_{lower} = |r| - 1 \tag{6.21}$$

For example, for a given product containing six parts that are installed/removed in groupings (e.g., directions) $r_k = (-y, +x, -y, -y, +x, +x)$, the resulting best-case value would be $2 - 1 = 1$ (e.g., one possible R_{lower} solution containing the optimal single change of product direction would be $\langle -y, -y, -y, +x, +x, +x \rangle$). In the specific case where the number of unique groupings is one less than the total number of parts n, the upper bound on the direction metric would be given by

$$R_{upper} = |r| \quad \text{where } |r| = n - 1 \tag{6.22}$$

Otherwise, the metric varies depending on the number of parts having a given grouping category and the total number of grouping types. It is bounded by

$$|r| \leq R_{upper} \leq n-1 \quad \text{where } |r| < n-1 \tag{6.23}$$

For example, six parts installed/removed in groups $r_k = (+x, +x, +x, -y, +x, +x)$ would give an R_{upper} value of 2 as given by the lower bound of Equation 6.20 with a solution sequence of $\langle +x, +x, -y, +x, +x, +x \rangle$. Six parts installed/removed in groups $r_k = (-y, +x, -y, -y, +x, +x)$ would give an R_{upper} value of $6 - 1 = 5$ as given by the upper bound of Equation 6.20 with a solution sequence of $\langle -y, +x, -y, +x, -y, +x \rangle$, for example.

In the special case where each part has a unique grouping, the metrics for R_{lower} and R_{upper} are equal and are given by

$$R_{lower} = R_{upper} = n - 1 \quad \text{where } |r| = n \tag{6.24}$$

6.5.2.9 Efficacy Index Metric, EI

The primary mathematical evaluation tool developed for comparative quantitative analysis of solution sequences is shown in Equation 6.25 [34]. From the area of statistical quality control, the Efficacy Index is the ratio of the difference between a calculated metric x and its worst-case value x_{worst} to the difference between the best-case metric value x_{best} and the worst-case metric value, which is then expressed as a percentage. This is described by

$$EI_x = \frac{100 \cdot |x_{worst} - x|}{|x_{worst} - x_{best}|} \quad \text{where } x_{best} \neq x_{worst} \tag{6.25}$$

(with the vertical lines in Equation 6.25 representing absolute value versus cardinality as seen elsewhere in this chapter; this use of absolute value provides a more general formulation that allows the use of MAX or MIN in representing best and worst case). This generates a value between zero and 100%, indicating the percentage of optimum for any given metric. The caveat that x_{best} not be equal to x_{worst} protects from a divide by zero; if x_{best} is equal to x_{worst}, the value $EI = 100\%$ should be used by default.

Finally, it should be noted that the values generated using Equation 6.25 can also be calculated using the actual best-case and worst-case values if they are known, instead of the theoretical bounds as given by Equations 6.1 through 6.24; this type of analysis is demonstrated in Section 6.2.5.

6.5.2.10 Additional Ancillary Formulae

Additional formulae [26] used in line balancing include the calculation of the cycle time CT as

$$CT = \frac{\text{production time available per day}}{\text{units of output required per day}} \tag{6.26}$$

with [11] the cycle time bounded by

$$\text{MAX}\{PT_k\} \le CT \le \sum_{k=1}^{n} PT_k \quad \forall k \in P \tag{6.27}$$

(this may further be constrained as $CT \in \mathbf{N}$). The production lead time LT is given [26] as

$$LT = CT \times NWS \tag{6.28}$$

6.5.2.11 Summarized Formulae

The unified line-sequencing metrics (summarized in Tables 6.1 and 6.2 [33]) are therefore given as B, I, LE, SI, U, H, D, and R as well as CT, LT, and NWS.

TABLE 6.1

Similar Assembly- and Disassembly-Sequencing Formulae

Title	Formula	Objective
Line Balance (Strict)	$B = \sqrt{\sum_{j=1}^{NWS} (CT - ST_j)^2}$	MIN
Line Balance (Conventional)	$I = \sum_{j=1}^{NWS} (CT - ST_j)$	MIN
Line Efficiency	$LE = \dfrac{\sum_{j=1}^{NWS} ST_j}{NWS \cdot CT}$	MAX
Smoothness Index	$SI = \sqrt{\sum_{j=1}^{NWS} [\text{MAX}\{ST\} - ST_j]^2}$	MIN
Utilization (note: $U = LE$)	$U = \dfrac{\sum_{k=1}^{n} PT_k}{NWS \cdot CT}$	MAX
General Binary Identifying	$H = \sum_{k=1}^{n} (k \cdot h_{PS_k})$	MIN or MAX
General Ordinal Ranking	$D = \sum_{k=1}^{n} (k \cdot d_{PS_k})$	MIN or MAX
General Adjacency Grouping	$R = \sum_{k=1}^{n-1} R_k$	MIN

TABLE 6.2

Ancillary Similar Assembly and Disassembly Formulae

Title	Formula
Cycle time	$CT = \dfrac{\text{production time available per day}}{\text{units of output required per day}}$
Production lead time	$LT = CT \times NWS$
Efficacy Index	$EI_x = \dfrac{100 \cdot \lvert x_{worst} - x \rvert}{\lvert x_{worst} - x_{best} \rvert}$

NWS is readily observed from a given sequence, while *B, I, LE, SI, U, H, D,* and *R* are calculated using a given assembly or disassembly sequence and their associated formulae.

6.6 Assembly-Line and Disassembly-Line Quantitative Differences

Assembly and disassembly lines also exhibit quantitative distinctions. These measurable differences are demonstrated in this section in two ways [33]. One of these ways is in the calculation of the computational complexity involved in finding ideal sequences, where disassembly lines can be seen to have more possible solutions than assembly lines. The second way is demonstrated through the use of the previously seen similar formulae applied to the assembly and disassembly of a case-study product resulting in differing sequences (i.e., the disassembly sequence not being the reverse of the assembly sequence), differently selected metrics, different metric priority ranking, and ultimately, different metric scores.

6.6.1 Complexity Theory Formulations

While adding restrictions makes a problem more complex in the general sense that an additional constraint is something else to consider, it does not necessarily make it more complex in the mathematical sense. For example, adding precedence constraints to the bin-packing problem not only makes it similar in structure to an assembly- or disassembly-sequencing problem; it also would seem to add complexity (i.e., there is something else to consider—enforcement of the precedence constraints—in any potential solution). However, adding precedence constraints cannot increase the (mathematical) complexity, because it does not increase the number of solutions to consider; in fact, it typically reduces them. There can be no more than $n!$ orderings (with this being the case if there are no precedence constraints), and adding any precedence constraints reduces this, the extreme being a solution that has precedence constraints entirely in series, giving only one possible solution (e.g., only one feasible solution, such as $\langle 1, 2, 3, 4, 5 \rangle$, where 2's predecessor is 1, 3's predecessor is 2, etc.), even though there are n parts having a maximum search space of $n!$ (here 5! or 120). However, assembly and disassembly sequencing are generally considered to be NP-complete problems [11].

Even though both are seen to be NP-complete, the upper bounds on the size of their number of possible solutions (and hence, their search space and ultimately, their time complexity) are different [33]. While the minimum number of solution sequences is one in each case, there can be as many as $n!$ possible solution sequences (again, this being the exceptional case of there being no precedence constraints) for assembly, and even more for disassembly, due to the possibility of partial disassembly. Complete disassembly considers as many as $n!$ possible solution sequences, while, for example, additionally considering disassembly consisting of only removing two (assumed to be always accessible) parts would add to the possible solutions to be considered and calculated as a permutation of subsets (of two in this example). The upper bound on the total number of possible sequences for disassembly is therefore the sum of permutations of all subsets, that is, $P_n^n + P_{n-1}^n + P_{n-2}^n + \ldots + P_1^n$. However, in manufacturing, it can be seen that sequences that remove all of the parts are indistinguishable from sequences that remove all but one of the parts; therefore, P_{n-1}^n (which is equal to $n!$) represents a duplicate sequence and can be ignored. The upper bound is then $P_n^n + P_{n-1}^n + P_{n-2}^n + \ldots + P_1^n - n!$ or $(n! + n! + P_{n-2}^n + \ldots + P_{n-(n-2)}^n + n) - n!$, which, when simplified and re-ordered, can be concisely written as $\sum_{k=1}^{n-1} P_k^n$ or slightly expanded to $n! + \sum_{k=1}^{n-2} P_k^n$ to readily provide an intuitive comparison with assembly's $n!$ search space. The number of assembly sequences is therefore bounded as

$$1 \leq \text{assembly sequences} \leq n! \tag{6.29}$$

while the number of disassembly sequences is bounded as

$$1 \leq \text{disassembly sequences} \leq n! + \sum_{k=1}^{n-2} \frac{n!}{(n-k)!} \tag{6.30}$$

These unique assembly and disassembly metrics are summarized in Table 6.3.

TABLE 6.3

Unique Assembly and Disassembly Formulae

Title	Formula
Assembly search-space bounds	$1 \leq \text{assembly sequences} \leq n!$
Disassembly search-space bounds	$1 \leq \text{disassembly sequences} \leq n! + \sum_{k=1}^{n-2} \frac{n!}{(n-k)!}$

6.6.2 Case Study

6.6.2.1 Product Data

A notional product has been previously developed for use as a simple case study [33]. This small—consisting of only five parts—product has been designed to readily illustrate the application of the unified metrics as well as to demonstrate possible differences, even on a very small scale, between assembly and disassembly sequences for application to a paced line.

The item has several precedence relationships (e.g., parts B AND C need to be installed prior to part E) and is assembled and disassembled on paced lines, both of which are operated at a speed that allows a cycle time of 10 time units (e.g., seconds) for each workstation to perform its required tasks. The case study instance is seen in Table 6.4 with the precedence relationships displayed in Figure 6.1.

At this point, it can be seen that there is nothing unique about the product in terms of assembly or disassembly. In terms of its knowledge base, disassembly is the same as assembly (note that this can be seen as potentially unrealistic, as assembly times for each part could be expected to differ from disassembly times, further indicating the unique natures of assembly and disassembly), and in terms of the precedence diagrams, disassembly is simply the reverse of assembly in this example.

6.6.2.2 Case-Study Metric Selection and Application of Metric Prototypes

For this case study, balance is calculated using B alone (i.e., not using LE, SI, U, or I), and H, D, and R will be formulated first in their original format (i.e., hazardous-part position in sequence, demanded-part position in sequence, and number of product orientation changes, and listed as H [hazardous], D [demand], and R [direction]). (While B is used alone here as an example, the other criteria can certainly be used alongside as well, though keeping in mind that a B-optimal result must be I-optimal as well, and recalling that $LE = U$.) To demonstrate the use of the prototypes in developing new metrics, and to provide a more realistic study, three additional metrics are developed and used: one from each of the three prototype categories. Based on the H metric, H (fragile) will be used to measure any assembly sequence's performance in installing any fragile parts as late as possible in the sequence. Based on the D metric, D (cost) will be used to measure any assembly sequence's performance in installing any high-cost parts as late as possible in the sequence. Finally, based on the R metric, R (tool) will be used to measure the assembly sequence's and the disassembly sequence's performance in installing any parts requiring the same tool adjacent to each other in the sequence.

The use of some criteria selected uniquely for the evaluation of the assembly-sequence result (e.g., H [fragile] and D [cost]) and some uniquely to the evaluation of the disassembly-sequence result (e.g., H [hazardous] and D

TABLE 6.4

Knowledge Base of the Product Instance

Part	PT	Assembly Predecessors	Disassembly Predecessors	H Hazardous	H Fragile	D Demand	D Cost	R Direction	R Tool
A	5	–	D	–	–	1	1	y	S
B	2	–	E	–	–	0	1	z	W
C	6	–	E	–	–	1	1	y	W
D	3	A	–	–	Yes	2	2	x	G
E	9	B, C	–	Yes	–	3	1	x	S

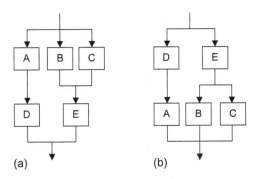

FIGURE 6.1
Assembly (a) and disassembly (b) diagrams.

[demand]) provides one example of differences in assembly and disassembly sequencing.

6.6.2.3 Numerical Analysis

With five parts, the assembly search space is 5! or 120, while the disassembly search space is potentially $5! + P_3^5 + P_2^5 + 5 = 205$; only complete disassembly will be considered here, to further limit the differences between assembly and disassembly for this example, and therefore, the disassembly search space is also 5! or 120. To determine all of the feasible solutions and sort them by performance, a search algorithm was used. The H-K search heuristic [11] works by skipping solutions by a predetermined, fixed amount to reduce the size of the search space. Especially effective in finding initial solutions in a search space where there is no information that many metaheuristics could exploit to build on (e.g., problems such as the initial search in the grid-based, strategic two-player guessing game Battleship), H-K increments solutions (e.g., a sequence permutation) from end to beginning according to an assigned skip size ψ. For example, with $n = 4$, giving the set of the solution space elements as $P = \{1, 2, 3, 4\}$ and no precedence constraints, instead of considering the 4! = 24 possible permutations, only five are visited by the single-phase H-K with $\psi = 2$: $PS_k = \langle 1, 2, 3, 4 \rangle$, $PS_k = \langle 1, 4, 2, 3 \rangle$, $PS_k = \langle 3, 1, 2, 4 \rangle$, $PS_k = \langle 3, 1, 4, 2 \rangle$, and then $PS_k = \langle 3, 4, 1, 2 \rangle$.

Because of the small size of the case study's search space (i.e., 120), the skip size ψ was set to 1 for the instance used in this chapter, effectively making H-K an exhaustive search checking all solutions. Of the 120 possible assembly sequences, only 20 are feasible; of the 120 possible disassembly sequences, again, only 20 are feasible. As such, just 17% of the case study's possible sequences provide a possible solution. From these subsets of results, maximum and minimum results for each metric were found for both the assembly and disassembly cases. For example, the sequence $\langle A, C, B, D, E \rangle$ gave a minimum part-installation (i.e., assembly) direction value of 2, while the sequence $\langle A, B, C, D, E \rangle$ gave a maximum part-installation direction value of 4. All actual (as opposed to theoretical) maximum and minimum values can be seen in Table 6.5 (idle time—which is calculated in the same way as Line Balance [Conventional] *I*—and the number of workstations are not listed, as they are accounted for by Line Balance [Strict] *B*).

The differences in the maximum and minimum results in Table 6.5 provide another indication of differences between assembly-line balancing and disassembly-line balancing.

6.6.2.4 Multi-Criteria Considerations

By considering multiple items in determining an assembly or disassembly sequence, the difference between the two becomes more apparent [33]. In considering the multiple objectives of each problem, this chapter's demonstration makes use of one of the more intuitive selection processes: preemptive (lexicographic) goal programming. Here, the level of balance will be the primary consideration, and additional objectives are only considered subsequently; that is, the heuristic first seeks to select the best-performing measure of balance solution; equal balance solutions are then evaluated for the second metric; equal balance and secondary metric solutions are evaluated for the tertiary metric; and so on.

In terms of metric priorities, the assembly version of the problem instance seen here is considered to be next concerned with, after balance, the placement of any fragile or delicate components as late as possible in the assembly sequence (i.e., MAX *H* [fragile]). The next consideration is then selected as reducing the number of tool changes along the line (i.e., MIN *R* [tool]), then to install high-cost components as late as possible (i.e., MAX *D* [cost]) to minimize inventory costs, and finally, to minimize the number of product orientation changes along the line (i.e., MIN *R* [direction]). Hazardous parts may not be of concern, as all assembly components are new, while part

TABLE 6.5

Upper and Lower Metric Bounds (Actual) for all Possible Outcomes in the Cases of Assembly and Disassembly for the Five-Part Product Instance

	Assembly		Disassembly	
	MAX	MIN	MAX	MIN
B	8.89	3	8.89	3
H (hazardous)	5	3	3	1
H (fragile)	5	2	4	1
D (demand)	28	24	18	14
D (cost)	20	17	19	16
R (direction)	4	2	4	2
R (tool)	4	2	4	2

demand does not apply, as obviously, every one of the parts is needed for assembly.

In general, disassembly may be more concerned with a different sequence. Disassembly here will be concerned with—after balancing the line— removing hazardous parts early to ensure that they do not adversely affect any demanded components, removing high-demand components as soon as possible, product orientation, and finally, tool considerations. Part-cost considerations don't apply here, as all parts (it is assumed that the end-of-life product is complete) are already installed, and so there are no inventory considerations as would be found with assembly. Fragile parts in an end-of-life product may be already broken and, if needed, will be accounted for in the demand criteria. The number of tool changes may be a consideration; however, the condition of end-of-life products often requires tools and/or techniques that differ from those of assembly, so a variety of tools might be expected at each workstation regardless. Table 6.6 summarizes the priorities in the order selected for use in this case study.

Even neglecting to consider that partial disassembly may be more efficient, the differences in objectives (i.e., MIN versus MAX; Table 6.6) provide another example of differences in sequencing assembly and disassembly lines.

6.6.2.5 Results

The H-K heuristic generated all 20 feasible sequences for each (i.e., assembly and disassembly). The assembly sequence ⟨B, C, E, A, D⟩ provided the optimal balance measure of 3 (spread over three workstations and having an idle time of 5 time units) with optimal fragile-part placement (i.e., last), optimal number of tool changes (i.e., two), optimal cost (i.e., 20), and sub-optimal direction (i.e., four direction changes). The disassembly sequence ⟨E, D, A, C, B⟩ provided the optimal balance measure of 3 (also in three workstations and having an idle time of 5 time units) with optimal hazardous-part placement (i.e., first), optimal removal of demanded parts (i.e., score of 14), optimal direction changes (i.e., two), and sub-optimal number of tool changes (i.e., three). Figure 6.2 demonstrates each solution structure, while all scores of interest are listed in Tables 6.7 and 6.8 [33].

TABLE 6.6

Sequence Considerations, Priorities (High [Top] to Low [Bottom]), and Objectives

Assembly	Disassembly
MIN *B*	MIN *B*
MAX *H* (fragile)	MIN *H* (hazardous)
MIN *R* (tool)	MIN *D* (demand)
MAX *D* (cost)	MIN *R* (direction)
MIN *R* (direction)	MIN *R* (tool)

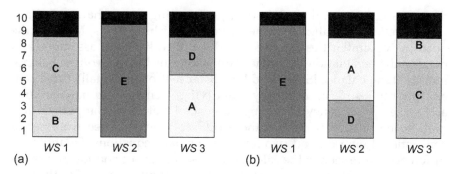

FIGURE 6.2
Assembly (a) and disassembly (b) solutions with $CT = 10$.

TABLE 6.7

Metric Scores for the Optimal Assembly Sequence ⟨B, C, E, A, D⟩

	MIN *B*	**MAX *H* Fragile**	**MIN *R* Tool**	**MAX *D* Cost**	**MIN *R* Direction**
Score	3	5	2	20	4
EI (%)	100	100	100	100	50

TABLE 6.8

Metric Scores for the Optimal Disassembly Sequence ⟨E, D, A, C, B⟩

	MIN *B*	**MIN *H* Hazardous**	**MIN *D* Demand**	**MIN *R* Direction**	**MIN *R* Tool**
Score	3	1	14	2	3
EI (%)	100	100	100	100	50

Differences between assembly and disassembly can be seen in the determined sequences (the disassembly sequence is not the reverse of the assembly sequence in this example), differently selected metrics, different metric priority ranking, and ultimately, different metric scores.

Due to the multi-criteria nature of any assembly- or disassembly-sequence solution, differing criteria dictate the optimal solution for a given product. As such, it is unlikely that a disassembly sequence would be the reverse of the same product's assembly sequence, as demonstrated with this very simple product example.

6.7 Conclusions

With disassembly becoming more and more relevant, this chapter provided an overview of assembly and disassembly and then compared them qualitatively and quantitatively, confirming many shared similarities as well as formalizing numerous distinguishing items. Many of the quantitative similarities were seen in the unified listing of assembly- and disassembly-evaluation formulae. This listing included two line-balance metrics (Line Balance [Strict] and Line Balance [Conventional]), three general prototypes (General Binary Identifying, General Ordinal Ranking, and General Adjacency Grouping), a general statistical comparison formula to be used with any of these (Efficacy Index), three well-known conventional metrics, and two familiar ancillary equations. Quantitative differences were seen in the calculation of search-space bounds for assembly and disassembly lines as well as in a case-study example. For the case study, two examples of each of the prototypes were demonstrated—three from previous disassembly research efforts and three newly developed ones—and these six example metrics were selected, along with other items from the unified formulae, for application to the case study. From this group, a total of five metrics were selected for their applicability to assembly of the case study, and five were selected for disassembly. Each set of five was then uniquely prioritized according to a notional decision-maker's criteria, with the case-study sequencing results demonstrating the use of the metrics and illustrating some of the differences that exist between assembly lines and disassembly lines.

References

1. Gutjahr, A. L. and Nemhauser, G. L. 1964. An algorithm for the line balancing problem. *Management Science* 11(2): 308–315.
2. Elsayed, E. A. and Boucher, T. O. 1994. *Analysis and Control of Production Systems.* Upper Saddle River, New Jersey: Prentice Hall.
3. Scholl, A. 1995. *Balancing and Sequencing of Assembly Lines.* Heidelberg, Germany: Physica-Verlag.
4. Ponnambalam, S. G., Aravindan, P., and Naidu, G. M. 1999. A comparative evaluation of assembly line balancing heuristics. *The International Journal of Advanced Manufacturing Technology* 15: 577–586.
5. Boysen, N., Fliedner, M., and Scholl, A. 2008. Assembly line balancing: Which model to use when? *International Journal of Production Economics* 111(2): 509–528.
6. Ilgin, M. A. and Gupta, S. M. 2012. *Remanufacturing Modeling and Analysis.* Boca Raton, Florida: CRC Press.
7. Johnson, M. R. and Wang, M. H. 1995. Planning product disassembly for material recovery opportunities. *International Journal of Production Research* 33(11): 3119–3142.
8. Vujosevic, R., Raskar, T., Yetukuri, N. V., Jothishankar, M. C. and Juang, S. H. 1995. Simulation, animation, and analysis of design assembly for maintainability analysis. *International Journal of Production Research* 33(11): 2999–3022.

9. Brennan, L., Gupta, S. M. and Taleb, K. N. 1994. Operations planning issues in an assembly/disassembly environment. *International Journal of Operations and Production Management* 14(9): 57–67.
10. Gupta, S. M. and Taleb, K. 1994. Scheduling disassembly. *International Journal of Production Research* 32(8): 1857–1866.
11. McGovern, S. M. and Gupta, S. M. 2011. *The Disassembly Line: Balancing and Modeling.* New York: McGraw-Hill.
12. Altekin, F. T. 2017. A comparison of piecewise linear programming formulations for stochastic disassembly line balancing. *International Journal of Production Research* 55(24): 7412–7434.
13. Kalayci, C. B., Polat, O. and Gupta, S. M. 2016. A hybrid genetic algorithm for sequence-dependent disassembly line balancing problem. *Annals of Operations Research* 242(2): 321–354.
14. Kazancoglu, Y. and Ozturkoglu, Y. 2018. Integrated framework of disassembly line balancing with green and business objectives using a mixed MCDM. *Journal of Cleaner Production* 191(1): 179–191.
15. Mete, S., Cil, Z. A., Agpak, K., Ozceylan, E. and Dolgui, A. 2016. A solution approach based on beam search algorithm for disassembly line balancing problem. *Journal of Manufacturing Systems* 41(1): 188–200.
16. Pistolesi, F., Lazzerini, B., Mura, M. D. and Dini, G. 2018. EMOGA: A hybrid genetic algorithm with extremal optimization core for multiobjective disassembly line balancing. *IEEE Transactions on Industrial Informatics* 14(3): 1089–1098.
17. Battaïa, O. and Dolgui, A. 2013. A taxonomy of line balancing problems and their solution approaches. *International Journal of Production Economics* 142: 259–277.
18. Gungor, A. and Gupta, S. M. 1999. Issues in environmentally conscious manufacturing and product recovery: A survey. *Computers and Industrial Engineering* 36(4): 811–853.
19. Ilgin, M. A. and Gupta, S. M. 2010. Environmentally conscious manufacturing and product recovery (ECMPRO): A review of the state of the art. *Journal of Environmental Management* 91(3): 563–591.
20. Lambert, A. J. D. 2003. Disassembly sequencing: A survey. *International Journal of Production Research* 41(16): 3721–3759.
21. Lambert, A. J. D. and Gupta, S. M. 2005. *Disassembly Modeling for Assembly, Maintenance, Reuse, and Recycling.* Boca Raton, Florida: CRC Press.
22. Ozceylan, E., Kalayci, C. B., Gungor, A. and Gupta, S. M. in press. Disassembly line balancing problem: A review of the state of the art and future directions. *International Journal of Production Research.* DOI: 10.1080/00207543.2018.1428775
23. Wang, H.-F. and Gupta, S. M. 2011. *Green Supply Chain Management: Product Life Cycle Approach.* New York: McGraw Hill.
24. Gupta, S. M. 2013. *Reverse Supply Chains: Issues and Analysis.* Boca Raton, Florida: CRC Press.
25. Gupta, S. M. and Ilgin, M. A. 2018. *Multiple Criteria Decision Making Applications in Environmentally Conscious Manufacturing and Product Recovery.* Boca Raton, Florida: CRC Press.
26. Finch, B. 2008. *Operations Now: Supply Chain Profitability and Performance.* New York: McGraw-Hill.
27. Nahmias, S. 2009. *Production and Operations Analysis.* New York: McGraw-Hill/Irwin.

28. Tapping, D. 2003. *The Lean Pocket Guide*. Chelsea, Michigan: MCS Media.
29. Bourjault, A. 1987. Methodology of assembly operation: A new approach. *Abstracts of the 2nd International Conference on Robotics and Factories of the Future*. San Diego, California: 34–45.
30. Güngör, A. and Gupta, S. M. 2002. Disassembly line in product recovery. *International Journal of Production Research* 40(11): 2569–2589.
31. McGovern, S. M. and Gupta, S. M. 2003. 2-opt heuristic for the disassembly line balancing problem. *Proceedings of the SPIE International Conference on Environmentally Conscious Manufacturing III*. Providence, Rhode Island: 71–84.
32. McGovern, S. M. and Gupta, S. M. 2006. Deterministic hybrid and stochastic combinatorial optimization treatments of an electronic product disassembly line. *Applications of Management Science* Vol. 12. K. D. Lawrence, G. R. Reeves, and R. Klimberg, eds. North-Holland Amsterdam: Elsevier: 175–197.
33. McGovern, S. M. and Gupta, S. M. 2015. Unified assembly- and disassembly-line model formulae. *Journal of Manufacturing Technology Management* 26(2): 195–212.
34. McGovern, S. M. and Gupta, S. M. 2007. Combinatorial optimization analysis of the unary NP-complete disassembly line balancing problem. *International Journal of Production Research* 45(18–19): 4485–4511.
35. McGovern, S. M., Gupta, S. M. and Kamarthi, S. V. 2003. Solving disassembly sequence planning problems using combinatorial optimization. *Northeast Decision Sciences Institute Conference*. Providence, Rhode Island: 178–180.

7

Environmentally Friendly and Economical Disassembly Parts Selection for Material Recycling by Goal Programming

Yuki Kinoshita, Tetsuo Yamada, and Surendra M. Gupta

CONTENTS

7.1 Introduction

The depletion of natural resources has become more serious, because the demand for natural resources is increasing as world population growth and economic development cause increasing demand for products and services (Yamada, 2012). Thus, assembly manufacturing, which is employed for products such as home electrical appliances, automobiles, and smartphones, is facing changes from mass production and large-scale consumption to environmentally conscious manufacturing (Ilgin and Gupta, 2010). These changes are caused by the desire to preserve natural resources through the promotion of recycling for end-of-life (EOL) products. Recycling can be defined as the recovery of scrap materials from EOL products (Lambert and Gupta, 2005). It is one of the key methods for material circulation. However, the U.S. Environmental Protection Agency reported that more than 250 million tons of EOL product are discarded each year, even though most materials in the EOL products are still valuable in the United States (Nasr, 2017). This situation means that two-thirds of recyclable materials in the EOL products become trash in the United States (Nasr, 2017).

Another environmental issue is global warming (IPCC, 2014). The CO_2 emissions generated by manufacturing have become a serious concern that must be addressed worldwide. In 2015, for the first time in human history, not only developed nations but also emerging countries at the Conference of Parties (COP) 21 meeting held in Paris agreed to control CO_2 emissions (United Nations Framework Conversation on Climate Change). Each country is obligated to set targets for CO_2 reduction, thereby engaging in ambitious efforts to curb climate change. In this context, recycling is effective to reduce not only the consumption of natural resources but also additional CO_2 emissions from the production of materials by replacing virgin material production with material recycling.

With regard to material recycling, collected EOL assembly products must be disassembled into separate parts for each material type by disassembly operations. Disassembly is defined as a process in which a product is separated into its components and/or subassemblies by nondestructive or semide-structive operations (Lambert and Gupta, 2005). The reason why disassembly is an essential phase for material recycling is that each material requires different recycling processes to recover its value. Further, the type of material determines the recycling and CO_2 saving rates (Igarashi et al., 2014b; Hiroshige et al., 2002; Hitachi, Ltd.). The recycling rate is the ratio of recyclable weight against the whole product weight (Igarashi et al., 2014a), while the CO_2 saving rate is defined as the volume of CO_2 emissions saved by replacing the CO_2 emissions for virgin material production (Igarashi et al., 2014b). Thus, recycling contributes to reduction of disposal weight and CO_2 emissions as well as virgin material consumption. Although disassembly is an unavoidable phase of recycling and plays an important role, the automation of disassembly operations is confronted with many challenges due to the variable quality and structure of returned products and the variability of tasks (Agrawal and Tiwari, 2008). Therefore, manual disassembly has proved to be the most efficient method (Opaltić et al., 2010). This situation means that the disassembly cost increases because of the high labor cost, especially in developed countries. Although it is desirable to disassemble all parts of EOL products to maximize the CO_2 saving and recycling rates from an environmental viewpoint, it is difficult for recycling factories to achieve this goal from an economic perspective. Thus, a trade-off relationship exists between environmental loads and cost reduction for recycling.

To establish environmentally friendly and economical recycling factories, disassembly parts selection (Igarashi, Yamada and Inoue, 2014a; Igarashi et al., 2014b; Igarashi et al., 2016), which involves the selection of disassembly parts for recycling, is often conducted in recycling factories (Yamada, 2008). The selected parts are removed from EOL products manually, which entails costs as well as recycling and CO_2 saving rates. Non-selected parts are then crushed for disposal. The cost of crush operations can be regarded as minimal and/or as zero cost assumed (Igarashi, Yamada and Inoue, 2014a). Therefore, the objective of environmentally friendly and economical disassembly parts selection is defined to enable the combinations of disassembled parts with higher recycling or CO_2 saving rates and lower recycling costs to be decided. Thus, satisficing rather than optimizing is required, because the trade-off relationship ensures that simultaneous improvement in all the objectives cannot occur (Messac, 2015). Hillir and Lieberman (2005) mention that "satisficing as a combination of the words 'satisfactory' and 'optimizing' is much more prevalent than optimizing in actual practice." A satisficing solution is a solution whereby the values of all criteria are sufficient for a decision-maker, even though these values are not the best for each objective.

Goal programming (Gupta and Ilgin, 2018) is one of the methods for resolving a multi-criteria decision-making problem. In this regard, it can find satisficing solutions for the trade-off problem. In addition to the trade-off relationship between environmental loads and cost reduction, a disassembly precedence relationship among the parts of an assembly product exists (Lambert and Gupta, 2005) and generally increases disassembly costs, because all preceding parts need to be removed by disassembly operations so as to remove a certain part (Lambert and Gupta, 2005). Thus, even though some parts have higher CO_2 saving or recycling rates and lower recycling costs, total recycling cost becomes unprofitable if these parts have multiple preceding parts.

Igarashi, Yamada and Inoue (2014a) and Igarashi et al. (2014b) propose two different environmental objective functions for environmentally friendly and economical disassembly parts selection: recycling and CO_2 saving rates. These environmental indices can improve different but related global environmental issues, such as material starvation and global warming, simultaneously (Kinoshita et al., 2018).

However, recycling and CO_2 saving rates depend on the types and weights of material. Recycling cost depends not only on these types and weights but also on disassembly tasks such as unscrewing and moving up (Hiroshige et al., 2002; Hitachi, Ltd.). The types and weights are included in a bill of materials (BOM) at the assembly phase. A BOM lists all the subassemblies, parts, raw materials, components, and bulk products (Institute of Industrial and Systems Engineers). By adding environmental and disassembly information such as costs and CO_2 saving and recycling rates, a disassembly BOM also plays an important role in environmentally friendly and economical disassembly parts selection, because each part has different CO_2 saving and recycling rates and costs. Hence, it is desirable to construct the disassembly BOM that includes costs and CO_2 saving and recycling rates at recycling factories to promote material circulation with an affordable cost.

Thus, the challenges of disassembly parts selection are which parts should be disassembled, how disassembled parts should be determined, what indices should be used for an environmentally friendly and economical process, and how the trade-off relationship problem for environmental loads and cost reduction should be evaluated to find a satisficing solution.

This chapter proposes and compares two types of bi-objective environmentally friendly and economical disassembly parts selection by using goal programming so as to maximize the CO_2 saving or recycling rates while minimizing the recycling costs. The chapter is organized as follows. Section 7.2 explains the objectives of environmentally friendly and economical disassembly parts selection and a trade-off relationship between environmental loads and cost reduction. Moreover, the disassembly BOM and precedence relationships are explained in Section 7.2. Section 7.3 describes the procedures of the environmentally friendly and economical disassembly parts selection and formulates the bi-objective disassembly parts selection by goal programming. Section 7.4 illustrates a numerical example using a cell phone and compares the results of the two types of bi-objective disassembly parts selection. Section 7.5 contains the conclusions and ideas for future research.

7.2 The Problem of Disassembly Parts Selection

Disassembly is an operation for removing the parts from assembly products. To recover the value of materials contained in EOL products, disassembly is an essential phase for material recycling. The assembly process has to be complete, while the disassembly process does not always have to be carried out completely due to technical and economic restrictions (Özceylan et al., 2018). Moreover, the objective of the disassembly is to retrieve material value from selected disassembly parts instead of all parts being removed. Additionally, disassembly operations are implemented manually because of the complexity of EOL product structure and the sequences of precedence relationships of the assembled parts; thus, disassembly costs tend to be higher because of labor costs. Consequently, disassembly parts selection is often carried out at recycling factories, where only selected parts are removed from EOL products by disassembly operations for recycling (Yamada, 2008). When disassembly parts selection is implemented, three indices and disassembly precedence relationships (McGovern and Gupta, 2011) should be taken into account for two types of environmental issues, such as material starvation and global warming. A detailed explanation of the objectives and the required information is given in the following subsection.

7.2.1 Environmental and Economic Objectives

Disassembly parts selection is conducted to retrieve material value from EOL products in an environmentally friendly and economical way. Additionally, each part of an EOL product has different CO_2 saving and recycling rates, because these rates depend on the material's type, and weight. Further, even though CO_2 saving and recycling rates depend on a material's type and weight, the values of these rates differ for each part. Thus, the selected parts can differ if the environmental objective is switched. In this regard, there are several research questions related to environmentally friendly and economical disassembly parts selection: (1) What differences are observed in the behaviors of recycling cost as CO_2 saving or recycling rates increases? What differences are observed for selected parts in the two different bi-objectives? (2) What parts should be selected for disassembly? What features are in the selected key parts?

7.2.1.1 Recycling Cost

One economic objective is recycling costs. The recycling costs for each part can be estimated as the sum of the costs and the revenue from the material's sale (Hiroshige et al., 2002; Hitachi, Ltd.). The sum of the costs consists of labor for disassembly and costs for disposal and landfill (Hiroshige et al., 2002; Hitachi, Ltd.), while the revenue is earned from the material's sale. Thus, recycling can be profitable if the revenue is higher than the sum of the costs. According to the Recyclability Evaluation Method (REM) (Hiroshige et al., 2002; Hitachi, Ltd.), if the type of disassembly operation, the weight, and the type of material are inputted for each part, the REM software can estimate the recycling rate and cost for each part.

7.2.1.2 Recycling and CO_2 Saving Rates

To harmonize environmental and economic objectives for disassembly parts selection, environmental objectives are required. One of the important objectives is the recycling rate for material circulation. The recycling rate for each part is defined as the ratio of recyclable weight compared with the whole product's weight based on the REM (Hiroshige et al., 2002; Hitachi, Ltd.). Hence, maximizing the total recycling rate by disassembly parts selection contributes to minimizing the disposal weight. According to the REM, the recycling rate depends on the type of materials and the weight for each part (Hiroshige et al., 2002; Hitachi, Ltd.).

In the case of a certain part made from materials that are difficult to recycle, the recycling rate becomes 0%. For example, the recycling rate for parts made of rubber or cloth/fiber becomes 0%. Thus, the disassembly for all parts does not always achieve a 100% recycling rate because of the nature of the materials and current technological/economic restrictions. The maximum achievable recycling rate is decided when a material is selected during a product's design phase.

Another important environmental objective is the CO_2 saving rate for preventing global warming. The CO_2 saving rate for each part can be defined as the volume of CO_2 that can be reduced compared with the total CO_2 volume for the whole product if recycled material is used instead of virgin material (Igarashi et al., 2014b). Thus, maximizing the CO_2 saving rate is considered to minimize additional CO_2 emissions from virgin material production. CO_2 volumes for each part can be estimated using life cycle assessment (LCA) (Rebitzer et al., 2004), which is a methodological framework for estimating and assessing the environmental impacts attributable to the life cycle of a product, such as climate change, stratospheric ozone depletion, and the depletion of resources. Based on LCA , the Life Cycle Inventory (LCI) database has been developed to provide representative unit process data at national and regional levels to measure the greenhouse gas (GHG) emissions, including CO_2 emissions, of a wide range of industries (Sugiyama et al., 2005). According to the LCI database, CO_2 emissions in the material production phase also depend on the type of material and the weight (Itsubo Laboratory; Yoshizaki et al., 2014).

One of the LCI databases has input–output (I/O) tables that calculate environmental loads, including CO_2 emissions for certain products, using an exchange-of-value basis among industrial sectors (Itsubo Laboratory; Yoshizaki et al., 2014). Yoshizaki et al. (2014) propose an estimation method for material-based CO_2 emissions using the LCI database with these I/O tables in China and Japan (Itsubo Laboratory). According to this method, the

CO_2 emissions in the material production phase can be calculated by matching each part's material types in the assembled product with the unit process data in the LCI database (Itsubo Laboratory).

7.2.1.3 *Trade-Off and Satisficing between Environmental Loads and Costs*

It is generally known that a trade-off relationship exists between environmental loads and costs (Gupta and Ilgin, 2018; Utara et al., 2017; Kinoshita et al., 2018). As previously explained in Sections 7.2.1.1 and 7.2.1.2, there is an economic index—the recycling costs—and two environmental indices—the CO_2 saving and recycling rates—in the process of environmentally friendly and economical disassembly parts selection.

Table 7.1 shows the trade-off relationship between environmental and economic objective functions in environmentally friendly and economical disassembly parts selection. As shown in Table 7.1, the recycling cost consists of three costs and one revenue. The revenue is denoted as a negative value, so that the recycling costs can be negative if the total revenue from material sales is higher than the sum of these costs. Thus, the recycling costs should be minimized to obtain a positive profit through the revenue from the material's sale. On the other hand, the CO_2 saving and recycling rates should be maximized to reduce disposal weight and additional CO_2 emissions for virgin material production. As the number of parts selected for disassembly is increased, the total recycling cost basically increases, but the total CO_2 saving and recycling rates can be increased except in the case of parts with positive profit. From the economic viewpoint alone, one of the solutions is that all parts should be crushed without a disposal cost; however, in this case, the total CO_2 saving and recycling rates become 0%. From an environmental perspective, it is desirable to disassemble all the parts; however, the total recycling cost becomes higher. Thus, there is an unavoidable trade-off relationship between environmental loads and costs. This is known as *multi-criteria decision-making* (Gupta and Ilgin, 2018), where there is no unique solution that maximizes all objectives simultaneously (McGovern and Gupta, 2011). Messac (2015) pointed out that "a set of solutions called *Pareto Optimal Solutions* form the complete solution set of the optimization problem."

7.2.2 Goal Programming

Multi-criteria decision-making often results in conflict and trade-off relationships (Messac, 2015). Even though decision-makers are usually eager to achieve several goals simultaneously, no optimal solution exists for the trade-off problem (McGovern and Gupta, 2011). Pareto optimal solutions instead of the optimal solution are obtained for trade-off problems; thus, decision-makers are required to decide on a satisficing solution that reflects their preferences for certain goals by comparing the solutions in terms of their effectiveness and feasibility from viewpoints that are not part of the

TABLE 7.1

Trade-Off Relationships between Environmental and Economical Objective Functions in the Environmentally Friendly and Economical Disassembly Parts Selection

Types of Objective Function		Environmental Objective Functions		Economic Objective Function			
Optimization direction		Maximization		Minimization			
					Recycling costs		Revenue
					Cost breakdown		
Name of objective functions		CO_2 saving rate	Recycling rate	Disassembly cost	Disposal cost	Landfill cost	Revenue from material sale
Options of disassembly parts selection	Disassembly for material recycling	Increase	Increase	Increase	Increase	Increase	Increase
	Crush for disposal	Decrease	Decrease	Decrease	Decrease	Decrease	Decrease

optimization (Fushimi et al., 1987). Goal programming (Gupta and Ilgin, 2018; Fushimi et al., 1987) is one of the methods for resolving multi-criteria decision-making problems.

By setting only sufficient and tolerable levels for each goal, goal programming can evaluate different objective functions easily, even though the functions have different scales or units, such as the environmental loads and costs. Moreover, goal programming can seek different Pareto optimal solutions by changing only the target ranges for each goal. One of the advantages of goal programming is that satisficing solutions can be obtained with fewer numerical experiments than in the ε-constraint method. The ε-constraint method prioritizes a primary objective while expressing other objectives as constraints with ε (Eskandarpour et al., 2015). This method is well adapted to the extension of a single-objective economic approach to bi-objective models integrating environmental or social criteria (Eskandarpour et al., 2015). However, it requires many numerical experiments due to changing ε to obtain satisficing solutions (Kinoshita et al., 2016).

7.2.3 Disassembly Information

Some of the information required for material recycling operations differs from that needed for assembly manufacturing, because each type of material requires a different recycling process. With regard to material recycling, the material types of each part are more important. However, they are already determined when the material types and the assembly operations are chosen at the product design and assembly manufacturing phases. This results in different CO_2 saving and recycling rates and costs for each part. Hence, this information should be contained in a BOM for disassembly as well as the BOM for assembly manufacturing.

With regard to disassembly operations, disassembly precedence relationships should be considered for disassembly parts selection to retrieve the material value from disassembled parts in an environmentally friendly and economical way under precedence relationships among disassembly parts.

7.2.3.1 Disassembly Bill of Materials with Environmental Loads and Recycling Costs

A BOM lists all subassemblies, parts, raw materials, components, and bulk products (Institute of Industrial and Systems Engineers), and also plays an important role in assembly and material requirement planning (MRP) (Nof et al., 1997).

On the other hand, the information for each part listed in a BOM affects assembly processes and costs. In the case of environmentally friendly and economical parts selection, the CO_2 saving and recycling rates, and the cost for each part, are required as input data. Thus, when the environmental loads and disassembly information are added to the assembly BOM, a disassembly BOM is also constructed as an effective tool for recycling factories. Table 7.2

TABLE 7.2

Disassembly BOM with Environmental Loads and Recycling Costs: the Case of a Cell Phone

No.	Part Name	Material Type	Disassembly Operation	Weight (g)	CO_2 Saving Rate e_j (%)	Recycling Rate r_j (%)	Recycling Cost c_j
1	Battery cover	PC	[move up]	1.00	0.65	0.49	3.94
2	Battery	Battery	[move up]	58.10	7.21	8.57	5.28
3	Back case	PC	[unscrew 4]	1.00	0.65	0.49	36.51
4	Board	Circuit board	[move up]	85.40	7.98	42.07	−38.78
5	Microphone	SUS	[move up]	0.50	0.82	0.25	3.94
6	Camera	Zinc alloy	[move up]	5.30	1.68	2.61	3.90
7	Main button	PC	[move up]	1.00	0.65	0.49	3.94
8	Number buttons	PC	[move up 12]	1.00	0.65	0.49	9.60
9	Junction	SUS	[move up]	47.50	78.08	23.40	3.56
10	Front case	PC	[unscrew 4][move up]	1.00	0.65	0.49	36.51
11	LCD	Glass	[move up]	1.00	0.00	0.49	3.93
12	Speaker	SUS	[move up]	0.60	0.99	0.30	3.94
	Total			203.40	100.00	80.14	76.27
	Average			16.95	8.33	6.68	6.36
	Standard deviation			28.15	21.18	12.46	18.05

presents a disassembly BOM in the context of a cell phone, including part name, material type, disassembly operation, weight, CO_2 saving, and recycling rates and costs. It is found from Table 7.2 that Parts #4 (board) and #9 (junction) are made of circuit board and Steel Use Stainless (SUS) and have the highest recycling and CO_2 saving rates, respectively, among all parts. Additionally, Part #4 (board) has the lowest recycling costs among all parts.

7.2.3.2 Disassembly Precedence Relationship

The disassembly precedence relationship ordering of tasks/parts according to their immediate predecessors provides a visual representation of precedence constraints and of possible disassembly sequences (McGovern and Gupta, 2011). To remove a certain part, all preceding parts must be disassembled first because of disassembly precedence relationships. Thus, key parts in environmentally friendly disassembly parts selection, which can be defined as parts with higher CO_2 saving or recycling rates but lower recycling costs, should be disassembled.

Figure 7.1 illustrates a disassembly precedence relationship in the context of a cell phone. Each large box in Figure 7.1 represents one part. The three squares in each box show CO_2 saving and recycling rates and costs for each part, respectively. The arrow represents the disassembly precedence relationship. Thus, for instance, to remove Part #4 (board), whose CO_2 saving and recycling rates and costs are 7.98%, 42.07%, and −38.78, respectively, all

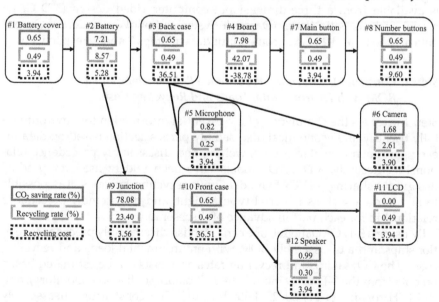

FIGURE 7.1

Disassembly precedence relationship with CO_2 saving and recycling rates and costs: the case of a cell phone.

disassembly preceding parts such as #1 (battery cover), #2 (battery), and #3 (back case) also have to be disassembled simultaneously. Therefore, the total CO_2 saving and recycling rates and cost for the four parts become 16.48%, 51.62%, and 6.95, respectively.

7.3 Environmentally Friendly and Economical Disassembly Parts Selection Using Goal Programming

This section integrates the procedures of the environmentally friendly and economical disassembly parts selection based on Kinoshita et al. (2016) for recycling rate and costs, and Kinoshita et al. (2018) for CO_2 saving rate and recycling costs. Next, the disassembly parts selection is formulated using goal programming.

7.3.1 Procedure of Environmentally Friendly and Economical Disassembly Parts Selection by Goal Programming

The integrated procedure of environmentally friendly and economical disassembly parts selection consists of three steps, as treated in Kinoshita et al. (2016) and Kinoshita et al. (2018) and shown in Figure 7.2. The squares in Figure 7.2 mean input and output data for each step. The input data at Step 1 is available from a three-dimensional computer aided design (3-D CAD) model such as SolidWorks (Dassault Systèmes SolidWorks Corp.). Output data at Steps 1 and 2 also become input data at Steps 2 and 3, respectively.

Step 1: Construct Disassembly Precedence Relationships and a BOM with Environmental Loads and Recycling Costs

Step 1 involves the completion of the essential information for environmentally friendly and economical disassembly parts selection based on data for each part such as material type, weight, and disassembly precedence relationship. Recently, 3-D CAD models have been widely used for product design. By sharing 3-D CAD models with recycling factories, it is possible to obtain data such as material type, weight, and disassembly precedence relationship for each part in advance of disassembly.

By using a 3-D CAD model, one can establish disassembly precedence relationships and a disassembly BOM with environmental loads and recycling costs. The CO_2 saving and recycling rates and costs can be estimated based on data from the 3-D CAD model, the LCI database (Itsubo Laboratory), and REM (Hiroshige et al., 2002; Hitachi, Ltd.). The constructed disassembly BOM includes the recycling costs and environmental information at Step 1. This information becomes the input data of the environmentally friendly and economical disassembly parts selection at Step 2.

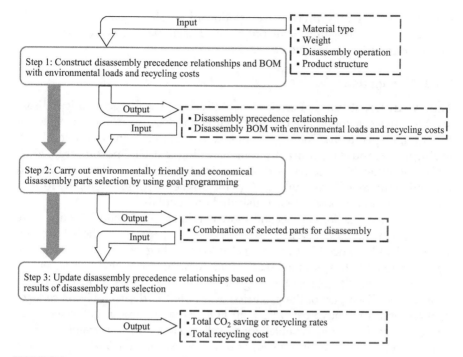

FIGURE 7.2
The integrated procedure of environmentally friendly and economical disassembly parts selection by goal programming with input and output data.

Step 2: Conduct Environmentally Friendly and Economical Disassembly Parts Selection using Goal Programming

Step 2 conducts environmentally friendly and economical disassembly parts selection using goal programming. Either the CO_2 saving rate or the recycling rate is selected as an environmental index for environmentally friendly and economic objective functions. Then, disassembly parts selection has two objective functions: minimizing the total recycling cost and maximizing the total CO_2 saving or recycling rates. To seek satisficing solutions for the bi-objectives, goal programming is applied to set tolerable and sufficient levels for each goal. By determining sufficient levels, goal programming finds one solution, which is greater/lower than the tolerable level for all goals, for each combination of target ranges.

Step 3: Update Disassembly Precedence Relationships Based on the Results of Disassembly Parts Selection

Step 3 updates the disassembly precedence relationships based on the solutions for selected parts obtained at Step 2. The canceled parts in the environmentally friendly and economical disassembly parts selection are removed from the disassembly precedence relationships. The updated disassembly precedence relationships have only the chosen parts selected with CO_2 saving or recycling rates and costs.

7.3.2 Formulation

The two different types of environmentally friendly and economical disassembly parts selection have one environmental and one economic objective function, respectively. One of the bi-objectives is to maximize the total CO_2 saving rate, E, and to minimize the total recycling cost, C (Kinoshita et al., 2018), while the other bi-objective is to maximize the total recycling rate, R, and minimize the total recycling cost, C (Kinoshita et al., 2016). Here, the formulation of the first bi-objective is illustrated and explained.

The objective functions are set and shown in Equations 7.1 and 7.2. e_j and c_j are the CO_2 saving rate and recycling costs, respectively, for part j. x_j is the 0–1 decision variable. This becomes 1 if part j is selected for recycling; otherwise, x_j becomes 0 (see Equation 7.3). It is assumed that part j is removed manually by disassembly operation j. Then, the total CO_2 saving rate, E, and the total recycling cost, C, can be increased. Each part of the produced assembly has disassembly precedence relationships. To remove part j from an EOL assembly product, all precedence parts, i, must also be disassembled for recycling. Hence, the constraint for disassembly precedence relationships is set based on Nof et al. (1997), as shown in Equation 7.4. Equation 7.4 ensures constraint of the precedence relationships.

$$E = \sum_{j}^{N} e_j x_j \rightarrow \text{Max} \tag{7.1}$$

$$C = \sum_{j}^{N} c_j x_j \rightarrow \text{Min} \tag{7.2}$$

$$x_j = \{0,1\} \quad j \in J \tag{7.3}$$

$$x_j \leq x_i \quad i \in P_j \tag{7.4}$$

The two objective functions in the process of environmentally friendly and economical disassembly parts selection have a trade-off relationship. The solution for a trade-off problem is generally not unique, because different trade-off levels may be desirable (Messac, 2015). Thus, Pareto optimal solutions instead of the optimal solution are sought.

To obtain the Pareto optimal solutions by simultaneously evaluating both objective functions, for which different units and scales exist, goal programming is applied to the bi-objective disassembly parts selection (Kinoshita et al., 2018; Kinoshita et al., 2016). Goal programming requires the transposition of the objective functions to the constraints with sufficient and tolerable levels for each criterion to establish an aggregate objective function.

A summary of the notation is given here.

E_0/E_s: Tolerable/sufficient total CO_2 saving rate
C_0/C_s: Tolerable/sufficient total recycling cost
d_1^+ / d_1^- : Positive/negative deviation from the sufficient CO_2 saving rate, E_s
d_2^+ / d_2^- : Positive/negative deviation from the sufficient recycling cost, C_s
d: Maximum deviational variable
β: Parameter to weight the average and the maximum of d

The aggregate objective function minimizes the differences between the values of the objective functions and the sufficient levels to seek the Pareto optimal solutions. By changing only the target ranges, which are defined as the differences between sufficient and tolerable levels, other solutions can be obtained. The detailed formulation by goal programming is explained as follows.

1. The first goal is to maximize the total CO_2 saving rate, E.

    The total CO_2 saving rate, E, is equal to or greater than the tolerable total CO_2 saving rate, E_0. It tries to achieve the sufficient total CO_2 saving rate, E_s, by minimizing the negative deviation variable from the sufficient total CO_2 saving rate, d_1^- . Since the total CO_2 saving rate is maximized, the sufficient total CO_2 saving rate, E_s, is determined to be greater than the tolerable total CO_2 saving rate, E_0, as shown in Equation 7.5. Equation 7.6 ensures that the total CO_2 saving rate, E, is equal to or greater than the tolerable total CO_2 saving rate, E_0. The terms d_1^+ and d_1^- in Equation 7.7 are positive values and denote the difference between the sufficient total CO_2 saving rate, E_s, and the total CO_2 saving rate, E. Thus, either the positive d_1^+ or the negative d_1^- deviation variable becomes 0. Additionally, the coefficient $(E_s - E_0)$ is used for normalizing each goal.

    Goal: minimize d_1^- .
    Subject to:

$$E_s > E_0 \tag{7.5}$$

$$E \geq E_0 \tag{7.6}$$

$$E + (E_s - E_0)(d_1^- - d_1^+) = E_s \tag{7.7}$$

2. The second goal is to minimize the total recycling cost, C.

    The total recycling cost, C, is equal to or lower than the tolerable total recycling cost, C_0. It tries to achieve the sufficient total recycling cost, C_s, by minimizing the positive deviation variable from the sufficient total recycling cost, d_2^+ . In contrast to the total CO_2 saving rate, the sufficient total recycling cost, C_s, is determined to be lower than the tolerable total recycling cost, C_0, as shown in Equation 7.8, because the total recycling cost is minimized. The total recycling cost, C, is equal to or lower than the tolerable total recycling cost, C_0, as shown in Equation 7.9. Similarly to Equation 7.7, the positive and negative deviation variables d_2^+ and d_2^- and the coefficient $(R_s - R_0)$ are determined in Equation 7.10. The total recycling cost, C, approaches the sufficient total recycling cost, C_s, by minimizing d_2^+.

Goal: minimize d_2^+.

Subject to:

$$C_s < C_0 \tag{7.8}$$

$$C \leq C_0 \tag{7.9}$$

$$C + (C_0 - C_s)(d_2^- - d_2^+) = C_s \tag{7.10}$$

To solve the environmentally friendly and economical disassembly parts selection, the aggregate objective function is determined as Equation 7.11. The aggregate objective function minimizes not only the average of d_1^- and d_2^+ but also the maximum deviation value, d, simultaneously to improve the worst criterion value. The parameter β in Equation 7.11 is a parameter to weight the average and maximum of the deviation variables d. The recommended setting of the parameter β is 0.5 (Kinoshita et al., 2016). Equations 7.12 and 7.13 ensure that the value of the maximum deviation variable d becomes the same as the value of either d_1^- or d_2^+, whichever is the greater.

$$\beta \frac{d_1^- + d_2^+}{2} + (1 - \beta)d \rightarrow \text{Minimize} \tag{7.11}$$

$$d \geq d_1^- \tag{7.12}$$

$$d \geq d_2^+ \tag{7.13}$$

$$d_1^+, d_1^-, d_2^+, d_2^- \geq 0 \tag{7.14}$$

$$0.0 \leq \beta \leq 1.0 \tag{7.15}$$

In the case of a bi-objective for maximizing the total recycling rate, R, and minimizing the total recycling cost, C, the environmental objective function, as shown in Equation 7.1, is switched to Equation 7.16. The r_j in Equation 7.16 denotes the recycling rate at part j. Moreover, it is necessary to set an approximate sufficient and tolerable total recycling rate in Equations 7.5 through 7.7.

$$R = \sum_{j}^{N} r_j x_j \rightarrow \text{Max} \qquad (7.16)$$

7.4 Numerical Example

This section considers a cell phone (Kinoshita et al., 2016; Igarashi, Yamada and Inoue 2014a) as a case study in the context of environmentally friendly and economical disassembly parts selection. The cell phone consists of 12 original parts, as shown in Table 7.2. If all these parts are disassembled for recycling, the CO_2 saving and recycling rates and overall cost are 100% (=E_{max}), 80.14% (=R_{max}), and 89.40, respectively. The disassembly precedence relationships with CO_2 saving and recycling rates and costs are shown in Figure 7.1.

7.4.1 Example of Problem and Parameter Setting

To seek Pareto optimal solutions using goal programming, target ranges for each criterion are required by setting sufficient and tolerable levels. By changing the target ranges, other alternative solutions can be found. According to Kinoshita et al. (2016) and Kinoshita et al. (2018), the target range of the environmental objective functions is changed, although one of the total recycling costs is fixed. A total of four patterns of target ranges are enough to obtain Pareto optimal solutions in this case. Thus, the tolerable and sufficient total recycling cost are determined as the sum of the negative recycling cost ($C_0 = 115.05$) and the sum of the positive profit ($C_s = -38.78$) for the cell phone. With regard to CO_2 saving and recycling rates, 10 different target ranges are determined, based on feasible and maximum total CO_2 saving/recycling rates, as shown in Table 7.3. For instance, to implement a Pattern 3 "division into three areas", one of the tolerable total CO_2 saving rates is set as $E_0 = 33\%$, while the sufficient one is set as $E_s = 66\%$.

By using the mathematical programming package, Numerical Optimizer (NTT DATA Mathematical Systems Inc.), all numerical experiments are performed by the same desktop computer with the following specifications: Windows 7 with Intel(R) Core(TM) I7-2600 CPU@3.40 GHz.

7.4.2 Results of Two Different Types of Bi-Objective Disassembly Parts Selection in the Case of the Cell Phone

This section discusses and compares the selected parts in two different bi-objective disassembly parts selections to examine whether the total recycling cost shows a different trend as the total CO_2 saving or recycling rate increases. Two different types of bi-objective disassembly parts selection

TABLE 7.3

Tolerable and Sufficient CO_2 Saving/Recycling Rates for Each Target Range

Patterns	All Ranges	Division into Two Areas		Division into Three Areas			Division into Four Areas			
Target Ranges (%)	0–100	0–50	50–100	0–33	33–66	66–100	0–25	25–50	50–75	75–100
Tolerable total CO_2 saving rate E_0 (%)	0.00	0.00	50.00	0.00	33.00	66.00	0.00	25.00	50.00	75.00
Sufficient total CO_2 saving rate E_s (%)	100.00	50.00	100.00	33.00	66.00	100.00	25.00	50.00	75.00	100.00
Tolerable total recycling rate R_0 (%)	0.00	0.00	40.07	0.00	26.45	52.89	0.00	20.04	40.07	60.11
Sufficient total recycling rate R_s (%)	80.14	40.07	80.14	26.45	52.89	80.14	20.04	40.07	60.11	80.14

using goal programming are prepared for the cell phone: 1) recycling rate and cost, and 2) CO_2 saving rate and recycling cost.

Table 7.4 shows the results of environmentally friendly and economical disassembly parts selection in a disassembly BOM in the case of a cell phone. "X" in Table 7.4 denotes the parts selected for recycling by two different types of bi-objective disassembly parts selection. These selected parts are disassembled manually for recycling; then, the CO_2 saving and recycling rates and costs can be increased, while other non-marked parts are crushed without cost.

7.4.2.1 Results of Combinations of the Selected Parts for Disassembly

As shown in Table 7.4, it can be observed that three different solutions, containing different combinations of selected parts with different recycling rates and costs, are obtained in the bi-objective for recycling rate and cost. In contrast, although the target ranges differ, only one solution is obtained in the bi-objective for CO_2 saving rate and cost.

By focusing on the selected parts, it can be seen that Parts #1 (battery cover), #2 (battery), #3 (back case), and #4 (board) are always selected for all solutions of the bi-objectives, as shown in Table 7.4. One of the reasons why Part #4 (board) is selected is that it consists of the circuit board and has the lowest recycling costs: −38.78. The other three parts (#1 [battery cover], #2 [battery], and #3 [back case]) are disassembly preceding parts of Part #4 (board), as shown in Figure 7.1; thus, they must be disassembled to remove Part #4 (board). The negative value of the recycling costs means that recycling revenue is earned when the recycled materials within parts are all sold. Part #4 (board) is the only part among all parts to obtain recycling sales revenue. It is difficult to earn a positive profit for the other parts, because their disassembly costs are higher than their recycling sales revenue. It is found that the total recycling cost for all solutions becomes lower than 15 by selecting Part #4 (board).

7.4.2.2 Comparison of Bi-Objectives for CO_2 Saving Rate and Recycling Cost versus Recycling Rate and Cost

To examine whether the total recycling cost shows a different trend as the CO_2 saving or recycling rate increases, the behaviors of the total recycling cost for the CO_2 saving rate and the total recycling rate are shown in Figure 7.3a and 7.3b, respectively, for the bi-objective disassembly parts selections. The total CO_2 saving rate in the bi-objective for recycling rates and costs is estimated by adding the CO_2 saving rate for each selected part based on the disassembly BOM, as shown in Table 7.2. Similarly to the estimation method for the total CO_2 saving rate, the total recycling rate in the bi-objective for the CO_2 saving rates and costs is also estimated. Thus, four different types of solutions are plotted, as shown in Figure 7.3a and 7.3b.

When the behaviors of the total recycling cost of the CO_2 saving and recycling rates are compared, the same trends are observed. This means that the

TABLE 7.4

Results of Environmentally Friendly and Economical Disassembly Parts Selection in a Disassembly BOM: Case of a Cell Phone

No.	Part Name	CO_2 saving Rate e_j (%)	Recycling Rate r_j (%)	Recycling Costs c_j	1) All ranges 0–100%	2) Division into two areas 0–50%	50–100%	3) Division into three areas 0–33%	33–66%	66–100%	4) Division into four areas 0–25%	25–50%	50–75%	75–100%
1	Battery cover	0.65	0.49	3.94	X	X	X	X	X	X	X	X	X	X
2	Battery	7.21	8.57	5.28	X	X	X	X	X	X	X	X	X	X
3	Back case	0.65	0.49	36.51	X	X	X	X	X	X	X	X	X	X
4	Board	7.98	42.07	−38.78	X	X	X	X	X	X	X	X	X	X
5	Microphone	0.82	0.25	3.94										
6	Camera	1.68	2.61	3.90						X				X
7	Main button	0.65	0.49	3.94										
8	Number buttons	0.65	0.49	9.60										
9	Junction	78.08	23.40	3.56	X		X			X			X	X
10	Front case	0.65	0.49	36.51										
11	LCD	0.00	0.49	3.93										
12	Speaker	0.99	0.30	3.94										
	Total CO_2 saving rate				94.56	16.48	94.56	16.48	16.48	96.24	16.48	16.48	94.56	96.24
	Total recycling rate				75.02	51.62	75.02	51.62	51.62	77.63	51.62	51.62	75.02	77.63
	Total recycling cost				10.51	6.95	10.51	6.95	6.95	14.41	6.95	6.95	10.51	14.41

Bi-objective for recycling rate and cost — Pattern — Target Ranges

TABLE 7.4 (CONTINUED)

Results of Environmentally Friendly and Economical Disassembly Parts Selection in a Disassembly BOM: Case of a Cell Phone

No.	Part Name	CO_2 saving Rate e_j (%)	Recycling Rate r_j (%)	Recycling Costs c_j	1) All ranges 0–100%	2) Division into two areas 0–50%	50–100%	3) Division into three areas 0–33%	33–66%	66–100%	4) Division into four areas 0–25%	25–50%	50–75%	75–100%
1	Battery cover	0.65	0.49	3.94	X	X	X	X	X	X	X	X	X	X
2	Battery	7.21	8.57	5.28	X	X	X	X	X	X	X	X	X	X
3	Back case	0.65	0.49	36.51	X	X	X	X	X	X	X	X	X	X
4	Board	7.98	42.07	-38.78	X	X	X	X	X	X	X	X	X	X
5	Microphone	0.82	0.25	3.94										
6	Camera	1.68	2.61	3.90										
7	Main button	0.65	0.49	3.94										
8	Number buttons	0.65	0.49	9.60										
9	Junction	78.08	23.40	3.56	X	X	X	X	X	X	X	X	X	X
10	Front case	0.65	0.49	36.51										
11	LCD	0.00	0.49	3.93										
12	Speaker	0.99	0.30	3.94										
	Total CO_2 saving rate				94.56	94.56	94.56	94.56	94.56	94.56	94.56	94.56	94.56	94.56
	Total recycling rate				75.02	75.02	75.02	75.02	75.02	75.02	75.02	75.02	75.02	75.02
	Total recycling cost				10.51	10.51	10.51	10.51	10.51	10.51	10.51	10.51	10.51	10.51

Pattern — Bi-objective for Saving CO_2 Rate vs. Cost

total recycling cost generally increases as the CO_2 saving and recycling rates are increased. However, there is a different trend for the ranges between the highest/lowest total recycling and CO_2 saving rates. It is observed that the total recycling rates in all four solutions are plotted from 51.62% to 77.63%, while the total CO_2 saving rates in all four solutions are plotted from 16.48% to 94.56%. Thus, the plotted range of the total CO_2 saving rate becomes wider than that of the total recycling rate. It seems that there is a certain part with a much higher CO_2 saving rate, such as Part #9 (junction), and it is not always selected for disassembly in the bi-objective for recycling rate and cost.

7.4.2.3 Key Parts for Each Bi-Objective Disassembly Parts Selection

This section identifies a reason why the plotted range of the total CO_2 saving rate becomes wider than that of the total recycling rate by focusing on the selected parts with each bi-objective. This situation would be caused by key parts, which are defined as parts with higher CO_2 saving or recycling rates but lower recycling cost, in the two bi-objective disassembly parts selection. The key parts can have large impact on decision of the combination for disassembly. In terms of the CO_2 saving rate and recycling costs, Parts #4 (board) and #9 (junction) are considered as key parts, since they have the lowest recycling costs and highest CO_2 saving rate, −38.78 and 78.08%, respectively, of all parts. The recycling costs and CO_2 saving rate for Parts #4 and #9 comprise 25% and 78%, respectively, of those of the whole product. That is, the total recycling cost is decreased by 25%, while the total CO_2 saving rate is increased by 78%, if the two key parts are selected simultaneously. Thus, the two key parts are prioritized to be selected for disassembly in the bi-objective for CO_2 saving rate and recycling cost. By selecting only the two key parts simultaneously, the total CO_2 saving, E, and total recycling cost, C, can achieve the both sufficient levels simultaneously. Therefore, even though ten different target ranges are set through four patterns, there is only one combination for disassembly including the two key parts. Then, the total CO_2 saving rate reaches 94.56% with an affordable

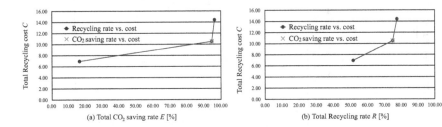

FIGURE 7.3
(a) Behaviors of the recycling cost for the CO_2 saving rate: a case of bi-objective optimization by goal programming. (b) Behaviors of the recycling cost for the recycling rate: a case of bi-objective optimization by goal programming.

recycling cost, 10.51, which is 86% lower than in the case when all parts are disassembled.

Similarly, to the case of the bi-objective for CO_2 saving rate and recycling cost, Parts #4 (board) and #9 (junction) are also the key parts in the bi-objective for recycling rate and costs, since they have the first and second highest recycling rate, respectively, among all parts. In contrast to the bi-objective for CO_2 saving rate and recycling cost, there is a priority for part selection between the two key parts in the bi-objective for recycling rate and cost. The reason is that Part #4 (board) has a recycling cost more than 11 times lower than that of Part #9 (junction). Thus, Part #4 should be prioritized for disassembly in terms of the recycling rate and costs, and then, Part #9 (junction) should be disassembled to achieve a much higher total recycling rate. On the other hand, Part #9 (junction) also accounts for 78.08% of the CO_2 saving rate in the whole product. Even though there is a higher priority for disassembly between the key parts #4 (board) and #9 (junction) in the bi-objective for recycling rate and cost, Part #9 (junction) is always selected for disassembly in the bi-objective for CO_2 saving rate and costs.

From the discussion about the case study, there are two main findings. The first finding is that the cell phone has the same two key parts in both bi-objectives for the CO_2 saving rate and recycling cost and for recycling rate and costs. The second is that there is a different priority for the selected parts between the two key parts in the two different bi-objectives. Therefore, it is desirable to locate the key parts separately from other parts in the product design phase so that they can be removed without preceding parts for disassembly.

7.5 Conclusions and Future Research

This chapter presented environmentally friendly and economical disassembly parts selection by goal programming, which determined the combination of selected parts for disassembly to achieve higher CO_2 saving or recycling rates with an affordable recycling cost. As illustrated by the case study, higher total CO_2 saving or recycling rates could be achieved with the affordable total recycling cost by selecting key parts. There was a trade-off relationship between environmental loads and cost reduction for material recycling. Therefore, it was demonstrated that environmentally friendly and economical disassembly parts selection could obtain satisficing solutions using goal programming.

Future studies should expand the proposed bi-objective disassembly parts selection to a multi-objective method, including CO_2 saving and recycling rates and cost, and adapt to the demand for recycled and virgin material for remanufacturing by prioritizing the parts for disassembly, such as in a disassembly-to-order system (Lambert and Gupta, 2005).

Acknowledgments

The authors would like to thank Mr. Seiichi Fujita and Hitachi Ltd. for providing the REM software and Prof. Norihiro Itsubo at Tokyo City University for providing the LCI database.

References

Agrawal, S. and Tiwari, M.K. (2008), A Collaborative Ant Colony Algorithm to Stochastic Mixed-model U-shaped Disassembly Line Balancing and Sequencing Problem, *International Journal of Production Research*, Vol.46, No.6, pp.1405–1429.

Dassault Systèmes SolidWorks Corp, www.solidworks.com/ (accessed on August 27, 2018).

Eskandarpour, M., Dejax, P., Miemczyk, J. and Péton, O. (2015), Sustainable Supply Chain Network Design: An Optimization-Oriented Review, *Omega*, Vol.54, pp.11–32.

Fushimi, T., Fukukawa, T. and Yamaguchi, T. (1987), *Goal Programming for Management: Concept and Applications*, Morikita Publishing Co., Ltd., Tokyo, Japan (in Japanese).

Gupta, S.M. and Ilgin, M.A. (2018), *Multiple Criteria Decision Making Application in Environmentally Conscious Manufacturing and Product Recovery*, CRC Press, Boca Raton, FL, ISBN: 978-1-4987-0065-8.

Hillier, F.S. and Lieberman, G.J. (2005), *Introduction to Operations Research 8th edition*, McGraw Hill Higher Education, New York, NY, ISBN: 0-07-252744-7.

Hiroshige, Y., Nishi, T. and Ohashi, T. (2002), Recyclability evaluation method, *Proceedings of the ASME 2002 International Mechanical Engineering Congress and Exposition*, p.835, New Orleans, LA, November.

Hitachi, Ltd., EcoAssist, www.ecoassist.com/HTML_n/option/rem/rem_tr/pp frame.htm (accessed on August 26, 2018) (in Japanese).

Igarashi, K., Yamada, T., Gupta, S.M., Inoue, M. and Itsubo N. (2016), Disassembly System Modeling and Design with Parts Selection for Cost, Recycling and CO_2 Saving Rates using Multi Criteria Optimization, *Journal of Manufacturing Systems*, Vol.38, pp.151–164.

Igarashi, K., Yamada, T. and Inoue, M. (2014a), 2-stage Optimal Design and Analysis for Disassembly System with Environmental and Economic Parts Selection using the Recyclability Evaluation Method, *International Journal of Industrial Engineering and Management Systems*, Vol.13, No.1, pp.52–66.

Igarashi, K., Yamada, T., Itsubo N. and Inoue, M. (2014b), Optimal Disassembly System Design with Environmental and Economic Parts Selection for CO_2 Saving Rate and Recycling Cost, *International Journal of Supply Chain Management*, Vol.3, No.3, pp.159–171.

Ilgin, M.A. and Gupta, S.M. (2010), Environmentally Conscious Manufacturing and Product Recovery (ECMPRO): A Review of the State of the Art, *Journal of Environmental Management*, Vol.91, No.3, pp.563–591.

Institute of Industrial and Systems Engineers, Terminology, www.iise.org/Details. aspx?id=2402 (accessed on August 26, 2018).

IPCC (2014), Fifth Assessment Report of Climate Change, Synthesis Report, www. ipcc.ch/report/ar5/syr/ (accessed on August 26, 2018).

Itsubo Laboratory, Life Cycle Inventory Database, www.yc.tcu.ac.jp/~itsubo-lab/ (accessed on August 26, 2018) (in Japanese).

Kinoshita, Y., Yamada, T., Gupta, S.M., Ishigaki, A. and Inoue M. (2016), Disassembly Parts Selection and Analysis for Recycling Rate and Cost by Goal Programming, *Journal of Advanced Mechanical Design, Systems, and Manufacturing*, Vol.10, No.3, DOI:10.1299/jamdsm.2016jamdsm0052.

Kinoshita, Y., Yamada, T., Gupta, S.M., Ishigaki, A. and Inoue M. (2018), Analysis of Cost Effectiveness by Material Type for CO_2 Saving and Recycling Rates in Disassembly Parts Selection using Goal Programming, *Journal of Advanced Mechanical Design, Systems, and Manufacturing*, Vol.12, No.3, DOI:10.1299/jamdsm.2018jamdsm0080.

Lambert, A.J.D.F. and Gupta, S.M. (2005), *Disassembly Modeling for Assembly, Maintenance, Reuse, and Recycling*, CRC Press, Boca Raton, FL.

McGovern, S.M. and Gupta, S.M. (2011), *The Disassembly Line: Balancing and Modeling*, McGraw Hill, New York, NY, ISBN: 978-0-07-162287-5.

Messac, A. (2015), *Optimization in Practice with MATLAB® for Engineering Students and Professionals*, Cambridge University Press, New York, ISBN: 978-1-107-10918-6.

Nasr, N. (2017), Redefining Manufacturing for a Modern Economy, *Industrial and System Engineering at Work*, Vol.49, No.3, p.24.

Nof, S.Y., Wilhelm, W.E. and Warnecke, H. (1997), *Industrial Assembly*, Chapman & Hall, London, ISBN: 0-412-55770-3.

NTT DATA Mathematical Systems Inc., Numerical Optimizer Brand New Package of Mathematical Programming, www.msi.co.jp/english/index.html (accessed on August 26, 2018).

Opaltić, M., Kljajin, M. and Vučković, K. (2010), Disassembly Layout in WEEE Recycling Process, *Strojarstvo*, Vol.52, No.1, pp.51–58.

Özceylan, E., Kalayci, C.B., Güngör, A. and Gupta, S.M. (2018), Disassembly Line Balancing Problem: A Review of the State of the Art and Future Directions, *International Journal of Production Research*, DOI:10.1080/00207543.2018.1428775

Rebitzer, G., Ekvall, T., Frischknecht, R., Hunkeler, D., Norris G., Rydberg, T., Schmidt, W.-P., Suh, S., Weidema, B.P. and Pennington, D.W. (2004), Life Cycle Assessment Part 1: Framework, Goal and Scope Definition, Inventory Analysis, and Applications, *Environment International*, Vol.30, No.5, pp.701–720.

Sugiyama, H., Fukushima, Y., Hirao, M., Hellweg, S. and Hungerbühler, K. (2005), Using Standard Statistics to Consider Uncertainty in Industry-Based Life Cycle Inventory Databases, *International Journal of Life Cycle Assessment*, Vol.10, No.6, pp.399–405.

United Nations Framework Conversation on Climate Change, The Paris Agreement, http://bigpicture.unfccc.int/#content-the-paris-agreemen (accessed on August 26, 2018).

Urata, T., Yamada, T., Itsubo, N. and Inoue, M. (2017), Global Supply Chain Network Design and Asian Analysis with Material-based Carbon Emissions and Tax, *Computers and Industrial Engineering*, Vol.113, pp.779–792.

Yamada, T. (2008), Design Issues for Inverse Manufacturing Systems in Japanese Cases, *Northeast Decision Science Institute 2008 Annual Meeting*, Brooklyn, NY, USA, CDROM, pp.551–556.

Yamada, T. (2012), Design of Closed-loop and Low-carbon Supply Chains for Sustainability, In Takakuwa, S., Son, N.H. and Minh, N.D. (Eds), *Manufacturing and Environmental Management*, National Political Publishing House, Hanoi, Vietnam, pp. 211–221, ISBN: 978-604-57-0000-6.

Yoshizaki, Y., Yamada, T., Itsubo, N. and Inoue M. (2014), Material Based Low-carbon and Economic Supplier Selection with Estimation of CO_2 Emissions and Cost using Life Cycle Inventory Database, *Innovation and Supply Chain Management*, Vol.66, No.4, pp.159–170.

8

Modelling Uncertainty in Remanufacturing

Aybek Korugan

CONTENTS

8.1 Introduction

The remanufacturing process comprises all activities that bring used products, subassemblies, and parts back to a reusable condition in which they continue to fulfill their function. These processes have initially been used to maintain very expensive machinery and systems such as those in the aviation industry and the military (Guide and Srivastava, 1997). In recent decades, remanufacturing practices have also been adopted for consumer goods in an attempt to reduce the environmental impact of mass consumption on natural resources and to minimize the generation of waste. Furthermore, many players embark on the remanufacturing business for its profitability, since the total effort required to overhaul a returned product is significantly less than that of manufacturing a new product. As larger systems and multiple ownerships enter the equation, the remanufacturing processes encounter higher levels of uncertainty in both demand and supply operations.

Remanufacturing activities present a new and unique set of problems for the design and control of production systems. From collecting and inspecting products that have reached the end of their useful lives (cores) to disassembly, reprocessing, and resale activities, many challenges arise. Yet, the profitability of this business attracts independent companies as well as original equipment manufacturers (OEMs). When OEMs remanufacture their own products, they become a hybrid manufacturing (HM) system with an extra set of management issues arising from shared resources and demand base. Thus, we can consider HM to the most general form of production activities in the literature so far and explain the uniqueness of all other forms of production layouts as a modification of HM systems. Figure 8.1 graphically demonstrates the general phases and material flow of HM. HM is in its most complex form when both remanufacturing and new product manufacturing activities are conducted under the same roof. Yet, OEMs may prefer to use dedicated facilities for remanufacturing. Let us term such a facility an *original equipment remanufacturer* (OER). The material flow and layout of OERs are designed around remanufacturing activities only. Along with the disassembly process, they have a machine park and an assembly process dedicated to processing cores. However, they predominantly reprocess their own products. As the remanufacturing business is lucrative, independent remanufactures also collect and

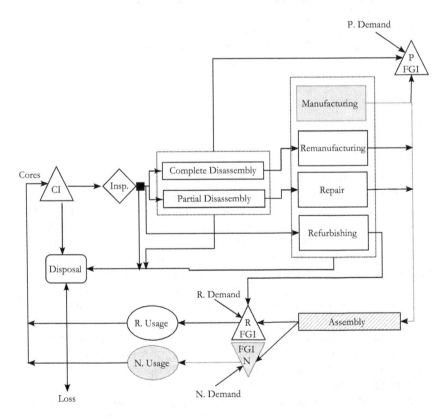

FIGURE 8.1
HM system.

process cores. Independent remanufacturing (IR) facilities have the same general layout as OERs. They receive cores from customers, disassemble them, and reprocess them using dedicated resources. Yet, IRs are subject to more uncertainties due to lack of information. They usually concentrate on a product group and collect various brands. Depending on their contract with the OEMs of these products, they may or may not have access to product specifications and assembly/disassembly and machining information. On the other hand, OERs have all this information for the product types they are working on. Furthermore, they can supply spare parts for remanufacturing more easily.

The complexities of remanufacturing activities are listed by Guide (2000) as the uncertain timing and quantity of returns, the need to balance returns with demands, the disassembly of returned products, the uncertainty in materials recovered from returned items, the requirement for a reverse logistics network, the complication of material matching restrictions, the problems of stochastic routings for materials for remanufacturing operations, and highly variable processing times. Six of these characteristics directly affect the throughput of a remanufacturing facility. Therefore, any facility design or production plan has to consider the level and structure of the uncertainty these complexities introduce to the system. A traditional manufacturing system also encounters uncertainties due to synchronization and routing issues faced during production as well as the demand processes. These uncertainties are amplified significantly in remanufacturing, since here also, the supply timing and quality are stochastic, the condition of cores can complicate disassembly efforts, extracted parts require nonstandard machining and reprocessing efforts in both processing time and number of jobs, the varying quality of recovered parts can add extra stress to machines and tools, and reassembly efforts may be slowed down by specific requirements. Thus, when these characteristics are not properly embedded into models that design remanufacturing systems, the resulting processes will have lower throughput rates and higher variance.

The essential objective of a production system is to meet the demand in a timely and accurate way. To this end, its throughput function has to be understood well. Since remanufacturing systems face uncertain core return processes as well as random demands, they pose a more challenging problem than traditional production systems. In this chapter, our aim is to classify the nature of the uncertainties that arise in the remanufacturing process and to discuss relevant methods for developing better design and control methods at an operational level. In the next section, we will consider the differences and similarities of remanufacturing systems with respect to the level of uncertainties they are exposed to. In Section 3, we will consider the structure of a remanufacturing facility in terms of material and information flows. In Section 4, we will further analyze the remanufacturing function and discuss relevant research. Then, in the final section, we will point out the achievements and shortcomings of the work done so far and consider further research ideas. As the reverse supply chain problem is vast, we will limit ourselves to studying remanufacturing systems and will not extend our scope to include the design of reverse logistics systems.

8.2 Uncertainty-Based Classification of Remanufacturing Systems

Figure 8.1 depicts the major operations of an HM system. HM defines the most general form of a production structure in terms of information and material flow. The material flow starts with the OEM manufacturing and selling new products. After a random time of use, cores are collected for remanufacturing with a probability $r < 1$, since some portion of the cores may have been sold to the second-hand market, disposed of, or simply not returned by the consumer. Collected cores are placed in the core inventory (CI) or are discarded based on an admittance policy. Admitted products are inspected and routed to be refurbished, repaired, or remanufactured according to their condition. Refurbishing products does not require any disassembly, while repair requires partial disassembly, and remanufacturing is conducted after the core is completely disassembled. During disassembly, parts and subassemblies are reassessed and routed to the machine park of the production system based on their individual machining needs. Repair, remanufacturing, manufacturing, and refurbishing activities use the same machine park. When the reprocessing of used parts is completed, or new parts are manufactured, they are sent either to the product assembly process or to the spare parts inventory (PFGI). Assembled products are kept in different inventories for new (NFGI) and remanufactured (RFGI) finished goods. When a demand for a product class arises, it is fulfilled from its respective inventory.

In a traditional production system, information flow starts with the demand occurrence. All decisions are aimed at successfully satisfying the demand. While a remanufacturing system has the same objective, the core arrivals start an independent information flow, since they have the potential of satisfying the demand with minimal effort. Therefore, the information about the arrival and condition of the core influences the decisions on new product manufacturing and used product remanufacturing. The return rate of cores is based on the number of products in use, average time of use, and return probability r. When a core arrives, the information on its condition further affects disassembly, remanufacturing, and reassembly decisions as well as the new component production decisions for HR and OEM systems. A remanufacturing facility has to be designed to accommodate the uncertainties carried by the information related to cores. Therefore, remanufacturing systems make an extra effort to collect information about core return rates and conditions. Here, HM and OER systems have the advantage of knowing the sales figures, average usage time, and reliability of the components of the products that are sold by their system.

When new product manufacturing and remanufacturing activities are separated, an OER process is obtained. Here, although production resources are different, all new and remanufactured products sold by the system will eventually feed the return rate of OER. Also, depending on the policies, new parts and/or new products can be used to satisfy the remanufacturing part and product demand. Therefore, the state of remanufacturing affects the new product manufacturing decisions of the OEM. When new product manufacturing is eliminated, we obtain the model of an IR that receives return flows from the market. IRs concentrate on specific product types and collect products of different brands. Therefore, even though product types are the same brand, specific disassembly and reprocessing requirements generate more product classes and setups. Also requesting new spare parts from OEMs may not be as seamless as it is for OERs.

There are two types of systems that receive their products with a return probability $r=1$. The first type is a maintenance and repair system that is only capable of repairing and remanufacturing cores. Such a system receives a broken component and replaces it with a working one from the inventory immediately to bring the equipment that is down back to operation as soon as possible. Then, it repairs the broken component to replenish the inventory. The system is not a competitor but a customer of the OEM. Therefore, the information for component repair and equipment maintenance is accessible. Also, despite the uncertainty in the timing and severity of failures, the number and condition of components and the amount of usage are monitored by the system. Therefore, the failure occurrences and severities are easier to predict. Since such systems have been studied in the literature quite extensively (Wang, 2002; Guide and Srivastava, 1997), we do not include a more detailed discussion about them in this chapter.

OEMs that lease their products or provide a service using their products comprise the second type of systems with deterministic return processes. This type of business structure is called *servicizing* (Rothenberg, 2007). Here, the OEM retains the ownership of the product and either leases the functionality of the product to a user or provides a service that includes using its product. At the end of the contract term, the product is returned for remanufacturing. Many automotive companies lease their products for one term and then sell them as certified preowned vehicles after refurbishing them, while systems such as AB Electrolux (Electrolux, 1999), Caterpillar, Xerox, IBM, and Bombardier (Rothenberg, 2007; Örsdemir, et al., 2017) offer the functionality of their products as part of a service to users. All of these systems receive cores at the end of a deterministic contract term and use them again after remanufacturing. In both cases, the return process carries less uncertainty regarding the condition of the core and almost no uncertainty about the timing and quantity of returns.

The uncertainties and complexities of remanufacturing processes defined by Guide (2000) can be extended to include the challenges of using shared resources and the availability of information by distinguishing major types of remanufacturing environments. We can summarize the level of uncertainties for HM, OER, and IR systems in a qualitative manner, as given in Table 8.1. Here, we compare these systems by adding the ownership of the core, where, S stands for cores that are returns of products previously owned by customers, and O represents the products that are owned by the OEM or its distributors and are used for servicizing. Thus, HM-S and OER-S process cores returned by their previous owners while HM-O and OER-O receive cores at the end of lease terms.

As presented in Table 8.1, IR systems face higher uncertainty and complexity in almost all areas, since they do not have exclusive access to product specifications for the cores they receive. In addition, they cannot collect any information on how well the cores were maintained before being returned. This kind of information is also inaccessible for HM-S and OER-S systems unless an information collecting sensor is embedded in the product prior to sales (Ilgın and Gupta, 2011). On the other hand, depending on the terms of the service contract, HM-O and OER-O systems can monitor the condition of cores during their use by providing maintenance or enforcing usage constraints. Thus, among the types of cores, these carry the lowest amount of unknowns into the remanufacturing line. Also, their return times are known except for contract breaches or buyouts, e.g., automobile leasing. While HM-S and OER-S systems face the same kind of uncertainty as IR systems regarding quality of cores, they have more information on component reliability and the number of products in use. Therefore, they can make better predictions about the quality, quantity, and timing of core returns. HM-S, OER-S, and IR systems experience the same amount of uncertainty in demand flows, as the information can only be collected through traditional forecasting methods. However, HM-O and OER-O systems can improve these estimations by collecting data about customers that tend to buy new service at the end of their contracts.

The uncertainties in core disassembly and remanufacturing times, material recovery rates, and remanufacturing routing complexities are directly related

TABLE 8.1

Relative Levels of Uncertainty in Remanufacturing Systems

	HM-S	HM-O	OER-S	OER-O	IR
Core quality and quantity	Med	Low	Med	Low	High
Core timing	Med	None	Med	None	High
Demand	High	Med	High	Med	High
Disassembly times	Med	Low	Med	Low	High
Material recovery	Med	Low	Med	Low	High
Remanufacturing routing	Med	Low	Med	Low	High
Remanufacturing times	Med	Low	Med	Low	High
Setup quantity and times	High	Med	Med	Low	High
Machine sharing	High	Med	Med	Low	Med
Machine breakdowns	Med	Low	Med	Low	High

to the condition of cores. Thus, they are the lowest for HM-O and OER-O systems, higher for HM-S and OER-S systems, and the highest for IR systems. The quantity and duration of setups are related to the number of product classes and priority policies. Here, S based systems will encounter higher uncertainty then O based systems, since they experience higher uncertainty in core quality and quantity, while HM systems will have more classes and lower priority for remanufacturing than OER systems, since they are primarily occupied with new product manufacturing. IR systems will always have the highest uncertainty in setups, as they process multiple brands and versions of the same product type with the lowest amount of information among all systems in question. On the other hand, the complexities arising from machine sharing are the highest with HM-S systems, as OER and IR systems have dedicated resources for remanufacturing, and HM-O systems have fewer uncertainties for remanufacturing routing. Finally, the uncertainty in machine breakdowns is on a par with the uncertainty in core quality for all systems, since lower quality cores drive machines to tool and calibration failures more often.

8.3 Structure of Remanufacturing Systems

As depicted in Figure 8.1, a remanufacturing process consists of a disassembly, reprocessing, and reassembly process. Here, the disassembly process is the unique addition to production systems. Güngör and Gupta (2001) state that this process is not the inverse of an assembly process due to the uncertain and divergent nature of material and information flows, since a core is dismantled into its many subparts. While an assembly process combines all parts to supply the demand for one product, the disassembly process will extract components from one core to supply multiple demand sources. In many remanufacturing systems, the demand for disassembled components may come not only from the product to be reassembled but also from external requests for spare parts. Based on the comprehensive list of issues provided by Güngör and Gupta (2002), a disassembly process faces random operation times, random part yields in quality and quantity, random routings, including reworks due to stuck or missing parts in a core, and an imbalance in part demand due to spare part demands along with remanufacturing process demands. Furthermore, as some types of component defects are difficult to detect, final yield still carries some uncertainty. As the authors state, installing buffers between stations will enable the line to synchronize tasks.

IR systems encounter the highest level of uncertainties related to disassembly systems, as they have very little information about the state of cores and the product specifications. Furthermore, they usually process more than one brand and version of the same product type. Thus, they face multiple classes and steeper learning curves and setups. To discuss the effects of these uncertainties on the performance measures of an IR facility, consider an arbitrary disassembly line as given in Figure 8.2. Here, the IR system processes two types of cores, C_1 and C_2. A core C_i, $i = 1, 2$ is picked from CI and directed to its respective buffer in front of the first disassembly station (DS_1) after inspection. When the queue in front of the core is depleted, and DS_1 is working on type i, the core enters the station for the first disassembly task. After a random time, the part or parts are disassembled and placed in the part buffer P_jC_i. Then, the rest of the core is placed in its respective buffer for further disassembly by DS_2. When everything goes well, the parts are collected in part buffers, and the core reaches the end of the disassembly line sequentially. However, starting from the first buffer, the process can face many problems. If DS_1 processes type i more slowly or prioritizes the other core type, the buffer for type i starts accumulating cores and increasing the work-in-process. Eventually, the buffer reaches its limit and cannot admit new cores sent by the inspection station. In this case, either the station stops and waits for the buffer to be reduced or it switches to the other core type. Yet, the system continues to receive C_is to the CI. Eventually, if this problem lasts long enough, either the CI will be filled predominantly with C_is or the system will start disposing of cores of type i, depending on how CI is shared by core types. A similar result will be observed for both cores when a disassembly station stops working. In that case, both core buffers swell to eventually block machines upstream of the station.

Another problem is encountered when either more or fewer parts than required are obtained from a component disassembly process. This case will cause uneven levels at P_jC_i buffers. If one P_jC_i buffer receives unevenly more parts and becomes full, then the next disassembly of a C_i will block the DS_j station until a demand removes parts from the buffer. The blocking of DS_j will eventually cause the upstream servers to block and the downstream servers to starve. Uneven demand arrivals will also cause the same problem. Finally, the complications arising from potential defects of a core may generate new disassembly sequences with reentrant lines and rework,

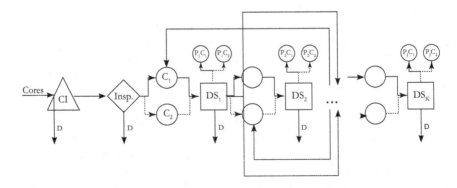

FIGURE 8.2
Disassembly in an IR system. C_i: Core type i, DS_k: Disassembly station k, P_jC_i: Part j of core i, D: Disposal $i = 1, 2; j = 1, 2, \ldots J; k = 1, 2, \ldots K$.

adding further delays to the cycle time of the disassembly process. HM-S and OER-S systems face the same problems as the IR system unless they can monitor the condition of a core with sensors or service contracts. Their only advantage is that they have the information about the original product structure, which will be useful in devising better disassembly sequences. However, HM-O and OER-O systems have the information about the condition of the core, since they have access to maintenance records. Therefore, most routings and disassembly tasks are known before a core is dismantled.

One advantage of IR and OER systems over HM systems is that they have a dedicated machine park for reprocessing disassembled components. However, as an IR system has to reprocess different brands with only experience based knowledge on machining tolerances and component design specifications, processing times and uncertainties are elevated. In Figure 8.3, we present a depiction of a remanufacturing process that works on parts and subassemblies stemming from two distinct types of cores sent from a disassembly process. Here, component P_1C_1 is routed either to machine M_1 or directly to M_3, depending on its condition. Thus, $(1 - q)$ proportion of all P_1C_1 components have to wait both for the processing time of M_1 and in the queue for $P_1C_{1,2}$. Component P_1C_2 is processed on machines M_2, M_3, and M_1 with probability r, while with $(1 - r)$, some components need a rework on M_2. The rework on M_2 generates two classes of the same component that compete for the service. Such sequences pose challenging problems for production line control and analysis. Another issue that further complicates the analysis is the reliability of machines. Random machine failures are common in production systems. In remanufacturing systems, the probability of machine failures increases due to the uncertain condition of the parts being processed. The unscheduled stops in production flow may result in throughput disruptions.

The reassembly of remanufactured parts follows a similar pattern as the assembly process of a new product, as given in Figure 8.4, since the majority

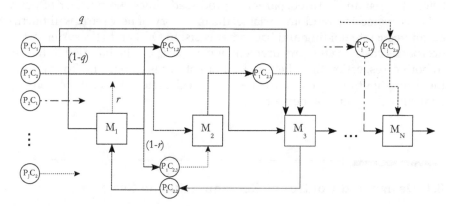

FIGURE 8.3
Remanufacturing in an IR/OER system. M_n: Machine n, $n = 1, 2, ...N$, $P_jC_{i,r}$: Queue for part j of core i after operation r, r, $s = 1, 2, ...R$.

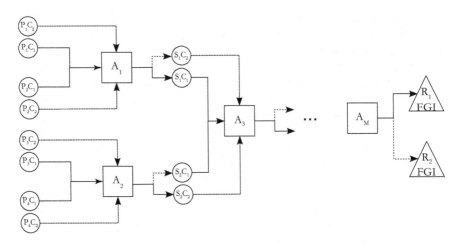

FIGURE 8.4

Reassembly in an IR/OER system. A_m: Assembly Station m, $m = 1, 2, ..., M$, $S_u C_i$: Subassembly u of core i, $u = 1, 2, ..., U$.

of quality and reliability related uncertainties are all but eliminated up to this point. However, cores sent to repair are randomly routed through stations, since they are partially disassembled based on the repair type they need. Also, the imbalance in the quantity of remanufactured parts ready for reassembly slows down the process, as starvations occur for some parts. Either the independent remanufacturer can remanufacture as many products as the minimum number of components and sell the remaining parts to the spare parts market, or it can order new parts to increase the number of remanufactured products. The lead time for new parts will always be longer than the remanufacturing time of these parts. To synchronize new and remanufactured parts in reassembly, the order for new parts has to be given before the remanufactured parts are processed. Since the number of parts to be recovered is a random variable, the inventory of new parts will fluctuate and generate holding and backorder costs. In OER and HM systems, the decision is easier, as the procurement of new parts can be handled in house. In both cases, estimating the required quantities is important. To this end, the throughput rates of all parts have to be calculated. This can be done by analyzing the queueing network.

8.4 Design and Control of Remanufacturing Systems

As in traditional production systems, the objective of remanufacturing systems is to satisfy the demand for remanufactured products in a timely manner while keeping costs at a minimum. In this quest, the extra challenge remanufacturing systems face is the uncertainty pertaining to core returns. Also, the addition of a disassembly line further complicates the design and control of these processes. In the modelling and analysis of these processes, two main approaches are commonly used for determining operational policies. The first and most commonly used approach is to balance the input of core returns with the procurement or manufacturing of new products to supply the demand by only considering CI and FGI levels, the procurement/ production rate, and the core return rate. Since these studies aim at controlling the input and output inventories, we group them as *inventory models*. The second approach aims at modelling the remanufacturing facility in more detail, as presented in the previous section. The uncertainties and delays in the remanufacturing facility are taken into account. The interaction between random events in disassembly and the rest of the process are studied. We group the studies using the second approach under *queueing network models*.

8.4.1 Inventory Models

One of the most important objectives of remanufacturing systems is to balance returns with demands. As cores replace raw materials in these systems, the challenge becomes to plan and control the system under uncertain demand and return flows. Starting with the earliest works on remanufacturing systems, many studies concentrate on balancing returns with demands using inventory control models. The major difference in these models arises from modelling the remanufacturing and procurement processes. One class of studies represents either one or both of these processes by lead times independently of order or production amounts so as to be able to consider fixed ordering costs in the cost function. We discuss them under *lead time models*. The second class of studies incorporates finite processing rates into the model and establishes a time–quantity relation between order amounts and production. These are the *capacitated inventory models*. Both types of model reduce a complex convolution of random variables that define remanufacturing processes to an aggregate rate or lead time value. While this assumption has the potential for generating inaccurate estimates, it enables researchers to build tractable models for studying various demand and return scenarios and the optimality of control mechanisms.

8.4.1.1 Lead Time Models

These models use lead times for the procurement or production of new products and the remanufacturing of cores. They assume that inventories are either periodically or continuously reviewed. The model structure enables fixed and variable costs to be incorporated. Initial models start with uncorrelated demand and return rates. However, they assume that return probability $r < 1$. Therefore, an outside procurement to satisfy the demand is always needed. In most models, the demand does not distinguish between new and remanufactured products. Yet, some models include distinct demands and product substitution. Such models are more useful for the analysis of HM systems. Further extensions generalize the return and demand processes to consider correlation among them. Here, we discuss some of the most significant models in the literature. A comprehensive review can be found in Akçalı and Çetinkaya (2011) and Ilgın and Gupta (2010).

One of the first models was proposed by Muckstadt and Isaac (1981). The model first considers a single-item single-echelon inventory system that receives independent stochastic demand and return rates. The demand is supplied either by returns or with new products. As the demand rate is higher than the return rate, the difference is procured at a constant lead-time. A continuous review (Q, r) policy is applied, and the optimal values are calculated under the return flows. The results obtained from the single-echelon model are then applied to a two-echelon model in which the upper echelon supplies the lower echelon retailers that satisfy the demand and receive returns.

van der Laan et al. (1996) consider a continuous review (s, Q) inventory control problem similar to Muckstadt and Isaac (1981). They assume that demands and returns follow independent Poisson processes, and any difference is procured externally following a fixed lead time. They initially consider a repair facility that processes all returns and model it as an $M/M/c$ or an M/G/queue that has the same output rate as the return rate. Then, to add the disposal option, they model the repair facility as an $M/M/c/c + N$ queue and propose an (s, Q, N) inventory control policy. Finally, they conduct a comparative study between inventory policies with and without disposal and show that disposal is a necessary action for cost minimization.

In (van der Laan and Salomon, 1997), the authors formulate general PUSH and PULL inventory control systems under a similar demand structure to that given by van der Laan et al. (1996), where in PUSH, as soon as the CI reaches a target level, it is processed and sent to FGI, while in PULL remanufacturing, it does not start before the FGI goes below a trigger level, s_R. Both new products and remanufactured products arrive following fixed and independent lead times. The initial model is analyzed using independent demand and return processes. Then, a correlation for demand and return distributions is added. The study indicates that the disposal option is essential for achieving maximum system efficiency, since it reduces variability. Also, they conclude that PULL strategies are superior only when CI has a significantly lower value than finished goods. In van der Laan et al. (1999), as an extension to the previous study, they numerically evaluate the effects of stochastic lead time duration and lead time variability on total expected costs and show that the manufacturing lead time duration has a higher impact on cost, while the remanufacturing lead time variability increases cost. Also, they state that the PULL control strategy almost always outperforms the PUSH control strategy under stochastic lead times.

Fleischmann et al. (2002) consider a basic (s, Q) continuous review inventory system with independent Poisson demands and returns. They represent the return process by modelling positive and negative demand occurrences. In the model, manufacturing lead time is deterministic, but remanufacturing lead time is neglected, order cost is fixed, and holding and backlogging costs are linear, but remanufacturing cost is neglected. They show that conventional (s, Q) policies remain optimal when introducing Poisson item return flows. For the same system, they propose an optimization algorithm to compute the control parameters for an order up to level (s, S) policy given in (Fleischmann and Kuik, 2003).

One of the earliest periodic inventory review models for systems with return flows is developed by Simpson (1978). In this paper, he studies a system where items arrive at a separate remanufacturing facility and can be either disposed of or held for some time before they are remanufactured, considering the tradeoff between material savings due to reuse and additional inventory carrying costs. Then, he proves the optimality of a three-parameter control policy to control order, repair, and disposal with independent demand and return rates but without fixed costs and lead times. Inderfurth (1997) shows that the policy is also optimal for non-stochastic and identical non-zero lead times modelling procurement and remanufacturing processes. A comparison of the lead times for the two processes shows that the deviation between two lead times is a critical factor for the level of complexity of the optimal policy, since different lead times increase the number of dimensions of the underlying Markov model.

Buchanan and Abad (1998) assume that returns are a stochastic fraction of the number of items in use for each period, and the usage time is exponentially distributed. They derive an optimal procurement policy based on the on-hand inventory and the number of items in use for a finite horizon. Kiesmüller and van der Laan (2001) also consider a correlation between returns and demands in a periodic review setting. Here, both demand and return flows follow a Poisson distribution, where returns depend on previous demands. All lead times are constant, and cores are either remanufactured or disposed of following a constant probability. The authors compare the case of dependent returns with the case of independent returns in a finite planning horizon and numerically show that the average cost is smaller when a dependence exists.

DeCroix et al. (2005) model negative demand occurrences in a multi-echelon series system that receives independent demands and returns. They show that a base stock echelon is still optimal for the infinite horizon problem. As an alternative to the echelon base stock policy, they also discuss a policy that uses only local information for a base stock policy. Also, they show that when upper echelons receive returns, their base stock level reduces to lower echelon values.

8.4.1.2 Capacitated Models

The major advantage of lead time models is to consider fixed order costs in the optimization. Yet, when we consider OER and HM systems, the procurement occurs in house. Therefore, a fixed order cost is usually not an issue, while the finite processing capacity cannot be disregarded. Most of the models consider a production rate and periodic review of inventory levels in their work. Therefore, queueing system based models are commonly used for these problems. However, in some cases, to analyze optimal operational policies and/or policy structures, some researchers also use stochastic dynamic programming based models with finite production capacities. While most models do not consider a distinction between remanufactured and new products, some consider independent demands and substitution among them. Such models are well suited for the analysis of HM systems.

One of the first models to consider returns and capacitated processing is presented by Heyman (1977). Here, a single-echelon continuous review inventory system is modelled using an $M/M/1/N$ queue, where returns are assumed to arrive following a Poisson process and demands occur one by one following an independent exponentially distributed time and are satisfied as long as there is a returned product in the queue. Returns are accepted in the system if the inventory of returns does not exceed N and are disposed of otherwise. The objective is to determine the optimal inventory level N that minimizes the total inventory cost using a push production control. The model includes a disposal option but does not consider the production and remanufacturing lead times. Korugan and Gupta (1998) expand this model to a two-echelon inventory system with independent Poisson return and demand processes, where returns are collected at the lower echelon and transferred to the upper echelon following an exponential delay. Then, they are remanufactured after another exponentially distributed time before being placed in the FGI. The FGI also receives new items from a source after an exponential time. The authors model this process as an open queueing network with finite buffers and calculate performance measures using the expansion methodology (Kerbache and Smith, 1987).

Yuan and Cheung (1998) consider an inventory control problem in the retail and rental business that experiences Poisson demand arrivals and exponentially distributed return interarrival times that are correlated with demands. Customers return the leased product with a probability less than one, as they may opt to keep the product. This system is a good example of HM-O and OER-O systems. The authors model this process using a queueing system that operates following an (s, S) control policy. All returns are accepted in the system, and any outside procurement occurs instantaneously. At the end of their use, items are either returned or kept by the customers with a fixed probability. The model is analyzed using matrix geometric methods, and an algorithm for optimizing replenishment parameters is proposed. In another study that considers demand and return correlations, Toktay et al. (2000) analyze an industry problem in the Kodak single use camera remanufacturing case. They construct a closed queueing network model that represents the closed loop supply chain for the product. Using this model, they study the effects of various system parameters such as informational structure, procurement delay, demand rate, and length of the product's life cycle.

Bayındır et al. (2003) consider a remanufacturing system that supplies a Poisson demand based on an $(S-1, S)$ continuous review inventory control policy. They model the system as a queueing network using M/G/queues that represent procurement lead time, preprocessing, product use, remanufacturing, and assembly processes. Then, they extend their model to include finite capacity production rates using $M/M/c$ queues. They show that under uncapacitated procurement systems, there is no need to remanufacture to reduce inventory related costs.

Remanufacturing becomes feasible only when all production processes have finite capacity and remanufacturing is quicker. In a second study, Bayındır et al. (2005) relax the "as good as new" assumption of remanufactured products for an HM system. They consider two customer classes and two product classes as new and remanufactured with a common capacity constraint. They model the system for an $(S-1, S)$ inventory control policy and downward product substitution, where a remanufactured demand may be satisfied by a new product. The main aim is to investigate the system conditions and find the level of use for the remanufacturing option that provides profit improvement.

Korugan and Gupta (2014) model an OER-S system that supplies the same demand and that does not differentiate between new and remanufactured products. They model remanufacturing and manufacturing processes with two separate exponential servers. The remanufacturing process receives returns, while manufacturing is assumed to always have raw material. All products are sent to the FGI. The authors propose a CONWIP control mechanism with adaptive kanbans that increase and decrease their numbers based on the inventory level, as proposed in (Gupta and Al-Turki, 1997).

Stochastic dynamic programming models are also used for the generation of operational policies. These policies provide good guidance and managerial insight. Gong and Chao (2013) construct a finite horizon stochastic dynamic programming model to analyze the optimal periodic review inventory policies of an HM system that has finite capacities for remanufacturing and manufacturing activities in each period. They show that when there is a remanufacturing capacity and a manufacturing capacity available, the optimal inventory control policies are to remanufacture either down to an optimal level of CI or to the maximum capacity of remanufacturing facility and manufacture new products up to an upper level of FGI.

Flapper et al. (2012) consider an HM system that remanufactures cores and manufactures new products. The return of cores is announced in advance and realized after an exponential time with a probability. Arriving cores are instantaneously remanufactured and placed in the FGI. Demand follows a Poisson process and does not distinguish between new and remanufactured products. They model a two-dimensional infinite horizon Markov decision process (MDP) that keeps track of the FGI level and the number of announced returns. Then, they show that the optimal production policy depends on the announced products, and the upto level reduces as the announced products increase for a fixed return probability. Zerhouni et al. (2013) relax the instantaneous procurement lead time assumption of Cheung and Yuan (2003) by considering capacitated production to analyze the impact of ignoring dependency between demands and returns. Yet, for the sake of tractability, they assume instantaneous lead times of product returns. Here, they show that when the dependency is ignored, the optimal production policy is still base stock. Yet, when the dependency is considered, the base stock level decreases with the information of potential returns. Korugan et al. (2017) generate a model to measure the impact of knowing the number of products in use. To this end, they construct an MDP model similar to that in (Zerhouni et al., 2013) and numerically compare the impact of fixed return rate estimates with knowing the load dependent return rate at time t. They show that when return probabilities are below 0.5, the impact of bad estimates and fixed base stock policies is low.

8.4.2 Queueing Network Models

The majority of the research aimed toward remanufacturing systems relies on estimating either a lead time or a throughput rate for the output of the system, as presented in the previous section. The motivation behind this approach comes from similar models constructed for traditional manufacturing systems. Although most of the uncertainty these systems face stems from demand processes, the lack of synchronization and unexpected stops in the system generate a throughput variance that cannot be dismissed (Tan, 1999). When additional uncertainties that define the characteristics of remanufacturing systems are considered, it is not difficult to conclude that the throughput variance will be quite large. Therefore, a more detailed model of the process will better explain the behavior of remanufacturing systems.

A successful design for a remanufacturing system should take into account the characteristics listed in Table 8.1 and the type of remanufacturing system that is studied. IRs encounter the highest level of uncertainties and number of product classes among all system types, while OER-O systems experience relatively fewer uncertainties and no resource sharing problems. Thus, when designing remanufacturing systems with dedicated resources, these two systems represent the two extremes. On the other hand, the most challenging problems in designing HM systems will be encountered in routing remanufacturing products through machining resources shared with new product manufacturing tasks. All of these problems will directly affect the throughput and yield of remanufacturing systems. Therefore, a design methodology has to consider workload dependent lead times, lead time fluctuations due to missing components, random routings of components, machine breakdowns, and quality issues.

Queueing networks have been useful in designing manufacturing systems, since they allow models to consider capacitated systems, stochastic relations, and material and information flow (Dallery and Gershwin, 1992). In these analyses, important performance measures (work in process [WIP] and inventory levels, service levels, and average cycle times) can be calculated under the uncertainty of demand and unexpected processing delays. Based on these measures, machine types and quantities and buffer levels that minimize system variance while reaching target performance levels can be determined. We can extend these analysis methods to model remanufacturing systems.

When queueing networks are used to model production systems, usually, the buffers are considered to be finite. When the buffer between two tandem machines is full, a job that is completed by the upstream machine is not discarded, but it forces the upstream machine to stop working. This phenomenon is called *blocking*. Similarly, when an upstream machine does not work for a long time while the downstream machine works, the intermediate buffer is emptied. Then, the downstream machine cannot work, as it is starved. These dependencies make the exact analysis of queueing networks complicated (Altıok, 1997). Even for a Markovian queueing system with 10 tandem machines and nine intermediate buffers, each with capacity of 10, we will have to solve for 10^9 equations to find the steady-state distribution. When machines also have up and down states, this value increases to $2^{10} \times 10^9$. Therefore, the analysis requires either an approximation or the help of simulation. The most common approximate analysis methods for these processes are decomposition (Gershwin, 1994), aggregation (Li and Meerkov, 2009), and expansion (Kerbache and Smith, 1987). For a detailed discussion of these methods and an introduction of alternative methods, we refer the reader to (Li et al., 2009).

The majority of queueing network and simulation models for remanufacturing systems are generated to study the disassembly process, as it uniquely defines the remanufacturing activity. The disassembly process encounters the majority of core related uncertainties, starting from disassembly sequences and core routings. The demand received by the process is imbalanced due to uncertain recovery probabilities of parts and external demand arrivals for spare parts. Even for a balanced line, the workflow is not always sequential, as some parts may skip stations due to severe failures and come back. Also, such failures combined with hazardous material can temporarily withhold a station from work. Thus, these stations experience random workflow, processing times, and failures as well as multiple job types.

Kızılkaya and Gupta (1998) look at a disassembly cell control problem where tandem disassembly workstations disassemble parts out of a core sequentially. Each workstation has one input buffer for cores waiting for disassembly and two output buffers, one for disassembled parts and one for the processed core. The demand is observed independently at each part buffer, causing the pull process to be triggered from multiple sources. The authors construct a kanban control mechanism with withdrawal kanbans that pull the core in the station, part kanbans that pull parts out of the station to meet the demand, and disassembled core kanbans that advance the core through the line. They also devise a control policy that increases and decreases the kanban sizes based on the fluctuations of demand. To test the efficiency of this policy, they devise a simulation model for the system and compare it with a fixed kanban size policy. They report that although the WIP level of the flexible kanban policy is slightly elevated, it has a much higher service level than the fixed kanban policy.

Udomsawat et al. (2004) also consider a kanban control mechanism for a disassembly line. The line they consider has internal random routings between stations and external random routings from the inspection station to the disassembly line. All disassembly stations can receive cores directly from outside for further processing. Also, demand for disassembled parts is independent, uneven, and random. All stations have the same average speed, yet each task is completed in a random time. To cope with this random structure of the problem, they use the flexible kanban control methodology developed by Gupta and Al-Turki (1997) and Gupta et al. (1999). They propose two types of kanbans to control the flow of disassembled components and the remainder of cores after disassembly. Then, using a simulation model, they compare the flexible kanban control system with a push type control policy where cores are released to the system to meet a target demand rate. They show that the adaptive multi-kanban control mechanism performs better for the disassembly environment with respect to fill rates as well as WIP levels.

Kızılkaya and Gupta (2004) extend their work by defining a more advanced dynamic kanban control mechanism geared toward the disassembly process. In their model, they consider the uncertainties related to parts, operation times, and demand They introduce a quality failure rate for functional quality problems of components and add the quantity based issues such as extra, skipping, and disappearing components. They define a methodology that determines capture and release threshold levels for extra kanbans and minimum and maximum kanban quantities. Then, they compare this method with the method in (Kızılkaya and Gupta, 1998) using a simulation model. They first balance the disassembly line with the help of a disassembly line balancing technique developed by (McGovern and Gupta, 2003). Their results show that the new method performs better in a disassembly line in terms of both WIP and fill rates.

Udomsawat and Gupta (2005) analyze a disassembly line subject to sudden breakdowns of its stations resulting in blocking and starvation of other stations in the line. The material and demand flow is the same as in (Udomsawat et al. 2004). They propose a multi-kanban control mechanism as before and generate a component kanban routing method based on the inventory position of candidate inventories. With this method, they aim to minimize the probability of starvation and blocking in the system. To see the effectiveness of this method, using simulation, they compare it with a push controlled system that has finite buffers. The results show that the multi-kanban mechanism holds 78% less inventory than the traditional push control system, while both systems maintain equal fill rates. In a subsequent simulation study, Udomsawat and Gupta (2006) test this mechanism further with various routing scenarios in the disassembly line. They measure the effectiveness of the mechanism using average inventory levels, average service level, and average waiting time of backorders. Their findings verify the results in their earlier paper under all scenarios. Nakashima and Gupta (2012) advance the multi-kanban control mechanism for disassembly further by incorporating withdrawal kanbans into stations.

Disassembly line balancing assigns the workload to disassembly stations. Thus, it is one of the main determinants of the disassembly line throughput and efficiency. The effectiveness of all control mechanisms is bounded by the accuracy of disassembly line balancing methods. To measure the impact of alternative disassembly line balancing algorithms, Kızılkaya and Gupta (2005) construct a disassembly line model using the kanban control mechanism they have developed in (Kızılkaya and Gupta, 2004). They report that the Greedy algorithm and the AEHC algorithm (McGovern and Gupta, 2005) perform better than the 2-Opt Heuristic (McGovern and Gupta, 2003).

Ilgın and Gupta (2011) study the effect of sensor embedded cores on the disassembly process. They analyze the disassembly line using the multi-kanban control methodology of (Udomsawat and Gupta, 2006). They consider a computer disassembly facility with three stations, exponential service times, and no random routings. They assume that both demand and returns follow Poisson processes, and the testing times are normally distributed. When a buffer is full, any arriving part is considered excess and sent to recycling. Thus, the system is not blocked. Embedded sensors state the condition of components before the assembly, enabling partial disassembly. The authors test the effect of sensor embedded products using simulation. As expected, the extra information gathered from sensors helps the system attain significant cost reductions.

Dingeç and Korugan (2013) consider the imbalanced demand problem encountered in disassembly systems. When a core has a missing or nonfunctioning component, the decision of whether to partially disassemble a second core to satisfy the demand for the component is encountered. The authors use a stochastic analysis of a kanban controlled disassembly production system to establish a good counter for the overflow items. To this end, they model and analyze a stylized queueing network using synchronization queues (Di Mascolo, Frein, and Dallery, 1996). By using this method, they calculate the expected number of unused and partially disassembled cores, components obtained from cores, and outstanding component demand. Based on these performance measures, they conduct a cost–benefit analysis of the partial disassembly decision. They show that there exists a threshold value for the marginal profitability above which partial disassembly is feasible. They also show that direct disposal of overflow items is never feasible, and prioritizing overflows does not affect the expected total cost.

The remanufacturing job shop also encounters random routings, processing times, and failures stemming from the uncertain condition of the core. Efforts to classify products for their quality and condition lead to nontrivial prioritization rules. Guide et al. (2005) propose a stylized model for a remanufacturing shop that processes two products, where product A consists of two components, while product B is a single component product. Product B and one of the two components of product A are processed by the same server. The authors use $M/G/1$ queues to model both servers and assume that the disassembly and assembly of A are instantaneous. The objective of the study is to determine dispatching rules for minimizing the total weighted average sojourn times, where the weights determine the importance of the product type. They first show that delaying the release of jobs from disassembly to match parts only increases the sojourn times. Then, they derive the constrained optimal priority rule for the facility that produces two part types for some cases. Also, they show that when both products have the same weight in the measure, then the priority rule is only marginally better than the FCFS rule.

Souza et al. (2002) propose a multi-class queueing model for a remanu-facturer that either remanufactures products or sells them as is, based on the core quality grade. They look at the optimal product mix decision with respect to the service level the remanufacturer provides. To this end, they calculate the average flow times of each demand type. The operation is trig-gered by a demand arrival. Once the product goes through sorting, it is either sold as is or sent to the remanufacturing process that is suitable for its quality condition: superior, average, or inferior. They show that the product mix decision is nontrivial, and in some cases, grading and selling cores as is may be more profitable. Also, at an operational level, a dynamic dispatching rule helps maintain a desired service level.

Behret and Korugan (2009) model a HM system that grades cores into three categories with respect to their return condition. They assign each cat-egory a different remanufacturing rate reflecting their condition. To analyze this system, they construct an open queueing network with finite buffers. Here, they assume stochastic processing times for the system and indepen-dent random return and demand processes. They calculate optimal buffer levels using a simulation and compare the system with a hybrid network that does not classify cores into quality grades. They show that quality grad-ing increases the savings in total cost when return probabilities are above a threshold value. They also report that prioritizing among quality grades increases savings.

Another complication that disrupts remanufacturing system throughput is setups and machine failures. While setups can delay the throughput of one product type, failures affect all types. Also, part quality can change the machine function to a state where it continues to work yet produces bad quality jobs. Such failures will change the yield and the throughput of the system.

Aksoy and Gupta (2005) consider a remanufacturing system that processes returns to meet a demand. Both arrival processes are assumed to be Poisson, and the demand rate is less than the return rate. The difference is supplied externally at a rate equal to the difference of return and demand rates for an additional cost. To analyze the system, they construct an open queueing network model with finite buffers at each station. All servers work for an independent exponential time if they are in working condition. They may fail during operation exponentially and are fixed after an independent exponentially distributed time. When a machine stays down long enough, the buffers downstream of the server will be depleted and cause servers that feed from them to be starved. Eventually, the production stops. Similarly, the buffer upstream can get full and may cause the server or servers that feed it to get blocked. Blocking can propagate upstream, causing returns to fill the CI and the system to start rejecting returns. Since a rejected return is a lost opportunity, a cost is associated with it. To avoid this problem, buffer levels have to be determined carefully. To this end, the authors propose a near optimal buffer allocation algorithm. The algorithm distributes a total buffer capacity N to the buffers in the system while minimizing the total expected cost of the system. The total expected cost is obtained by calculating core disposal and rejection rates, outside procurement and lost sales rates, average inventories, and processing rates. To this end, the open queueing network with finite buffers is analyzed using the expansion methodology.

Aksoy and Gupta (2011) consider a remanufacturing system that processes returns to meet a demand. Both arrival processes are assumed to be Poisson, and the demand rate is less than the return rate. The difference is supplied externally at a rate equal to the difference of return and demand rates for an additional cost. To analyze the system, they construct an open queueing network model with finite buffers at each station. All servers work following an N policy, whereby they switch off as soon as they finish all remanufacturing jobs and do not start remanufacturing until N parts are in the queue. This delay can model both the servers working on other tasks, such as new part manufacturing and machine failures. When a buffer is full, the preceding server is blocked after it finishes a job. If the machine before the CI is blocked, and the CI is full, arriving cores cannot be admitted. They incur an additional opportunity cost. The control parameters of this remanufacturing process are the buffer sizes, as the maximum total amount of cores, WIP, and finished goods cannot exceed the sum of all buffer sizes. When the buffer sizes increase, the effect of N policy on the total throughput declines, yet the average inventories and cycle times increase. The authors define a cost function that minimizes expected total cost of disposal and rejection of cores, processing at each station, lost sales of demand, inventory holding, and procurement with respect to buffer levels. They analyze this problem using the expansion methodology (Kavuşturucu and Gupta, 1998, 1999). The problem they define can be either an OER-S or an IR, as the demand difference is procured from outside, and server vacations indicate that the server is working on another job type.

Korugan et al. (2013) consider the machine and quality failures in the remanufacturing cell of an HM system. They first model the failures of a single machine receiving new and remanufactured parts of the same type using a Markov chain, in which new parts take longer to process, while remanufactured products cause the machine to fail faster. When the machine fails, either it stops and is fully repaired or it deteriorates to produce bad quality parts until it is detected and taken offline. They extend the single model to a two-machine one-buffer model, where they analyze the throughput and yield of the system by extending the work of Kim and Gershwin (2005) to remanufacturing systems.

Takahashi et al. (2014) consider the remanufacturing process of an OER or IR where cores are either disassembled or sold as used products. Disassembled cores are placed in the common parts inventory of assembly of new products. Also, new parts are procured for this inventory. All interoccurrence times of events are assumed to follow independent exponential distributions, and all inventories are finite. Unsatisfied demand is lost, and arriving cores are discarded, when CI is full. Also, remanufacturing and manufacturing processes have a faster and slower average rate. The authors define an expected total cost function for inventory holding, processing, disposal, and lost sales costs, with which they calculate the related performance measures for a pull policy using Markovian stationary analysis. Then, they optimize the buffer sizes and processing speeds.

8.5 Evaluation of the Current State and Future Directions

Remanufacturing has become a premier business in the world economy. While many countries provide incentives, more and more consumers opt to buy services rather than products. An increasing number of OEMs incorporate product designs that consider remanufacturing processes and build products that can last through multiple cycles of reprocessing activities. New methods for monitoring product condition while in use are being explored. Consequently, the number and type of products that are remanufactured are increasing. The interest in and need for the analysis of remanufacturing systems is also increasing rapidly. So far, many studies that model and analyze the essential problems of remanufacturing systems have been published. The inventory problems and uncertainty of core returns have been studied thoroughly from various aspects. Many tactical decision problems, such as disassembly scheduling, have been addressed. A detailed list of studies can be found in the review studies of Ilgın and Gupta (2010) and Akçalı and Çetinkaya (2011).

Frequent changes in product designs, along with a fast paced consumption of goods, generate a diverse and changing core inflow for remanufacturing. While minor product updates bring minor additions to the remanufacturing shop floor, more significant design changes require a redesign for the processes in remanufacturing. Since, in many businesses, such, changes are encountered almost every 6 months to a year, a formal methodology to redesign remanufacturing processes is required. Developing such a methodology first demands an understanding of the impact of uncertainty in remanufacturing. To this end, the sources of uncertainties and their magnitudes have to be determined, based on the type of the remanufacturing business. In this chapter, we have proposed a starting point for such an understanding. Further studies are required to give a more detailed picture of the uncertainties remanufacturing systems encounter.

Second, the operational link among the effects of these uncertainties has to be properly determined. Thus, the link between random events triggered by cores has to be presented and analyzed clearly for a good estimate of the process throughputs and yields. To this end, more detailed models that consider the capacitated nature of production have to be constructed for remanufacturing systems. The links between disassembly, reprocessing, and reassembly have to be well defined. The propagation of variance originating from random processing times, routings, qualities, yields, and failures has to be well accounted for. Also, the effect of processing multiple versions and brands of a core has to be considered.

A proper analysis of remanufacturing systems using capacitated models provides support for strategic, operational, and tactical decisions. When opening an IR, along with market conditions and return probabilities of cores, the throughput function of potential remanufacturing facilities has to be considered, since the main advantage of remanufacturing lies in the significantly short cycle times. Similarly, when an OEM ponders the decision of remanufacturing its own product, the advantages and disadvantages of opening a separate facility can be measured by analyzing alternative designs of HM and OER systems. Once the facility is opened, the buffer sizes and control of material and information flows can be established using the same models.

References

Akçalı, E., and S. Çetinkaya. 2011. "Quantitative models for inventory and production planning in closed-loop supply chains." *International Journal of Production Research* 49 (8): 2373–2407.

Aksoy, H.K., and S. M. Gupta. 2005. "Buffer allocation plan for a remanufacturing cell." *Computers and Industrial Engineering* 48: 657–677.

Aksoy, H.K., and S. M. Gupta. 2011. "Optimal management of remanufacturing systems with server vacations." *International Journal of Advanced Manufacturing Technology* 54: 1199–1218.

Altıok, T. 1997. *Performance Analysis of Manufacturing Systems. Springer Series in Operations Research.* Springer Science + Business Media.

Bayındır, Z. P., N. Erkip, and R. Güllü. 2003. "A model to evaluate inventory costs in a remanufacturing environment." *International Journal of Production Economics* 81/82: 597–607.

Bayındır, Z. P., N. Erkip, and R. Güllü. 2005. "Assessing the benefits of remanufacturing under one-way substitution." *Journal of the Operational Research Society* 56 (2): 286–296.

Behret, H., and A. Korugan. 2009. "Performance analysis of a hybrid system under quality impact of returns." *Computers and Industrial Engineering* 56 (2): 507–520.

Buchanan, D. J., and P. L. Abad. 1998. "Optimal policy for a periodic review returnable inventory system." *IIE Transactions* 30: 1049–1055.

Cheung, K. L., and X. M. Yuan. 2003. "An infinite horizon inventory model with periodic order commitment." *European Journal of Operational Research* 146: 52–66.

Dallery, Y., and S. B. Gershwin. 1992. "Manufacturing flow line systems: A review of models and analytical results." *Queueing Systems* 12: 3–94.

DeCroix, G., J. S. Song, and P. Zipkin. 2005. "A series system with returns: Stationary analysis." *Operations Research* 53 (2): 350–362.

Di Mascolo, M., Y. Frein, and Y. Dallery. 1996. "An analytical method for performance evaluation of kanban controlled production systems." *Operations Research* 44 (1): 50–64.

Dingeç, K. D., and A. Korugan. 2013. "A stochastic analysis of asynchronous demand in disassembly processes of remanufacturing systems." *European Journal of Industrial Engineering* 7 (2): 175–205.

Electrolux. 1999. "Electrolux offers 7,000 households free washing machines." Accessed July 9 2018. www.electroluxgroup.com/en/electrolux-offers-7000- households-free-washing-machines-1885/.

Flapper, S. D. P., J. P. Gayon, and S. Vercraene. 2012. "Control of a production-inventory system with returns under imperfect advance return information." *European Journal of Operational Research* 218: 392–400.

Fleischmann, M., and R. Kuik. 2003. "On optimal inventory control with independent stochastic item returns." *European Journal of Operational Research* 151: 25–37.

Fleischmann, M., R. Kuik, and R. Dekker. 2002. "Controlling inventories with stochastic item returns: A basic model." *European Journal of Operational Research* 138 (1): 63–75.

Gershwin, S. B. 1994. *Manufacturing Systems Engineering.* Prentice Hall.

Gong, X., and X. Chao. 2013. "Technical Note—Optimal Control Policy for Capacitated Inventory Systems with Remanufacturing." *Operations Research* 61 (3): 603–611.

Guide, V. D. R., Souza G. C., and E. A. van der Laan. 2005. "Performance of static priority rules for shared facilities in a remanufacturing shop with disassembly and reassembly." *European Journal of Operational Research* 164: 341–353.

Guide, V. D. R., and R. Srivastava. 1997. "Repairable inventory theory: Models and applications." *European Journal of Operational Research* 102: 1–20.

Guide, V. D. R. 2000. "Production planning and control for remanufacturing: Industry practice and research needs." *Journal of Operations Management* 18:467–483.

Güngör, A., and S. M. Gupta. 2001. "A solution approach to the disassembly line balancing problem in the presence of task failures." *International Journal of Production Research* 39 (7): 1427–1467.

Güngör, A., and S. M. Gupta. 2002. "Disassembly line in product recovery." *International Journal of Production Research* 40 (11): 2569–2589.

Gupta, S. M., and Y. A. Y. Al-Turki. 1997. "An algorithm to dynamically adjust the number of kanbans in a stochastic processing times and variable demand environment." *Production Planning and Control* 8 (2): 133–141.

Gupta, S. M., Y. A. Y. Al-Turki, and R. F. Perry. 1999. "Flexible kanban system." *International Journal of Operations and Production Management* 19 (10): 1065–1093.

Heyman, D. P. 1977. "Optimal disposal policies for a single-item inventory system with returns." *Naval Logistics Quarterly* 24: 385–405.

Ilgın, M. A., and S. M. Gupta. 2010. "Environmentally conscious manufacturing and product recovery (ECMPRO): A review of the state of the art." *Journal of Environmental Management* 91: 563–591.

Ilgın, M. A., and S. M. Gupta. 2011. "Performance improvement potential of sensor embedded products in environmental supply chains." *Resources, Conservation and Recycling* 55:580–592.

Inderfurth, K. 1997. "Simple optimal replenishment and disposal policies for a product recovery system with leadtimes." *OR Spektrum* 19: 111–122.

Kavuşturucu, A., and S. M. Gupta. 1998. "A methodology for analyzing finite buffer tandem manufacturing systems with N-policy." *Computers and Industrial Engineering* 34 (4): 837–848.

Kavuşturucu, A., and S. M. Gupta. 1999. "Expansion method for the throughput analysis of open finite manufacturing/queueing networks with N-policy." *Computers and Operations Research* 26 (13): 1267–1292.

Kerbache, L., and J. M. Smith. 1987. "The generalized expansion method for open finite queueing networks." *European Journal of Operational Research* 32: 448–461.

Kiesmüller, G. P., and E. A. van der Laan. 2001. "An inventory model with dependent product demand and returns." *International Journal of Production Economics* 72: 73–87.

Kim, J., and S. B. Gershwin. 2005. "Integrated quality and quantity modeling of a production line." *Operations Research Spectrum* 27: 287–314.

Kızılkaya, E., and S. M. Gupta. 1998. "Material flow control and scheduling in a disassembly environment." *Computers and Industrial Engineering* 35 (1–2): 9396.

Kızılkaya, E., and S. M. Gupta. 2004. "Modeling Operational Behavior of a Disassembly System." In *Proceedings of the SPIE International Conference on Environmentally Conscious Manufacturing IV*, edited by S. M. Gupta, Vol. 5583 of *Proceedings of SPIE*, 79–93. SPIE.

Kızılkaya, E., and S. M. Gupta. 2005. "Impact of Different Disassembly Line Balancing Algorithms on the Performance of Dynamic Kanban System for Disassembly Line." In *Proceedings of the SPIE International Conference on Environmentally Conscious Manufacturing V*, edited by S. M. Gupta, Vol. 5997.

Korugan, A., S. Ata, and M. Fadıloğlu. 2017. "The impact of orbit dependent return rate on the control policies of a hybrid production system." In *Proceedings of the SMMSO 2017*, 201–208.

Korugan, A., K. D. Dingeç, T. Önen, and N. Y. Ateş 2013. "On the quality variation impact of returns in remanufacturing." *Computers and Industrial Engineering* 64: 923–936.

Korugan, A., and S. M. Gupta. 1998. "A multi-echelon inventory system with returns." *Computers and Industrial Engineering* 35 (1–2): 145–148.

Korugan, A., and S. M. Gupta. 2014. "An adaptive CONWIP mechanism for hybrid production systems." *International Journal of Advanced Manufacturing Technology* 74: 715–727.

Li, J., D. B. Blumenfeld, N. Huang, and J. B. Alden. 2009. "Throughput analysis of production systems: Recent advances and future topics." *International Journal of Production Research* 47 (14): 3823–3851.

Li, J., and S. Meerkov. 2009. *Production Systems Engineering.* Springer Science + Business Media, LLC.

McGovern, S. M., and S. M. Gupta. 2003. "2-Opt Heuristic for the Disassembly Line Balancing Problem." In *Proceedings of the SPIE International Conference on Environmentally Conscious Manufacturing III,* edited by S. M. Gupta, 71–84.

McGovern, S. M., and S. M. Gupta. 2005. "Local Search Heuristics and Greedy Algorithm for Balancing a Disassembly Line." *International Journal of Operations and Quantitative Management* 11: 2.

Muckstadt, J. A., and M. H. Isaac. 1981. "An analysis of single item inventory systems with returns." *Naval Research Logistics Quarterly* 28: 237–254.

Nakashima, K., and S. M. Gupta. 2012. "A study on the risk management of multi Kanban system in a closed loop supply chain." *International Journal of Production Economics* 139: 65–68.

Örsdemir, A., V. Deshpande, and A. K. Parlaktürk. 2017. "Is servicization a win-win strategy? Profitability and environmental implications of servicization." in review.

Rothenberg, S. 2007. "Sustainability through servicizing." *MIT Sloan Management Review* 48 (2): 83–89.

Simpson, V. P. 1978. "Optimum solution structure for a repairable inventory problem." *Operations Research* 26 (2): 270–281.

Souza, G. C., M. E. Ketzenberg, and V. D. R. Guide. 2002. "Capacitated remanufacturing with service level constraints." *Production and Operations Management* 11 (2): 231–248.

Takahashi, K., Y. Doi, D. Hirotani, and K. Morikawa. 2014. "An adaptive pull strategy for remanufacturing systems." *Journal of Intelligent Manufacturing* 25 (4): 629–645.

Tan, B. 1999. "Variance of the output as a function of time: Production line dynamics." *European Journal of Operational Research* 117: 470–484.

Toktay, L. B., L. M. Wein, and S. A. Zenios. 2000. "Inventory management of remanufacturable products." *Management Science* 46 (11): 1412–1426.

Udomsawat, G., and S. M. Gupta. 2006. "Controlling Disassembly Line with Multi- Kanban System." In *Proceedings of the SPIE International Conference on Environmentally Conscious Manufacturing VI,* edited by S. M. Gupta, Vol. 6385.

Udomsawat, G., S. M. Gupta, and Y. A. Y. Al-Turki. 2004. "Multi-Kanban Model for Disassembly Line with Demand Fluctuation." In *Proceedings of the SPIE International Conference on Environmentally Conscious Manufacturing III,* edited by S. M. Gupta, Vol. 5262.

Udomsawat, G., and S. M. Gupta. 2005. "The Effect of Sudden Server Breakdown on the Performance of a Disassembly Line." In *Proceedings of the SPIE International Conference on Environmentally Conscious Manufacturing V*, edited by S. M. Gupta, Vol. 5997.

van der Laan, E. A., R. Dekker, and M. Salomon. 1996. "An (s,Q) inventory model with remanufacturing and disposal." *International Journal of Production Economics* 46/47: 339–350.

van der Laan, E. A., and M. Salomon. 1997. "Production planning and inventory control with remanufacturing and disposal." *European Journal of Operational Research* 102: 264–678.

van der Laan, E. A., M. Salomon, and R. Dekker. 1999. "An investigation of lead time effects in manufacturing/remanufacturing systems under simple PUSH and PULL control strategies." *European Journal of Operational Research* 115 (1): 195–214.

Wang, H. 2002. "A survey of maintenance policies of deteriorating systems." *European Journal of Operational Research* 139: 469–489.

Yuan, X. M., and K. L. Cheung. 1998. "Modeling returns of merchandise in an inventory system." *OR Spectrum* 20: 147–154.

Zerhouni, H., J. P. Gayon, and Y. Frein. 2013. "Influence of dependency between demands and returns in a reverse logistics system." *International Journal of Production Economics* 143 (1): 62–71.

9

Impact of Buffer Size and Remanufacturing Uncertainties on the Hybrid System Performance Measures

H. Kıvanç Aksoy and Surendra M. Gupta

CONTENTS

9.1 Introduction

Environmental regulations, customer consciousness, shorter product life cycles, and extensive competition in the global markets have directed manufacturers to focus on their supply chains. The integration of used products into the existing supply chains by various forms of recovery options (remanufacturing, reconditioning, and refurbishment) reduces supply chain costs as a whole. Nevertheless, uncertainties in timing, quantity and quality of returned products complicate the reverse portion of the supply chain as well as the serviceable parts inventory control (Fleishmann et al., 2000). Thierry et al. (1995) specified the goal of product recovery management as "to recover as much of the economic (and ecological) value as reasonably possible, thereby reducing the ultimate quantities of waste." The authors provided various cases from different industries that are applying remanufacturing processes for used products. Alternative processes for used items are remanufacturing, cannibalizing, refurbishing, and recycling. Remanufacturing can be defined as "an industrial process in which worn-out products are restored to like-new conditions." Therefore, the remanufacturing option delivers the quality criteria of brand new goods from recovered parts and assemblies. Conversely, recycling can be defined as "a process performed to retrieve the material content of used and non-functioning products without retaining the identity of the cores." This chapter examines levels of buffering and production capacity decisions to cope with uncertainties through the various stages of a remanufacturing system. We consider a hybrid system in which manufacturing and remanufacturing operations are occurring together with single item remanufacturable returns and stochastic demand. In a hybrid system, it is critical that remanufacturing and disposal decisions for the returned products satisfy non-stationary demand. Uncertainty is introduced into the remanufacturing system from different sources: time, amount, and quality of the reclaimed items.

Currently, there is a significant amount of literature about product recovery and remanufacturing system modeling. Geyer et al. (2007) examine the economic feasibility of remanufacturing where the recovered items can be exchanged for the new product. Rubio and Corominas (2008) consider a lean manufacturing setting through deterministic and stationary demand and suggest a model by which manufacturing and remanufacturing capacities can be controlled. Yang et al. (2016) studied a procurement and remanufacturing problem for a multi-product recoverable system. The authors used a nonlinear programming approach to balance the economic and environmental benefits.

Remanufacturing operations are exposed to substantial uncertainties due to variations in the condition, timing, and quantity of the returned products. These variations also generate uncertainties during the recovery operations, such as remanufacturing process time, recovery rate, and output of the system. As Steeneck and Sarin (2013) pointed out, the per-unit production cost of remanufactured products is affected not only by the quantity and quality of end-of-life products but also by the quantity of remanufactured products. Therefore, it should be modeled as a function of both prices. Robotis et al. (2012) focused on uncertainties and their effects on the remanufacturing cost. A major source of this kind of uncertainty is the unpredictable qualities of the returned cores. The authors showed that the technological abilities of remanufacturing companies play a significant part in the decision process. Bulmus et al. (2013) investigated the remanufacturing effect on capacity and manufacturing choices. The authors obtained optimal manufacturing and remanufacturing quantities for a two-epoch model with manufacturing in both epochs and the decision in the second to remanufacture products, which are returned to the system in the last part of the first epoch. Testa and Iraldo (2010) summarized the strategic motivations driving managers to greener supply chain management, such as positive corporate image, increased efficiency, and innovation leadership. Subramoniam et al. (2013)

highlighted that the management of returned cores in the remanufacturing process is one of the most critical issues for effective remanufacturing operations. Deng et al. (2017) built a resource evaluation model on a remanufacturing process for end-of-life construction machinery under uncertainty in the recycling price. Carter and Ellram (1998) review reverse logistics operations, which comprise planning, implementing, and controlling the reverse flow of materials and the management of information through the inverse supply chain. The authors emphasize the significance of the decisions through forward and backward material flow. Rubio et al. (2008) examine and present major features of research papers in the area of reverse logistics. Ilgin and Gupta (2010) examined timely works in the field of environmentally responsible production and remanufacturing. Govindan et al. (2015) reviewed recently published articles in reverse logistics. Gupta and Lambert (2008) explored problems for environmentally friendly manufacturing, and Gupta (2013) concentrated on reverse supply chain issues and analysis. The book by Pochampally et al. (2009) explored various areas and issues of closed-loop reverse logistics and supply chains. Dubey et al. (2017) systematically reviews the literature on sustainable supply chain management drivers. Also, the authors discuss the use of alternative research methods to address questions related to sustainable supply chain management drivers, and they propose and illustrate the use of total interpretive structural modeling. Liao et al. (2017) considered procurement and demand uncertainties for a joint manufacturing and remanufacturing system. The authors classified returned items according to quality levels and directed products to remanufacturing operations to optimize the joint system total profit.

In this chapter, we examine a hybrid system for a single remanufacturable product with a stochastic return of used products and demand for remanufactured items. We model the system as an open queuing network (OQN) representation and examine each station separately through the network. Then, we use expansion methodology to analytically examine the system. It is assumed that the demand and return processes of cores are independent and normally distributed with known mean and variance. The major objective of this chapter is, in the presence of the aforementioned uncertainties of the remanufacturing system, to examine the impact of the remanufacturing system capacity and buffer sizing on the system's performance measures, such as expected total cost, expected throughput rate, expected processing (remanufacturing) time, and expected work-in-process (WIP) inventory. To this end, we model the hybrid system with an OQN with limited buffers and reliable servers (Aksoy and Gupta, 2005, 22011). To investigate the remanufacturing system, we use the decomposition principle and expansion methodology (Gupta and Kavusturucu, 1998, 2000, Kavusturucu and Gupta, 1999). Additionally, we analyzed the effect of buffering and capacity increase on the system performance measures with various phases of product useful life. To analyze the complete characteristics of the model, we use the return and demand patterns through the typical life span of a remanufacturable item. For this purpose, Vander Laan and Salomon (1997) present a diagram for a characteristic life cycle for a recoverable product, which has five phases: introduction, growth, maturity, decline, and terminal.

The chapter is organized as follows. In Section 9.2, we introduce the hybrid system model and remanufacturing operations. In Section 9.3, we present the expansion methodology in brief to obtain the analytical results for the remanufacturing system and derive the system performance measures. In Section 9.4, we present the numerical analysis and results for the system through the life cycle stages of the remanufacturable item. Finally, we summarize the results and conclusions in Section 9.5.

9.2 Model Description and Formulation

Tang and Naim (2004) modeled a manufacturing/remanufacturing system, examined the system's performance using a control engineering perspective, and showed that clarity of information helps to obtain successful results from the system. Kwak and Kim (2017) presented a model for integrated pricing and production planning for a line of new and remanufactured products in a competitive market. They used a mixed-integer programming model and assumed a buyback program as a take back strategy that optimizes the buyback prices, selling prices, and detailed production plans simultaneously. The main objective of the model is to maximize the total profit, but the model also considers how much environmental impact can be avoided by remanufacturing option of used items. The OQN model that we have considered for a hybrid system is a group of service stations where returned items come for service at various rates and require processing through unequal operation periods.

We model the hybrid system by means of a queuing network as shown in Figure 9.1. Here, we use an OQN model with finite buffers and reliable stations to define the remanufacturing system. We assume that used items return to the collection station, and demand for remanufactured items occurs independently. Here, we take into account a remanufacturable single module item. When returned cores are collected by the system, they are directed to the pre-sorting and testing station, and then, collected used products are directed to the disassembly station. In hybrid systems, returned cores generate the main raw material source of the system. To begin the disassembly operation, returned items are tested, and with a stochastic recovery ratio r they are channeled to the remanufacturing stations. The remanufacturing shop accomplishes the different recovery procedures according to the varying condition of the returned used items. Subsequently, recovered parts/assemblies are forwarded to the serviceable parts inventory station to fulfill the customer demand together with brand new items. Returned items that do not satisfy the defined quality level for retrieval and parts that are useless after

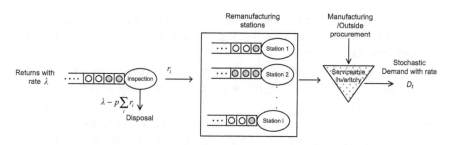

FIGURE 9.1
Queueing network model for remanufacturing system.

disassembly are either sent to landfill or sold as recyclable material. There are two distinct inventory locations in the system; the return product inventory and the serviceable inventory. The return product inventory comprises post-used returned items from consumers and the serviceable inventory comprises remanufactured products where the stochastic demand is fulfilled. By definition, recovered items are considered to be "like new" items, and they come with the same quality, warranty, and selling price.

In Figure 9.1, (r_i) denotes the recovery rate of returned cores from the end user. For hybrid systems, the low recovery rate of returned cores does not constitute a significant issue in satisfying the demand from serviceable inventory, since the serviceable inventory of remanufactured parts can be coordinated with the new item procurement option by means of an effective information flow from the used product collection phase. On the other hand, high fluctuation in the recovery rate of returned products complicates successful serviceable inventory coordination of these two sources: remanufactured and new parts. We consider that the core recovery rate in successive periods is an independent and identically distributed (i.i.d) stochastic variable shown by r_i. In Figure 9.1, r_i symbolizes the recoverable rate of cores that are acquired from used products, and $(1 - r_i)$ corresponds to the scrap rate. We also assume that the recovery rate distribution function follows a normal distribution, and its parameters depend on the return product life cycle stage, but it is totally independent of the return product amount. Moreover, we assume that the distribution function of the recovery rate is not affected by the arrival rate of the returned cores. The probability density function and cumulative density function of the recovery rate of returned products are denoted as $f(r_i)$ and $F(r_i)$, respectively, with mean $\bar{r}$ and standard deviation σ_r.

Various processes play an important role in remanufacturing planning and inventory control of the remanufacturing system. These processes and their associated complexities can be summarized as follows:

- *Return process*: Collection of used products and components. Time, quantity, and quality of returned items are the major uncertainty factors.

- *Disassembly and testing process*: All returned products are disassembled to part level, and after testing, reusable parts are directed to the remanufacturing shop.
- *Recycling and disposal process*: After testing, returned products that are not recoverable are either sent to the recycling process or disposed of as scrap.
- *Remanufacturing process*: Due to the unknown condition of the returned products, various shop floor operations are performed by different servers with varying time and routings inside the remanufacturing shop.
- *Serviceable inventory*: This process coordinates remanufactured and new items to satisfy demand. Variations in the reusable rate of the returned products and system efficiency are the major factors that affect the coordination of the remanufacturing and outside procurement processes.

In this chapter, we consider the remanufacturing scheme as an OQN, which is presented in Figure 9.1. To analyze the system, we first decompose the network and investigate each server separately (Figure 9.2.). Then, we enlarge the isolated station by adding an extra holding station in front of every station. It is assumed that these nodes work with zero processing time and an infinite buffer capacity. In this way, these additional nodes process arrivals (jobs) that cannot be accepted by the downstream station. Therefore, arrivals that are processed by the holding nodes wait there until the first space in the downstream station becomes available. After each station has been investigated, the relation of each station with the remaining part of the system can be examined (Gupta and Kavusturucu, 1998, 2000, Kavusturucu and Gupta, 1999). Expansion methodology is briefly explained in the next section.

9.2.1 Model Assumptions

In this chapter, we examine a single unit remanufacturable product. Postconsumption or returned items reach the hybrid system from outside through the inspection and sorting station and follow the necessary remanufacturing operations through the system. When returned cores are collected by the

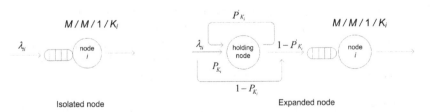

FIGURE 9.2
Isolated and expanded server.

system, they are directed to the pre-sorting and testing station, and then, the collected used products are directed to the disassembly station. In hybrid systems, returned cores generate the main raw material source of the system. To begin the disassembly operation, returned cores are tested, and with a stochastic recovery ratio r, they are channeled to remanufacturing stations. The remanufacturing shop performs different recovery procedures according to the varying condition of the returned used items. Subsequently, recovered parts/assemblies are forwarded to the serviceable parts inventory station to fulfill the customer demand together with brand new items. It is assumed that after remanufacturing operations, all recovered items satisfy the same quality standards as new ones.

It is assumed that the core returns to the hybrid system and the demand rate follow independent probability distributions. Demand rate γ and return rate, λ_{ar} are exponentially distributed. Additionally, we assume that the arrival process to each station is a renewal process. Additional assumptions are that each station has a finite buffer space, denoted by B_i, and each service station operates with exponential service rate μ_i according to the first come first serve (FCFS) service discipline.

9.2.2 Analysis of the Hybrid System

Due to the previously mentioned uncertainties and complications of the remanufacturing system, the optimization of a hybrid system's performance is a challenge. One of the methods to reduce the effect of uncertainties on the hybrid system's performance measures is to increase the available number of buffer slots at the servers that are experiencing inadequacies. Nevertheless, various actual system situations and physical restrictions place limits on the number of obtainable buffer slots. Although the system's total expected cost is one of the major performance criteria of the hybrid system, system output rate, WIP inventory, and expected operation duration are equally significant. In this study, we resort to a buffering approach to deal with the unavoidable uncertainties of the remanufacturing systems. By means of the buffering approach, one can regulate the WIP inventory level against variability in the hybrid system (So, K., 1989).

We model the hybrid system as an OQN and use the expansion method to examine it. To obtain the throughput rate (TH_i) of the whole remanufacturing system, we employ expansion methodology. A brief discussion of the expansion method is given in the subsequent section, while details of the technique and essential derivations for manufacturing systems can be found in Gupta and Kavusturucu (2000) and Aksoy and Gupta (2005).

9.3 Expansion Method

Expansion Methodology is a robust and effective approximation technique developed by Kerbache and Smith (1988) for calculating the throughput rate of finite queueing systems. Later, Kavusturucu and Gupta (1999) and Gupta and Kavusturucu (2000) used this method for finite buffered queueing systems for production lines with server unavailability. When an analytical solution for a queueing system does not exist, the decomposition principle is broadly used to analyze the queueing networks. Here, first, system stations are separated, and the essential parameters of every single station are calculated independently. After the analysis of each station is accomplished, the collaboration of each station with the other stations of the system can be revised.

Next, the subsequent sections provide the steps of the analytical method and the computation of the system's output rate. We used the following notation for calculation of the network parameters.

Notation:

α_i	Failure ratio of station i
β_i	Restore ratio of station i
B_i	Capacity of station i
γ	Demand rate
i	Station index no, $(i=1,..., I)$
K_i	Capacity size of station i
L_i	Mean amount of waiting parts at station i
Lq_i	Mean amount of wait in line items at station i
λ_r	Return rate of used items
λh_i	Arrival ratio of jobs to the holding station
λ_i	Growth ratio at station i
λj_i	Directly accept ratio of jobs to station i
λt_i	Effective arrival ratio to station i
μ_i	Process time at station i
P_{Ki}	Probability of K_i jobs at station i
P'_{K_i}	Feedback blocking probability at station i
P_{qsi}	Probability of s_i jobs at station i. ($q=0$, station is up and $q=1$, station is down)
r_i	Recovery rate
ρ_I	Utilization rate $(\lambda t_i / \mu_i)$.
th_i	Throughput ratio at station i $(i=1,..., I)$

9.3.1 Analysis of the Network

The first stages of the expansion method are to decompose the system nodes and analyze them separately. In Figure 9.2, $M/M/1/K_i$ denotes the queueing representation of exponentially distributed arrival and service rates of the finite capacity single server station. After isolation of each station, we abstractly enlarge the station by adding an extra holding station in front of each station's limited waiting line. The purpose of this extra node is to record the number of rejected jobs from the main station due to the shortage of buffer spaces and to process jobs with zero processing time and with an infinite buffer capacity. Here, if there is an available buffer space for station i, arriving jobs directly join this station's waiting line with a probability of $1 - P_{K_i}$. Conversely, if there is no available buffer space for station i, arriving jobs are rejected by the station for processing and routed to the holding node with a probability of P_{K_i}. These jobs wait at the holding station until there is an available place at that station. From this point of view, the holding station can theoretically house an infinite number of jobs that are rejected by station i due to the unavailability of the buffer area. Once there is an available buffer slot, items are directed to the waiting line of this station with a probability of $1 - P'_{K_i}$.

9.3.2 Calculation of Network Parameters

The isolated and expanded $M/M/1/K_i$ node i is given in Figure 9.2. Gupta and Kavusturucu [24] provide the steady-state equalities for P_{qs_i} as follows (see Figure 9.3 for the Markov Chain for this system).

$$\lambda t_i P_{00_i} = \mu_i P_{01_i} \tag{9.1}$$

$$(\lambda t_i + \mu_i + \alpha_i)P_{0s_i} = \lambda t_i P_{0,s_i-1} + \mu_i P_{0,s_i+1} + \beta_i P_{1,s_i} \quad 1 \le s_i \le K_i - 1 \tag{9.2}$$

$$(\mu_i + \alpha_i)P_{0K_i} = \lambda t_i P_{0,K_i-1} + \beta_i P_{1,K_i} \tag{9.3}$$

$$(\lambda t_i + \beta_i)P_{11_i} = \alpha_i P_{01_i} \tag{9.4}$$

$$(\lambda t_i + \beta_i)P_{1s_i} = \alpha_i P_{0s_i} + \lambda t_i P_{1,s_i-1} \quad 2 \le s_i \le K_i - 1 \tag{9.5}$$

$$\beta_i P_{1K_i} = \alpha_i P_{0K_i} + \lambda t_i P_{1,K_i-1} \tag{9.6}$$

$$P_{10_i} = 0 \tag{9.7}$$

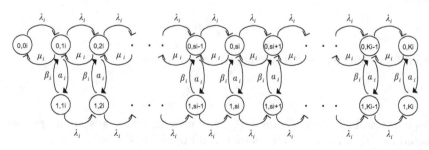

FIGURE 9.3
Transition diagram of $M/M/1(BD)/K_i$ queueing system.

The boundary condition is given by

$$\sum_{q=0}^{1}\sum_{s_i=0}^{K_i} P_{qs_i} = 1 \tag{9.8}$$

The analytical steady state resulting from the *M/M/1(BD)/K* model provides the following expressions for P_{qs_i} and P'_{K_i} :

$$P_{01_i} = \frac{\lambda t_i}{\mu_i} P_{00_i} \tag{9.9}$$

$$P_{0s_i} = \left(\frac{\lambda t_i}{\mu_i}\right)\left\{P_{0,s_i-1} + \frac{\alpha_i}{\lambda t_i + \beta_i}\left[\sum_{m=1}^{s_i-1} P_{0m}\left(\frac{\lambda t_i}{\lambda t_i + \beta_i}\right)^{s_i-m-1}\right]\right\} \quad 2 \le s_i \le K_i \tag{9.10}$$

$$P_{10_i} = 0 \tag{9.11}$$

$$P_{11_i} = \frac{\alpha_i}{\lambda t_i + \beta_i} P_{01_i} \tag{9.12}$$

$$P_{1s_i} = \frac{\alpha_i}{\lambda t_i + \beta_i}\left[\sum_{m=1}^{s_i} P_{0m}\left(\frac{\lambda t_i}{\lambda t_i + \beta_i}\right)^{s_i-m}\right] \quad 2 \le s_i \le K_i - 1 \tag{9.13}$$

$$P_{1K_i} = \left(\frac{\lambda t_i}{\beta_i}\right)\left(\frac{\alpha_i}{\lambda t_i + \beta_i}\right)\left[\sum_{m=1}^{K_i-1} P_{0m}\left(\frac{\lambda t_i}{\lambda t_i + \beta_i}\right)^{K_i-m-1}\right] + \left(\frac{\alpha_i}{\beta_i}\right)P_{0K_i} \tag{9.14}$$

$$P_{00_i} = 1 - \sum_{q=0}^{1}\sum_{s_i=1}^{K_i} P_{qs_i} \tag{9.15}$$

Probability of s_i items (jobs) at the station i is denoted by P_{s_i} and calculated as follows:

$$P_{s_i} = P_{0s_i} + P_{1s_i} \quad 0 \le s_i \le K_i \tag{9.16}$$

From Equations 9.10 and 9.14, one can obtain P_{K_i} easily:

$$P_{K_i} = P_{0K_i} + P_{1K_i} \tag{9.17}$$

Delaying probability at station i, P'_{K_i}, and growth rate λ_i at station i are estimated by this formulation (Labetolle and Pujolle, 1980):

$$\lambda_i = \lambda j_i - \lambda h_i(1 - P'_{K_i}) + \alpha_i + \beta_i \tag{9.18}$$

$$P'_{K_i} = \left(2 - \frac{\lambda_i(r_{2_i}^{K_i} - r_{1_i}^{K_i}) - (r_{2_i}^{K_i-1} - r_{1_i}^{K_i-1})}{\mu_i(r_{2_i}^{K_i+1} - r_{i1}^{K_i+1}) - (r_{2_i}^{K_i} - r_{1_i}^{K_i})} \right)^{-1} \tag{9.19}$$

where

$$\lambda j_i = \lambda t_i (1 - P_{K_i}) \tag{9.20}$$

$$\lambda h_i = \lambda t_i P_{K_i} \tag{9.21}$$

$$r_{1_i} = \frac{\left[(\lambda_i + 2\mu_i) - \sqrt{z_i} \right]}{2\mu_i} \tag{9.22}$$

$$r_{2_i} = \frac{\left[(\lambda_i + 2\mu_i) + \sqrt{z_i} \right]}{2\mu_i} \tag{9.23}$$

$$z_i = (\lambda_i + 2\mu_i)^2 - 4\lambda_i\mu_i \tag{9.24}$$

9.3.3 Calculation of the System Output

In expansion methodology, each station is examined separately; consequently, the output of each station is obtained independently. The output of station i is obtained as follows (Gupta and Kavusturucu, 2000):

$$TH_i = (L_i - Lq_i)\mu_{i_i} + \lambda j_i (1 - P'_{K_i})^{\rho_i + \rho_{i-1}} (1 - P_{K_i}) \tag{9.25}$$

If station i is forking into M parallel routes, the throughput rate can be obtained as follows:

$$TH_i = r_{ij}((L_i - Lq_i)\mu_{i_i} + \lambda j_i (1 - P'_{K_i})^{\rho_i + \rho_{i-1}} (1 - P_{K_i})), \quad j = 1, 2, \ldots, M \tag{9.26}$$

If M parallel routes are integrating into a single station, the throughput rate can be obtained as follows:

$$TH_i = \sum_{j=1}^{M} ((L_i - Lq_i)\mu_{i_i} + \lambda j_i (1 - P'_{K_i})^{\rho_i + \rho_{i-1}} (1 - P_{K_i})) \tag{9.27}$$

where:
  the average number of parts in station i

$$L_i = \sum_{s_i=0}^{K_i} s_i P_{si} \tag{9.28}$$

the average number of parts in the queue at station i

$$Lq_i = \sum_{s_i=1}^{K_i} (s_i - 1)P_{0s_i} + \sum_{s_i=1}^{K_i} s_i P_{1s_i} = L_i - \sum_{s_i=1}^{K_i} P_{1s_i} \tag{9.29}$$

When the throughput for station i is obtained, it turns into the arrival rate of the next station. Hence, the output of the latest station denotes the throughput of the whole network.

9.3.4 Other Performance Measures

In this section, we derive the steady-state performance measures of the system.

An important performance measure of the system is WIP inventories. E_{WIP} can be derived from Equations 9.5 through 9.13.

$$E_{WIP} = \sum_{i=1}^{I} L_i = \sum_{i=1}^{I} \sum_{s_i=0}^{K_i} s_i P_{si} \tag{9.30}$$

where P_{si} denotes the probability of s items waiting for service at station i:

$$P_{si} = \frac{\lambda t_i}{\mu_i} P_{00_i} + \left(\frac{\lambda t_i}{\mu_i}\right) \left[P_{0,s_i-1} + \vartheta_i \left(\sum_{m=1}^{s_i-1} P_{0m} \omega^{s_i-m-1} \right) \right]$$

$$+ \vartheta_i P_{01_i} + \vartheta_i \sum_{m=1}^{s_i} \left(P_{0m} \omega^{s_i-m} \right) \tag{9.31}$$

where

$$\vartheta_i = \frac{\alpha_i}{\lambda t_i + \beta_i} \text{ and } \omega_i = \frac{\lambda t_i}{\lambda t_i + \beta_i} \tag{9.32}$$

Another important performance measure is expected time-in-process (the average time spent in the system), and it can be derived as follows:

$$E_{PT} = \sum_{i=1}^{I} \left(\mu_i + \frac{Lq_i}{\lambda t_i} \right) \tag{9.33}$$

where expected number of parts in the queue at station i (Lq_i) is as follows:

$$Lq_i = \sum_{s_i=1}^{K_i} \left[(s_i - 1) \left(\frac{\lambda t_i}{\mu_i} \right) \left(P_{0,s_i-1} + \vartheta_i \sum_{m=1}^{s_i-1} \left(P_{0m} \omega_i^{s_i-m-1} \right) \right) \right]$$

$$+ \sum_{s_i=1}^{K_i} \left[s_i \vartheta_i \sum_{m=1}^{s_i} P_{0m} \omega_i^{s_i-m} \right] \tag{9.34}$$

9.4 Numerical Experiments

To capture the full characteristics of the model, we use the demand and return rates during a typical life cycle of a remanufacturable product, which are defined by Van der Laan and Salomon (1997). The authors use the following life cycle stages, which are depicted in Figure 9.4 and can be explained as follows:

I- The introduction: in this phase, the demand rate rises, but the return rate is nearly zero.

II- The growth: in this phase, the demand rate rises significantly, whereas the return rate gradually starts to rise.

III- The maturity phase: in this phase, both the demand and the return rate keep a steady-state position.

IV- The decline phase: in this phase, the demand rate declines quickly, but the return rate could gradually start to decline.

V- The terminal stage: in this phase, no demand occur any longer, while the return rate could be present.

To assess the effect of buffer size on the remanufacturing system's performance, we defined the expected cost per period, which comprises the variable and fixed remanufacturing and outside procurement costs, disassembly, testing, disposal and remanufacturing costs, holding costs for serviceable inventory, and lost sales costs. The following notation is used for long-term steady-state cost function:

$$E(TC|r_i) = c_p E(R_t) + c_{dis} E(dis) + c_h E(S_t) + c_l E(L_s)$$
$$+ c_r E(Rm_t) + c_m E(P_t)$$

(9.35)

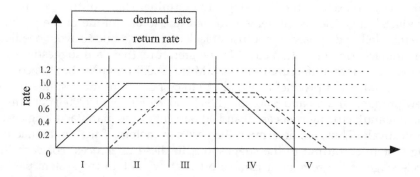

FIGURE 9.4
Typical life cycle of a remanufacturable product. (From van der Laan, E., Salomon, M. Production planning and inventory control with remanufacturing and disposal. *Eur. J. Oper. Res.* 1997, 102, 264–278. With permission.)

$E(R_t)$	The expected rate of the returned products is represented by the arrival rate of returned products to the remanufacturing system.
$E(dis.)$	The expected rate of disassembled products is estimated by the throughput rate of the first station.
$E(S_t)$	The expected serviceable inventory level of the remanufacturing system is estimated by the average queue length of the serviceable inventory where the demand is satisfied.
$E(L_s)$	The expected rate of lost sales is estimated by the starving probability of the serviceable inventory and demand rate.
$E(Rm_t)$	The expected rate of the remanufactured parts.
$E(P_t)$	The estimated amount of procured/manufactured new items.

Cost parameters are

c_p	Acquisition cost of cores ($/product)
C_{dis}	Disassembly cost ($/product)
c_h	Inventory holding cost for cores($/product/time)
c_l	Lost sales cost ($/product/time)
c_r	Remanufacturing cost ($/product)
c_m	Cost of new product ($/product)

The performance measures for recovery rate variations are assessed and this information is updated through the life cycles of the remanufacturable products with the following cost parameters: purchasing cost of returned products ($c_p = 6$), disassembly cost ($c_{dis} = 4$), inventory holding cost for serviceable items ($c_h = 1$), lost sales cost for unfulfilled demand ($c_l = 5$), remanufacturing operation cost ($c_r = 10$), and cost of procured/manufactured items ($c_m = 30$). In our analysis, we exclude the first stage (the introduction stage) of the recoverable products' life cycle, since there are no return items during the first stage, and the whole demand is satisfied by new products. Likewise, we exclude the fifth stage (the terminal stage) of the recoverable products' life cycle, as all items returned due to end-of-life of the product are recycled or disposed of because of lack of demand and to avoid needless remanufacturing operation costs. In the literature, there are suggestions for the value of remanufactured product. Mitra (2007) remarks that the cost of a remanufactured product is usually 40 to 60 percent of the cost of a brand new product. 31Laan and Salomon (1997) and Zanoni et al. (2006) determine the remanufacturing costs as 50 and 40 percent of the manufacturing costs, respectively. Thus, we determine the cost parameters of the remanufacturing system according to the suggestions in these references. For each life cycle stage of the remanufacturable product, we obtain the system performance measures according to the following total numbers of buffer slots among the five system stations: $N = 12, 15, 18$. Here, for the optimum allocation of the total buffer spaces among the system's servers, we resort to the optimal buffer allocation algorithm (BAP) (Aksoy and Gupta, 2005). The BAP algorithm distributes the available number of buffer slots among the system stations to minimize the expected total system cost (E(TC)). We also obtain the other system performance measures: expected WIP inventory (E(WIP)) and expected system process time (E(PT)). In Tables 9.1 through 9.3, E(TC) stands for the long-run expected system cost, E(WIP) stands for the expected WIP inventory in the system, and E(PT) stands for the expected processing time (time spent in the system).

Table 9.1 shows the performance measures of the remanufacturing systems for the second stage (growth stage) for mean rate of return (λ_{ar}) and demand rate (D_t) for the following parameters: $\lambda_{ar} = 0.2, 0.4, 0.6, 0.8$ and $D_t = 0.8, 1.0$. We assume that the recovery rate for returned cores is normally distributed with coefficient of variation $c_v = 0.2, 0.4$ and 0.6, successively.

Figure 9.5 depicts the expected system cost and WIP inventory levels for the growth stage, where total buffer slots $N = 12, 15$, and 18 distributed optimally among the system stations.

TABLE 9.1

System Performance Measures for Growth (Second) Stage

	N = 12 (3-3-2-2-2)			N = 15 (4-3-3-3-2)			N = 18 (4-4-4-3-3)		
λ_r, D_t, cv_r	E(TC)	E(WIP)	E(PT)	E(TC)	E(WIP)	E(PT)	E(TC)	E(WIP)	E(PT)
(0.2,0.8,0.2)	58.82	7.56	8.32	60.03	8.48	8.51	62.30	8.56	8.71
(0.2,0.8,0.4)	56.35	7.84	8.58	58.90	8.76	8.84	61.17	8.65	8.92
(0.2,0.8,0.6)	54.12	8.18	8.81	57.24	9.02	9.30	60.26	8.78	9.14
(0.2,1.0,0.2)	60.41	7.92	9.11	62.78	8.94	9.63	64.92	9.03	9.83
(0.2,1.0,0.4)	59.17	8.11	9.43	61.83	9.36	9.89	63.97	9.43	10.34
(0.2,1.0,0.6)	57.28	8.34	9.90	60.05	9.77	10.36	63.03	9.92	11.26
(0.4,0.8,0.2)	61.43	8.86	10.31	66.21	9.83	10.82	67.71	10.23	11.76
(0.4,0.8,0.4)	60.72	9.15	10.43	64.76	10.12	11.28	66.56	10.82	12.42
(0.4,0.8,0.6)	60.02	9.42	10.57	63.11	10.43	11.83	65.39	11.30	12.78
(0.4,1.0,0.2)	64.85	9.84	10.82	67.38	10.86	11.98	68.10	11.48	12.91
(0.4,1.0,0.4)	63.29	9.91	11.23	65.62	11.17	12.35	67.82	11.53	13.37
(0.4,1.0,0.6)	62.82	10.23	11.54	64.20	11.38	12.51	63.23	11.75	13.64
(0.6,0.8,0.2)	65.23	10.58	12.07	70.53	11.73	12.72	71.32	12.11	13.88
(0.6,0.8,0.4)	64.51	10.83	12.41	68.91	11.92	12.87	70.83	12.62	14.17
(0.6,0.8,0.6)	63.28	11.05	12.84	67.14	12.14	13.04	70.47	12.84	14.42
(0.6,1.0,0.2)	67.66	11.31	13.20	71.21	12.34	13.26	73.82	12.98	14.73
(0.6,1.0,0.4)	65.81	11.49	13.74	70.94	12.68	13.48	72.92	13.31	14.85
(0.6,1.0,0.6)	64.32	11.84	13.88	69.49	12.91	13.63	70.34	13.72	15.11
(0.8,0.8,0.2)	70.47	12.18	14.13	72.98	13.35	13.80	74.26	14.08	15.32
(0.8,0.8,0.4)	68.93	12.54	14.39	71.45	13.52	14.02	73.78	14.38	15.54
(0.8,0.8,0.6)	67.48	12.75	14.47	70.38	13.83	14.27	72.36	14.59	15.78
(0.8,1.0,0.2)	71.13	13.07	14.71	73.12	14.12	14.83	75.73	14.82	15.98
(0.8,1.0,0.4)	70.57	13.32	14.92	72.73	14.41	15.19	74.41	15.06	16.23
(0.8,1.0,0.6)	69.34	13.44	15.16	70.95	14.59	15.36	72.90	15.32	16.57

TABLE 9.2

System Performance Measures for Maturity (Third) Stage

λ_r, D_t, cv_r	N = 12 (3-3-2-2-2)			N = 15 (4-3-3-3-2)			N = 18 (4-4-4-3-3)		
	E(TC)	E(WIP)	E(PT)	E(TC)	E(WIP)	E(PT)	E(TC)	E(WIP)	E(PT)
(0.9,1.0,0.1)	107.83	11.28	14.52	109.11	12.37	14.83	112.83	14.13	14.93
(0.9,1.0,0.2)	105.95	11.95	14.85	108.32	12.79	15.08	110.56	14.56	15.21
(0.9,1.0,0.3)	104.32	12.43	15.13	107.28	13.58	15.31	109.75	14.88	15.43
(0.9,1.0,0.4)	110.67	12.82	15.32	112.78	14.21	15.48	113.18	15.41	15.87
(0.9,1.0,0.5)	109.86	13.57	15.48	111.93	14.84	15.75	112.03	15.87	16.12
(0.9,1.0,0.6)	107.90	14.18	15.79	110.87	15.46	15.82	110.96	16.33	16.30
(0.9,1.0,0.7)	113.78	14.57	16.21	114.17	16.02	16.25	114.48	16.78	16.52
(0.9,1.0,0.8)	112.56	14.96	16.37	112.86	16.37	16.41	112.04	17.41	16.69
(0.9,1.0,0.9)	110.13	15.39	16.62	111.51	16.96	16.73	110.18	17.73	16.88

Table 9.2 shows that the performance measures of the remanufacturing systems for the third stage (maturity stage) for mean rate of return $\left(\lambda_{ar}\right)$ and demand rate (D_t) are steady for the following parameters: $\lambda_{ar} = 0.9$ and $D_t = 1.0$. We assume that the recovery rate for returned cores is normally distributed with coefficient of variation $c_v = 0.1, 0.2, 0.3, 0.4, 0.5, 0.6, 0.7, 0.8,$ and $0.9,$ successively.

TABLE 9.3

System Performance Measures for Decline (Fourth) Stage

λ_r, D_t, cv_r	N = 12 (3-3-2-2-2)			N = 15 (4-3-3-3-2)			N = 18 (4-4-4-3-3)		
	E(TC)	E(WIP)	E(PT)	E(TC)	E(WIP)	E(PT)	E(TC)	E(WIP)	E(PT)
(0.8,0.8,0.2)	70.47	12.18	14.13	72.98	13.35	13.80	74.26	14.08	15.32
(0.8,0.8,0.4)	68.93	12.54	14.39	71.45	13.52	14.02	73.78	14.38	15.54
(0.8,0.8,0.6)	67.48	12.75	14.47	70.38	13.83	14.27	72.36	14.59	15.78
(0.8,0.6,0.2)	68.24	12.42	14.16	71.21	13.56	13.97	72.65	14.23	15.54
(0.8,0.6,0.4)	67.16	12.06	13.86	70.18	13.27	13.71	71.27	13.97	15.31
(0.8,0.6,0.6)	65.42	11.65	13.72	68.53	13.02	13.53	70.08	13.76	15.05
(0.6,0.6,0.2)	66.35	11.19	13.54	69.46	12.81	13.12	70.62	13.52	14.82
(0.6,0.6,0.4)	64.19	10.73	13.21	68.23	12.65	12.84	69.80	13.34	14.73
(0.6,0.6,0.6)	63.24	10.32	12.98	67.11	12.30	12.76	67.46	13.17	14.58
(0.6,0.3,0.2)	64.76	9.98	12.81	69.03	11.96	12.53	68.22	12.89	14.36
(0.6,0.3,0.4)	63.32	9.73	12.63	67.96	11.84	12.41	67.64	12.75	14.20
(0.6,0.3,0.6)	61.15	9.45	12.24	66.34	11.61	12.20	66.71	12.52	14.01
(0.4,0.3,0.2)	62.47	9.13	11.79	67.34	11.23	11.94	67.82	12.30	13.68
(0.4,0.3,0.4)	61.69	8.81	11.62	66.17	11.02	11.65	67.18	12.16	13.52
(0.4,0.3,0.6)	60.02	8.56	11.35	64.85	10.78	11.32	66.41	11.94	13.34
(0.4,0.1,0.2)	62.35	8.24	11.08	65.24	10.37	11.14	67.26	11.76	13.20
(0.4,0.1,0.4)	60.64	8.06	10.84	64.31	10.11	10.86	65.83	11.59	12.91
(0.4,0.1,0.6)	59.40	7.83	10.63	63.26	9.84	10.63	64.34	11.27	12.64

Figure 9.6 depicts the expected system cost, process time, and WIP inventory levels for the maturity stage, where total buffer slots $N = 12$, 15 and 18 distributed optimally among the system stations.

Table 9.3 shows that the performance measures of the remanufacturing systems for the fourth stage (decline) for mean rate of return (λ_{ar}) and demand rate (D_t) are steady for the following parameters: $\lambda_{ar} = 0.8, 0.6, 0.4$ and $D_t = 0.8$, 0.6, 0.3, 0.1. We assume that the recovery rate for returned cores is normally distributed with coefficient of variation $c_v = 0.2, 0.4$, and 0.6, successively.

Figure 9.7 depicts the expected system cost and WIP inventory levels for the decline stage. where total buffer slots $N = 12$, 15, and 18 distributed optimally among the system stations.

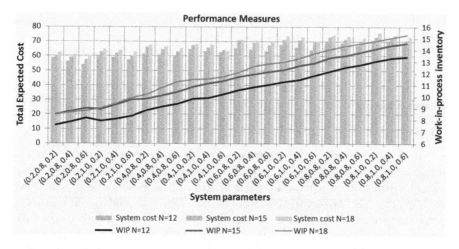

FIGURE 9.5
System performance measures for growth stage.

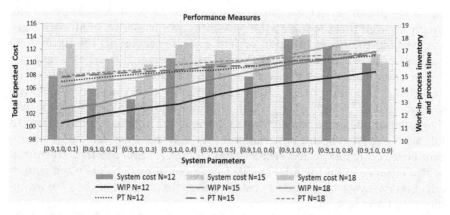

FIGURE 9.6
System performance measures for maturity stage.

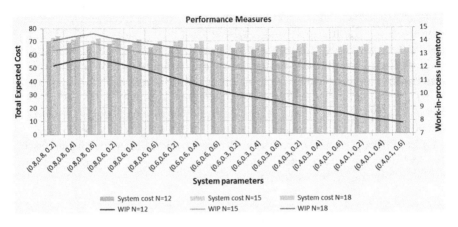

FIGURE 9.7
System performance measures for decline stage.

9.5 Results and Conclusions

In this chapter, we analyzed the hybrid system and investigated the effect of buffer size on dealing with the typical uncertainties of a remanufacturing system through the various life cycle stages of the recoverable product. We modeled the remanufacturing system as an OQN and analyzed it using the expansion method. To identify the entire effect of buffering through various demand and core return rates, we resorted to the typical life cycle of a remanufacturable product as defined by Van der Laan and Salomon (1997). The results of the experiments suggested that the recovery rate (r) and its coefficient of variation in conjunction with a used product return rate (λ_{ar}) has a significant effect on the system's expected total cost. Experiments clearly showed that the higher the reusability rate (r) with a small coefficient of variation, the lower the total system cost. In general, as the return rate increases, the expected total cost decreases. Moreover, a lower recovery rate coefficient of variation decreases the system's expected cost and reduces the expected processing time. Additionally, when used product return rates are low, which occurs during the growth stage, the total cost is relatively insensitive to variations in the recovery rate. Conversely, a high used product return rate with high coefficient of variation in the core recovery rate has a significant effect on the expected system total cost. In addition to these results, it is also observed that the total available number of buffer slots has a similar effect on the system's expected cost. This is a direct result of the WIP inventory effect on the system.

There are certain assumptions in this research that can be relaxed for upcoming potential research topics. In this study, we assumed that product return rate and demand are independent random variables. Nevertheless, certain products, especially those with a shorter life cycle, could be examined for a dependent return and demand pattern.

References

Aksoy, H. K. and Gupta, S. M. Buffer allocation plan for a remanufacturing cell. *Comput. Ind. Eng.* 2005, 48, 657–677.

Aksoy, H. K. and Gupta, S. M. Optimal management of remanufacturing systems with server vacations. *Int. J. Adv. Manuf. Tech.* 2011, 54, 1199–1218.

Bulmus, S. C., Zhu, S. X., and Teunter, R. Capacity and production decisions under a remanufacturing strategy. *Int. J. Prod. Econ.* 2013, 145, 359–370.

Carter, C. R. and Ellram, L. M. Reverse logistics: A review of the literature and framework for future investigation. *J. Bus. Logist.* 1998, 19, 85–102.

Deng, Q., Liao, H., Xu, B., and Liu, X. The resource benefits evaluation model on remanufacturing processes of end-of-life construction machinery under the uncertainty in recycling price. *Sustainability* 2017, 9, 1–21.

Dubey, R., Gunasekaran, A., Papadopoulos, T., Childe, S. J., Shibin, K. T., and Wamba, S. F. Sustainable supply chain management: Framework and further research directions. *J. Clean. Prod.* 2017, 142, 1119–1130.

Fleischmann, M., Krikke, H. R., Dekker, R., and Flapper, S. D. P. A characterisation of reverse logistics networks for product recovery. *Omega-Int. J. Manage. S.* 2000, 28, 653–666.

Geyer, R., Van Wassenhove, L. N., and Atasu, A. The economics of remanufacturing under limited component durability and finite product life cycles. *Manage. Sci.* 2007, 53, 88–100.

Govindan, K., Soleimani, H., and Kannan, D. Reverse logistics and closed-loop supply chain: A comprehensive review to explore the future. *Eur. J. Oper. Res.* 2015, 240, 603–626.

Gupta, S. M. and Kavusturucu, A. Modeling of finite buffer cellular manufacturing systems with unreliable machines. *Int. J. Ind. Eng.* 1998, 5, 265–277.

Gupta, S. M. and Kavusturucu, A. Production systems with interruptions, arbitrary topology and finite buffers. *Ann. Oper. Res.* 2000, 93, 145–176.

Gupta, S. M. and Lambert, A. J. D. (Editors). *Environment Conscious Manufacturing.* CRC Press, Boca Raton, Florida, 2008, ISBN: 9780849335525.

Gupta, S. M. (Editor). *Reverse Supply Chains Issues and Analysis.* CRC Press, Boca Raton, Florida, 2013, ISBN: 978-1-4398-9903-8.

Ilgin, M. A. and Gupta, S. M. Environmentally conscious manufacturing and product recovery (ECMPRO): A review of the state of the art. *J. Environ. Manage.* 2010, 91, 563–591.

Kavusturucu, A. and Gupta, S. M. Analysis of manufacturing flow lines with unreliable machines. *Int. J. Comput. Integ. M.* 1999, 12, 510–524.

Kerbache, L. and Smith, J. M. Asymptotic behavior of the expansion method for open finite queueing networks. *Comput. Oper. Res.* 1988, 15, 157–169.

Kwak, M. and Kim, H. Green profit maximization through integrated pricing and production planning for a line of new and remanufactured products. *J. Clean. Prod.* 2017, 142, 3454–3470.

Labetolle, J. and Pujolle, G. Isolation method in a network of queues. *IEEE T. Software Eng.* 1980, 6, 373–380.

Liao, H., Deng, Q., and Wang, Y. Optimal acquisition and production policy for end-of-life engineering machinery recovering in a joint manufacturing/remanufacturing system under uncertainties in procurement and demand. *Sustainability* 2017, 9, 1–19.

Mitra, S. Revenue management for remanufactured products. *Omega-Int. J. Manage. S.* 2007, 35, 553–562.

Pochampally, K. K., Nukala, S., and Gupta, S. M. *Strategic Planning Models for Reverse and Closed-Loop Supply Chains.* CRC Press, Boca Raton, Florida, 2009, ISBN: 9781420054781.

Robotis, A., Boyacı, T. and Verter, V. Investing in reusability of products of uncertain remanufacturing cost: The role of inspection capabilities. *Int. J. Prod. Econ.* 2012, 140, 385–395.

Rubio, S. and Corominas, A. Optimal manufacturing–remanufacturing policies in a lean production environment. *Comput. Ind. Eng.* 2008, 1, 234–242.

Rubio, S., Chamorro, A., and Miranda, F. J. Characteristics of the research on reverse logistics (1995–2005). *Int. J. Prod. Res.* 2008, 46, 1099–1120.

So, K. On the efficiency of unbalancing production lines. *Int. J. Prod. Res.* 1989, 27, 717–729.

Steeneck, D. W. and Sarin, S. C. Pricing and production planning for reverse supply chain: A review. *Int. J. Prod. Res.* 2013, 51, 6972–6989.

Subramoniam, R., Huisingh, D., Chinnam, R. B., and Subramoniam, S. Remanufacturing decision-making framework (RDMF): Research validation using the analytical hierarchical process. *J. Clean. Prod.* 2013, 40, 212–220.

Tang, O. and Naim, M. M. The impact of information transparency on the dynamic behavior of a hybrid manufacturing/remanufacturing system. *Int. J. Prod. Res.* 2004, 42(19), 4135–4152.

Testa, F. and Iraldo, F. Shadows and lights of GSCM (green supply chain management): Determinants and effects of these practices based on a multinational study. *J. Clean. Prod.* 2010, 18, 953–962.

Thierry, M., Salomon, M., van Nunen, J., and van Wassenhove, L. Strategic issues in product recovery management. *Calif. Manage. Rev.* 1995, 37, 114–135.

van der Laan, E. and Salomon, M. Production planning and inventory control with remanufacturing and disposal. *Eur. J. Oper. Res.* 1997, 102, 264–278.

Yang, C., Liu, H., Ji, P., and Ma, X. Optimal acquisition and remanufacturing policies for multi-product remanufacturing systems. *J. Clean. Prod.* 2016, 135, 1571–1579.

Zanoni, S., Ferretti, I., and Tang, O. Cost performance and bullwhip effect in a hybrid manufacturing and remanufacturing system with different control policies. *Int. J. Prod. Res.* 2006, 44, 3847–3862.

10

A Manufacturing–Remanufacturing System with Cannibalization and Market Expansion Effects

Aya Ishigaki, Tetsuo Yamada, and Surendra M. Gupta

CONTENTS

10.1 Introduction

The design of a closed-loop supply chain in the context of recycling or reusing promotes social responsibility and supports competitive abilities by making it possible for companies to offer sustainable products and services. However, to maintain a closed-loop supply chain, it is important to secure and control returned products (Gupta, 2013; Gupta and Ilgin, 2018; Ilgin and Gupta, 2010; Ilgin and Gupta, 2012; Kurilova-Palisaitiene and Sundin, 2014; Pochampally et al., 2009). That is, manufacturers need to plan production while understanding not only customer demand for newly manufactured and remanufactured products, but also the characteristics of returned products. Korugan and Gupta (1998) propose a two-stage inventory system and design an inventory system that uses an open-type queuing network model. Minner (2001) assumes that demand and returns are stationary and follow a normal distribution with a known mean and standard deviation. Mitra (2009, 2012) suggests a decision model for economic order quantity based on the assumption that the demand and returned product quantities follow a normal distribution. When remanufacturing products, there are two methods to follow: either a newly manufactured product is produced by reusing and recycling parts, or a remanufactured product is produced by replacing degraded or outdated parts. The latter is sold as a remanufactured product at a lower price than the newly manufactured product. Therefore, a cannibalization effect may occur in which the demand for newly manufactured products decreases. That is, consumers who would have originally purchased the newly manufactured products may instead purchase remanufactured products at a lower price. This section presents a manufacturing–remanufacturing system to decide a production plan and inventory control policy in consideration of the quantity of reusable products affected by past demand and the cannibalization effect.

10.2 The Model

10.2.1 New Product Diffusion Model

The Bass model was designed for the purpose of describing and predicting the time course of the number of sales of new products and has become the foundation of many studies (Bass, 1969). The Bass model is based on the following assumptions:

1. A repetitive purchase can be ignored during a planning period.
2. The number of customers is equal to the number of purchases.
3. A market consists of two kinds of customer: the innovator, who makes their own decision to purchase, and the imitator, whose decision is influenced by an existing customer according to the demonstration effect.
4. An innovator's purchase probability is constant.
5. The purchase probability of the imitator at period t is proportional to the probability of an existing customer from period 0 to t.
6. The size of a potential market is constant.

A probability density function of newly manufactured products at period t using the Bass model can be expressed as follows:

$$f(t) = \frac{p(p+q)^2 e^{-(p+q)t}}{(p + qe^{-(p+q)t})^2},$$

(10.1)

where

$f(t)$:   probability density function of newly manufactured products at period t

p: coefficient of innovation
q: coefficient of imitation

10.2.2 General Demand Model

Because demand tends to decrease as the price of a product increases, the demand model shown in Equation 10.2 is used in many studies:

$$D(P) = M - bP, \qquad (10.2)$$

where
$D(P)$: potential market size at price P
P: price of products
M: potential market scale
b: price sensitivity

10.2.3 Demand Model with Cannibalization

In this section, we present a demand model for newly manufactured products and remanufactured products that are affected by price while taking into consideration cannibalization and market expansion effects. The following notation is used to formulate the demand with the cannibalization effect:

P_1: price of newly manufactured products
P_2: price of remanufactured products
γ: cannibalization rate
$d_n(t)$: demand for newly manufactured products at period t
$d_r(t)$: demand for remanufactured products at period t
st: sales starting period of remanufactured products

We define the prices of newly manufactured and remanufactured products as P_1 and P_2, respectively. Using Equation 10.2, it is clear that $D(P_1) < D(P_2)$, as we assume that $P_1 > P_2$. The increased part of the market size $D(P_2) - D(P_1)$ due to the price falling from P_1 to P_2 can be considered as purchasing remanufactured products. Because the customer who does not purchase at the price P_1 originally purchases at price P_2, it is said that the market has been expanded. On the other hand, when remanufactured products are sold at a lower price than newly manufactured products, the demand for newly manufactured products decreases due to the cannibalization effect, assuming that the cannibalization rate γ is defined as the degree of demand of newly manufactured product reduction by cannibalization. When the sale of remanufactured products starts, $D(P_1)$ is divided into the market $(1 - \gamma)D(P_1)$ of newly manufactured products and the market $\gamma D(P_1)$ of remanufactured products, respectively. Finally, the demand for newly manufactured products and remanufactured products in period t, considering cannibalization and market expansion effects, is denoted by the following equations:

$$d_n(t) = \begin{cases} D(P_1)f(t), & t < \Delta t \\ (1-\gamma)D(P_1)f(t), & t \geq \Delta t \end{cases}'$$ (10.3)

$$d_r(t) = \begin{cases} 0, & t < \Delta t \\ \left[b(P_1 - P_2) + \gamma D(P_1)\right]f(t), & t \geq \Delta t \end{cases}.$$ (10.4)

Figure 10.1 shows the demand when it is set as $M = 10{,}000$, $b = 0.2$, $P_1 = 6000$, $P_1 = 4000$, $p = .005$, $q = 0.1$, $st = 30$, and $\gamma = 0.3$. The market is expanded by the sale of remanufactured products having started at period 30. The demand for newly manufactured products is reduced by 30 percent according to the cannibalization effect.

10.2.4 Production Planning

In this section, we present a manufacturing–remanufacturing system. The basis of our model is a manufacturing–remanufacturing model by Okuda et al. (2018), and some scenarios are considered using this model. The recovery period of product k recovered at the jth time, $T(k, j)$, is calculated by adding the use period of each product $U(k, j)$ when the product was sold for period t.

$$T(k,j) = t + U(k,j)$$ (10.5)

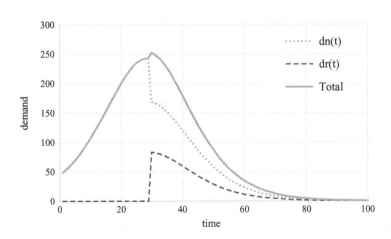

FIGURE 10.1
Demand for newly manufactured products and remanufactured products.

To calculate the quantity of reusable products and disposals, we introduce an indicator function χ_t, which takes the value of 1 when products are recovered from period $t-1$ to t, and 0 otherwise.

$$\chi_t\{T(k,j)\} = \begin{cases} 1, & t-1 \le T(k,j) < t \\ 0, & otherwise \end{cases}. \tag{10.6}$$

Here, it is assumed that a product can be remanufactured a maximum of n times. In other words, the products are discarded when returned for the $(n+1)$th time. Next, we define $S_n(t)$ and $S_r(t)$ as the sales quantity of newly manufactured and remanufactured products at period t. The quantity of reusable and disposal products at period t is defined as $R(t)$ and $W(t)$, respectively, as follows:

$$R(t) = r \sum_{i=1}^{S(t)} \sum_{j=1}^{n} \chi_t\{T(i,j)\}, \tag{10.7}$$

$$W(t) = r \sum_{i=1}^{S(t)} \chi_t\{T(i,n+1)\}, \tag{10.8}$$

where

$S(t)$: total sales until period t ($S(t) = \sum_{k=1}^{t}(S_n(k)+S_r(k))$),

r: return rate

We defined $M_n(t)$ and $M_r(t)$ as the quantity of newly manufactured and remanufactured products, respectively, at period t. A production capacity upper limit is set for the production facility, and the quantity of products is balanced.

$$M_n(t) = \begin{cases} d_n(t+l_n), & d_n(t+l_n) \le m_n \\ m_n, & d_n(t+l_n) > m_n \end{cases},$$

$$M_r(t) = \begin{cases} d_r(t+l_r), & d_r(t+l_r) \le m_r \\ m_r, & d_r(t+l_r) > m_r \end{cases}, \tag{10.9}$$

where
l_n: lead time for manufacturing
l_r: lead time for remanufacturing
m_n: production capacity of manufacturing
m_r: production capacity of remanufacturing

Finally, the quantities of inventory, shortages, and sales of products are shown as follows:

$$I_n(t) = I_n(t-1) + M_n(t-l_n) - S_n(t), \tag{10.10}$$

$$I_r(t) = I_r(t-1) + M_r(t-l_r) - S_r(t), \tag{10.11}$$

$$I_u(t) = I_u(t-1) + R(t) - M_r(t), \tag{10.12}$$

$$L_n(t) = d_n(t) - S_n(t), \tag{10.13}$$

$$L_r(t) = d_r(t) - S_r(t), \tag{10.14}$$

$$S_n(t) = \begin{cases} d_n(t), & d_n(t) \le I_n(t-1) + M_n(t-l_n) \\ I_n(t-1) + M_n(t-l_n), & d_n(t) > I_n(t-1) + M_n(t-l_n) \end{cases}, \tag{10.15}$$

$$S_r(t) = \begin{cases} d_r(t), & d_r(t) \le I_r(t-1) + M_r(t-l_r) \\ I_r(t-1) + M_r(t-l_r), & d_r(t) > I_r(t-1) + M_r(t-l_r) \end{cases}, \tag{10.16}$$

where
$I_n(t)$: inventory of newly manufactured products at period t
$I_r(t)$: inventory of remanufactured products at period t
$I_u(t)$: inventory of reusable products at period t
$S_n(t)$: sales quantity of newly manufactured products at period t
$S_r(t)$: sales quantity of remanufactured products at period t
$L_n(t)$: shortage of newly manufactured products at period t
$L_r(t)$: shortage of remanufactured products at period t

The total profit of this system can be derived by the following equation:

$$\Pi = \sum_{t=1}^{H} \{ S_n(t)P_1 + S_r(t)P_2 - (M_n(t)C_n + M_r(t)(C_r + C_d) + W(t)C_w)$$

$$- (I_n(t)C_{hn} + I_r(t)C_{hr} + I_u(t)C_{hu} + L_n(t)C_{sn} + L_r(t)C_{sr}) \}, \tag{10.17}$$

where
C_n: production cost of newly manufacturing product per unit
C_r: production cost of remanufacturing product per unit
C_d: decomposition cost of product per unit
C_{hn}: inventory holding cost of newly manufacturing product per unit per period
C_{hr}: inventory holding cost of remanufacturing product per unit per period
C_{hu}: inventory holding cost of reusable product per unit per period
C_{sn}: shortage cost of newly manufacturing product per unit per period
C_{sr}: shortage cost of remanufacturing product per unit per period

10.3 Numerical Example

In this section, a numerical experiment is performed to investigate the economic efficiency of a manufacturing–remanufacturing system with cannibalization effect.

The demand for newly manufactured and remanufactured products changes not only with the cannibalization rate but also with the sales starting period. Furthermore, when demand for products changes, the number of collections of used products also changes. Therefore, it is necessary to predict the time change of demand and the number of collections of used products and to determine the production planning and sales starting period of remanufactured products.

Rai and Singh (2006) show that the relationship between automobile mileage and downtime adhered well to a logarithmic normal distribution. We assume that the use period of each product is generated as a random number according to a normal distribution $N(\mu, \sigma)$. The parameters used in this section are shown in Table 10.1.

The price of remanufactured product P_2 is expressed using a discount rate for the price of a newly manufactured product P_1. The discount rate changed by 0.1–0.9. Moreover, Ovchinnikov (2011) shows the two kinds of relationships between discount rate and cannibalization rate: the consumers' willingness to pay (WTP) type and the U-shaped type. The WTP type is traditional consumer behavior, and the cannibalization rate increases with the increase in the discount rate. On the other hand, it is known that profits will be increased by incorporating inverted U-shaped customer behavior. We used the relation shown in Table 10.2 to investigate the effect of these settings.

The other parameters were set as follows:

Lead time for manufacturing and remanufacturing = 1; maximum number of remanufacturing cycles = 2; planning horizon = 150; production cost of manufacturing and remanufacturing per unit = (130, 90); decomposition cost of used product per unit = 10; disposal cost of used product per unit = 10; inventory holding cost per unit per period of manufactured product, remanufactured product, and used product = (30, 15, 15); and shortage cost per unit per period of manufactured product and remanufactured product = (15, 10).

TABLE 10.1

Parameter Setting

p	0.005	b	0.2
q	0.1	r	0.516
P_1	250	μ	5
M	5000	σ	1

TABLE 10.2

Relationship between Discount Rate and Cannibalization Rate

	γ	
Discount Rate	WTP	U-shape
0.1	0.35	0.35
0.2	0.65	0.65
0.3	0.70	0.47
0.4	0.82	0.43
0.5	0.82	0.23
0.6	0.82	0.18
0.7	0.82	0.06
0.8	0.90	0.12
0.9	0.95	0.18

Production capacity was investigated by ten units from 10 to 110, and the one with the maximum profit was selected.

Table 10.3 shows the result for *st* and total profit in the case when the cannibalization rate is a WTP type. In this case, the total profit becomes the maximum when the discount rate is 0.2 and *st* = 25.

Table 10.4 shows the costs and revenues for *st* in the case when the cannibalization rate is WTP type (discount rate = 0.2). If the sales starting period of remanufactured products is too early, a shortage of remanufactured products will occur. If the sales starting period is too late, the amount of inventory of reusable products will increase. In the case of coefficient of innovation $p = .005$ and coefficient of imitation $q = 0.1$, total demand increases and becomes the maximum at $t = 30$. Then, even if the sales starting period of remanufactured products is delayed, the production cost and revenue of remanufactured products increase until $t = 30$. However, the amount of inventory of reusable products increases greatly when the sales starting period is late, and then, the total profits decrease.

TABLE 10.3

Total Profit for Discount Rate and Sales Starting Period (WTP)

st	Discount Rate								
	0.1	0.2	0.3	0.4	0.5	0.6	0.7	0.8	0.9
5	180,330	274,125	210,300	100,355	86,530	73,620	61,740	12,105	−16,770
10	202,880	299,365	237,635	128,755	112,475	97,515	82,775	32,585	2,445
15	198,100	330,750	268,065	164,805	145,835	126,900	109,110	58,345	26,480
20	180,055	359,700	298,755	203,970	181,750	155,815	133,190	82,840	48,210
25	119,185	360,980	309,515	227,570	201,775	175,480	139,415	97,685	62,475
30	60,135	278,575	255,070	200,865	179,075	134,985	101,070	63,175	20,150

TABLE 10.4

Costs and Revenues for st (Cannibalization Rate is WTP Type, Discount Rate = 0.2)

st	Profit ($)	Production Cost ($)		Disassembly Cost ($)	Holding Cost ($)			Shortage Cost ($)		Disposal Cost ($)	Total Cost ($)	Revenue ($)		Total Revenue ($)
		New	Remanu-facturing		New	Remanu-facturing	Reusable	New	Remanu-facturing			New	Remanu-facturing	
5	274,125	235,170	88,740	9,860	0	0	15,045	0	21,440	5,070	375,325	452,250	197,200	649,450
10	299,365	255,060	94,500	10,500	0	0	16,425	0	19,270	5,380	401,135	490,500	210,000	700,500
15	330,750	284,700	105,750	11,750	0	0	27,480	0	15,750	6,320	451,750	547,500	235,000	782,500
20	359,700	325,390	118,260	13,140	0	0	54,300	0	11,220	6,540	528,850	625,750	262,800	888,550
25	360,980	369,980	129,960	14,440	0	0	110,685	765	5,980	7,510	639,320	711,500	288,800	1,000,300
30	278,575	419,640	143,460	15,940	0	0	258,360	1,605	90	8,130	847,225	807,000	318,800	1,125,800

Table 10.5 shows the costs and revenues for discount rate in the case when the cannibalization rate is WTP type ($st = 25$). If the discount rate increases, demand increases due to the market expansion effect. Since the price of remanufactured products will decrease when the discount rate increases, the revenue decreases. These examples are not concerned with the sales starting period of remanufactured products, and total profits are always high when the discount rate is 0.2. On the other hand, if a discount rate exceeds 0, revenue decreases gradually. This is because total profit decreases with the decrease in the price of remanufactured products, and the shortage of remanufactured products increases with the increase in demand for remanufactured products.

Table 10.6 shows the result for st and total profit in case when the cannibalization rate is an inverted U-shape. In this case, total profit reaches the maximum when the discount rate is 0.3 and $st = 20$ and the minimum when the discount rate is 0.7. This is because of the price of remanufactured products being low and the cannibalization rate reaching its minimum.

10.4 Other Models

Souza (2013) discusses the pricing of newly manufactured and remanufactured products and insists that it should take into consideration both the cannibalization and the market expansion effects. Nanasawa and Kainuma (2017) investigate the cannibalization effect in a manufacturing–remanufacturing system. They illuminate the profitability of the system by considering a two-stage scenario in which only new products are sold in the first stage, and both new and remanufactured products are sold in the second stage. Atasu et al. (2008) investigate the impact of competition between original equipment manufacturers, the existence of green consumers, and the change in market size on the profitability of remanufacturing. Ovchinnikov (2011) analyzes the pricing strategy for a firm that is considering putting remanufactured products on the market together with new products. This study estimates the number of consumers who would switch from purchasing a new product to purchasing a remanufactured product at a lower price and shows that it is an inverted U-shape. Zhou et al. (2017) develop a model for solving the pricing problem of the latest generation of remanufactured products and the old generation of newly manufactured products. Okuda et al. (2018) design a manufacturing–remanufacturing system with cannibalization effect and investigate the influence of the price of remanufactured products, cannibalization rate, and sales starting period of remanufactured products on the total profit and remanufacturing rate of our system.

TABLE 10.5

Costs and Revenues for Discount Rate (Cannibalization Rate is a WTP Type, $st = 25$)

Discount rate	Profit ($)	Production Cost ($)		Disassembly Cost ($)	Holding Cost ($)			Shortage Cost ($)		Disposal Cost ($)	Total Cost ($)	Revenue ($)		Total Revenue ($)
		New	Remanu-facturing		New	Remanu-facturing	Reusable	New	Remanu-facturing			New	Remanu-facturing	
0.1	119,185	291,850	89,100	9,900	0	0	243,720	23,865	1,110	5,270	664,815	561,250	222,750	784,000
0.2	360,980	369,980	129,960	14,440	0	0	110,685	765	5,980	7,510	639,320	711,500	288,800	1,000,300
0.3	309,515	352,560	126,810	14,090	0	0	105,660	450	7,970	7,520	615,060	678,000	246,575	924,575
0.4	227,570	302,250	103,590	11,510	0	0	88,170	510	14,340	5,960	526,330	581,250	172,650	753,900
0.5	201,775	306,670	109,710	12,190	0	0	91,800	0	13,710	6,270	540,350	589,750	152,375	742,125
0.6	175,480	306,670	105,840	11,760	0	0	87,540	0	14,180	5,880	531,870	589,750	117,600	707,350
0.7	139,415	306,670	108,630	12,070	0	0	93,600	0	13,890	6,000	540,860	589,750	90,525	680,275
0.8	97,685	274,690	90,270	10,030	0	0	81,945	0	18,470	5,310	480,715	528,250	50,150	578,400
0.9	62,475	254,280	84,510	9,390	0	0	76,320	0	20,740	4,760	450,000	489,000	23,475	512,475

TABLE 10.6

Total Profit for Discount Rate and Sales Starting Period (Inverted U-Shape)

	Discount Rate								
st	0.1	0.2	0.3	0.4	0.5	0.6	0.7	0.8	0.9
5	180,330	274,125	361,270	294,405	−41,160	−63,950	−160,870	−112,665	−97,875
10	202,880	299,365	380,655	302,020	−43,625	−63,245	−143,610	−121,350	−76,305
15	198,100	330,750	395,750	320,850	−33,330	−68,910	−169,720	−95,480	−99,680
20	180,055	359,700	403,685	329,035	−37,435	−84,085	−171,410	−114,620	−106,115
25	119,185	360,980	287,960	155,600	−63,345	−82,125	−277,065	−143,460	−110,530
30	60,135	278,575	65	−196,755	−72,870	−78,545	−313,495	−148,705	−108,875

10.5 Conclusions

This chapter presented a demand model that is dependent not only on the price of remanufactured products but also on the sales starting period of remanufactured products. In this chapter, the Bass model and the cannibalization rate according to the discount rate of the remanufactured product price were used to design the demand model. As a result of numerical examples using the relation between the two kinds of discount rates and the cannibalization rate, the optimal discount rate and sales starting period of remanufactured products were determined.

References

Atasu, A., Sarvary, M. and Van Wassenhove, L. N., "Remanufacturing as a marketing strategy", *Management Science* 54, 1731–1746, 2008.

Bass, F. M., "A new product growth model for consumer durables", *Management Science* 15, 215–227, 1969.

Gupta, S. M., "*Reverse Supply Chains: Issues and Analysis*", CRC Press, Boca Raton, Florida, ISBN: 978-1439899021, 2013.

Gupta, S. M. and Ilgin, M. A., "*Multiple Criteria Decision Making Applications in Environmentally Conscious Manufacturing and Product Recovery*", CRC Press, Boca Raton, Florida, ISBN: 978-1498700658, 2018.

Ilgin, M. A. and Gupta, S. M., "Environmentally conscious manufacturing and product recovery (ECMPRO): A review of the state of the art", *Journal of Environmental Management* 91, 563–591, 2010.

Ilgin, M. A. and Gupta, S. M., "Remanufacturing Modeling and Analysis", CRC Press, Boca Raton, Florida, ISBN: 9781439863077, 2012.

Korugan, A. and Gupta, S. M., "A multi-echelon inventory system with returns", *Computers & Industrial Engineering* 35, 145–148, 1998.

Kurilova-Palisaitiene, J. and Sundin, E., "Challenges and opportunities of lean remanufacturing", *International Journal of Automation Technology* 8, 644–652, 2014.

Minner, S., "Strategic safety stocks in reverse logistics supply chains", *International Journal of Production Economics* 71, 417–428, 2001.

Mitra, S., "Analysis of a two-echelon inventory system with returns", *Omega* 37, 106–115, 2009.

Mitra, S., "Inventory management in a two-echelon closed-loop supply chain with correlated demands and returns", *Computers and Industrial Engineering* 62, 870–879, 2012.

Nanasawa, T. and Kainuma, Y., "Quantifying the cannibalization effect of hybrid manufacturing/remanufacturing system in closed-loop supply chain", *Procedia CIRP* 61, 201–205, 2017.

Okuda, A., Ishigaki, A., Yamada, T. and Gupta, S. M., "Inventory management in a manufacturing-remanufacturing system with cannibalization and stochastic returns", *LogForum* 14, 113–125, 2018.

Ovchinnikov, A., "Revenue and cost management for remanufactured products", *Production and Operation Management* 20, 824–840, 2011.

Pochampally, K. K., Nukala, S. and Gupta, S. M., "*Strategic Planning Models for Reverse and Closed-loop Supply Chains*", CRC Press, Boca Raton, Florida, ISBN: 9781420054781, 2009.

Rai, B. and Singh, N., "Customer-rush near warranty expiration limit and nonparametric hazard rate estimation from known mileage accumulation rates", *IEEE Transactions on Reliability* 55, 480–489, 2006.

Souza, G. C., "Closed-loop supply chains: A critical review, and future research", *Decision Science* 44, 53–80, 2013.

Zhou, L., Gupta, S. M., Kinoshita, Y. and Yamada, T. "Pricing decision models for remanufactured short-life cycle technology products with generation consideration", *Procedia CIRP* 61, 195–200, 2017.

11

Warranty Fraud in a Remanufacturing Environment

Aditya Pandit and Surendra M. Gupta

CONTENTS

11.1 Introduction

Advances in technology have fueled a rise in electronics and thus endowed customers with access to inexpensive, high-quality consumer goods. The abundance of high-quality and inexpensive products has also altered consumers' behavior. One noticeable change is that now, products are quite often disposed of before they actually spoil or fail. This leads to products becoming obsolete in a much shorter time even though they still have remaining life. Consequently, there is a shortened product life cycle, which leads to a steady degradation of natural resources to compensate for the ever-increasing demands of customers and introduces even more waste into the environment.

Environmental legislation has encouraged firms to move away from disposal and more toward end-of-life (EOL) strategies. Over the past few decades, changing legislation as well as competitive market forces has driven companies to involve themselves in more eco-friendly activities. Environmentally conscious manufacturing can be carried out at any stage of the product's life, from a product's design phase to its EOL, which are all instrumental in getting a product to meet environmental standards. The management of waste is becoming a problem with an ever-burgeoning population. An issue related to environmentally conscious manufacturing and product recovery (ECMPRO), which focuses on minimizing the amount of waste that is ultimately sent to landfills by extracting usable material through EOL processes such as recycling (Gungor and Gupta, 1999; Ilgin and Gupta, 2010). It is for these among other reasons that EOL processes should be conducted with the aim of maximizing recycling, reducing the total amount of landfilled materials, and controlling the disposal of hazardous materials, all while still remaining profitable.

A field related to ECMPRO is environmentally responsible manufacturing (ERM). ERM has been defined as an economically driven, integrated approach to the reduction and elimination of all waste associated with the design, manufacture, use, and/or disposal of products and materials (Curkovic and Landeros, 2000; Handfield et al., 1997; Melnyk et al., 2001). By keeping waste to a minimum, the firm can reduce disposal costs and permit requirements, avoid environmental fines, boost profits, discover new business opportunities, rejuvenate employee morale, and protect and improve the state of the environment (Hanna et al., 2000).

One such waste stream arises from the presence of fraudulent activities in the supply chain, which not only generates excessive costs but also requires time and resources to deal with. Frauds in the new product industry have been generally well covered in recent literature (Mu and Carroll, 2016; Green and Choi, 1997; Shih et al., 2011; Zhang et al., 2010); however, issues of fraud in the remanufacturing industry have yet to be explored in a meaningful way. This chapter covers the basics of fraud and ways to mitigate it to reach the goal of responsible manufacturing.

11.2 Literature Review

There exists a trove of scientific papers and journals that discuss the different areas of ECMPRO. An extensive review was conducted by Gungor and Gupta (1999), which was later updated by Ilgin and Gupta (2010). The role of enforcing ECMPRO in the industry is through government regulations and through public pressure arising from concerns over environmental degradation.

Similarly, a core understanding of ERM is the recognition that pollution, irrespective of its type and form, is waste. Strategies such as Total Quality Management and Just-In-Time have defined waste as any activity or product that consumes resources or creates costs without generating any form of off-setting stream of value (Porter, 1991; Porter and Van der Linde, 1995).

The subject of EOL was thus first explored in response to the increasing levels of industrial wastes accumulating worldwide. There was a strong need for new guidelines and disposal methods. Some notable strategies that were developed in response to this phenomenon included design for reman-ufacture, design for disassembly, and design for assembly (Veerakamolmal and Gupta, 2000). A number of avenues for approaching the EOL products recovery problem have been proposed by Lambert (2003), Lambert and Gupta (2002), and Xiong et al. (2008). Before one decides to go through with an EOL process, it is important to check whether the product can be repaired. If the product cannot be brought back to a functional state, one or more of the EOL processes should be available to the owner. Recycling, remanufacturing, and reuse are the primary EOL activities that a decision maker considers. The majority of recoverable waste comes from electronic waste, and as a conse-quence, many methods have been proposed to deal with it effectively.

When it comes to reuse, knowing whether or not a product is reusable can be an issue. Breaking down a product or "disassembly" plays an important role in remanufacturing and recycling. Go et al. (2011) presents a review of several disassemblability methods, including EOL value and time for disassembly. Hatcher et al. (2011) reviewed the different approaches to remanufacturing, including predicting what remanufacturing needs may arise in the future. In a related paper, Ahmed et al. (2013) proposed the idea that there exists an optimal number of times that a product can be recovered, which establishes the finite number of times that a product may be remanufactured.

Remanufacturing is in essence a process of disassembly and recovery. It aims at replacing and repairing worn-out and obsolete components and brings the product back to new condition. Of all the EOL processes, remanufactur-ing involves the most work, and consequently, remanufactured products have better quality and reliability compared with repaired and reused products. This can be partly attributed to the fact that the process of remanufacturing requires disassembly (i.e., the total dismantling of the product) and then reas-sembly of its components, during which any worn or spoilt components are replaced. Remanufacturing is currently most frequently applied to consumer electronics, which involve complex electro-mechanical and mechanical prod-ucts with cores that, when recovered, will have value added to them that is high relative both to their market value and to their original cost (Lund, 1985). Remanufacturing is even better than recycling from an environmental aspect, in that remanufacturing preserves the embodied energy that has been used to shape the components for their first life, but in recycling, some energy is expended in converting products into their raw materials. It was estimated that a remanufactured product requires only one-quarter of the energy used in its initial formation (Lund, 1985). Therefore, in addition to the material being reused, the energy required to produce a remanufactured product is significantly lower than for a manufactured product. Although the environmental advantages are clear, there are other benefits from remanufacturing. While remanufactured products can boast many benefits, consumers are still hesitant to purchase remanufactured products. Because of misconceptions held by consumers, manufacturers often search for market mechanisms to encourage consumers to purchase their products.

Warranty has in the past been used as a tool for competitive marketing. Many manufacturers and researchers have explored a host of ways to make a product more appealing by experimenting with warranty policies: doing things such as adding additional services, extending the periods, offering favorable terms, and so on. Podolyakina (2017) identified the relative level of cost incurred by the manufacturer to fully satisfy the consumer's warranty expectation. The competitive strategy that is based on adding services is sometimes referred to as *servitization*. A customer perception of what a warranty is called also affects their willingness to purchase a product. Wilkes and Wilcox (1981) conducted an empirical survey to identify, if a consumer was presented with a product (a microwave oven) with a limited warranty versus one with a full warranty, which they would find more appealing. They noted that the product with the limited warranty was seen as less desirable. When it comes to price, Chen et al. (2012) explored the competiveness of several pricing scenarios, in one of which the product prices remained the same, but the warranty services were different.

While the consumer never interacts directly with the manufacturer but only through a retailer, there is no doubt that the marketing the manufacturer is conducting is aimed at the consumer and not at any of the intermediaries. The consumer relies on the manufacturer more than they do on the retailer regarding the nature and quality of the goods, and this fact has strongly influenced courts in warranty cases (Southwick, 1963). The majority of the extant literature has been focused on warranties with respect to the new product industry. Many of the same issues have also been tackled in the remanufacturing sector as well. Alqahtani and Gupta (2017a) considered a two-dimensional warranty policy with the objective to maximize consumer confidence and minimize cost to the remanufacturer. Yeh and Fang (2015) attempted to decide on the best marketing strategy to integrate decisions such as pricing, warranty service, and production with the goal of maximizing profits. Unfortunately for the warranty provider (WP), there are other parties, such as customers and maintenance service agents (SAs), who are also trying to maximize their own profits. This may lead to overinflated prices, which may fit under the umbrella of competitive pricing but may just as easily fall under the category of fraud.

Vendors typically lose 3 to 5 percent of revenue to warranty and support abuse, according to an AGMA (alliance for grey market and counterfeit abatement) study. Warranty fraud is a significant problem affecting motor vehicles and other consumer products having multiple components that are the subject of a warranty. In general, one can define fraud as a deliberate action or mistake made by a person or a group of persons in the knowledge that the error may result in some benefits that are not to individuals or entities or other parties (Ernst and Young, 2009). Fraud can also be seen as the misrepresentation, storage, or negligence of a truth for the purpose of manipulating a financial statement to harm a company or organization; this also includes embezzlement, theft, or any attempt to steal or unlawfully obtain, abuse, or harm the assets of an organization (Abdullahi and Mansor, 2015).

The two prevalent classical fraud theories are (i) the fraud triangle theory and (ii) the fraud diamond theory. This comparison is important to assist anti-graft bodies and organizations in formulating a practical strategy to prevent and investigate organizational frauds. When the two fraud theories are compared, it can be surmised that if there are significant financial benefits to be gained and limited risk of getting caught, there are some people and companies who will try to take advantage of the opportunity, resulting in fraud. This can occur in the context of both individuals and companies.

Fraud prediction requires a large amount of product life cycle data, which often is not available. Sensors are often employed to monitor products during their life cycles and to remotely and continuously track their usage patterns. Integrating sensors into products can help produce vital data related to the conditions of products and their components, and this information can later on be used to inform EOL decision-making. Ondemir and Gupta (2014a) investigated how sensors and radio-frequency identification (RFID) tags could be used to assist product recovery operations and propose an advanced remanufacturing-to-order and disassembly-to-order (ARTODTO) system for EOL sensor-embedded products (SEPs). Ondemir and Gupta (2014b) extended this concept to use the Internet of Things in a formulated mixed integer goal programming model. Dulman and Gupta (2018) proposed that the information collected by the sensors could also be used to estimate and predict product failures, thereby helping to improve maintenance operations. It was theorized by Kurvinen et al. (2016) that sensors might also show potential in catching warranty-related fraud. The concept of sensor implementation to assist in warranty-related activities has been recently explored by Alqahtani and Gupta (2017b) in developing warranty policies. It would then stand to reason that SEPs could be one possible solution in dealing with fraud.

11.3 Actors and Victims of Fraud

Table 11.1 shows the key factors that are important in the context of fraud. Most people and companies have higher integrity and will not take advantage of the opportunity. Additionally, the likelihood and consequences of

TABLE 11.1

Key Factors That Decide Potential Fraud

Factors for	Factors Against
Opportunity	Consequences of getting caught
Financial potential	Risks of getting caught
Lack of integrity	

getting caught have an impact on the chances of fraud taking place. With the current level of mobile and social media technology, fraudsters have access to a larger number of potential victims and a statistically better likelihood of finding people who will eventually fall into the trap. There are many ways of viewing the problem of fraud; Figure 11.1 shows the multitude of ways in which fraud may be categorized.

Fraud can potentially exist in any sectors where a monetary transaction occurs. These transactions may occur over multiple media such as mail, wire, phone, and more recently, the Internet. Fraud can also be carried out by almost any of the parties involved in the transaction. When it comes to dealing with fraud, any actions taken typically fall under either fraud avoidance or fraud deterrence. One way of tackling fraud when the seller is responsible is through government legislation. In the United States, organizations such as the Securities and Exchange Commission (SEC) and the Federal Trade Commission (FTC) are responsible for monitoring and punishing fraud. Fraud is also monitored and investigated at the more local level. Practices such as internal audits and random inspections help in rooting out any discrepancies, as it is in the interest of companies to, at the very least, give the appearance (to their investors) that they take such threats seriously.

When the guilty party is the consumer, frauds are usually rooted out through investigations carried out by the defrauded party. Traditionally, companies use a predetermined set of business rules to evaluate claims that are sent to them. But smart fraudsters can work around any publicly known set of rules to their own advantage. Historically, statistical fraud detection methods have been useful in handling fraud. They can be further subdivided into supervised and unsupervised methods. In supervised methods, models are constructed based on a historical data set with known fraudulent and non-fraudulent cases. Using

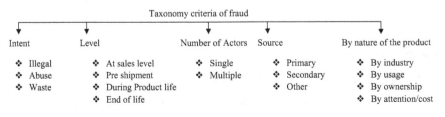

FIGURE 11.1
Taxonomy criteria of fraud.

defined criteria and threshold values, a new observation can be assigned as being either fraudulent or non-fraudulent. Widely used statistical classification methods such as linear discriminant analysis and neural network methods have been shown to be effective tools in such supervised situations (Hand, 1981, 1997; McLachlan, 1992; Ripley, 1996; Webb, 1999). Hawkins et al. (2011) propose a hybrid approach combining business rules, anomaly detection, advanced analytics, and social network analysis into hybrid fraud algorithms to score each claim. This frees up auditors to look at claims that are 100 percent fraudulent and not some random selection of claims.

In general cases, one assumes that fraud occurs between two players, namely, the seller and the buyer; however, it is more complex when we talk about fraud in industry. Often, product manufacturers are required to outsource services to outside companies or service providers. A typical remanufactured product warranty servicing scenario (Figure 11.2) (Kurvinen et.al, 2016) is considered, wherein a WP offers a warranty on a remanufactured product to a customer, which also shows a host of other parties that may be involved in the act of fraud. The level of trust that a company has in a third party service provider can help in avoiding or quantifying the level of fraud. Trust models serve as decision criteria for whether to decide to co-operate with an external agent. Trust can be modeled by considering factors such as intent, competence, availability, and promptness. Barber et al. (2003) dealt with establishing an initial level of trust with a SA prior to any form of interaction of the company

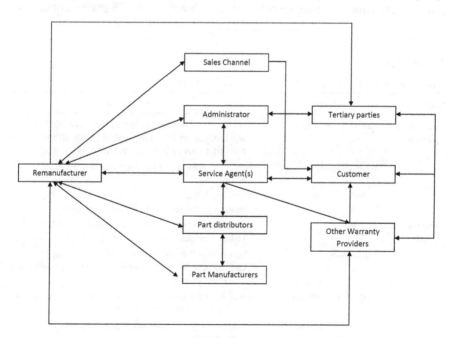

FIGURE 11.2
Key parties involved in a warranty servicing chain.

with the said agent. The most prominent types of fraud are insurance fraud, financial fraud, and business fraud, and the types of fraud that they involve are distinct and may offer clues as to how to solve warranty-related frauds.

The primary players involved in a remanufacturing fraud scenario are the WP, the SA, and the customer; the remaining parties of the chain can be subdivided into secondary and tertiary parties, and their roles will be described in Table 11.2.

11.4 Frauds against the Warranty Provider

Fraud impacts all parties involved in the supply chain: the WP, the customers, and other parties in the service network. Fraud is a very large research topic, and many of the issues surrounding fraud have been enumerated and expanded on; however, to narrow down the scope of fraud, only fraud against the WP (in this case, the remanufacturer) is being considered. This section describes the scale of fraud and its effect on the WP. The different types of fraud that a WP may have to deal with are outlined in Table 11.3. While fraud can have a significant impact on a company's overall profitability, its effects often manifest themselves in different ways. These hidden consequences may be divided into direct and indirect consequences.

TABLE 11.2

Other Parties Involved in a Warranty Servicing Chain

Category	Name	Description
Secondary parties	Part manufacturers	Produce the parts and other materials needed in the warranty servicing. They sell the parts either directly to SA or through distributors.
	Sales channel	Modes in which products are delivered to customers.
	Administrator	Deals with the various organizational activities related to the warranty servicing process.
Tertiary parties	Leasers	Lease products for use by customers when their failed products are under repair.
	Inspectors	Act on behalf of the WP to verify the causes of defects and determine whether they are covered by warranty or not.
	Logistics companies	Deal with the transport of failed and repaired items and with the delivery of parts.
	Underwriters and insurers	Provide the financial backing for warranty operations.
	Other interested parties	These include the government and shareholders.

TABLE 11.3

Fraud Where the WP is the Victim, Considering Both the Motivation and Method (Primary)

Fraud Source	Motivation	Method
Customer	Refund or replacement	Unjustified return or replacement of item that is not faulty or is a fake
	Service cost avoidance	Getting out of warranty products repaired under warranty
	Extra products or earning	Claiming and reselling parts or replacement items
	Service level improvement	Claiming better service than they are entitled to
Service agent	Extra revenue	Creating fictitious claims
	Extra revenue	Intentionally conducting out of warranty service at WP's expense
	Extra revenue	Inflating the price of an existing claim through various methods
	Extra revenue	Intentional overselling or use of too many parts
	Extra revenue	Using or reselling WP-owned parts obtained by unnecessary claims disassembly, or returned products
	Service cost avoidance	Using counterfeit or unauthorized parts or products
	Service cost avoidance	Not doing all the necessary actions under the service contract
	Service cost avoidance	Unnecessarily changing parts to minimize diagnostics effort
	Service cost avoidance	Using unqualified technicians to reduce costs

11.4.1 Direct Consequences

These refer to how fraud affects the WP's bottom-line by overinflating service costs. In one scenario, only part of the claim may be covered by warranty, although service is still provided by the SA and charged to the WP. Such claims can also relate to activities that never happened and where the claim was simply fabricated. In other cases, the cost of repair in individual claims can be inflated. The claim as such may be valid, but it may include inflated labor, spare parts, or other costs. There are also cases wherein an excess of maintenance was done and parts were consumed, but the work done may have been unnecessary and/or not covered by warranty.

11.4.2 Indirect Consequences

It is common practice for field data to be used to take corrective measures when problems arise. Repair data received from SAs are a key source of information for research. However, if the repair data include an abundance of fictitious claims, it would be next to impossible to distinguish between real quality problems and fake problems that arise from fraudulent claims. Therefore, sorting out fact from fiction might delay corrective actions. It might also result in unnecessary and highly expensive product recalls and reduce the effectiveness of predictive maintenance. Further on, it can lead to costly engineering changes, additional quality improvement activities with the part suppliers, and in the worst case, terminating profitable products or product families that incorrectly seem to be loss making. Warranty fraud can also affect the WP's reputation and damage its brand. This is the case, for example, when customers are wrongly denied warranty service or receive poor service due to fraud.

11.5 Tackling Fraud against the Warranty Provider

The various types, consequences, and problems relating to fraud have been enumerated in previous sections. The ways of combating fraud have not yet been properly addressed. There are many problems in dealing with fraud; the more common problems may fall into one of three categories:

- With the investigation process: depending on the parties involved, the approach to investigation will be different.
- With punishing fraud: depending on the nature of the party responsible for fraud, the avenues of punishment available will vary.
- With the nature of fraud: frauds can be committed in many different ways, each with varying levels of success and payoff, and they cannot all be dealt with in the same manner.

In the past, the issues of fraud have been modeled using techniques such as game theory, and while these have been instructive in providing a basic understanding of the problem, a more complex and detailed model is required to fully capture this issue. A number of different types of fraud (where the WP is the victim) can be modeled, but to illustrate the fraud modeling process, we consider only the scenario where the SA commits the fraud, and the WP is the victim of the said fraud.

11.5.1 Experiment Model

A discrete event simulation model was constructed with a number of SAs, each submitting multiple claims to a warranty administrator (who acts as the go-between for the SA and the WP). As described in Figure 11.3, the claim validation process runs parallel to the warranty servicing process.

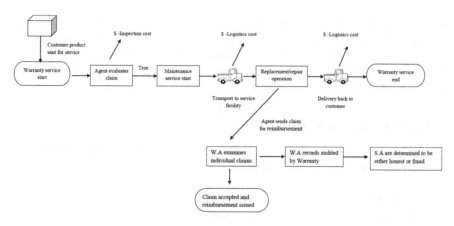

FIGURE 11.3
Warranty servicing with claim validation.

A number of factors influence the outcome of decisions at each stage of the claim validation process. The various factors (and the reasoning behind them) are listed in the following subsection.

11.5.1.1 The Service Agent

The SA submits multiple claims to the administrator. The claims can be either true or false (fraudulent). The probability of a fraud occurring is dependent on three factors:

- Previously escaped: if the SA has previously committed a fraud without being penalized, it is assumed that the agent will be bolder (more likely to commit fraud) the next time they make a claim.
- Previously penalized: if the SA has previously committed a fraud and was penalized, it is assumed that the agent will be more careful (less likely to commit fraud) the next time they make a claim.
- Total number of claims: it is assumed that the probability of fraud increases proportionally with the number of claims (especially if the SA has never been penalized in the past).

11.5.1.2 The Auditing Process

The auditing process is a two-stage process (for the purpose of the model). The first is a more general review of all the aspects of an SA's performance, from efficiency to customer satisfaction. (The probability of discovering fraud is less likely if only this stage is completed.)

The secondary inspection is a focused audit that makes note of the basics of the service rendered (service expenditure, labor cost, prior record of claims, etc.).

In addition, it is a more detailed investigative audit process that may involve multiple queries between the investigator and the SA to determine that the claim can be verified (or found to be false). All claims pass through the first stage, whereas the second is reserved for cases where there is cause for concern that a fraud has been committed.

11.5.1.3 The Claim Investigator

The inspector is assumed to be prone to error. This, therefore, leads to four separate outcomes of the investigation:

- Investigator catches fraud that exists.
- Investigator misses fraud that exists.
- Investigator finds the claim to be true.
- Investigator falsely charges a true claim.

In addition, it is assumed that multiple inspectors are being employed, whose experience and competence vary. To represent this variability, four types of inspectors are considered

- Competent
- Expert
- Incompetent
- Novice

11.5.1.4 Secondary Inspection (Focused Audit)

The secondary inspection can be triggered due to a number of different reasons:

- Random inspection: from time to time, claims may be randomly selected to go through a secondary fraud inspection.
- Inspection triggered by warning signs: if certain parameters (such as a suspicious number of claims within a fixed time period, or if the claim value is higher than the projected costs) deviate from standard values, this might trigger an inspection of the SA.
- Inspection triggered by lack of inspection: if a number of SA claims go through without a need for inspection (either because the claims show no warning flags or if they were never selected for a random inspection), there is a chance that an inspection is triggered (this probability increases as more claims go unreviewed by the secondary inspectors).

11.5.1.5 Sensor Behavior

- Claim data on record: as the sensor has better records of the claim (dates, times, locational data, etc.) it will be more likely to accurately determine whether the submitted claims are overinflated. However, we assume that there is still a small scope for error (from the SA due to poor record keeping) leading to mismatched data that might result in a false flag.
- Prior criminal record: The prior record of the SA (only of caught fraud, not of committed fraud) will influence the decision on whether to accept the claims as true or to refer to secondary inspection.

11.5.2 Design of Experiment

Based on the different factors that have been laid out, the flow of the claim investigation process in regular systems is depicted in Figure 11.4. The inspection structure of the sensor embedded systems is more complex than those of the regular systems. Using the information provided by the sensors, the claim validation processes can be planned differently. In regular systems, fraud is caught during the second stage of investigation.

In a sensor embedded system, fraud can be caught (and later confirmed by the investigator) before reaching this stage. While the sensor can assist in fraud detection, we do not assume that it can replace manual investigation. The flow of claims in an SEP system is depicted in Figure 11.5.

With the flow of the claim review process firmly established, next, the details of the time- and cost-dependent processes are defined. The costs that are considered for this model include the revenue costs and the costs to the remanufacturer. Costs to the remanufacturer include the costs for audit (inspection costs for primary and secondary inspection) as well as logistics costs (related to maintenance activities emanating from a fraudulent claim) as well as other related costs (such as service costs for maintenance activities). Additionally, when a fraud is committed, we consider that fraud amount to be a loss to the remanufacturer (cost of uncaught fraud). In the case of SEP, it would be necessary to include the cost of sensors as well. The sources of revenue that are considered are primarily from the cost of penalizing fraud. This is not to say that many other sources of revenue do not exist (sales, additional warranty and out of warranty service costs, etc.). Table 11.4 covers some of the costs (inspection related) that were employed in this simulation model. When a fraud is identified, it is assumed that a penalty cost is applied on a case-by-case basis. While penalty policies often vary, in this case, we assume that the penalty is proportional to the amount by which the WP is defrauded. Table 11.5 covers the range of the penalties that may be applied to agents, which is dependent on where the fraud amount lies in the predetermined range.

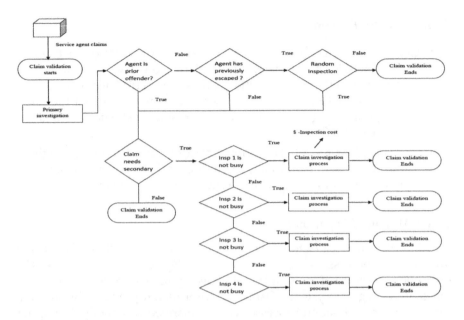

FIGURE 11.4
Warranty service investigation process.

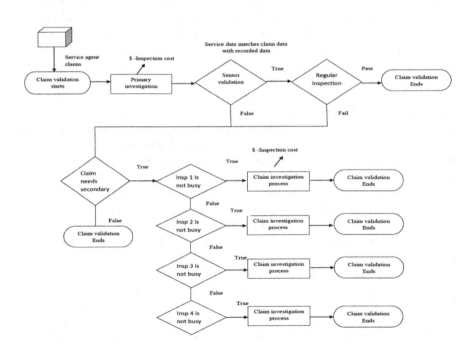

FIGURE 11.5
Warranty service investigation process (sensor embedded).

Along with cost, the other factor to be considered is the various time-dependent processes. These may include the different inspection process times as well as arrival rates (frequency of fraud audits). Table 11.6 summarizes the process times related to the claim audit. We do not consider maintenance and related logistics times. Process time does not assume a lag (lead time) between when the decision to audit is made and when it actually starts; that is, it assumes that the validation begins instantaneously.

It is unrealistic to assume that an agent's past history with the investigation process would not bias their future decision making. To that end, the effects of past outcomes on future decisions have been summarized in Table 11.7.

TABLE 11.4

Costs from Inspections

Assumed Costs	Dollar Amount ($)
Cost/audit	5
Cost/inspection	15
Fraud amount	Uniform distribution (5,50)

TABLE 11.5

Costs from Inspections (Penalty)

Fraud Range($)	Penalty Costs ($)
0–25	30
25–50	60
>50	100

TABLE 11.6

Process Times (Distribution)

Assumed Times	Distribution	Parameter(s) (Hours)
Primary audit	Triangular	(0.2,0.5,0.7)
Secondary inspection	Triangular	(0.5,1.0,1.5)
Arrival rate	Poisson	3

TABLE 11.7

Fraud Decision Outcomes

Service Agent History	Effect on Subsequent Fraud Probability	
	Caught	Uncaught
First claim is true	Falsely charged (no effect)	No effect
First claim is false	Charged (reduces probability)	Emboldened (increases probability)
Subsequent claim is true	Falsely charged (no effect)	Ideal scenario (no effect)
Subsequent claim is false	Charged (reduces probability)	Emboldened (increases probability)
Selected for random inspection	Sent for inspection (probability is reset)	Escapes inspection (probability increments for the next claim)

Additionally, it is assumed that the selection criteria for random inspections also do not remain the same for all cases.

The functions that determine the probability in each case are dependent on a number of factors (as summarized in Table 11.8). As claims are submitted for review, it is assumed that earlier claims have an impact on later claims. For example, the SA may submit false claims earlier on and be caught, which will bias later claims to be more true than false. The reverse is also assumed to hold true (i.e., uncaught fraud causes later claims to be more false than true).

Having discussed the behavior of the SAs with respect to fraud and the investigation process, next, the behavior of the inspectors with respect to fraud and the investigation process is modeled. As outlined in the previous section, it is assumed that investigators will be categorized into four types. These are differentiated from each other based on their success rate at correctly detecting fraud (Table 11.9). In addition to accounting for the probability of not detecting actual fraud (Type II error), the probability of falsely charging an agent (Type I error) is accounted for.

TABLE 11.8

Modeling Claim Probability

Claim Scenario	Nature	Probability (%)
Is the first claim true?	Constant	85
Is a subsequent claim true if first claim was true?	Constant	85
Does a claim require a random inspection?[a]	Incremental increase	$100*(1 - e^{(-0.3*Randomprob)})$
Is a claim fraudulent (if previous was false but not caught by inspection)?[b]	Incremental increase	$100*(1 - e^{(-0.3*Claim\ no)})$
Is a claim fraudulent (if previously caught)?	Incremental decrease	$100*(claim\ no + 1)^{-1.5}$

[a] Randomprob: a simulation (non-negative integer with a starting value of 1) attribute used to denote whether an SA has been recently selected for random inspection; it increments each time the SA is not selected and resets once they are selected for inspection.

[b] Claim no: a simulation (non-negative integer with a starting value of 1) attribute used to denote the specific claim of the SA that is being audited.

TABLE 11.9

Types of Inspector (Secondary)

Type	Probability of Fraud Detection (%)	Probability of Falsely Charging SA (%)
Competent	80	10
Expert	90	5
Incompetent	65	15
Novice	70	15

Discrete event simulation was used to model the normal (base) and SEP systems. Arena 14.7 simulation software (Rockwell, Austin, TX, USA) was used for the modeling process. For validation, the models were run by assigning extreme values to variables, and corresponding performance measures were observed with these runs. For example, if the probability of detecting fraud is increased near to 1 (a perfect inspection), the number of subsequent frauds being committed by the SA decreases dramatically. Similarly, if the inspection probabilities are set to be below 0.5, over time, the probability of committing frauds increases over the simulation run for each SA. The run length of the simulation experiments was 365 days, which is approximately 1 year. SEP systems and regular (non-sensor) systems were introduced, and the design of experiments study was explained. The performance measures that were used to calculate these values are shown in the following list.

Total profit = total revenue − total cost

Total revenue = penalty revenue

Total cost = inspection cost + cost of audit + uncaught fraud

11.5.3 Simulation Results and Conclusion

For each system, both normal and SEP, experiments were carried out, and the data pertaining to the total profit, inspection cost, and penalty and fraud costs were tracked. Table 11.10 contrasts the difference between the base scenario and the SEP scenario by describing statistics pertinent to fraud detection and inspections.

The data indicated that the use of sensors significantly reduced the cost of the inspection process. There were certain parameters that did not follow this pattern; for example, in normal systems; the inspection cost for the simulation period was $3585, while this was reduced to $3795 in the SEP systems. Table 11.11 presents the average values of the performance measures mentioned earlier as well as the total cost for both systems.

Preliminary results show that the sensor embedded system shows a statistically significant improvement over the base scenario with respect to fraud detection. A number of correlations between different factors were also observed. There is a negative correlation between penalty value and total number of frauds being committed. There also exists a positive correlation between inspection cost and the total cost. In summary, it is possible to use sensors not to just to combat, but also to better track fraud. Sensors also provide additional benefits, because they can be used to gain an economic advantage in a closed-loop supply chain system.

TABLE 11.10

Fraud Detection Statistics

Service Agent Claims Statistics	Base Case	With Sensors	Percentage Improvement (%)
Uncaught false claims	63	50	26
Uncaught false claims (only manual)	63	39	N/A
Uncaught false claims (with sensor)	–	11	N/A
Falsely charged	24	23	4.3
Caught fraud (from investigation)	40	43	7.5
Total general audits	500	500	–
Total claims flagged by sensors	–	73	N/A
Total inspection	239	253	5.9
True claims (from investigation)	164	178	8.34
Average time in system	9.3638 min	9.6601 min	3.164
No. of SA claims that fool sensors	–	13	N/A
No. of true SA claims that are flagged by sensors	–	54	N/A
Approved claims	436	434	0.5
Max. queue length (primary)	2	1	50
Max. queue length (secondary)	3	2	33

TABLE 11.11

Fraud Detection Statistics

Measure	Base System ($)	Sensor Embedded System ($)
Penalty costs	1400	1505
Inspection costs	3585	3795
Uncaught fraud costs	2205	1750
Total costs	8290	8045

11.6 Conclusion

Fraud is a sometimes overlooked issue in both manufacturing and remanufacturing environments. This chapter described some of the literature surrounding the issues of fraud and warranties. This review showed that it should be the goal of any responsible manufacturer to tackle the issue of fraud in the warranty service industry. The problems in dealing with fraud as well as current and possible future methods in combating fraud were laid out. And finally, an approach to mitigate fraud against the WP was proposed. This has been an overlooked problem in the area of remanufacturing, and further exploration would prove to be beneficial to all the parties involved.

References

Abdullahi, R., Mansor, N., 2015, "Fraud triangle theory and fraud diamond theory. Understanding the convergent and divergent for future research", *International Journal of Academic Research in Accounting, Finance and Management Sciences*, Vol. 5(4), pp. 30–37.

Ahmed, M. A., Saadany, E., Jaber, M. Y., Bonney, M., 2013, "How many times to remanufacture?", *International Journal of Production Economics*, Vol. 143(2), pp. 598–604, ISSN 0925-5273.

Alqahtani, A. Y., Gupta, S. M., 2017a, "Warranty as a marketing strategy for remanu-factured products", *Journal of Cleaner Production*, Vol. 161, pp. 1294–1307

Alqahtani, A. Y., Gupta, S. M., 2017b, "Optimizing two-dimensional renewable warranty policies for sensor embedded remanufactured products", *Journal of Industrial Engineering and Management*, Vol. 10(2), pp. 145–187.

Barber, K. S., Fullam, K., Kim, J., 2003, *"Challenges for Trust, Fraud and Deception Research in Multi-agent Systems"*, The Laboratory for Intelligent Processes and Systems Electrical and Computer Engineering, the University of Texas at Austin.

Chen, X., Li, L., Zhou, M., 2012, "Manufacturer's pricing strategy for supply chain with warranty period-dependent demand", *Omega*, Vol. 40(6), pp. 807–816.

Curkovic, S., Landeros, R., 2000, "An environmental Baldrige?" *Mid-American Journal of Business*, Vol. 15(2), pp. 63–76.

Dulman, M. T., Gupta, S. M., 2018, "Evaluation of maintenance and EOL operation performance of sensor-embedded laptops", *Logistics*, Vol. 2(1), p. 3.

Ernst & Young, (2009, "Detecting Financial Statement Fraud". Retrieved: 2 August 2014 from www.ey.com/Publication/vwLUAssets/FIDSFI Detecting Financial Statement Fraud.pdf/$FILE/FIDSFI_detectingFinanceStatementFraud.pdf.

Go, T. F., Wahab, D. A., Ab Rahman, M. N., Ramli, R. R., Azhari, C. H., 2011, "Disassemblability of end-of-life vehicle: A critical review of evaluation methods", *Journal of Cleaner Production*, Vol. 19(13), pp. 1536–1546, ISSN 0959-6526.

Green, B. P., Choi, J. H., 1997, "Assessing the risk of management fraud through neu-ral network technology", *Auditing—a Journal of Practice & Theory*, Vol. 16(1), pp. 14–28.

Gungor, A., Gupta, S. M., 1999, "Issues in environmentally conscious manufacturing and product recovery: A survey", *Computers & Industrial Engineering*, Vol. 36(4), pp. 811–853.

Hand, D. J., 1981, *"Discrimination and Classification"*, Wiley, New York, NY.

Hand, D. J., 1997, *"Construction and Assessment of Classification Rules"*, Wiley, Chichester, UK.

Handfield, R. B., Walton, S. V., Seegers, L. K., Melnyk, S. A., 1997, "Green value chain practices in the furniture industry", *Journal of Operations Management*, Vol. 15(4), pp. 293–315.

Hanna, M. D., Newman, R. W., Johnson, P., 2000. "Linking operational improve-ment through employee involvement", *International Journal of Operations and Production Management*, Vol. 20(2), pp. 148–165.

Hatcher, G. D., Ijomah, W. L., Windmill, J. F. C., 2011, "Design for remanufacture: A literature review and future research needs", *Journal of Cleaner Production*, Vol. 19(17–18), pp. 2004–2014.

Hawkins, T., Arnum, E., Froning, D., 2011, "Using Analytics to Uncover Claims Errors and Fraud", *Insights from the third webcast in the 2011 Supply Chain Leadership Series*, SAS Conclusions Paper.

Ilgin, M. A., Gupta, S. M., 2010, "Environmentally conscious manufacturing and product recovery (ECMPRO): A review of the state of the art", *Journal of Environmental Management*, Vol. 91(3), pp. 563–591.

Kurvinen, M., Töyrylä, I., Murthy, D. N. P., 2016, "Warranty Fraud Management: Reducing Fraud And Other Excess Costs In Warranty And Service Operations", Wiley, Hoboken, NJ.

Lambert, A. J. D., 2003, "Disassembly sequencing: A survey", *International Journal of Production Research*, Vol. 41(16), pp. 3721–3759.

Lambert, A. J. D., Gupta, S. M., 2002, "Demand-driven disassembly optimization for electronic products", *Journal of Electronics Manufacturing*, Vol. 11(2), pp. 121–135.

Lund, R., 1985, "Remanufacturing: The Experience of the United States and Implications for Developing Countries", UNDP Project Management Report 2, World Bank Technical Paper No 31, pp. 24–34.

McLachlan, G. J., 1992, "Discriminant Analysis and Statistical Pattern Recognition", Wiley, New York, NY.

Melnyk, S A., Sroufe, R., Montabon, F., 2001, "How does management view environmentally responsible manufacturing?", *Production and Inventory Management Journal*, pp. 55(10).

Mu, E., Carroll, J., 2016, "Development of a fraud risk decision model for prioritizing fraud risk cases in manufacturing firms", *International Journal of Production Economics*, Vol. 173, pp. 30–42.

Ondemir, O., Gupta, S. M., 2014a, "A multi-criteria decision making model for advanced repair-to-order and disassembly-to-order system", *European Journal of Operational Research*, Vol. 233(2), pp. 408–420.

Ondemir, O., Gupta, S. M., 2014b, "Quality management in product recovery using the Internet of Things: An optimization approach", *Computers in Industry*, Vol. 65(3), pp. 491–504.

Podolyakina, N., 2017, "Estimation of the relationship between the products reliability, period of their warranty service and the value of the enterprise cost", *Procedia Engineering*, Vol. 178, pp. 558–568.

Porter, M. E., 1991, "America's green strategy", *Scientific American (April)*, Vol. 168.

Porter, M. E., Van der Linde, C., 1995, "Green and competitive: Ending the stalemate", *Harvard Business Review*, Vol. 73(5), pp. 120–134.

Ripley, B. D., 1996, "Pattern Recognition and Neural Networks", Cambridge University Press, Cambridge, UK.

Shih, K. H., Cheng, C. C., Wang, Y. H., 2011, "Financial information fraud risk warning for manufacturing industry—using logistic regression and neural network", *Romanian Journal of Economic Forecasting*, Vol. 14(1), pp. 54–71.

Southwick, A. F., 1963, "Mass marketing and warranty liability", *Journal of Marketing*, Vol. 27(2), pp. 6–12.

Veerakamolmal, P., Gupta, S. M., 2000, "Design for Disassembly, Reuse and Recycling", *Green Electronics/Green Bottom Line: Environmentally Responsible Engineering*, edited by Lee Goldberg, Butterworth-Heinemann; (Newnes), Chapter 5, 69–82, ISBN: 0-7506-9993-0.

Webb, A. R., 1999, "Statistical Pattern Recognition", Arnold, London, UK.

Wilkes, R. E., Wilcox, J. B, 1981, "Limited versus full warranties: The retail perspective", *Journal of Retailing*, Vol. 57, pp. 65–76.

Xiong, Y., Lau, K., Zhou, X., Schoenung, J. M., 2008, "A streamlined life cycle assessment on the fabrication of WC–Co cermets", *Journal of Cleaner Production*, Vol. 16(10), pp. 1118–1126.

Yeh, C. W., Fang, C. C., 2015, "Optimal decision for warranty with consideration of marketing and production capacity", *International Journal of Production Research*, pp. 1–16.

Zhang, H., Hu, Y., Zhou, Z., 2010, "Prevention of resource trading fraud in manufacturing grid: A signalling games approach", *International Journal of Computer Integrated Manufacturing*, Vol. 23(5), pp. 391–401.

12

Price Models for New and Remanufactured High-Technology Products across Generations

Liangchuan Zhou and Surendra M. Gupta

CONTENTS

12.1 Introduction

12.1.1 Background

Driven by the high-technology revolution, people's lifestyle is becoming more and more diverse and convenient. In the past, customers shopped for groceries, food, and consumer goods in grocery stores or supermarkets; nowadays, more and more individuals shop online. Previously, face-to-face communication only happened in a common physical space, such as a café or park; at present, communicators can also see each other through FaceTime using smartphones. Likewise, customers' appetite for life innovation promotes high-technology development. Because of the speed of innovation, newer-generation high-technology products often include more functions while running faster. In addition, as product technology becomes more complex, users often experience a simplified interface. Driven by market competition, manufacturers can refresh models every year to make sure their products stay abreast of the latest technology level and fashion trend (Aytac and Wu, 2013). Customers are often eager to purchase the newest version and retire the older ones even while the early products still have much residual value. Both manufacturers' innovation and customers' purchase behaviors promote social and economic developments. However, rapid development also leads to a serious e-waste problem. Solutions are needed to deal with a large amount of disposed-of outdated products. Government regulations to control the e-waste problem are increasing the manufacturers' disposal costs for electrical products. In this situation, manufacturers are appealing to customers to return used products for remanufacturing and are trying to extract residual value from used parts while maintaining a balance among the environment, society, and the economy. Various related research fields were addressed in earlier times, including product disassembly, material recovery, and design for environment (Gungor and Gupta, 1999). Then, the study areas were extended to closed-loop supply chain, remanufacturing, and supplier selection (Ilgin and Gupta, 2010). Remanufacturing is a process of restoring components to a like-new functional state. It is a way to transform a disposal burden into a business opportunity.

12.1.2 Market Situation

For high-technology products, manufacturers launch new models while the early ones are still available in the market. Meanwhile, manufacturers go through the remanufacturing process for returned products, upgrade them with the latest technology, and sell them as remanufactured items in the remanufactured market. Depending on the timing of return, remanufactured products can belong to different generations. As a result, new and remanufactured products belonging to different generations co-exist in the same market, appealing to customers in various segments. Additionally, warranty becomes a market strategy for remanufactured products, which adds power to market competition with new items (Alqahtani and Gupta, 2017). Pricing a portfolio of new and remanufactured products belonging to different generations is one of the primary market issues for manufacturers and associated retailers.

With the development of e-commerce, a secondary market issue is the competition between physical and online channels. Some customers prefer retailer shopping, while other customers like online shopping better. Manufacturers have an opportunity to create a separate sale-channel strategy that caters to the needs of these two customer segments.

12.1.3 Customer Segments and Purchase Behavior

Customers in different categories exhibit different purchase behaviors, including which product and which purchase approach they will choose. This study assumes that high-end customers are eager to obtain and pay more for recently released products; low-end customers are willing to own and pay less for used products; and middle-level customers are seeking outdated new products or remanufactured products with a price between brand new and used products. These middle-level customers are the targets of this study. Within the middle-level category, customers are classified into two segments: technology-savvy and quality-conscious. Technology savvies prefer to pay more for remanufactured products belonging to later technology, while quality-conscious customers prefer new products belonging to earlier generations. For the purchase approach, customers' choices are based on various factors such as retailer's reputation, price, and shopping convenience.

12.1.4 Price-Decision Methods

Price models are based on theories and practices. In a theoretical price model, the demand function is the critical part. One of the most famous demand functions for high-technology products is the Bass model (Bass, 1969). The Bass model is a traditional diffusion model in which the demand trend for new products goes through initial, mutual, and diffusion phases. This means that the demand for recently launched products will decrease significantly after the mutual phase, when the new generation is about to released. Nowadays, the Bass model is still widely used in pricing decisions. Several of its applications are included in the Literature Review section. Another widely used model is the customer-surplus value model. The demand is dependent on the differential between the price and the customer's perceived value for the product. A product with a higher value surplus receives more demand than a product with a lower value surplus. Negative value surplus represents little demand. Customer discrete choice models are also used, such as the hierarchical pricing decision model (Ding et al., 2016) and the conditional multinomial logit choice model (Kwak and Kim, 2013). These demand models are based on customers' choices according to the product's characteristics in the context of a competing product. Additionally, different sale-channels have different channel powers that influence the theoretical demand model. Examples of pricing models are included in the Literature Review section.

However, most theoretical models are not validated by analysis of customer behavior using real-world data (Watson, 2008). Researchers have implemented empirical studies and found that the results contradicted the assumptions of the original models (Guide and Van Wassenhove, 2009, Guide and Li, 2010, Abbey et al., 2015). A more practical price model based on empirical studies is needed. For creating practical price models, the regular differential price between new and remanufactured products of multiple generations in a real market needs to be observed. According to a previous survey, the difference between remanufactured products and similar new product is between 30% and 40% (Ilgin and Gupta, 2012). Andrew-Munot et al. (2015) point to a more obvious gap, which is between 45% and 65%. However, this study does not only focus on the difference between new and remanufactured products but also keeps an eye on the product generation difference. The competition between new products belonging to an earlier generation and remanufactured products belonging to a later generation and the price decision of the two types of products are more complicated than what has been addressed in previous research. Therefore, new studies are needed.

12.1.5 Outline

The main objective of this study is to develop theoretical price models and practical models for new and remanufactured products across generations. In the following sections, previous research on high-technology products regarding theoretical price decisions, direct sale-channel effects, and online price analysis will be provided. However, pricing decisions for high-technology products from multiple generations have not been studied previously. This chapter will develop models for different types of products across generations and shed light on dual-channel effects. Real-world data from eBay are used to develop the practical price models.

12.2 Literature Review

12.2.1 Price Decision for Short-Lifecycle Products

Numerous studies have been conducted on remanufactured durable goods, while short-lifecycle products have received less attention (Gan et al., 2014). Gan et al. undertook a series of studies on pricing decisions for short-lifecycle products (Gan et al., 2015, Gan et al., 2017, Gan and Pujawan, 2017,

Gan et al., 2018). Demand functions are time dependent, derived from the Bass model. In 2015, they conducted a study on price decisions for new and remanufactured products in a single-channel closed-loop supply chain. Prices are optimized in four scenarios: retailer, collector, manufacturer, and joint supply chain. Reducing the price for new products in the demand decrease phase under the supply chain scenario is not recommended by the authors (Gan et al., 2015). One year later, they extended the research by taking a separate sale-channel into account. New products are sold through the retailer, while remanufactured products are sold directly by the manufacturer. Compared with the single sale-channel strategy, the separated sale-channel approach increases the profit under the supply chain scenario (Gan et al., 2017b). Later, a Manufacturer-Stackelberg model was developed by providing different levels of warranty to the remanufactured products. The study illustrates an optimal warranty level regardless of the initial warranty level set at the beginning of the retailer profit optimization model. Additionally, a higher demand expansion effectiveness coefficient of the warranty level increases the supply chain profit (Gan et al., 2017a). However, the quantity of remanufactured products is restricted by the number of qualified used cores. These three papers do not include the constraint of availability of used cores. In 2018, they developed the model by examining the uncertainties concerning the quality and quantity of acquired cores. The profitability in each scenario is affected by the quality of used cores, the collecting price, the shortage cost, and the remanufacturing cost. Meanwhile, reducing the variance of random yield contributes to a lower profit for the collector (Gan et al., 2018).

These discoveries in the remanufacturing of short-lifecycle products are interesting. However, with high-technology products, as a case of short-life-cycle products, product models belonging to different generations exist in the market simultaneously. The generation effect is one of the essential factors for price decisions. For the remanufacturing strategy, upgrading is a competitive approach to challenge the sales of new products. After the Bass model being created, Norton and Bass continued working on and developing the model to generations of high-technology products (Norton and Bass, 1987). Recently, some researchers have touched on this point. Bhattacharya, Guide, and Van Wassenhove optimize the retailer's profit by determining the optimal order quantities for new and remanufactured products. In the model, the remanufacturer remanufactures and upgrades products using returned and unsold products belonging to earlier generations (Bhattacharya et al., 2006). Galbreth, Byaci, and Verter take the quality of returned cores and production designs into account. They explain pros and cons of fast product innovation, find an incentive to reuse recycled parts when the cost of designing reusable products is up (Galbreth et al., 2013). Kwak and Kim conduct a market positioning research problem for remanufactured products. The study includes part upgrading, production design, and market driving (Kwak and Kim, 2013). The optimal upgrade decision for remanufactured products can be captured by the discrete choice demand model and conjoint analysis on product generational differences, selling price, and product status. However, according to the existing publications, the competition between upgraded remanufactured products and outdated new products has received less attention.

12.2.2 New and Remanufactured Products in Dual-Channel Supply Chain

With the development of the Internet, manufacturers have obtained an opportunity to sell products directly to customers, while selling products through retailers was the only way for manufacturers in the past. Series of studies have been conducted to analyze the advantages and disadvantages of different sale-channel strategies for new and remanufactured products. For instance, scientists have compared three strategies: a single-channel strategy through an independent retailer, a dual-channel strategy selling new products online and selling remanufactured products via a retailer, and a dual-channel strategy selling remanufactured products online and selling new products via a retailer (Wang et al., 2016). They recommend the separated sale-channel approach, because it brings more benefit to the manufacturer and the customers than the single-channel strategy. It is suggested that manufacturers analyze the remanufacturing cost, customers' acceptance of remanufactured products, and the online inconvenience cost before making decisions on the channel distribution for new and remanufactured products in the dual-channel supply chain system. Gan et al. examine a separate sale-channel for two types of products, as described in the previous paragraph Gan et al., 2017b). Another paper covers the dual-channel policy for both new and remanufactured products in the scenarios of retailer-Stackelberg, manufacturer-Stackelberg, and Nash game (Gao et al., 2016). They find that in the retailer-Stackelberg scenario, the wholesale price, retail price, and retailer's profit are decreased with an increase in customer acceptance of the direct channel, while the direct online sales price and the manufacturer's profit are increased. However, the study of price decisions for new and remanufactured products across generations in the dual-channel closed-loop supply chain is still a blank.

12.2.3 Empirical Study for Pricing New and Remanufactured Products

According to intuition, remanufactured products will be cheaper than new products of the same model. However, optimal prices cannot be decided without empirical studies on consumers' purchase behavior. Abbey, Blackburn, and Guide Jr. conducted a study about customers' preference for remanufactured products. They classified customers into two segments: strong preference for new products (low price-sensitive) and indifferent preference between new and remanufactured products (high price-sensitive). The results show that new products are preferred to remanufactured versions in both segments. Even for those individuals who claim to be green customers, new products are still their first choice if the prices are appropriate. The price-sensitive group requires a large discount to purchase remanufactured products, while the low price-sensitive group has high willingness to pay (WTP) for new ones. Therefore, the authors suggest that manufacturers maximize profit by increasing the price of the new products and applying a high discount level for the remanufactured products. This joint pricing strategy aims to make the price gap between new and remanufactured products more significant. Besides, enlarging customers' perceived value differential between new and remanufactured products also brings benefit to the manufacturer (Abbey et al., 2015a). Agrawal, Atasu, and Ittersum extend the research with the consideration of third-party competition. They indicate increased perceived value of new products with the presence of a third party (Agrawal et al., 2015).

In the study of customers' purchase behavior regarding remanufactured products, there is an interesting discovery that green customers are less interested in purchasing remanufactured products than new products (Abbey et al., 2015a, Abbey et al., 2015). With education on environment protection and the knowledge of remanufactured products, customers' acceptance of remanufactured products can increase (Ilgin and Gupta, 2012). However, the purchase intention and the behavior are not always consistent. Khor and Hazen examine the intention–behavior relationship when customers purchase electrical and electronic equipment using a survey measurement approach (Khor and Hazen, 2017). They indicate that green customers have firm purchase intention but weak purchase behavior for remanufactured products, because they are unaware that remanufactured products are environmentally friendly products. Customers perceive an energy-efficient new product to be a better choice than a remanufactured product.

Although the majority of the population prefer to purchase new products, lower price is a trigger for green customers and price-sensitive customers to buy remanufactured products (Abbey et al., 2015a, Abbey et al., 2015b). Research on customer switching behaviors will provide references to the price decision for remanufactured products. Ovchinnikov (2011) finds that the fraction of consumers who switch from new to remanufactured products follows an inverted U-shape curve, implying that a significant price differential has an adverse effect on the switching behavior. Customers assume that remanufactured products are poor quality. Therefore, the sales of new products can avoid cannibalization from the sales of remanufactured items by enlarging the price differential (Ovchinnikov, 2011). This finding is consistent with the conclusion from Agrawal et al. (2015). Except for the price effect, customers' attitude toward remanufactured products shows a strong association between price and consumers' switching intention (Hazen et al., 2017).

The papers in the preceding paragraphs examine customer behavior associated with price decisions for new and remanufactured products by surveys or

experiments. Researchers provide plenty of managerial insights into remanufacturing strategy. Nowadays, more and more people are familiar with online
shopping. Customers' purchase behavior is captured automatically by computers. Frota Neto et al. (2016) gather the sales data of remanufactured, used,
and new iPods from eBay. They find that customers assume better quality for
remanufactured products than for used ones (Frota Neto et al., 2016). Then,
Xu et al. (2017) analyze the prices of remanufactured iPods from fixed price
transaction and auction data, studying the influence of e-service on customer
purchase behavior toward remanufactured iPods. They claim that posting
more pictures increases WTP for auction but plays a less important role in
fixed price transactions. An autopay service is less significant, while expedited
shipping enhances WTP (Xu et al., 2017). Subramanian and Subramanyam
(2012) analyze and identify the factors that influence the price differential
between new and remanufactured electronic products and reveal the importance of the seller's reputation (Subramanian and Subramanyam, 2012). Pang
et al. (2015) use the same method for data collection, build linear regression
price models, and test the price differential determinants. They also indicate
a significant effect of seller identity on the price (Pang et al., 2015).

Previous research provides analysis methods for consumers' purchase
behavior and price information for new and remanufactured products.
However, the development of high-technology products is rapid. The
situation where multi-generation products co-exist in the market is not well
considered in prior empirical studies.

12.3 Model Development

In this section, three models are developed by considering the generation effects
for new and remanufactured high-technology products (Zhou et al., 2017,
Zhou and Gupta, 2017, Zhou and Gupta, 2018). The first two models are theoretical models. They are developed from the demand diffusion function presented by Gan et al. (2015) and Gan et al. (2017b). The third one is a practical
model based on real data from eBay.

12.3.1 Theoretical Model

For convenience, three types of products are defined here:

- Type 1: new product belonging to an earlier generation
- Type 2: remanufactured product belonging to the latest generation
- Type 3: recently launched new product belonging to the latest
  generation

Customers are classified into three segments. Their purchase behaviors are described here:

- Price-sensitive quality-conscious: prefer Type 1 product
- Price-sensitive technology-savvy: prefer Type 2 product
- High-end quality-conscious: prefer Type 3 product

The demand curves are shown in Figure 12.1. The market for new products follows the dual rollover strategy. Type 1 product is still available in the market but goes to the decline phase when Type 3 product is launched. The market for remanufactured products follows the single rollover strategy. Old-generation models will be phased out and replaced by new models equipped with the latest technology. Therefore, the demand for remanufactured product stays in the increase phase. Zhou et al. described these two strategies in detail (Zhou et al., 2015). The models are built within the period between t_2 and t_4. D_{n12} represents the demand for first-generation new product in the decline phase, while D_{n21} represents the demand for second-generation new product in the increase phase. D_{r1} means the demand for first-generation remanufactured product, while D_{r2} represents that for the second generation.

The manufacturer produces both new and remanufactured products. The demand functions are as follows:

$$D(t) = D_{n12}(t) + D_{r1}(t) + D_{r2}(t)$$

$$D_{n12}(t) = \frac{U}{\lambda U(T4 - T2) + \delta} ; \quad T_2 \le t \le T_4$$

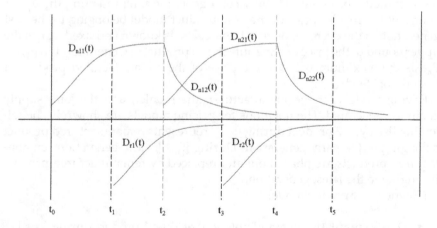

FIGURE 12.1
Demand curves of different types of products.

$$D_{r1}(t) = \frac{V}{1 + he^{-\eta V(t3-T2)}} \; ; \; T_2 \le t \le t_3$$

$$D_{r2}(t) = \frac{V}{1 + he^{-\eta V(T4-t3)}} \; ; \; t_3 \le t \le T_4$$

where

$$k = U/D_0 - 1; \; \delta = 1 + ke^{-\lambda U(T2)}$$

$$h = V/D_{r0} - 1; \; \varepsilon = 1 + he^{-\eta V(t3-t1)}$$

Notations for demand functions:

- U = Maximum possible demand for new product
- λ = Speed of demand change in a time function for new product
- D_o = Demand at the beginning of the product lifecycle when $t=0$
- V = Maximum possible demand for remanufactured product
- η = Speed of demand change in a time function for remanufactured product
- D_{ro} = Demand at the beginning of the product lifecycle where $t=t_1$ and $t=t_3$

It is assumed that the manufacturer and the retailer are in the supply chain system. The costs of producing new products belonging to different generations are similar. In addition, the costs of remanufacturing products that belong to different generations are similar as well. P_{n21} is the price of the new product model belonging to the second generation, representing the upper bound of the retailer price of the new product model belonging to the first generation in the decrease demand phase. P_{n21} is known and fixed. P_{n12} is the upper bound of the price of remanufactured product of Generation 1 in $[t_2, t_3]$. P_{n21} is the maximum value of the price of the remanufactured product of Generation 2 in $[t_3, t_4]$.

Pricing models for the manufacturer, the retailer, and the joint supply chain are generated. The notations for pricing models are shown in the following list. Type 2 product during $[t_2, t_3]$ represents remanufactured product belonging to the early generation. During $[t_3, t_4]$, early-generation remanufactured products are phased out and replaced by remanufactured product belonging to the latest generation.

Notations for pricing models:

- $D_{n12}(t)$: cumulative demand potential of Type 1 product during $[t_2, t_4]$
- $D_{n21}(t)$: cumulative demand potential of Type 3 product during $[t_2, t_4]$

- $D_{r1}(t)$: cumulative demand potential of Type 2 product $[t_2, t_3]$
- $D_{r2}(t)$: cumulative demand potential of Type 2 product $[t_3, t_4]$
- P_{n12}: retail price of Type 1 product during $[t_2, t_4]$
- P_{n21}: retail price of Type 3 product during $[t_2, t_4]$
- P_{r1}: price of Type 2 product during $[t_2, t_3]$
- P_{r2}: price of Type 2 product during $[t_3, t_4]$
- P_{nw}: wholesale price for new products
- P_{rw}: wholesale price of remanufactured product
- C_n: cost for producing new product
- C_r: cost for producing remanufactured product
- d_1: total demand for Type 1 product during $[T_2, T_4]$
- d_2: total demand for Type 2 product of Generation 1 during $[T_2, t_3]$
- d_3: total demand for Type 2 product of Generation 2 during $[t_3, T_4]$
- α_1: discount of generation obsolescence in price-sensitive quality-conscious customer's view
- α_2: discount of generation obsolescence in price-sensitive technology-savvy customer's view
- β_1: discount of remanufacturing inferiority in price-sensitive quality-conscious customer's view
- β_2: discount of remanufacturing inferiority in price-sensitive technology-savvy customer's view
- γ: direct channel preference rate

12.3.1.1 Basic Single-Channel Price Model across Generations

New and remanufactured products are sold in a single sale-channel in a closed-loop supply chain. The manufacturer produces new and remanufactured products in each generation and sells all types of products via the retailer at the wholesale price. The retailer sells products to customers at the retail price. Figure 12.2 shows the responsibilities and relationships in the system.

FIGURE 12.2
Closed-loop supply chain process with model elements.

Demand of Type 1 product in decline phase $[T_2, T_4]: d1$

$$= D_{n12}(t)*(1 - P_{n12} / P_{n21}).$$

(12.1)

Demand of Type 2 product during $[t_2, t_3]: d_2$

$$= D_{r1}(t)*(1 - P_{r1} / P_{n12})$$

(12.2)

Demand of Type 2 product during $[t_3, t_4]: d_3$

$$= D_{r2}(t)*(1 - P_{r2} / P_{n21})$$

(12.3)

Retailer's Model

$$\Pi R = \int_{T2}^{T4} \frac{U}{\lambda U(t - T2) + \delta} * \left(1 - \frac{Pn12}{Pn21}\right) * (Pn12 - Pnw) dt$$

$$+ \int_{T2}^{t3} \frac{V}{1 + he^{-\eta V(t - T2)} + \delta} * \left(1 - \frac{Pr1}{Pr21}\right) * (Pr1 - Prw) dt$$

$$+ \int_{T2}^{T4} \frac{V}{1 + he^{-\eta V(t - t3)} + \delta} * \left(1 - \frac{Pr2}{Pn21}\right) * (Pr2 - Prw) dt$$

(12.4)

$$= d1 * \left(1 - \frac{Pn12}{Pn21}\right) * (Pn12 - Pnw)$$

$$+ d2 * \left(1 - \frac{Pr1}{Pr12}\right) * (Pr1 - Prw)$$

$$+ d3 * \left(1 - \frac{Pr2}{Pn21}\right) * (Pr2 - Prw)$$

where

$$d1 = \frac{1}{\lambda} In\left(\frac{\lambda U(T4 - T2) + \delta}{\delta}\right)$$

$$d2 = \frac{1}{\eta} In\left(\frac{\varepsilon}{(1 + h)e^{-\eta V(t3 - T2)}}\right)$$

$$d3 = \frac{1}{\eta} In\left(\frac{\varepsilon}{(1 + h)e^{-\eta V(T4 - t3)}}\right)$$

Decision variables: P_{n12}, P_{r1}, P_{r2}
Parameters: P_{nw}, P_{rw}, P_{n21}, d_1, d_2, d_3
Constraints: $P_{r1} \leq P_{n12}$, $P_{r2} \leq P_{n21}$, $P_{n12} \leq P_{n21}$

Manufacturer's Model

The objective function is

$$\Pi_M = d1 * \left(1 - \frac{Pn12}{Pn21}\right) * (Pnw - Cn) + d2 * \left(1 - \frac{Pr1}{Pn12}\right) * (Prw - Cr)$$
$$+ d3 * \left(1 - \frac{Pr2}{Pn21}\right) * (Prw - Cr) \tag{12.5}$$

Decision variables: P_{nw}, P_{rw}
Parameters: P_{n12}, P_{r1}, P_{r2}, P_{n21}, d_1, d_2, d_3, C_n, C_r

Joint Profit Model

$$\Pi J = \Pi R + \Pi M$$

$$= d1 * \left(1 - \frac{Pn12}{Pn21}\right) * (Pn12 - Pnw)$$

$$+ d2 * \left(1 - \frac{Pr1}{Pn12}\right) * (Pr1 - Prw)$$

$$+ d3 * \left(1 - \frac{Pr2}{Pn21}\right) * (Pr2 - Prw)$$

$$+ d1 * \left(1 - \frac{Pn12}{Pn21}\right) * (Pnw - Cn)$$

$$+ d2 * \left(1 - \frac{Pr1}{Pn12}\right) * (Prw - Cr)$$

$$+ d3 * \left(1 - \frac{Pr2}{Pn21}\right) * (Prw - Cr) \tag{12.6}$$

Decision variables: P_{n12}, P_{r1}, P_{r2}, P_{nw}, P_{rw}
Parameters: d_1, d_2, d_3, P_{n21}, C_r, C_n

Numerical Example and Result

The data are partially adapted from the previous two papers (Gan et al., 2015 and Wang and Tung, 2011). Additionally, we assume that the maximum demand for the new product U is 1000. The initial demand $D_0 = 90$, $\lambda = 0.01$. The remanufactured product maximum demand utility $V = 500$, $D_{r0} = 50$,

$\eta=0.01$. The time is counted in months: $t_1=1$, $T_2=2$, $t_3=3$, $T_4=4$. The cumulative demand for Type 1 and Type 2 product in different periods is shown in Table 12.1.

Retailer's Optimization

Assuming $P_{n21}=[550, 650, 750]$, $P_{nw}=350$, $P_{rw}=150$, $C_n=200$, $C_r=50$, the optimal price for P_{n12}, P_{r1}, and P_{r2} and the objective value and the trend of prices in different values of P_{n21} are shown in Table 12.2.

The price gap between Type 1 and Type 2 products is larger if the selling price of Type 3 products increases. In addition, the price differential of Type 2 product between $[t_2, t_3]$ and $[t_3, t_4]$ becomes larger if the price of Type 3 products is higher.

Manufacturer's Optimization

Manufacturer's profit is optimized when the wholesale price for new and remanufactured products is equal to the retailer's price.

Joint Profit Optimization

Assume $C_n=200$, $C_r=[50]$. The optimal price for P_{n12}, P_{r1}, P_{r2}, P_{nw}, P_{rw}, and the objective values are shown in Table 12.3.

TABLE 12.1

Cumulative Demand Potential of Type 1 and Type 2 Products

Dn12 (t2, t3)	Dn12 (t3, t4)	Dr1	Dr2
240	64	438	270

TABLE 12.2

Optimal Retailer Prices of P_{n12}, P_{r1}, and P_{r2}

Decision Variable	$P_{n21}=550$	$P_{n21}=650$	$P_{n21}=750$
P_{n21}	541	610	678
P_{r1}	346	380	414
P_{r2}	350	400	450

TABLE 12.3

Optimal Solution for Joint Supply Chain

	$P_{n21}=550$	$P_{n21}=650$	$P_{n21}=750$
Objective Value	83,723	103,564	123,660
P_{n21}	473	541	609
P_{r1}	261	296	330
P_{r2}	300	350	400
P_{nw}	336	371	405
P_{rw}	156	173	190

In the joint profit optimization model, both Type 1 and Type 2 products are recommended to be sold at a lower price compared with the retailer model. The price gap of Type 2 products between $[t_2, t_3]$ and $[t_3, t_4]$ is larger than the values in the retailer model. If the selling price for recently released new products increases, the gap between new and remanufacture wholesale price is also increased. The original paper provides a more detailed analysis, discussion, and conclusion (Zhou et al., 2017).

12.3.1.2 Dual-Channel Effect

It is assumed that new products are sold by the retailer, while remanufactured products are sold online, operated by the manufacturer. The supply chain system is shown in Figure 12.3.

Then, the model is developed by adding the direct channel preference rate γ and considering the discount of generation obsolescence and remanufacturing inferiority in the view of technology-savvy and quality-conscious customers.

$$D_{n12}\left(t_2,t_3\right) = \frac{D_{n12}}{P_{n21}}\left[P_{n21} - \frac{P_{n12} - P_{r1}}{1-\beta_1}\right]; P_{r1} < \alpha_1\beta_1 P_{n21} \qquad (12.7)$$

$$D_{n12}\left(t_3,t_4\right) = \frac{D_{n12}}{P_{n21}}\left[P_{n21} - \frac{P_{n12} - P_{r2}}{\alpha_1 - \beta_1}\right]; P_{r2} < \beta_1 P_{n21} \qquad (12.8)$$

$$D_{n12}\left(t_2,t_3\right) = \frac{D_{n12}}{P_{n21}}\left[P_{n21} - P_{n12}\right]; \alpha_1\beta_1 P_{n21} \leq P_{r1} \leq \alpha_2\beta_2\gamma \bullet P_{n21} \qquad (12.9)$$

$$D_{n12}\left(t_3,t_4\right) = \frac{D_{n12}}{P_{n21}}\left[P_{n21} - P_{n12}\right]; \beta_1 P_{n21} \leq P_{r2} \leq \beta_2\gamma \bullet P_{n21} \qquad (12.10)$$

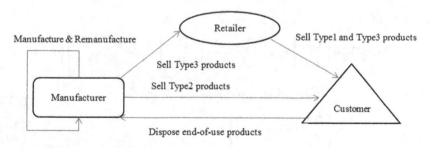

FIGURE 12.3
Closed-loop supply chain system with a separate sale-channel.

$$D_{r1}(t_2,t_3) = \frac{1}{P_{n21}}\left[D_{r1}\left(P_{n21-}\frac{\mathrm{Pr}1}{\gamma} \right) \right.$$

$$\left. + D_{n12}\left(\frac{P_{n12}-P_{r1}}{1-\beta_1} - \frac{P_{r1}}{\alpha_2\beta_2} \right) \right]; \quad P_{r1} < \alpha_1\beta_1 P_{n21} \tag{12.11}$$

$$D_{r2}(t_3,t_4) = \frac{1}{P_{n21}}\left[D_{r2}\left(P_{n21-}\frac{\mathrm{Pr}2}{\gamma} \right) \right.$$

$$\left. + D_{n12}\left(\frac{P_{n12}-P_{r2}}{\alpha_1-\beta_1} - \frac{P_{r2}}{\alpha_2\beta_2} \right) \right]; \quad P_{r2} < \beta_1 P_{n21} \tag{12.12}$$

$$D_{r1}(t_2,t_3) = \frac{D_{r1}}{P_{n21}}\left[P_{n21} - \frac{P_{r1}}{\gamma} \right]; \quad \alpha_1\beta_1 P_{n21} \le P_{r1} \le \alpha_2\beta_2\gamma \bullet P_{n21} \tag{12.13}$$

$$D_{r2}(t_3,t_4) = \frac{D_{r2}}{P_{n21}}\left[P_{n21} - \frac{P_{r2}}{\gamma} \right]; \quad \beta_1 P_{n21} \le P_{r2} \le \beta_2\gamma \bullet P_{n21} \tag{12.14}$$

Equations 12.7 and 12.8 represent the demand for Type 1 products during $[t_2,t_3]$ and $[t_3,t_4]$, when the price of Type 2 product is lower than the quality-conscious customers' value. Some customers in this segment will switch to buy Type 2 products. Equations 12.9 and 12.10 present the condition when the price of Type 2 product is higher than the quality-conscious customers' value but still lower than the technology-savvy customers' perceived value. Equations 12.11 through 12.14 are the demand during $[t_2,t_4]$ for Type 2 products in each condition.

The profit optimization models are generated accordingly in the three scenarios. The demand trend is dependent on price and customer perceived discount. The function is piece-wise dependent on customers' combined perceived value deduction on quality and technology obsolescence. During the period $[t_2, t_3]$, Type 2 products decrease in value because of the aging technology and lower quality, while during $[t_3, t_4]$, the value of the goods is only reduced because of their inferior quality.

Retailer's Model

$$\mathrm{Max}\ \Pi_R = \left(\frac{D_{n12}}{P_{n21}}\left[P_{n21} - \frac{P_{n12}-P_{r1}}{1-\beta_1} \right] + \frac{D_{n12}}{P_{n21}}\left[P_{n21} - \frac{P_{n12}-P_{r2}}{\alpha_1-\beta_1} \right] \right)$$

$$* \left(P_{n12} - P_{nw} \right); \quad \text{when } P_{r1}, P_{r2} < \alpha_1\beta_1 P_{n21}$$

$$= \left(\frac{D_{n12}}{P_{n21}}\left[P_{n21} - P_{n12} \right] \right) \tag{12.15}$$

$$* \left(P_{n12} - P_{nw} \right); \quad \text{when } \alpha_1\beta_1 P_{n21} \le P_{r1}, P_{r2} \le \alpha_2\beta_2\gamma \bullet P_{n21}$$

Decision variables: P_{n12}, P_{r1}, P_{r2}
Parameters: P_{n21}, P_{nw}, α_1, α_2, β_1, β_2, γ
Constraints: $P_{r1} \leq P_{n12}$, $P_{r2} \leq P_{n21}$, $P_{n12} \leq P_{n21}$, $\alpha_1 > \alpha_2$; $\beta_1 < \beta_2$; $\alpha_1 > \beta_1$

Manufacturer's Model

When $P_{r1}, P_{r2} < \alpha_1 \beta_1 P_{n21}$;

$$\text{Max } \Pi_M = \left(\frac{1}{P_{n21}} \left[D_{r1} \left(P_{n21-} \frac{P_{r1}}{\gamma} \right) + D_{n12} \left(\frac{P_{n12} - P_{r1}}{1 - \beta_1} - \frac{P_{r1}}{\alpha_2 \beta_2} \right) \right] \right) * (P_{r1} - C_r)$$

$$+ \left(\frac{1}{P_{n21}} \left[D_{r2} \left(P_{n21-} \frac{P_{r2}}{\gamma} \right) + D_{n12} \left(\frac{P_{n12} - P_{r2}}{\alpha_1 - \beta_1} - \frac{P_{r2}}{\beta_2} \right) \right] \right) * (P_{r2} - C_r)$$

$$+ \left(\frac{D_{n12}}{P_{n21}} \left[P_{n21} - \frac{P_{n12} - P_{r1}}{1 - \beta_1} \right] + \frac{D_{n12}}{P_{n21}} \left[P_{n21} - \frac{P_{n12} - P_{r2}}{\alpha_1 - \beta_1} \right] \right) * (P_{nw} - C_n)$$

When $\alpha_1 \beta_1 P_{n21} \leq P_{r1}$, $P_{r2} \leq \alpha_2 \beta_2 \gamma \bullet P_{n21}$;

$$\text{Max } \Pi_M = \frac{D_{r1}}{P_{n21}} \left[P_{n21} - \frac{P_{r1}}{\gamma} \right] * (P_{r1} - C_r) + \frac{D_{r2}}{P_{n21}} \left[P_{n21} - \frac{P_{r2}}{\gamma} \right] * (P_{r2} - C_r)$$

$$+ \left(\frac{D_{n12}}{P_{n21}} \left[P_{n21} - P_{n12} \right] \right) * (P_{nw} - C_n) \tag{12.16}$$

Closed-loop Supply Chain Model

$$\text{Max } \Pi_{clsc} = \Pi_R + \Pi_M \tag{12.17}$$

Numerical Example and Result

The cumulative demand potentials of Type 1 and Type 2 products are the same as in the basic model, as shown in Table 12.1. We assume that Cn = $200, Cr = $50, P_{n21} = $650, P_{nw} = $370, $\alpha_1 = 0.8$, $\alpha_2 = 0.7$, $\beta_1 = 0.7$, $\beta_2 = 0.8$, γ = 0.9. Tables 12.3 through 12.5 show the results of the retailer, the manufacturer, and the supply chain profit maximization model. The results are presented in Tables 12.4 through 12.6. They are varied by different values of α_1, α_2, β_1, β_2.

We can see that profit will be optimal in most cases when the price of Type 2 products is lower than quality-conscious customers' perceived value; the only exception is the condition in the retailer's model when the difference between generation discount levels in the two consumer groups is larger than that of the remanufacturing discount levels ($\alpha_1 - \alpha_2 > \beta_2 - \beta_1$). Profit will be optimal if Type 2 products are sold at prices lower than the quality-conscious

TABLE 12.4

Result of the Retailer's Model

Value of α and β	α1 = 0.8; α2 = 0.7; β1 = 0.7; β2 = 0.8		α1 = 0.8; α2 = 0.6; β1 = 0.7; β2 = 0.8		α1 = 0.8; α2 = 0.7; β1 = 0.6; β2 = 0.8	
Condition	$P_{r1} < \alpha_1 \beta_1 P_{n21}$ $P_{r2} < \beta_1 P_{n21}$	$P_{r1} < \alpha_1 \beta_1 P_{n21}$ $\beta_1 P_{n21} \leq P_{r2} \leq \beta_2 \gamma \cdot P_{n21}$	$P_{r1} < \alpha_1 \beta_1 P_{n21}$ $P_{r2} < \beta_1 P_{n21}$	$P_{r1} < \alpha_1 \beta_1 P_{n21}$ $\beta_1 P_{n21} \leq P_{r2} \leq \beta_2 \gamma \cdot P_{n21}$	$P_{r1} < \alpha_1 \beta_1 P_{n21}$ $P_{r2} < \beta_1 P_{n21}$	$\alpha_1 \beta_1 P_{n21} \leq P_{r1} \leq \alpha_2 \beta_2 \gamma \cdot P_{n21}$ $\beta_1 P_{n21} \leq P_{r2} \leq \beta_2 \gamma \cdot P_{n21}$
Pn12	456	468	455	468	462	511
Pri	364	364	364	364	312	312
Pr2	455	455	364	455	390	390
πR	16,321	12,732	12,512	12,732	11,968	9,291
Max. Profit*	*			*	*	

TABLE 12.5

Result of the Manufacturer's Model

Value of α and β	α1 = 0.8; α2 = 0.7; β1 = 0.7; β2 = 0.8		α1 = 0.8; α2 = 0.6; β1 = 0.7; β2 = 0.8		α1 = 0.8; α2 = 0.7; β1 = 0.6; β2 = 0.8	
Condition	$P_{ri} < \alpha_1 \beta_1$ $P_{n21} P_{r2} < \beta_1 P_{n21}$	$P_{ri} < \alpha_1 \beta_1 P_{n21}$ $\beta_1 P_{n21} \leq P_{r2} \leq \beta_2 \gamma \cdot P_{n21}$	$P_{ri} < \alpha_1 \beta_1$ $P_{n21} P_{r2} < \beta_1 P_{n21}$	$P_{ri} < \alpha_1 \beta_1 P_{n21}$ $\beta_1 P_{n21} \leq P_{r2} \leq \beta_2 \gamma \cdot P_{n21}$	$P_{ri} < \alpha_1 \beta_1$ $P_{n21} P_{r2} < \beta_1 P_{n21}$	$\alpha_1 \beta_1 P_{n21} \leq P_{ri} \leq \alpha_2 \beta_2 \gamma \cdot P_{n21}$ $P_{n21} \beta_1 P_{n21} \leq P_{r2} \leq \beta_2 \gamma \cdot P_{n21}$
Pn12	650	650	650	650	650	312
Pri	299	299	288	288	281	312
Pr2	357	455	351	455	323	390
πM	142,598	103,459	131,577	95,594	116,327	111,026
Max. Profit	*		*		*	

TABLE 12.6

Result of the Joint Supply Chain Model

Value of α and β	$\alpha1=0.8;\ \alpha2=0.7;\ \beta1=0.7;\ \beta2=0.8$		$\alpha1=0.8;\ \alpha2=0.6;\ \beta1=0.7;\ \beta2=0.8$		$\alpha1=0.8;\ \alpha2=0.7;\ \beta1=0.6;\ \beta2=0.8$	
Condition	$Pri < \alpha_1\,\beta_1$ $Pn21$ $Pr2 < \beta_1$ $Pn21$	$Pri < \alpha_1\,\beta_1\,Pn21$ $\beta_1\,Pn21 \le Pr2 \le \beta_2\,\gamma$ $\bullet\ Pn21$	$Pri < \alpha_1\,\beta_1$ $Pn21$ $Pr2 < \beta_1$ $Pn21$	$Pri < \alpha_1\,\beta_1\,Pn21$ $\beta_1\,Pn21 \le Pr2 \le \beta_2$ $\gamma \bullet Pn21$	$Pri < \alpha_1\,\beta_1$ $Pn21$ $Pr2 < \beta_1$ $Pn21$	$\alpha_1\,\beta_1\,Pn21 \le Pri \le \alpha_2\,\beta_2\,\gamma$ $\bullet\ Pn21\ PiPn21 \le Pr2 \le \beta_2$ $\gamma \bullet Pn21$
Pn12	422	437	407	422	456	510
Pri	258	265	242	249	260	318
Pr2	304	455	290	455	300	390
πc	103,287	95,439	95,649	89,613	103,838	93,342
Max. Profit*	*		*		*	

customers' perceived value in $[t_2, t_3]$ and higher than their perceived value in $[t_3, t_4]$. In the manufacturer's model, profit is optimal when the difference between generation discount levels in the two segments is the same as that of the remanufacturing discount levels ($\alpha_1 - \alpha_2 = \beta_2 - \beta_1$), and Type 2 products' price is lower than quality-conscious customers' perceived value. In the joint profit model shown earlier, profit is optimal when $\alpha_1 - \alpha_2 < \beta_2 - \beta_1$, and the discount level of Type 2 products is high enough to attract some of the quality-level consumers throughout the studied period (Zhou and Gupta, 2017).

Comparison between Single-channel and Separate-channel Models

Then, we compare the result with that of the basic model when the upper bound P_{n21} is \$650. In the retailer optimization model, optimal prices in the single channel environment are $P_{n12} = 610$, $P_{r1} = 400$, $P_{r2} = 380$. If a separate sale-channel is considered, the optimal prices for Type 1 products are lower in all the conditions. This implies the power of the direct sale-channel. In the single-channel model, the price of Type 2 products during $[t_3, t_4]$ is lower than the price during $[t_2, t_3]$, while the separate-channel model shows the opposite as the result of considering technology upgrades for remanufactured products. The high technology level increases the perceived value for Type 2 products.

12.3.2 Practical Price Model

Zhou and Gupta (2018) conduct empirical research by collecting sales data of Apple iPhones from eBay, finding price trends of different types of products, and identifying factors that significantly influence the prices. In addition, the quality depreciation rate and the technology depreciation rate are identified. The prices for new and remanufactured products from Generation 4 to Generation 7 are collected. They take seller-related (stars level and percentage of positive feedback), service-related (length of warranty and warranty cost), transaction-related (transaction quantity and number of reviewers), and product-related variables (product generation, condition, storage capacity, market positioning level, and innovation level) into account. More detailed descriptions can be found in the original paper.

12.3.2.1 Price Trends over Time

First, the price trend for new products belonging to different generations is extracted. Then, Equation 12.18 and Figure 12.4 show the price differential between the current price and the original price since launch. It is assumed that the price change of a new product is dependent on the technology depreciation rate. Equation 12.19 and Figure 12.5 show the technology depreciation curve.

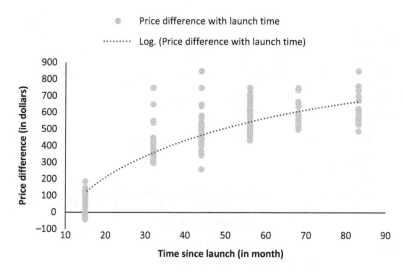

FIGURE 12.4
Price difference between the current price and the original price with time.

The price gap between the current rate and the original rate follows a logarithmic curve, while the technology depreciation rate correctly follows a polynomial curve. t represents the time since launch (in months).

$$\text{Price differential} = 320.98 \ln(t) - 750.1 \qquad (12.18)$$

$$\text{Current price for new} = 0.1009t^2 - 15.659t + 652.84 \qquad (12.19)$$

Quality obsolescence is studied by analyzing the price discount of remanufactured products compared with new products belonging to the same model.

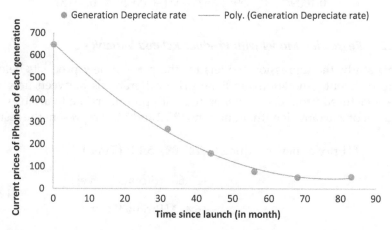

FIGURE 12.5
Current prices of new smartphones over time.

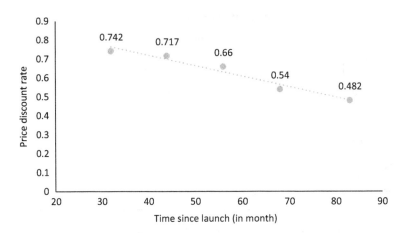

FIGURE 12.6
Price discount for the remanufactured product over time.

Figure 12.6 expresses the average price discount for remanufactured iPhone 4, iPhone 4S, iPhone 5, iPhone 5S, and iPhone 6 smartphones.

According to the curves in Figure 12.6, the price discount follows a linear regression model.

$$\text{Price discount} = -0.0055t + 0.9413 \qquad (12.20)$$

The average prices of remanufactured products belonging to different generations over time can be calculated by Equation 12.21:

$$\text{Price of the remanufactured product}$$
$$= \left(0.1009t^2 - 15.659t + 652.84\right) * \left(-0.0055t + 0.9413\right) \qquad (12.21)$$

12.3.2.2 Regression Model with Product-Related Variables

In this study, the regression models for the price of new products belonging to different generations and the price differentials between new and remanufactured products are generated with product-related variables and the factor of warranty length. Equations 12.22 and 12.23 represent the results.

$$f\left(\text{Price of new products}\right) = 247.09 - 5.13 * \left(\text{Time}\right)$$
$$+ 27.60 * \left(\text{Storage\_Level}\right)$$
$$+ 6.44 * \left(\text{Product\_Level}\right) \qquad (12.22)$$
$$+ 86.31 * \left(\text{Innovation\_Level}\right) + \varepsilon$$

$$f\left(\begin{array}{l}\text{price differential between new and}\\\text{remanufactured products of the same model}\end{array}\right)$$

$$= -294.3 + \text{In } 47.54 * (\text{Time}) - \text{In } 6.53 * (\text{Storage\_level}) \quad (12.23)$$

$$- \text{In } 16.99 * (\text{Product\_Level})$$

$$+ \text{In } 78.60 * (\text{Innovation\_Level}) + \varepsilon'$$

12.3.2.3 Factors Correlation and Interaction

One innovation of this study is that product-related variables including storage level, innovation level, and product level are considered in the model. In this paragraph, the correlation and interaction for these variables are shown. The original research paper presented detailed variable anlaysis (Zhou and Gupta, 2017). Table 12.7 exhibits the correlation between product-related variables and discounts from the launch price for new products, which represents technology depreciation. Table 12.8 shows a similar correlation between product-related variables with price discounts for remanufactured product from new product of the same model, which represents quality depreciation.

Regarding technology depreciation, time lapse, innovation level, and product level are significant factors, but storage level is not. The interaction

TABLE 12.7

Correlation Analysis for Price Discount of New Products

Effect	Num DF	Den DF	F Value	Pr > F
Storage_Level	2	267	0.13	0.8788
Innovation_Level	2	267	5.01	0.0073
Product_Level	2	267	3.75	0.0248
Time	5	267	163.19	<.0001
Storag*Innova*Product	6	267	8.85	<.0001

TABLE 12.8

Variables' Effects on Price Discount of Remanufactured Products

Effect	Num DF	Den DF	F Value	Pr > F
Condition	1	408	26.57	<.0001
Storage_Level	2	408	0.83	0.438
Innovation_Level	1	408	0.92	0.3375
Product_Level	1	408	1.68	0.1959
Time	5	408	61.01	<.0001
Condition*Time	7	408	3.89	0.0004
Storag*Innova*Product	9	408	3.89	0.0002

among storage, innovation, and product levels influences price discount significantly. Regarding quality depreciation, condition (seller-refurbished or manufacturer-refurbished) and time lapse are significant determinants, while product-related variables are not. However, the interaction among storage, innovation, and product levels also has an important effect.

12.3.2.4 Comparison with Theoretical Models

In the theoretical models, two product generations are analyzed. To check the validity of these models, the prices of Type 1 and Type 2 products are derived from the practical models. We assumed that the Type 1 product model has been released for 12 months (t = 12) within [t_2, t_3] and 18 months within [t_3, t_4]. The Type 2 product model has been released for 12 months within [t_2, t_3] and 6 months during [t_3, t_4].

According to the price curve formulas (Equations 12.19 and 12.21),

P_{n12} = \$479, P_{r1} = \$420 within [t_2, t_3]
P_{n12} = \$404, P_{r2} = \$511 within [t_3, t_4]

According to the regression models (Equations 12.22 and 12.23), assuming that storage, product, and innovation levels are the same with the neutral values of 2, 2, and 2, respectively,

P_{n12} = \$426, P_{r1} = \$177 within [t_2, t_3]
P_{n12} = \$395, P_{r2} = \$378 within [t_3, t_4]

In the theoretical model, the price of Type 2 product during [t_2, t_3] is lower than the price in [t_3, t_4]. The results of the practical models are consistent with this phenomenon. In the theoretical model, the price differential between new and remanufactured products is larger than that in the practical models. The value of the remanufactured product never exceeds the new products in the single-channel model, which is different from the real data price curve. However, in the separate sale-channel models, the supporting results can be found in joint supply chain models. When $\beta_1 \bullet P_{n21} < P_{r2} \leq \alpha_2 \beta_2 \gamma \bullet P_{n21}$, technology-savvy customers have the same or lower joint quality and technology depreciation as the quality-conscious customers (i.e., $\alpha_1^* \beta_1 \geq \alpha_2^* \beta_2$).

12.4 Managerial Insights and Conclusion

This chapter summarizes the development of theoretical and practical pricing models for new and remanufactured products by considering the high-technology generation factor. The single-channel model presents how generation development influences the price decision and reviews the price difference between Type 1 and Type 2 products. The separate sale-channel model illustrates the power of a direct sale-channel for remanufactured products. The practical models help to validate the two theoretical models. The results show some consistency in the price differential of remanufactured products between two time periods and some partial difference in price differential between new and remanufactured products.

The chapter provides knowledge for customers and guides them to purchase items at an appropriate price. The theoretical models can stimulate development of other price models that account for the product generation factor. The practical models help scientists to validate other price models and provide information for industry managers to support price decisions.

For future development, additional price-influencing factors can be added to the models. The constraint of acquiring cores is a common problem for both durable goods and short-lifecycle products. The quality and quantity of used cores can be added to the theoretical model in the future. Also, the competition factor cannot be ignored for pricing decisions. More data from other product brands can be added to practical models and used to support related theoretical models.

References

Abbey, J. D., Blackburn, J. D., and Guide Jr., V. D. (2015a). Optimal Pricing for New and Remanufactured Products. *Journal of Operations Management, 36,* 130–146.

Abbey, J. D., Meloy, M. G., Blackburn, J., and Guide Jr., V. D. (2015b). Consumer Markets for Remanufactured and Refurbished Products. *California Management Review* University of California, Berkeley, *57*(4), 26–42.

Agrawal, V. V., Atasu, A., and Van Ittersum, K. (2015). Remanufacturing, Third-Party Competition, and Consumers' Perceived Value of New Products. *Management Science, 61*(1), 60–72.

Alqahtani, A. Y., and Gupta, S. M. (2017). Warranty as a Marketing Strategy for Remanufactured Products. *Journal of Cleaner Production, 161,* 1294–1307.

Andrew-Munot, M., Ibrahim, R. N., and Junaidi, E. (2015). An Overview of Used-Products Remanufacturing. *Mechanical Engineering Research,* 12–23.

Aytac, B., and Wu, S. D. (2013). Characterization of Demand for Short Life-cycle Technology Products. *Annals of Operations Research, 203*(1), 255–277.

Bass, F. (1969). A New Product Growth for Model Consumer Durables. *Management Science, 13*(2), 203–223.

Bhattacharya, S., Guide, V. D., and Van Wassenhove, L. N. (2006). Optimal Order Quantities with Remanufacturing across New Product Generations. *Production and Operations Management, 15*(3), 421–431.

Ding, Q. D., Dong, C., and Pan, Z. (2016). A Hierarchical Pricing Decision Process on a Dual-Channel Problem with One Manufacturer and One Retailer. *International Journal of Production Economics, 175,* 197–212.

Frota Neto, J. Q., Bloemhof, J., and Corbett, C. (2016). Market Prices of Remanufactured, Used and New Items: Evidence from eBay. *International Journal of Production Economics, 171,* 371–380.

Galbreth, M., Byaci, T., and Verter, V. (2013). Product Reuse in Innovative Industries. *Production and Operations Management, 22*(4), 1011–1033.

Gan, S. S., and Pujawan, I. N. (2017a) Pricing and Warranty Level Decision for New and Remanufactured Short Life-cycle Products. *Jurnal Teknik Industri, 19*(1), 39–46.

Gan, S. S., Pujawan, I. N., Suparno, and Widodo, B. (2015). Pricing Decision for New and Remanufactured Short-life Cycle Products with Time-dependent Demand. *Operations Research Perspectives, 2,* 1–12.

Gan, S. S., Pujawan, I. N., Suparno, and Widodo, B. (2017b). Pricing Decision for New and Remanufactured Product in a Closed-loop Supply Chain with Separate Sales-channel. *International Journal of Production Economics, 190,* 120–132.

Gan, S. S., Pujawan, I. N., Suparno, and Widodo, B. (2018). Pricing Decision for Short Life-cycle Product in a Closed-loop Supply Chain with Random Yield and Random Demands. *Operations Research Perspectives, 5,* 174–190.

Gan, S. S., Pujawan, I., and Suparno. (2014). Remanufacturing of Short Life-cycle Products. *Operations and Supply Chain Management, 7*(1), 13–22.

Gao, J., Wang, X., Yang, Q., and Zhong, Q. (2016). Pricing Decision of a Dual-channel Closed-loop Supply Chain under Uncertain Demand of Indirect Channel. *Mathematical Problems in Engineering,* 1–13.

Guide Jr, V. D., and Li, J. (2010). The Potential for Cannibalization of New Products Sales by Remanufactured Products. *Decision Science, 41,* 547–572.

Guide Jr. V. D., and Van Wassenhove, L. N. (2009). The Evolution of Closed-loop Supply Chain Research. *Operations Research, 57,* 10–18.

Gungor, A., and Gupta, S. M. (1999). Issues in Environmentally Conscious Manufacturing and Product Recovery: A Survey. *Computers & Industrial Engineering, 36,* 811–853.

Hazen, B. T., Mollenkopf, D. A., and Wang, Y. (2017). Remanufacturing for the Circular Economy: An Examination of Consumer Switching Behavior. *Business Strategy and the Environment, 26,* 451–464.

Ilgin, M. A., and Gupta, S. M. (2010). Environmentally Conscious Manufacturing and Product Recovery (ECMPRO): A Review of the State of the Art. *Environmental Management, 91,* 563–591.

Ilgin, M. A., and Gupta, S. M. (2012). *Remanufacturing Modelling and Analysis.* CRC Press/Taylor & Francis Group, Boca Raton, Florida/London, UK.

Khor, K. S., and Hazen, B. T. (2017). Remanufactured Products Purchase Intentions and Behaviour: Evidence from Malaysia. *International Journal of Production Research, 55*(8), 2149–2162.

Kwak, K., and Kim, H. (2013). Market Positioning of Remanufactured Products with Optimal Planning for Part Upgrades. *Mechanical Design, 135*(1), 1–10.

Norton, J. A., and Bass, F. M. (1987). A Diffusion Theory Model of Adoption and Substitution for Successive Generations of High-technology Products. *Management Science, 33*(9), 1069–1086.

Ovchinnikov, A. (2011). Revenue and Cost Management for Remanufactured Products. *Production and Operations Management, 20*(6), 824–840.

Pang, G., Casalin, F., Papagiannidis, S., Muyldermans, L., and Yse, Y. (2015). Pricing Determinants for Remanufactured Electronic Products: A Case Study on eBay UK. . *International Journal of Production Research, 53*(2), 572–589.

Subramanian, R., and Subramanyam, R. (2012). Key Factors in the Market for Remanufactured Products. *Manufacturing & Service Operations Management, 14*(2), 315–326.

Wang, K. H., and Tung, C. T. (2011). Construction of a Model towards EOQ and Pricing Strategy for Gradually Obsolescent Products. *Applied Mathematics and Computation, 217*(16), 6926–6933.

Wang, Z. B., Wang, Y. Y., and Wang, J. C. (2016). Optimal Distribution Channel Strategy for New and Remanufactured Products. *Electronic Commerce Research, 16*(2), 269–295.

Watson, M. (2008). *A Review of Literature and Research on Public Attitudes, Perceptions, and Behavior Relating to Remanufactured, Repaired and Reused Products.* Sheffield, UK.: Center for Remanufacturing and Reuse, The University of Sheffield.

Xu, X., Zeng, S., and He, Y. (2017). The Influence of e-Service on Customer Online Purchasing Behavior toward Remanufactured Products. *International Journal of Production Economics, 187*, 113–125.

Zhou, E., Zhang, J., Gou, Q., and Liang, L. (2015). A Two Period Pricing Model for New Fashion Style Launching Strategy. *International Journal of Production Economics, 160*, 144–156.

Zhou, L., and Gupta, S. M. Jnl Remanufactur (2018). https://doi.org/10.1007/s13243-018-0054-x

Zhou, L., and Gupta, S. M. (2017). Pricing Decision for New and Remanufactured Products with Multiple Generations in a Dual-channel Supply Chain. *International Logistics and Supply Chain Congress.* Istanbul, Turkey.

Zhou, L., Gupta, S. M., Kinoshita, Y., and Yamada, T. (2017). Pricing Decision Models for Remanufactured Short-Life Cycle Technology Products with Generation Consideration. *Procedia CIRP, 61*, 195–200.

13

Applicability of Using the Internet of Things in Warranty Analysis for Product Recovery

Ammar Y. Alqahtani, Surendra M. Gupta, and Kenichi Nakashima

CONTENTS

13.1 Introduction

Many companies have become increasingly responsible for the management of products that have reached the end-of-use. This can be attributed to decreasing numbers of landfills and the rising cost of natural resources causing commercial and environmental problems. The use of end-of-use products (EOUP) provides a method through which companies can reduce the need for natural resources by recycling some of the parts in these obsolete products. Additionally, the cost of raw materials can be improved using EOUPs. The proper management of EOUPs requires cleaning, sorting, disassembling, component recovery, repair, and material handling to ensure that all operations run smoothly. It is vital to highlight that the condition of the EOUPs greatly determines which recovery option can be employed. In some situations, EOUPs with minor problems can be refurbished using new parts in certain areas. In contrast, those with significant damage need to be completely broken down and recycled as small components. Reverse logistics can be used to understand the uncertainty that influences the recovery option used. As a result, reverse logistics is important in remanufacturing. The main reason for the varied processes is the varying condition of the EOUPs that are returned to the company. The condition determines whether the products can be remanufactured or used as spare parts, or whether the components can be harvested.

The role of the Internet of Things (IoT) is to mitigate the complexity of the planning process that EOUPs require due to the uncertainty of their condition. One requirement of the IoT is the need for a network structure that allows the unique identification of components. The network allows the remote tracking and monitoring of all objects in various segments of the supply chain, including reverse logistics. The IoT requires the use of radio-frequency identification (RFID) as one of the vital components due to the ability to improve the tracking of these products. RFID chips are effective because they do not only collect information; they also store significant quantities of information in the sensors. This can be used to provide insight into the condition of the object for use in reverse logistics.

Sensors, such as those used in RFID chips, are devices that monitor the product and provide measures of calibrated dimensions, including but not limited to vibration, temperature, and pressure. Products that have been built with sensors embedded in them are called sensor embedded products (SEPs). They are built with the goals of data collection inbuilt in them to ensure that the length of their usefulness can be ascertained and their state during end-of-use can be readily established. Additionally, information on the amount of usefulness remaining can be used to assess how close the product is to becoming an EOUP. The data on the remaining usefulness can be used in ensuring that the right recovery models are adopted to make sure that the system criteria adopted optimize the products. The adoption of

RFID tags or specialized sensors can provide insight into the economic life of a product as well. The RFID chips and sensors can be used to monitor the main critical components, thereby providing information during the recovery phase. All the information stored in the tags, such as location, warranty terms, serial numbers, and beginning-of-life and middle-of-life information, can be accessed to provide insight into the best recovery process for the specific product.

Theoretically, there is no limit to the potential sensors that can be included. At present, additional sensors can be used to ascertain the environmental conditions, such as humidity, dust, and vibration, to which the product has been subjected. When combined with the service information, this can provide an empirical picture of the state of the product. If the product requires refurbishing only, it can be refurbished to change the worn-out components. If the damage is too great, it can be broken down for spare parts for other products. This information is quite important, but there is a need for a way of collecting this information using the lowest amount of manpower and without affecting client satisfaction during the lifetime of the product. This necessitates management of the life cycle with consideration of the multiple stakeholder needs throughout the various processes. The IoT offers a method of collecting this information. The design of the product can incorporate aspects such as early detection of the beginning-of-life and middle-of-life information, allowing the EOU operations department to determine the model that will be used in the individual product even before it has reached the factory at the product's end-of-life. This allows proactive decision making rather than time-consuming reactive decision making when the product reaches the end of its life cycle.

The system that uses SEPs to ascertain the recovery options at the product end-of-life is known as advanced remanufacturing to order (ARTO). ARTO systems use the SEP information to ensure that the material and component demands of the recovered product satisfy the system goals. In an ARTO system, the IoT can allow time-based product lifetimes to be ascertained beforehand to ensure adherence to minimum quality requirements. An additional benefit is that the remaining life of the components in the products can be clearly highlighted without the need for estimation. Considering that most of the customer requirements and expectations are linked to the warranty costs, the use of sensors can ensure that the products will always exceed the quality requirements while reducing the number of warranty claims.

The primary role of this chapter is to propose an ARTO model that can be used to ensure that the SEPs in the EOUPs are properly implemented. The model proposed in the study employs a mixed-integer method of programming that relies on physical, environmental, and financial goals. The most popular is the dryer system, which ensures that the relationship between the components can be used as a measure of the methodology that is selected.

The chapter's primary contribution is the presentation of a quantitative assessment of the effect of offering warranties on remanufactured items.

This is accomplished using a remanufacturer's perspective while at the same time proposing an appealing price to the buyer, thereby meeting the demands of two perspectives. While there are developmental studies on warranty policies for brand new products and a few on secondhand products, there exists no study that evaluates the potential benefits of warranties on remanufactured products in a quantitative and comprehensive manner. In the published literature, improved profit has been achieved by offering warranties for different policies to determine how much money can be invested in a warranty while still keeping it profitable overall. To that end, this chapter studies and scrutinizes the impact of offering renewing warranties on remanufactured products. Specifically, the chapter suggests a methodology that simultaneously minimizes the cost incurred by the remanufacturers and maximizes the confidence of the consumers in buying remanufacturing products.

Beyond these articulated aims, the rest of the chapter is divided up as follows: Section 13.2 listing all the related work from the literature review, Section 13.3 the reliability improvement warranty, Section 13.4 assumptions and notations, Section 13.5 preventative maintenance analysis, Section 13.6 the failures process, Section 13.7 warranty formulation, Section 13.8 system descriptions, Section 13.9 the design-of-experiments study, Section 13.10 results, and Section 13.11 conclusions.

13.2 Literature Review

13.2.1 Environmentally Conscious Manufacturing and Product Recovery

The issues of environmentally conscious manufacturing and product recovery (ECMPRO) have become increasingly prevalent in modern times, resulting in a substantial volume of research on the subject (Gungor and Gupta, 1999; Gupta and Lambert, 2008; Ilgin and Gupta, 2010). The growing importance of ECMPRO has been driven by environmental factors, public demands, and government regulation from the consumer/societal perspective. In terms of business, ECMPRO has been growing due to the potential to realize significant profits through the implementation of reverse logistics and resolutions to support product recycling. Manufacturers have noted the increasing level of consumer awareness of environmental issues and have responded through the institution of stricter environmental regulations and construction of facilities to minimize the amassing of waste through the recovery of EOUP materials and components (Gungor and Gupta, 2002).

Researchers have begun focusing on the myriad logistical issues encountered in product manufacturing when environmentally conscious activities are considered. Consequently, researchers have presented reviews of the many issues involved in environmentally conscious manufacturing and recovery (see Moyer and Gupta, 1997; Gupta, 2013; Ilgin et al., 2015; Gupta and Ilgin, 2018). The facet of greatest focus in the discourse on ECMPRO is the area of remanufacturing research, due largely to the significant role played by this facet in the overall recovery process. Lambert and Gupta (2005) have presented a comprehensive exploration of the various aspects involved in disassembly.

13.2.2 Review of RFID

The construction and integration of supply chain information systems can be used to achieve benefits for supply chain management. Thus, it is beneficial for the supply chain to implement the most up-to-date information systems in the market to gain a competitive advantage in the global arena (Edwards et al., 2001). According to research, it has been established that those organizations that take advantage of technology and deploy it in their supply chain functions are comparatively more successful than others (Shin and Eksioglu, 2015). This clearly proves that technologies that aid in redesigning and improving business operations are imperative for the sustainability of any organization in the international supply chain. Finkenzeller (2013) concluded that RFID technology has a number of uses ranging from the automation of operations, to container and automobile identification, to waste disposal. This clarifies why RFID technology has remained relevant over time as the classical technique for identifying objects.

13.2.3 Introduction to the Internet of Things

The Internet of Everything, the Industrial Internet of the Internet of Things, is a concept that envisions a network of machines and non-human-used devices that are constantly interacting with each other regardless of their position around the world. The main value of the paradigm is that full realization can only happen when devices can communicate with each other using aspects of business analytics, cloud computing, and enterprise systems to ensure that communication is almost seamless (Lee and Lee, 2015). According to Lund et al. (2014), the International Data Corporation (IDC) has projected an increase in demand by a 17.5 percent of the IoT infrastructure worldwide. Additionally, the infrastructure investment is around $1.9 trillion, but it is expected to rise to around $7.1 trillion by 2020. There are already numerous different competitive, societal, and technological pressures that are pushing firms to embrace the use of the IoT. Firms such as Walmart, Amazon, and Google are already using the IoT in some capacity. There is benefit to organizations embracing IoT due to the real-time operational benefits that it offers. Walmart, for example, has greatly embraced RFID to improve the operations management when it comes to the logistics and supply chain management.

The IoT industry has experienced great changes in the past 10 years. The factors that have caused the transformation include digital convergence, improved sensors, improved RFID technology, wireless technology improvements, and smartphone improvements (Talari et al., 2017). There are numerous examples of how the IoT has become an important factor in previously manual industries. Some examples include smart farms, self-drive cars, and smart metering, which have changed the manual methods of working in these industries to allow technology to be more widely employed. There is a growing need for methods of capturing real-time data using devices connected to the IoT. As with any technological evolution, there are some challenges that have arisen from the adoption of the IoT. Research by Gartner (2014) showed that there has been an increase in the data produced and stored in the IoT as more devices become connected. As a result, there is a likelihood that data centers will face numerous problems, such as breaches in security, consumer privacy, networking/warehousing issues, enterprise integration, and evolving server technologies. Developers whose niche is in IoT need to find solutions for these problems more quickly to ensure that the system can maintain its benefit to companies without compromising security or disrupting consumer trust. Proper due diligence is necessary to ensure that businesses understand the potential challenges presented by IoT adoption. This can allow companies to spend the required resources to ensure that the IoT can be integrated into the corporate model without causing more harm than good (Xia et al., 2012).

The IoT continues to grow each day, and the related technologies are also developing at the same rate. Concepts that were previously obscure are becoming more mainstream. The issues of artificial intelligence systems, cloud computing, robotics, and big data analytics are avenues where IoT has spurred tremendous growth (Gubbi et al., 2013). More technologies will continue being created and adopted with the objective of ensuring that almost all electronic devices can be used as an access point to monitor a product or a service. Furthermore, the IoT has seen the improvement of internet-based technologies with the aim of ensuring that devices continue to become more intelligent. Devices are being created with the ability to perform more tasks independently of human input (Mahdavinejad et al., 2018). The growth of smart homes, devices, and processes has been made possible using the IoT. These devices all require the IoT as the main point through which they can access information from other devices. Additionally, machine learning has been incorporated to ensure that devices can communicate with each other even without human information. However, one of the main components that have had to change to accommodate the IoT is networking protocols (Sethi and Sarangi, 2017).

Aside from that, the IoT allows integrated technology to provide solutions that were previously ineffective due to the amount of data that needed to be transferred and the electronic systems that were required to interact (Kopetz, 2011). These measures have boosted the retrieval, communication, and storage capabilities of device groups. The better the communication between the devices, the more effective the device groups. Networks, clouds, data, and devices are the main components in the technological innovation (Leung et al., 2014). One of the main motivations is that machines and devices that communicate with each other through the IoT can spur the next industrial revolution. Networks, robotic devices, and machines fitted with sensors will be able to perform complex processes without the inclusion of humans (Long and Kelley, 2010). This will improve the speed of operation, since computers can process decisions more quickly than humans. Additionally, when the processes have self-adoptive aspects, changes in areas such as supply chains may require little or no employee input. In some industries, these features have already been adopted. In the manufacturing industry, vehicles are now being produced mainly using robotic technology to increase speed and reduce errors. IoT incorporation can further streamline the manufacturing process (Wu et al., 2015).

One of the greatest challenges is how society will accept future factories. More modern factories are adopting the IoT technology. As a result, they have become more complex, as the integration of more processes continues. Additionally, the relationship between human workers and the integrated systems is expected to evolve, because the systems will be using real-time information (Jeschke et al., 2017). The result is less work for those who are working in smart factories as well as optimization of the resource consumption. There is a current estimate that a global smart factory may have an expected profit of around $67 billion in around the next 3 years. The expected increase in revenue will be 6 percent (Nativi and Lee, 2012). Additionally, the demand for better IoT integration is expected to spur the development of robotics, automation, communication, and virtual simulation in the modern manufacturing industry. Vendors are expected to increase their investment in IoT to $250 billion in 2020 (Sun, 2012). Clearly, market resource use and operational costs have been improved consistently over the past few years. When taking all these factors into account, this seems to indicate that the IoT is a necessary part of the advancement in technology as well as the champion for economic growth in the future.

13.2.4 Industry 4.0

An examination of the term *Industry 4.0*, as seen on a reliable online platform called "Industry 4.0," reveals that it is an industrial revolution in the fourth stage. In this phase, managers are entrusted with the responsibility of controlling and organizing the activities of different supply chain industries. It is inclusive of re-organizing the products' life cycle so that the customers' needs can be met perfectly (Liu and Xu, 2017).

The product life cycle in a supply chain starts with the generation of ideas and processing of the order, while production managers develop and manufacture the goods. Finally, the end product, as goods requested by the customer, is delivered to the access points for the consumer. The delivery of the product to the consumer initiates the processes and services of post-delivery, such as feedback about the consumer's experience. Therefore, the industrial revolution applied through Industry 4.0 is based on the integration of all participants in the process of the supply chain. Most important is the observance of achieving the delivery of valuable information and quality product and service delivery. The application of Industry 4.0 in a supply chain is a superb way of adding value optimally to the connection that exists between people, the optimization of processes, and products by supply chain companies in real time (Lasi et al., 2014).

As the supply chain process became complex, automation that involved the computerization of some processes of manufacturing evolved through growing technological innovations. The fourth revolution is a logical and natural extension of this computerized and automated evolution (Ivanov et al., 2016). In this revolution of the supply chain industry, cyber-physical systems have been initiated while adopting the technology and information used in the past three industry revolutions. However, in Industry 4.0, systems are sophisticated, in that they create a complex boundary between the world of advanced information and communication technology (the digital world) and the real world. In this case, the digital world is referred to as the *cyber-physical production systems* (CPPSs) (Lee et. al., 2015).

13.3 Reliability Improvement Warranty

The analysis of warranty costs for remanufactured products is complex in comparison with new and second-hand products due to the variable levels of use and maintenance history. Further, warranty policies similar to those for new and second-hand products may not be economically viable for the remanufacturer. To determine the prospective profitability of the chosen warranty format, it is necessary to test and compare warranty policies for remanufactured products to estimate the anticipated warranty cost that is associated with the policies. According to Alqahtani and Gupta (2017a,b), remanufacturers confront further issues, including the servicing strategies concerning remanufactured spare parts within the context of repair or replacement to address failures within the context of the warranty period.

Specifically, the warranty is an agreement between the manufacturer and the consumer by which the risk of product failure is addressed through correction or compensation on behalf of the manufacturer, insofar as the product issues are realized during the warranty period linked to the sale. Through the warranty, the product quality perception of the consumer is supported by the provision of performance guarantees (Choi and Ishii, 2010). In general, the warranty cost of a product is the same for all new items, insofar as the manufacturer has a well-established and effective quality control system.

While warranty costs are easily measurable, EOU products vary in value due to a number of variables, including age, maintenance history, and use, and thus, the warranty cost for a given remanufactured product is statistically unique (Alqahtani and Gupta, 2017c,d,e).

Within the context of the purchasing decision, buyers often compare the features of a product with competing brands offering a product of the same function. In some instances, competing brands may produce products that resemble one another in terms of cost, special characteristics, credibility of the product, insurance provided to the consumer, and quality (Hussain and Murthy, 2003). After the influence of sale factors is experienced, discount, warranty, and the availability of parts, repairs, and other services are then factored in. These elements are of significance in the purchasing decision, with the warranty allowing the buyer to further determine the level of reliability of a given product (Chattopadhyay and Murthy, 2004).

Consumers are increasingly aware of and demand warranties for remanufactured products due to a growing concern with product quality and an increasing level of environmental awareness on the part of the consumer (Yadav et al., 2003). This awareness is anticipated to increase the demand for remanufactured products in connection with the future costs of replacement/repair in the event that product failure is experienced. This highlights the importance of warranty management to remanufacturers of remanufactured products. Such manufacturers must effectively estimate the warranty costs, which must then be incorporated into the pricing structure, with failure to accomplish this potentially resulting in loss rather than profit through the sale of remanufactured items (Murthy, 2006).

The basic idea of a reliability improvement warranty (RIW) is to extend the notion of a basic consumer warranty to include guarantees on the reliability of the remanufactured item and not just on its immediate or short-term performance (Thomas and Richard, 2006). The intent of reliability improvement warranties is to negotiate warranty terms that will motivate a remanufacturer to continue improvements in reliability after a remanufactured product is delivered. In applications of RIW, it is essential that all terms be defined precisely and that methods for computing performance measures be negotiated and specified in the contract. Mean time between failures (MTBF) could be computed as a simple point estimate or as the lower confidence limit at some specified level of confidence, and so forth (Saleh and Marais, 2006).

Under RIW, the remanufacturer's fee is based on his ability to meet the warranty reliability requirements. Not all of these features are used in all procurements, of course. Furthermore, the terms of an RIW are quite specific to the individual transaction, so it is quite difficult to formulate a general RIW policy (Huang et al., 2007). For purposes of illustration, we list the following two somewhat simplified examples:

> *Policy 1:* Under this policy, the remanufacturer agrees to repair or provide replacements free of charge for any failed parts or units until time W

after purchase. In addition, the remanufacturer guarantees the MTBF of the purchased equipment to be at least M. If the computed MTBF is less than M, the remanufacturer will provide, at no cost to the buyer, (1) engineering analysis to determine the cause of failure to meet the guaranteed MTBF requirement, (2) engineering change proposals, (3) modification of all existing units in accordance with approved engineering changes, and (4) consignment spares for buyer use until such time as it shown that the MTBF is at least M (Gandara and Rich, 1977).

The following RIW provides for an initial period during which no MTBF guarantee is in effect followed by successive periods in which specific improvements in MTBF are required:

> *Policy 2:* under this policy, the remanufacturer agrees to repair or provide replacements for any failed parts or units until time W after purchase. In addition, the remanufacturer guarantees the MTBF of the purchased equipment to be as follows: no MTBF is guaranteed until time W_1 after date of first production delivery; during the period from W_1 to W_2 after first delivery, the MTBF is guaranteed to be at least M_1; from W_2 to W_3, the MTBF is guaranteed to be at least M_2; and from W_3 to W, the MTBF is guaranteed to be at least M_3 (with $0 < W_1 < W_2 < W_3 < W$ and $0 < M_1 < M_2 < M_3$). If during any period the MTBF guarantee is not met, the manufacturer will provide, at no cost to the buyer, engineering changes and product modifications as necessary to achieve the MTBF requirements.

13.4 Assumptions and Notations

Cost models for RIW reflect to some extent the wide diversity in terms of RIW contracts and the many cost elements that may be identified in the complex situation in which such warranties are employed. The models that have been developed, in fact, are often oriented to specific applications. This section starts with the model assumptions. Then, the notations of all the parameters used in this chapter are listed.

13.4.1 Assumptions

The following assumptions have been considered to simplify the analysis:

  i. The failures are statistically independent.
 ii. Every item failure under warranty period results in a claim.
iii. All claims are valid.
 iv. The failure of a remanufactured item is only a function of its age.

v. The time to carry out the replacement/repair action is relatively small compared with the mean time between failures.

vi. The cost to service a warranty claim (for repair/replacement of failed component) is a random variable.

13.4.2 Notations

W:	Warranty period
W_1:	Sub-interval of warranty period
C_o:	Operating cost of item
C_S:	Sale price of item
C_p:	Cost of remanufacturing an item
n:	Number of components in an item
RL:	Remaining life of item at sale
RL_i:	Remaining life of component i $(1 \leq i \leq n)$
U_i, L_i:	Upper and lower range of replacement component's remaining life
j:	Number of preventive maintenance (PM)
v:	Virtual remaining life
v_j:	Virtual remaining life after performing the jth PM activity
m:	Level of PM effort
$\delta(m)$:	Remaining life increment factor of PM with effort m
t:	Remaining life of remanufactured item at failure
$\Lambda(RL)$:	Intensity function for system failure
Λ_i:	Intensity function of non-stationary Poisson process
M_{iu}:	Renewal function associated with $F_{iu}(x)$
$E[.]$:	Expected value of expression within [.]
$F_i(x)$:	Failure distribution of a remanufactured component i
$F_{i1}(x)$:	Distribution function for times to first failure of component i
$F_{i2}(x)$:	Distribution function for times to subsequent failures of component i
$F_{iu}(x)$:	Distribution function for times to failure of remanufactured component used in replacement
$H(rl)$:	Distribution function for a remanufactured item
$H_i(rl)$:	Distribution function for a remanufactured component
$N(W; RL)$:	Number of failures over the warranty period with remaining life RL
$N_i(W; RL_i)$:	Number of failures for component i over the warranty period
$\Lambda(t)$:	Intensity function for system failure
$F_w(x)$:	Distribution function for the first failure in the period $[W_1, W)$ given by the excess remaining life of renewal process associated with failures in the period $[0, W_1)$
$C_d(W; RL)$:	Total warranty cost to remanufacturer
$C(m)$:	Cost of performing a PM with effort m
C_j:	Cost of replacement/repair jth failure, $j \geq 1$

13.5 Preventive Maintenance Analysis

Usually, PM activities involve a set of maintenance tasks, such as cleaning, systematic inspection, lubricating, adjusting and calibrating, replacing different components, and so on (Ben Mabrouk et al., 2016). The right PM activities can reduce the number of failures efficiently and as a result. reduce the warranty cost and increase customer satisfaction. This study adopts the modeling framework proposed by Kim et al. (2004) to model the effect of PM activities.

A series of PM activities of a remanufactured item are performed at remaining life $RL_1, RL_2, \ldots RL_j, \ldots$, with $RL_0 = 0$. Here, the effect of PM results in a restoration of the item, so that the item's virtual remaining life is effectively increased. The concept of virtual age is introduced in Kijima et al. (1988) and then extended in Kijima (1989). In this study, the jth PM only reimburses the damage accrued during the time between the $(j - 1)$th and the jth PM activities; as a result, an arithmetic reduction of virtual remaining life can be obtained (Martorell et al., 1999). Therefore, the virtual remaining life after performing the jth PM activity, that is, RL_j, is then given by

$$v_j = v_{j-1} + \delta(m)\left(RL_j - RL_{j-1}\right) \tag{13.1}$$

where

    m is the level of PM effort

    $\delta(m)$, $m = 0, 1, \ldots, M$, is the remaining life increment factor of PM with effort m

Note that the effect of PM depends on its level m, $0 \le m \le M$, and its relationship with the remaining life is characterized by the age-incremental factor $\delta(m)$. A larger value of m represents greater PM effort; hence, $\delta(m)$ is an increasing function of m with $\delta(0) = 0$ and $\delta(M) = 1$. More specifically, if $m = 0$, then $v_j = RL_j$, $j \ge 1$, which means that the item is restored to as bad as old (ABAO); if $m = M$, the item is restored back to as good as new (AGAN); while in a more general case, $m \in (0, M)$, the item is partially restored, that is, the PM activity is imperfect.

13.6 Failures Process

Most products are complex and made of multiple parts, so that an item can be viewed as a system consisting of several components. The failure of an item occurs due to the failure of one or more components. A remanufactured product or component is categorized in terms of two states: working or failed. The time intervals between consecutive failures are random variables and modeled by proper distribution functions. Interchangeably, the number of failures over time can be modeled by a suitable counting process.

The actions to make a failed item operational depend on whether the failed component(s) are repairable or not. In the case of a repairable component, the remanufacturer has the option of repairing it or replacing it with a remanufactured working component if available. If not, a new component will be used to rectify the claim. In the case of repairable components, the characterization of subsequent failures depends on the type of repair (e.g., minimal repair, imperfect repair, and so on). Similarly, in the case of a non-repairable component, the remanufacturer can use a remanufactured working component in the replacement to make the item operational.

The time to first failure of a remanufactured component depends on the mean remaining lifetime (MRL) and the PM of the component at the time of sale of the remanufactured product. If the sensor information on the EOU component indicates that it has never failed, or was always minimally repaired, then the remaining life of the component at sale is the same as that of the item. Usually, the MRL of a remanufactured component at sale differs due to the replacement or repair and maintenance actions. Therefore, the time to first failure under warranty needs to be defined. Let RL_i denote the remaining life of the remanufactured component i. There are two cases: either RL_i is known because of an embedded sensor or RL_i is unknown because it is a conventional product.

The sensor embedded in the item provides the remanufacturer with the MRL of the item at sale and the virtual remaining life due to upgrade and maintenance information. The item failure is modeled by a point process with intensity function Λ (RL), where RL represents the remaining life of the item. Λ (RL) is a decreasing function of RL, indicating that the number of failures increases as the remaining life decreases. The failures over the warranty period occur according to a non-stationary Poisson process with intensity function Λ (RL). This implies that N $(W; RL)$, the number of failures over the warranty period W for an item of remaining life RL at the time of sale and virtual remaining life v, is a random variable with

$$P\{N(W;RL)=n\}=\left\{\int_{v}^{v+W}\Lambda(RL)dRL\right\}e^{-\int_{v}^{v+W}\Lambda(RL)dRL}/n! \qquad (13.2)$$

The expected number of failures over the warranty period is given by

$$E\left[N(W;\ RL)\right]=\int_{v}^{v+W}\Lambda(RL)dRL \qquad (13.3)$$

ARENA 14.7 (a discrete event simulation and automation software developed by Systems Modeling and acquired by Rockwell Automation) is used to generate the remaining life of the remanufactured item at failure, (t_i), using a bivariate random number generator and time history of replacements under warranty and repeat sales over the simulation time interval. The ARENA simulation program yields the remaining life at failures under warranty, the virtual remaining life after PM activities, the number of replacements under warranty for each purchase, and the time between repeat purchases.

13.7 Warranty Formulation

13.7.1 Reliability Improvement Process

Let θ be a parameter of the failure distribution and the reliability increase as θ decreases. In the case of the exponential failure distribution, θ is the failure rate. For Weibull and gamma distributions, it is the scale parameter. As the development program continues, θ decreases, thereby improving the reliability of the product in the spirit of Duane, but the outcome $\tilde{\theta}(\tau)$, after a development period of τ is uncertain. Let θ_0 denote the initial value of θ, that is, the value before the development program is initiated, and θ_m the minimum achievable value after development for an infinite time.

Since the outcome of the development process is uncertain, $\tilde{\theta}(\tau)$ needs to be modeled as a random variable. We consider the following:

$$\tilde{\theta}(\tau) = \theta_0 - (\theta_0 - \theta_m) Z_\tau \tag{13.4}$$

where Z_τ is a random variable and is a function of the development time τ. One can model it in many other ways, and we discuss this briefly in the last section.

Note that we have used a "black-box" approach to modeling the reliability improvement, since we do not model the process itself. Rather, we simply model the uncertain outcome of the development process. We model Z_τ by

$$Z_\tau = \left[1 - exp(-p\tau)\right] Y \tag{13.5}$$

where $Y \in [0, 1]$ is a random variable distributed according to a beta distribution with parameters α and β, which are not dependent on τ. This implies that the density function for Y is given by

$$f_Y(y) = \left\{ \frac{\Gamma(\alpha + \beta)}{\Gamma(\alpha) \ (\beta)} \right\} y^{\alpha-1} (1-y)^{\beta-1} \tag{13.6}$$

and the expected value of Y is given by

$$E(Y) = \frac{\alpha}{\alpha + \beta} \tag{13.7}$$

The effect of τ, the development period, is modeled in a deterministic manner with $p>0$. This implies that conditional on Y, $E[Z\tau]$ increases, and $E\left[\tilde{\theta}(\tau)\right]$ decreases as τ increases.

The model is characterized by three parameters. As τ increases, the mean of $\tilde{\theta}(\tau)$ decreases, as is to be expected. The parameters of the beta distribution can be selected so that it yields not only the desired mean for $\tilde{\theta}(\tau)$ but also the desired variance. As a result, the model offers enough flexibility to model the uncertainty in the outcome of the development process.

13.7.2 Warranty Policy and Servicing

The items are sold with a free replacement warranty (FRW) policy with a warranty period T. Under this policy, the manufacturer rectifies all failures in the warranty period by either repairing the failed item or replacing it with a new one at no cost to the buyer. We assume that the product is repairable and that the manufacturer chooses to repair rather than replace. One can model the effect of repair actions differently. We consider the case where the failed items are repaired minimally, so that the failure rate of the item after repair is the same as that just before failure.

13.7.3 Cost Modeling

The development cost is a function of the development time τ. We assume that it is given by a linear function $C_s + C_t\tau$, where C_s is the fixed setup cost, and C_t is the variable cost per unit time.

Let C_m denote the production cost per item and Q the total number of items produced and sold subsequently. As a result, the development cost per item is $C_s + C_t\tau / Q$, and the total manufacturing cost per item is the sum of this and the production cost C_m.

The warranty cost per unit depends on the number of warranty claims over the warranty period and the cost of each repair. We model the cost of each repair by C_r, and this includes the cost of repair (labor and material) and the associated administrative costs of handling the claim. We model it as deterministic, but it can also be viewed as the expected value of random cost. The failures (and claims) occur randomly and are influenced by the warranty period and the reliability of the product, which in turn, is influenced by the development period. As a consequence, the expected warranty cost is a function of T and τ, and we denote it by $E\left[C_w(T;\tau)\right]$. In the next section, we derive an expression for this function.

13.7.4 Optimal Reliability Development

The optimal reliability development is obtained by minimizing $J(T;\tau)$, the total expected cost (the sum of the manufacturing cost and the expected warranty cost) per item. It is given by

$$J(T;\tau) = \frac{C_s + C_t\tau}{Q} + C_m + E\big[C_w(T;\tau)\big] \qquad (13.8)$$

when $\tau > 0$. The optimal development time τ^* is the value of τ that minimizes $J(T;\tau)$ given by Equation 13.8.

13.8 System Description

The ARTO system explored herein is a type of product recovery system considered through the product example of a sensor-embedded smartphone (SP). A series of recovery operations are presented in Figure 13.1 addressing various EOU SP condition levels. Reusable components may be necessary to cover product requirements within the context of refurbishing and repairing processes, with this ideally satisfying both internal and external component needs through the disassembly of recovered components. The ARTO system may intake three different classes of items: EOU products to undergo the recovery process, failed SEPs to be refurbished, or SEPs to receive maintenance activities.

Initially, EOU SPs enter the ARTO system for data retrieval through the use of a radio-frequency data reader stored in the database of the facility,

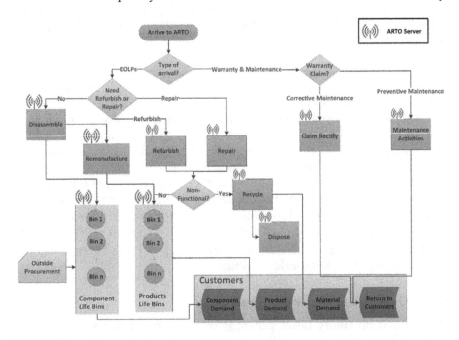

FIGURE 13.1
ARTO system's recovery processes.

after which the SPs are processed through a six-station disassembly line. To ensure the extraction of all components, complete disassembly is performed. Refer to Table 13.1 for the hierarchy of relationships among the components of the SP. The SP is comprised of nine components: the display and touchscreen, BB + XCR (baseband and transceiver chips), processor, battery, cameras, wireless device, NAND (non-volatile memory chip), SDRAM (dynamic random access memory), and transmission. Station disassembly times are determined by exponential distributions, the inter-arrival times for the demand of each component, and the inter-arrival times of EOU SPs. Following the retrieval of information, all EOUPs are shipped to station 1 for disassembly, or, in the event that the EOU only requires the repair of a particular component, it is directed to the relevant station.

Depending on the condition of the components, one of two disassembly options is chosen from the options of destructive or nondestructive disassembly. Should the disassembled component be nonfunctional, whether it is broken or its remaining life is too short, destructive disassembly is employed, ensuring that the other components' functionality is not negatively impacted. Consequently, the unit disassembly costs for a functional component are greater than for a nonfunctional component. Following disassembly, further component testing is unnecessary, as data are available within the embedded sensors to quantify the component's condition. There are two assumptions here: the assumptions that the demand and life cycle information for EOUPs are known and that the retrieval of information from sensors is less costly than inspection and testing operations.

The recovery options deployed vary depending on the overall condition and estimated remaining life of each SEP. Spare parts demands are provided for through recovered components, while material demands are provided for through the use of recycled products and components. Products and components that are recovered are then distributed into bins based on their remaining lifespans to be supplied to recovery operations as appropriate. Should a product or component be classified into a lower-remaining-lifespan bin,

TABLE 13.1

SP Components and Precedence Relationship

Component Name	Station	Code	Preceding Component
Display and touchscreen	1	A	—
BB + XCR	2	B	—
Processor	3	C	A, B
Battery	3	D	A, B, C
Cameras	4	E	A, B, C, D
Wireless device	5	F	A, B, C, D, F
NAND	5	G	F
SDRAM	6	H	D, F, H
Transmission	6	I	H

the value of the higher life is lost, exhibiting the importance of accurately determining the remaining life to optimize the economic return. Should a product, component, or material inventory level exceed the maximum inventory level for that particular class, it is classified as excess and either disposed of or used to meet material demands.

To meet product demand, repair and refurbish options must be carefully chosen. The functionality and completeness of an EOUP may be limited due to missing or nonfunctional components, which would then have to be replaced or replenished during the repair or refurbishment process to align with the particular remaining life requirements. EOUPs may also be comprised of components with lower remaining life than necessary and thus, may require replacement. Should SEP failure be realized during the warranty period, failed SPs arrive at the ARTO system to be analyzed for data retrieval through the facility's database. Following this, the SP is processed through the recovery operations applied to an EOUP.

During the final step, to support a reduction in the risk of failure, PM actions are performed during the warranty period. Within this study, should the remaining life of a remanufactured SP reach a predetermined value, the remanufactured SEPs are taken into the ARTO system for information retrieval from the radio-frequency data reader of the facility. After this, the SEPs undergo four maintenance activities, depending on the data collected from the sensors: adjustment, cleaning, measurements, and parts replacement. PM actions are performed with different degree of intensity (δ), which improve the remaining lives of the remanufactured SPs by δ units of time more than before the PM process. Should failures be experienced between two successive PM actions during the warranty period, no costs are realized by the consumer.

Herein, discrete-event simulation was used to identify an ideal implementation of a two-dimensional renewing warranty policy applied to remanufactured products. A specific product recovery system, the ARTO system, is deployed as an example of such a policy. Taguchi's orthogonal arrays provided the foundation for the design of the experiments in this study, representing the entirety of the recovery system to provide an opportunity to observe system behavior in varied experimental conditions. To identify the optimal strategy to be offered by the remanufacturer, a number of warranty and PM scenarios were analyzed through *t*-tests and Tukey pairwise comparison tests, in addition to one-way analysis of variance (ANOVA) for each scenario considered.

13.9 Design-of-Experiments Study

Ilgin and Gupta (2011) conducted a quantitative evaluation of SEPs in the context of disassembly line performance and demonstrated that smart SEPs are a viable solution to handling customer uncertainty pertaining to reman-ufactured products. In this study, this claim was tested on ARTO through the construction of a simulation model representing the full recovery sys-tem and the observed behavior within it under varying experimental con-ditions. Discrete-event simulation models were constructed through the ARENA program, Version 14.5. Fifty-one factors were employed in a three-level factorial design, with the levels defined as low, intermediate, or high. The three-level designs were employed to model possible curvature in the response function while also addressing the case of nominal factors that are realized at all three levels. Refer to Tables 13.2 and 13.3 for the param-eters, factors, and factor levels used to build the design-of-experiments study.

A significant number of experiments (5.185×10^{25}) are required to pres-ent a full-factorial design with 54 factors over three levels. Such a number would not be viable within the confines of this study, and thus, to reduce the number of experiments to a practical level, a relatively small set of possible variable combinations was employed in the study. Partial fraction experiments were employed, which helped with the selection method of an experiment's number, to yield the greatest amount of information possible concerning all factors that impact the performance parameter within the minimum number of experiments possible. Taguchi (1986) when engaging in such experiments employed particular guidelines and options, with a new means of conducting the experimental design presented in the form of using a special set of arrays named *orthogonal arrays* (OAs). OAs provide a means by which the minimal number of experiments to be conducted is identified. The minimum quantity of experiments required to conduct the Taguchi method may be calculated through the application of the degrees of freedom approach. Generally, OA is more efficient than other statistical designs.

Thus, the quantity of experiments must be greater than or equal to the sys-tem's degrees of freedom. Specifically, $L_{109}(3^{54})$ (i.e., $109 = [(\text{Number of levels} - 1) \times \text{Number of factors}] + 1$) OAs were selected due to the degrees of freedom in the ARTO system being 101, which means that 101 experiments are necessary to address the 54 factors on three different levels incorporated in the study. OA assumes that there is no interaction between any two factors among the 54 studied. Additionally, to support verification and validation, animations of the simulation models were constructed in concert with multiple dynamic and Contour Plots. Some 2000 replications over 6 months were used to run each experiment (at 8 hours a shift, one shift per day, and 5 days per week). Arena models were deployed to calculate the profit through the application of equation (13.9).

Furthermore, for validation and verification purposes, animations of the simulation models were built along with multiple dynamic and counters plots. Two thousand replications over 6 months (8 hours a shift, one shift a

TABLE 13.2

Parameters Used in the ARTO System

Parameters	Unit	Value	Parameters	Unit	Value
Backorder cost rate	%	40	Price for 3 years battery	$	30
Holding cost rate	$/hour	10	Price for 3 years cameras	$	120
Remanufacturing cost	$	1.5	Price for 3 years wireless device	$	50
Disassembly cost per minute	$	1	Price for 3 years NAND	$	40
Price for 1 year Display and touchscreen	$	20	Price for 3 years SDRAM	$	40
Price for 1 year BB + XCR	$	40	Price for 3 years transmission	$	130
Price for 1 year processor	$	10	Weight for display and touchscreen	lbs.	8
Price for 1 year battery	$	10	Weight for BB + XCR	lbs.	4
Price for 1 year cameras	$	85	Weight for processor	lbs.	2
Price for 1 year wireless device	$	30	Weight for battery	lbs.	2
Price for 1 year NAND	$	30	Weight for cameras	lbs.	6
Price for 1 year SDRAM	$	30	Weight for wireless device	lbs.	12
Price for 1 year transmission	$	10	Weight for NAND	lbs.	3
Price for 2 years display and touchscreen	$	30	Weight for SDRAM	lbs.	3
Price for 2 years BB + XCR	$	60	Weight for transmission	lbs.	6
Price for 2 years processor	$	24	Unit copper scrap revenue	$/lbs	0.6
Price for 2 years battery	$	24	Unit fiberglass scrap revenue	$/lbs	0.9
Price for 2 years cameras	$	110	Unit steel scrap revenue	$/lbs	0.2
Price for 2 years wireless device	$	36	Unit disposal cost	$/lbs	0.3
Price for 2 years NAND	$	36	Unit copper scrap Cost	$/lbs	0.3
Price for 2 years SDRAM	$	40	Unit fiberglass Scrap Cost	$/lbs	0.45
Price for 2 years transmission	$	120	Unit steel scrap Cost	$/lbs	0.1
Price for 3 years display and touchscreen	$	40	Price of 1 year SP	$	360
Price for 3 years BB + XCR	$	70	Price of 2 years SP	$	480

(Continued)

TABLE 13.2 (CONTINUED)

Parameters Used in the ARTO System

Parameters	Unit	Value	Parameters	Unit	Value
Price for 3 years processor	$	30	Price of 3 years SP	$	550
Operation costs for display and touchscreen	$	4	Operation costs for wireless device	$	1.66
Operation costs for BB + XCR	$	4	Operation costs for NAND	$	2.34
Operation costs for processor	$	2.8	Operation costs for SDRAM	$	0.6
Operation costs for battery	$	1.2	Operation costs for transmission	$	3.4
Operation costs for cameras	$	4	Operation costs for AC	$	55

day, and 5 days a week) were used to run each experiment. Arena models calculate the profit using the following equation:

$$\text{Profit} = SR + CR + SCR - HC - BC - DC - DPC$$
$$-TC - RMC - TPC - PMC - WC$$

(13.9)

where

SR   is the total revenue generated by the product, component, and material sales during the run time of the simulation

CR   is the total revenue produced through the collection of EOU SPs during the simulation run time

SCR   is the total revenue produced through selling scrap components during the simulated run time

HC   is defined as the total holding cost of components, materials, products, and EOU SPs within the run time of the simulation

BC   is the total backorder cost associated with products, materials, and components within the simulation run time

DC   is the total disassembly cost realized during the run time of the simulation

DPC   represents the total disposal cost of components, materials, and EOU SPs during the simulation run time

TC   is the total testing cost realized during the simulation run time

RMC   is the total remanufacturing cost of products during the simulation run time

TPC   represents the total transportation cost during the run time of the simulation

PMC   is the total PM cost that is realized during the simulation run time

WC   represents the total cost of the warranty.

TABLE 13.3

Factors and Factor Levels Used in Design-of-Experiments Study

No	Factor	Unit	Levels		
			1	2	3
1	Mean arrival rate of EOU SPs	Products/hour	10	20	30
2	Probability of repair EOUPs	%	5	10	15
3	Probability of a nonfunctional BB + XCR	%	10	20	30
4	Probability of a nonfunctional camera	%	10	20	30
5	Probability of a nonfunctional NAND	%	10	20	30
6	Probability of a nonfunctional transmission	%	10	20	30
7	Probability of a missing BB + XCR	%	5	10	15
8	Probability of a missing camera	%	5	10	15
9	Probability of a missing NAND	%	5	10	15
10	Probability of a missing transmission	%	5	10	15
11	Mean nondestructive disassembly time for station 1	Minutes	1	1	1
12	Mean nondestructive disassembly time for station 2	Minutes	1	1	1
13	Mean nondestructive disassembly time for station 3	Minutes	1	1	1
14	Mean nondestructive disassembly time for station 4	Minutes	1	1	1
15	Mean nondestructive disassembly time for station 5	Minutes	1	1	1
16	Mean nondestructive disassembly time for station 6	Minutes	1	2	2
17	Mean destructive disassembly time for station 1	Minutes	0	1	1
18	Mean destructive disassembly time for station 2	Minutes	0	1	1
19	Mean destructive disassembly time for station 3	Minutes	0	1	1
20	Mean destructive disassembly time for station 4	Minutes	0	1	1
21	Mean destructive disassembly time for station 5	Minutes	0	1	1
22	Mean destructive disassembly time for station 6	Minutes	1	1	1
23	Mean assembly time for station 1	Minutes	1	1	2
24	Mean assembly time for station 2	Minutes	1	1	2
25	Mean assembly time for station 3	Minutes	1	1	2
26	Mean assembly time for station 4	Minutes	1	1	1
27	Mean assembly time for station 5	Minutes	1	1	2
28	Mean assembly time for station 6	Minutes	1	2	2
29	Mean demand rate display and touchscreen	Parts/hour	10	15	20
30	Mean demand rate for BB + XCR	Parts/hour	10	15	20
31	Mean demand rate for processor	Parts/hour	10	15	20
32	Mean demand rate for battery	Parts/hour	10	15	20
33	Mean demand rate for camera	Parts/hour	10	15	20
34	Mean demand rate for wireless device	Parts/hour	10	15	20

(Continued)

TABLE 13.3 (CONTINUED)

Factors and Factor Levels Used in Design-of-Experiments Study

No	Factor	Unit	Levels		
			1	2	3
35	Mean demand rate for NAND	Parts/hour	10	15	20
36	Mean demand rate for SDRAM	Parts/hour	10	15	20
37	Mean demand rate for transmission	Parts/hour	10	12	20
38	Mean demand rate for 1 year SP	Products/hour	5	10	15
39	Mean demand rate for 2 years SP	Products/hour	5	10	15
40	Mean demand rate for 3 years SP	Products/hour	5	10	15
41	Mean demand rate for refurbished SP	Products/hour	5	10	15
42	Mean demand rate for material	Products/hour	5	10	15
43	Percentage of good parts to recycling	%	95	90	80
44	Mean metals separation process	Hour	1	1	2
45	Mean copper recycle process	Minutes	1	1	2
46	Mean steel recycle process	Minutes	1	1	2
47	Mean fiberglass recycle process	Minutes	1	1	2
48	Mean dispose process	Minutes	1	1	1
49	Maximum inventory level for SP	Products/hour	10	15	20
50	Maximum inventory level for refurbished SP	Products/hour	10	15	20
51	Maximum inventory level for SP component	Products/hour	10	15	20
52	Level of PM effort	—	0.5	0.6	0.7
53	Number of PM to perform	#	2	3	4
54	Time between PM	Months	1	2	3

13.10 Results

The results are divided into two parts. The first part deals with evaluating the effect of offering different warranty policies to help the decision maker choose the best warranty policy to offer, and the second part presents a quantitative assessment of the impact of SEPs on the warranty costs and policies to the remanufacturer.

13.10.1 Remanufacturing Warranty Policies Evaluation

In this part, the results to compute the expected number of failures and expected cost to the remanufacturer were obtained using the ARENA 14.7 program.

Table 13.4 presents the expected number of failures and the cost for remanufactured SP and components for extended FRW, pro-rata warranty (PRW),

TABLE 13.4A

Expected Number of Failures and Cost for Remanufactured SP's Components for Extended FRW, PRW, and Combination Policies

Components	W	Extended Free Replacement Warranty (FRW)						Extended Pro-Rata Warranty (PRW)						Extended Combination FRW/PRW					
		Expected probability of Failures			Expected Cost			Expected Probability of Failures			Expected Cost			Expected probability of Failures			Expected Cost		
		RL=1	RL=2	RL=3	RL=1	RL=2	RL=3	RL=1	RL=2	RL=3	RL=1	RL=2	RL=3	RL=1	RL=2	RL=3	RL=1	RL=2	RL=3
Display and touchscreen	0.5	0.5316	0.0035	0.0007	$7.48	$8.58	$6.86	0.6688	0.0044	0.0009	$10.78	$12.36	$9.86	0.4518	0.0029	0.0007	$8.20	$9.40	$7.50
	1	0.1066	0.0139	0.0064	$8.30	$9.40	$6.98	0.1341	0.0174	0.0080	$11.98	$13.54	$10.04	0.0905	0.0117	0.0054	$9.12	$10.30	$7.66
	2	0.1596	0.0309	0.0214	$12.46	$12.38	$7.18	0.2007	0.0387	0.0269	$17.94	$17.84	$10.36	0.1356	0.0262	0.0183	$13.68	$13.60	$7.90
BB + XCR	0.5	0.5253	0.0033	0.0041	$7.34	$8.52	$6.84	0.6607	0.0041	0.0052	$10.58	$12.28	$9.84	0.4464	0.0028	0.0035	$8.06	$9.36	$7.50
	1	0.1130	0.0135	0.0340	$8.66	$9.14	$6.94	0.1421	0.0171	0.0428	$12.48	$13.18	$9.98	0.0959	0.0116	0.0289	$9.50	$10.04	$7.60
	2	0.1532	0.0306	0.1147	$12.32	$12.16	$7.14	0.1926	0.0386	0.1443	$17.74	$17.50	$10.30	0.1302	0.0261	0.0974	$13.52	$13.34	$7.84
Processor	0.5	0.5189	0.0032	0.0221	$3.68	$3.44	$3.52	0.6527	0.0040	0.0278	$5.30	$4.96	$5.06	0.4409	0.0027	0.0188	$4.04	$3.78	$3.86
	1	0.1002	0.0140	0.1823	$4.84	$6.10	$3.60	0.1261	0.0175	0.2292	$6.96	$8.80	$5.16	0.0851	0.0118	0.1549	$5.32	$6.68	$3.94
	2	0.1469	0.0311	0.6130	$6.68	$7.50	$3.72	0.1846	0.0392	0.7711	$9.62	$10.82	$5.38	0.1248	0.0265	0.5210	$7.32	$8.24	$4.10
Battery	0.5	0.5189	0.0014	0.1180	$2.02	$1.98	$1.68	0.6527	0.0018	0.1485	$2.92	$2.84	$2.44	0.4409	0.0012	0.1003	$2.22	$2.18	$1.86
	1	0.0747	0.0141	0.9742	$2.92	$2.70	$1.86	0.0940	0.0177	1.2254	$4.22	$3.88	$2.68	0.0635	0.0120	0.8278	$3.22	$2.96	$2.04
	2	0.1340	0.0269	0.3992	$3.88	$3.84	$1.98	0.1686	0.0339	0.5021	$5.58	$5.54	$2.84	0.1139	0.0229	0.3392	$4.26	$4.22	$2.18
Cameras	0.5	0.5036	0.0033	0.6313	$7.66	$7.34	$7.18	0.6334	0.0041	0.7941	$11.04	$10.58	$10.34	0.4279	0.0028	0.5364	$8.40	$8.06	$7.88
	1	0.1092	0.0135	0.8189	$8.42	$7.86	$7.30	0.1373	0.0170	1.0300	$12.14	$11.32	$10.54	0.0927	0.0116	0.6958	$9.24	$8.62	$8.02
	2	0.1539	0.0311	0.0171	$11.84	$10.16	$7.38	0.1935	0.0392	0.0214	$17.04	$14.66	$10.64	0.1307	0.0265	0.0145	$13.00	$11.16	$8.10
Wireless device	0.5	0.5246	0.0035	0.7848	$2.40	$2.04	$1.98	0.6599	0.0045	0.9871	$3.44	$2.94	$2.88	0.4458	0.0030	0.6668	$2.64	$2.24	$2.20
	1	0.1021	0.0138	0.8257	$3.48	$2.92	$2.18	0.1284	0.0173	1.0386	$5.00	$4.22	$3.16	0.0867	0.0117	0.7017	$3.82	$3.22	$2.42
	2	0.1608	0.0311	0.0912	$4.02	$3.38	$2.30	0.2023	0.0391	0.1147	$5.80	$4.86	$3.34	0.1367	0.0265	0.0775	$4.42	$3.70	$2.54
NAND	0.5	0.5374	0.0032	0.8189	$4.58	$3.88	$3.72	0.6759	0.0040	1.0300	$6.60	$5.58	$5.38	0.4566	0.0027	0.6958	$5.04	$4.26	$4.10
	1	0.1174	0.0136	0.1665	$6.34	$4.52	$3.82	0.1477	0.0172	0.2094	$9.12	$6.54	$5.50	0.0998	0.0117	0.1415	$6.94	$4.98	$4.20

(Continued)

TABLE 13.4A (CONTINUED)

Expected Number of Failures and Cost for Remanufactured SP's Components for Extended FRW, PRW, and Combination Policies

Components	W	Extended Free Replacement Warranty (FRW)						Extended Pro-Rata Warranty (PRW)						Extended Combination FRW/PRW					
		Expected probability of Failures			Expected Cost			Expected Probability of Failures			Expected Cost			Expected probability of Failures			Expected Cost		
		RL=1	RL=2	RL=3	RL=1	RL=2	RL=3	RL=1	RL=2	RL=3	RL=1	RL=2	RL=3	RL=1	RL=2	RL=3	RL=1	RL=2	RL=3
SDRAM	2	0.1544	0.0309	0.4875	$7.88	$6.30	$4.02	0.1943	0.0388	0.6132	$11.34	$9.08	$5.80	0.1313	0.0263	0.4143	$8.64	$6.90	$4.42
	0.5	0.5425	0.0035	0.5834	$1.22	$0.96	$0.68	0.6824	0.0044	0.7339	$1.74	$1.36	$0.98	0.4610	0.0029	0.4957	$1.34	$1.04	$0.74
	1	0.1002	0.0137	0.8900	$1.88	$1.52	$0.82	0.1261	0.0173	1.1195	$2.72	$2.20	$1.18	0.0851	0.0117	0.7563	$2.06	$1.68	$0.90
	2	0.1525	0.0311	0.8222	$3.30	$2.20	$0.88	0.1919	0.0392	1.0343	$4.74	$3.18	$1.28	0.1296	0.0265	0.6987	$3.62	$2.44	$0.96
Transmission	0.5	0.5240	0.0035	0.0173	$5.32	$4.98	$4.76	0.6592	0.0044	0.0219	$7.66	$7.18	$6.86	0.4452	0.0029	0.0148	$5.84	$5.48	$5.24
	1	0.1060	0.0138	0.0912	$6.86	$6.44	$5.16	0.1332	0.0173	0.1147	$9.86	$9.26	$7.44	0.0900	0.0117	0.0775	$7.50	$7.06	$5.68
	2	0.1539	0.0310	0.8257	$9.32	$8.42	$5.34	0.1935	0.0389	1.0386	$13.44	$12.14	$7.70	0.1307	0.0264	0.7017	$10.24	$9.24	$5.86

TABLE 13.4B

Expected Number of Failures and Cost for Remanufactured SP for Extended FRW, PRW and Combination Policies

Components	W	Extended Free Replacement Warranty (FRW)						Extended Pro-Rata Warranty (PRW)						Extended Combination FRW/PRW					
		Expected Probability of Failures			Expected Cost			Expected Probability of Failures			Expected Cost			Expected Probability of Failures			Expected Cost		
		RL=1	RL=2	RL=3	RL=1	RL=2	RL=3	RL=1	RL=2	RL=3	RL=1	RL=2	RL=3	RL=1	RL=2	RL=3	RL=1	RL=2	RL=3
SP	0.5	0.6232	0.0045	0.0004	$113.74	$107.78	$106.84	0.7838	0.0058	0.0006	$131.66	$125.16	$159.74	0.3114	0.0021	0.0002	$110.02	$105.90	$104.98
	1	0.1602	0.0184	0.0029	$116.52	$117.70	$111.46	0.2016	0.0231	0.0035	$137.38	$137.62	$167.22	0.0629	0.0082	0.0012	$114.44	$115.56	$109.50
	2	0.2100	0.0409	0.0092	$131.52	$133.62	$115.30	0.2641	0.0515	0.0117	$161.42	$157.60	$170.44	0.0914	0.0185	0.0042	$132.92	$131.06	$111.26

and combination policies. In Table 13.4a and b, the expected number of failures represents the expected number of failed items per unit of sale. In other words, it is the average number of free replacements that the remanufacturer would have to provide during the warranty period per unit sold. The expected cost to the remanufacturer includes the cost of supplying the original item, C_s. Thus, the expected cost of warranty is calculated by subtracting C_s from the expected cost to the remanufacturer. For example, for $W=0.5$ and $RL=1$, the warranty cost for SP can be calculated as $113.74 (Table 13.4b) $C_s=\$113.74 - \$110.00 = \$3.74$, which is ([\$3.74/\$110.00] \times 100) = 3.40\%$ of the cost of supplying the item C_s which is significantly less than that $110.00, C_s. This may be acceptable, but the corresponding values for longer warranties are much higher. For example, for $W=2$ years and $RL=1$, the corresponding percentage is ([\$131.52 - \$110.00/\$110.00] \times 100) = 19.59\%$.

13.10.2 Impact of SEPs on Warranty Analysis

To assess the impact of SEPs on warranty cost, pairwise *t*-tests were carried out for each performance measure. Table 13.5 presents 95 percent

TABLE 13.5

ANOVA Table and Tukey Pairwise Comparisons for Warranty Cost

ANOVA: Warranty Cost

Null hypothesis All means are equal

Alternative hypothesis At least one mean is different

Significance level $\alpha = 0.05$

SUMMARY

Models	Count	Sum	Average	StDev	95% CI
Conventional Model	2000	353,113,950	176,556.98	675.40	(157977.3, 179653.8)
SEP Model FRW	2000	36,103,400	18,051.70	669.48	(14086.7, 21037.3)
SEP Model PRW	2000	86,975,360	43,487.68	681.49	(29522.2,46473.6)
SEP Model FRW/PRW	2000	63,543,280	31,771.64	668.45	(27806.6, 34757.4)

ANOVA

Source of Variation	SS	df	MS	F-Value	P-value
Model	2.42E + 13	3	5.25E + 12	62499126	0
Error	1.032E + 09	7996	83999		
Total	2.42E + 13	7999			

Tukey Pairwise Comparisons

Grouping Information Using the Tukey Method and 95% Confidence

Model	N	Mean	Grouping
SEP Model FRW	2000	18,051.70	A
SEP Model FRW/PRW	2000	31,771.64	B
SEP Model PRW	2000	43,487.68	C
Conventional Model	2000	176,556.98	D

Means that do not share a letter are significantly different.

TABLE 13.6

Results of Performance Measures for Different Models with Warranty and PM

Performance Measure	Conventional Model	Mean Value with Warranty (PM offered)		
		Sensor Embedded Model with FRW	Sensor Embedded Model with PRW	Sensor Embedded Model FRW/PRW
Holding cost	$375,385.55	$301,548.74	$317,111.26	$318,392.24
Backorder cost	$69,633.45	$60,654.40	$63,784.70	$64,042.36
Disassembly cost	$810,570.05	$643,094.96	$676,284.22	$679,016.10
Disposal cost	$131,308.02	$121,768.44	$128,052.74	$128,570.00
Testing cost	$241,762.49	N/A	N/A	N/A
Remanufacturing cost	$2,786,743.91	$1,797,936.76	$1,890,725.80	$1,898,363.46
Transportation cost	$70,316.93	$63,212.98	$66,475.32	$66,743.84
Warranty cost	$176,556.98	$18,051.70	$43,487.68	$31,771.64
Number of claims	83,583	23,962	30,974	29,586
PM cost	$13,630.88	$3,462.48	$6,363.96	$5,543.46
Total cost	$4,759,491.23	$3,033,692.46	$3,223,259.68	$3,222,029.10
Total revenue	$6,693,569.22	$7,452,158.07	$6,933,609.46	$7,677,871.58
Profit	$1,934,078.00	$4,418,465.61	$3,710,349.78	$4,455,842.48

confidence interval, t value, and p value for each test. According to these tables, SEPs achieve statistically significant savings in holding, backorder, disassembly, disposal, testing, remanufacturing, and transportation costs. In addition, SEPs provide statistically significant improvements in total revenue and profit. According to Table 13.6, the lowest average value of warranty costs, the number of warranty claims, and PM during the warranty period for remanufactured SPs across all policies are $18,051.70, 23,962 claims, and $3462.48, respectively, for the extended FRW warranty policy.

13.11 Conclusion

Sensors are implanted into SEPs during the initial production process. The value of sensors is realized through their ability to determine the best warranty policy and warranty period to present to consumers when selling remanufactured components and products. The remaining life and condition of components and products may be estimated prior to presenting a warranty based on the data collected through the sensors. Such information allows the remanufacturer to avoid unnecessary costs by enabling the remanufacturer to control the number of claims during warranty periods and to determine the appropriate PM policy to employ. In this chapter, the costs of reliability improvement policies were explored through the offering of PM for different periods. This chapter also addressed the impact of SEPs on the cost of warranties. Lastly, this chapter presented and analyzed a case study involving various simulation conditions to illustrate the applicability of the model.

References

Alqahtani, A. Y., and Gupta, S. M. (2017a). Warranty as a marketing strategy for remanufactured products. *Journal of Cleaner Production*, 161, 1294–1307.

Alqahtani, A. Y., and Gupta, S. M. (2017b). Warranty cost analysis within sustainable supply chain. In *Ethics and Sustainability in Global Supply Chain Management* (pp. 1–25). IGI Global.

Alqahtani, A. Y., and Gupta, S. M. (2017c). One-dimensional renewable warranty management within sustainable supply chain. *Resources*, 6(2), 16.

Alqahtani, A. Y., and Gupta, S. M. (2017d). Warranty and preventive maintenance analysis for sustainable reverse supply chains. *Journal of Management Science and Engineering*, 2(1), 69–94.

Alqahtani, A., and Gupta, S. M. (2017e). Optimizing two-dimensional renewable warranty policies for sensor embedded remanufactured products. *Journal of Industrial Engineering and Management*, 10(2), 145–187.

Ben Mabrouk, A., Chelbi, A., and Radhoui, M. (2016). Optimal imperfect preventive maintenance policy for equipment leased during successive periods. *International Journal of Production Research*, 1–16.

Chattopadhyay, G., and Murthy, D. N. P. (2004). Optimal reliability improvement for used items sold with warranty. *International Journal of Reliability and Applications*, 5(2), 47–57.

Choi, B., and Ishii, J. (2010). Consumer perception of warranty as signal of quality: An empirical study of power train warranties. *POSCO Research Institute & Amherst College Department of Economics* (March 2010), 3–5.

Edwards, P., Peters, M., and Sharman, G. (2001). The effectiveness of information systems in supporting the extended supply chain. *Journal of Business Logistics*, 22(1), 1–22.

Finkenzeller, K. (2003). *RFID Handbook: Fundamentals and Applications in Contact-Less Smart Cards and Identification*. John Wiley & Sons.

Gándara, A., & Rich, M. D. (1977). Reliability Improvement Warranties for Military Procurement (No. RAND/R-2264-AF). RAND CORP SANTA MONICA CALIF.

Gartner. (2014, March 19). Gartner says the Internet of Things will transform the data center. Retrieved from http://www.gartner.com/newsroom/id/2684616.

Gubbi, J., Buyya, R., Marusic, S., and Palaniswami, M. (2013). Internet of Things (IoT): A vision, architectural elements, and future directions. *Future Generation Computer Systems*, 29(7), 1645–1660.

Gungor, A., and Gupta, S. M. (1999). Issues in environmentally conscious manufacturing and product recovery: A survey. *Computers and Industrial Engineering*, 36, 811–853.

Gungor, A., and Gupta, S. M. (2002). Disassembly line in product recovery. *International Journal of Production Research*, 40, 2569–2589.

Gupta, S. M. (2013). *Reverse Supply Chains: Issues and Analysis*. CRC Press, Boca Raton, Florida.

Gupta, S. M., and Ilgin, M. A. (2018). *Multiple Criteria Decision Making Applications in Environmentally Conscious Manufacturing and Product Recovery*. CRC Press, Boca Raton, Florida.

Gupta, S. M., and Lambert, A. F. (Eds.). (2008). *Environment Conscious Manufacturing*. CRC Press, Boca Raton, Florida.

Huang, H. Z., Liu, Z. J., and Murthy, D. N. P. (2007). Optimal reliability, warranty and price for new products. *IIE Transactions*, 39(8), 819–827.

Hussain, A. Z. M. O., and Murthy, D. N. P. (2003). Warranty and optimal reliability improvement through product development. *Mathematical and Computer Modelling*, 38(11–13), 1211–1217.

Ilgin, M. A, Gupta, S. M., and Battaïa, O. (2015). Use of MCDM techniques in environmentally conscious manufacturing and product recovery: State of the art. *Journal of Manufacturing Systems*.

Ilgin, M. A., and Gupta, S. M. (2010). Environmentally conscious manufacturing and product recovery (ECMPRO): A review of the state of the art, *Journal of Environmental Management*, 91(3), 563–591.

Ilgin, M. A., and Gupta, S. M. (2011). Performance improvement potential of sensor embedded products in environmental supply chains. *Resources, Conservation and Recycling*, 55(6), 580–592.

Ivanov, D., Dolgui, A., Sokolov, B., Werner, F., and Ivanova, M. (2016). A dynamic model and an algorithm for short-term supply chain scheduling in the smart factory industry 4.0. *International Journal of Production Research*, 54(2), 386–402.

Jeschke, S., Brecher, C., Meisen, T., Özdemir, D., and Eschert, T. (2017). Industrial internet of things and cyber manufacturing systems. In *Industrial Internet of Things* (pp. 3–19). Springer, Cham.

Kijima, M. (1989). Some results for repairable systems with general repair. *Journal of Applied Probability*, 89–102.

Kijima, M., Morimura, H., and Suzuki, Y. (1988). Periodical replacement problem without assuming minimal repair. *European Journal of Operational Research*, 37(2), 194–203.

Kim, C. S., Djamaludin, I., and Murthy, D. N. P. (2004). Warranty and discrete preventive maintenance. *Reliability Engineering & System Safety*, 84(3), 301–309.

Kopetz, H. (2011). Internet of things. In *Real-Time Systems* (pp. 307–323). Springer, Boston, MA.

Lambert, A. J. D., and Gupta, S. M. (2005). *Disassembly Modeling for Assembly, Maintenance, Reuse, and Recycling*. CRC Press, Boca Raton, FL.

Lasi, H., Fettke, P., Kemper, H. G., Feld, T., and Hoffmann, M. (2014). Industry 4.0. *Business & Information Systems Engineering*, 6(4), 239–242.

Lee, J., Bagheri, B., and Kao, H. A. (2015). A cyber-physical systems architecture for industry 4.0-based manufacturing systems. *Manufacturing Letters*, 3, 18–23.

Leung, J., Cheung, W., and Chu, S. C. (2014). Aligning RFID applications with supply chain strategies. *Information & Management*, 51(2), 260–269.

Liu, Y., and Xu, X. (2017). Industry 4.0 and cloud manufacturing: A comparative analysis. *Journal of Manufacturing Science and Engineering*, 139(3), 034701.

Long, L. N., and Kelley, T. D. (2010). Review of consciousness and the possibility of conscious robots. *Journal of Aerospace Computing, Information, and Communication,* 7(2), 68–84.

Lund, D., MacGillivray, C., Turner, V., and Morales, M. (2014). Worldwide and regional Internet of Things (IOT) 2014–2020 forecast: A virtuous circle of proven value and demand. *International Data Corporation* (IDC), Tech. Rep., 1.

Mahdavinejad, M. S., Rezvan, M., Barekatain, M., Adibi, P., Barnaghi, P., and Sheth, A. P. (2018). Machine learning for Internet of Things data analysis: A survey. *Digital Communications and Networks,* 4(3), 161–175.

Martorell, S., Sanchez, A., and Serradell, V. (1999). Age-dependent reliability model considering effects of maintenance and working conditions. *Reliability Engineering & System Safety,* 64(1), 19–31.

Moyer, L. K., and Gupta, S. M. (1997). Environmental concerns and recycling/disassembly efforts in the electronics industry. *Journal of Electronics Manufacturing,* 7, 1–22.

Murthy, D. N. P. (2006). Product warranty and reliability. *Annals of Operations Research,* 143(1), 133–146.

Nativi, J. J., and Lee, S. (2012). Impact of RFID information-sharing strategies on a decentralized supply chain with reverse logistics operations. *International Journal of Production Economics,* 136(2), 366–377.

Saleh, J. H., and Marais, K. (2006). Highlights from the early (and pre-) history of reliability engineering. *Reliability Engineering & System Safety,* 91(2), 249–256.

Sethi, P., and Sarangi, S. R. (2017). Internet of Things: Architectures, protocols, and applications. *Journal of Electrical and Computer Engineering,* 2017.

Shin, S., and Eksioglu, B. (2015). An empirical study of RFID productivity in the US retail supply chain. *International Journal of Production Economics,* 163, 89–96.

Sun, C. (2012). Application of RFID technology for logistics on Internet of Things. *AASRI Procedia,* 1, 106–111.

Taguchi, G. (1986). *Orthogonal Arrays and Linear Graphs.* American Supplier Institute, Inc., Dearborn, Ml.

Talari, S., Shafie-khah, M., Siano, P., Loia, V., Tommasetti, A., and Catalão, J. P. (2017). A review of smart cities based on the Internet of Things concept. *Energies,* 10(4), 421.

Thomas, M. U., and Richard, J. P. P. (2006). Warranty-based method for establishing reliability improvement targets. *IIE Transactions,* 38(12), 1049–1058.

Wu, D., Rosen, D. W., Wang, L., and Schaefer, D. (2015). Cloud-based design and manufacturing: A new paradigm in digital manufacturing and design innovation. *Computer-Aided Design,* 59, 1–14.

Xia, F., Yang, L. T., Wang, L., and Vinel, A. (2012). Internet of Things. *International Journal of Communication Systems,* 25(9), 1101–1102.

Yadav, O. P., Singh, N., Chinnam, R. B., and Goel, P. S. (2003). A fuzzy logic based approach to reliability improvement estimation during product development. *Reliability Engineering & System Safety,* 80(1), 63–74.

14

Supplier Selection Model for End-of-Life Product Recovery: An Industry 4.0 Perspective

Ozden Tozanli, Elif Kongar, and Surendra M. Gupta

CONTENTS

14.1 Introduction

The ever-increasing demand for newer products coupled with shortened product life cycles results in growing demand for raw materials and high complexity in product recovery operations (Alshibli et al., 2017). The transformation requirements brought by these changes are primarily imposed by governments via rules and regulations and by society in general as a result of growing environmental awareness. These changes require addressing two major structural challenges: how manufacturers and consumers can become active participants in environmentally responsible product disposal activities, and how fast and efficiently manufacturers can respond to changing market and capital needs while preserving their environmental, economic, and social sustainability levels (Ilgin and Gupta, 2010b; Tozanli et al., 2017). One significant goal of end-of-life (EOL) product management as it relates to sustainability is to maintain environmentally and socially viable product recovery operations without reduction in economic well-being (Alshibli et al., 2017; Fiksel, 2009). Despite the fact that EOL product recovery is expected to exist within the field of manufacturing, it extends beyond traditional manufacturing, as it includes the collection, transportation, and management of EOL products. These topics are generally investigated under reverse logistics (Ondemir and Gupta, 2008). An efficient reverse logistics system that is integrated into a well-designed supply chain can ensure value creation in product recovery operations.

Today, the majority of supply chains fall short of meeting one or more of the requirements of competitiveness, such as cost efficiency, productivity, flexibility, adaptability, stability, and sustainability (Hofmann and Rüsch, 2017). This decreasing capability for value creation has triggered the replacement of traditional production and supply chain management with high-tech production strategies leading to an integrated approach known as *Industry 4.0*. The concept of Industry 4.0 has received attention from both academia and industry due to its ability to address the growing complexity of manufacturing and production operations by combining future-oriented production technologies with Internet of Things (IoT).

This chapter builds on the previous work published by Ondemir and Gupta (2014) and focuses on the supplier selection problem in the context of Industry 4.0. To this end, Industry 4.0 is first discussed from the point of view of sustainable product recovery. Following this, the integration of Industry 4.0 into the supplier selection problem is analyzed with the help of a numerical example. The example involves a disassembly-to-order (DTO) system, which is modeled as a multi-criteria decision-making problem and is solved via a goal programming (GP) model.

14.2 Industry 4.0

14.2.1 Introduction

Industry 4.0, also known as the fourth industrial revolution, is an innovative concept that aims at fully integrating industrial technologies into the supply chain to optimize the overall value generated. The concept first appeared under the name "Industrie 4.0" at the Hanover Trade Fair in 2011 as part of Germany's high-tech strategy initiatives based on autonomous,

knowledge-based, sensor-embedded, self-organized, and decentralized information technology (IT)-driven production systems (Hofmann and Rüsch,
2017). Four years following its first formal appearance in the academic arena
through the articles published by Kagermann et al., (2011), the term *Industry 4.0*
has become widely popular after its promotion by the Industrial Internet
Consortium in 2015. Since being listed as a main topic in the 2016 World
Economic Forum's agenda (Hofmann and Rüsch, 2017; Stock and Seliger, 2016),
the concept's popularity has been growing significantly. Confirming its
growing importance, Kagermann et al. (2012) emphasized that industrial
value creation today would require active participation in the Industry 4.0
era, since digital connectivity helps prepare companies for possible challenges and opportunities in future production operations. However, despite
its fast growth, the concept of Industry 4.0 is still a relatively unexplored field,
requiring further investigation to ensure its successful implementation.

As can be observed from Figure 14.1, Industry 4.0 uses various state-of-the-art
IT-based concepts in conjunction with modern corporate strategies and organizational structures. The concept simply implies disruptive innovation in
manufacturing systems ensuring the sustainability of value creation with
significant potential benefits.

Lasi et al. (2014) have categorized these potential benefits as application
(pull) and technology (push). In Lasi et al. (2014), application describes the
benefits from operative aspects such as individualization on demand, higher
flexibility in product development, and mass production, while technology
indicates certain innovative advantages such as advanced mechanization
and automation, and self-organized digital structures.

FIGURE 14.1
Fundamental components of Industry 4.0. (From Brettel, M., et al., *IJMIE*, 8, 37, 2014. With
permission.)

Decentralization in organizational structures for faster decision-making and resource efficiency from the economic and ecological aspects are also investigated under the pull strategy. Here, innovative technologies that lead to increasing mechanization and automation while reducing the complexity and hence, the cost of overall operations are also considered.

Digitalization and networking through the tools of actor- and sensor-data, simulation, digital protection, augmented reality, big data analytics, simultaneous information flow, and real-time coordination with a communication technology infrastructure are additional important technological benefits the concept can bring to operational practices.

Industry 4.0 puts forward several key concepts that yield sustainable value creation, including cyber-physical systems (CPS), self-organization, new systems distribution and procurement, new systems in the development of products and services, adaptation of human needs, and corporate social responsibility. The combination of these concepts often leads to the definition of a smart factory with varying levels of operational capabilities.

In general, a smart factory allows the core components of industry, such as machines, products, labor, and organization, to communicate with one another in an integrated network. This integration often leads to increasing capability of inbound and outbound logistics, manufacturing, production, and service operations (Lasi et al., 2014; Stock and Seliger, 2016). The following section elaborates on the key components of Industry 4.0 and its application to sustainable product management and logistics areas.

14.2.2 Applications of Industry 4.0 in Sustainable Product Life Cycle

As highlighted in the previous sections of this chapter, Industry 4.0 is an emerging concept that provides unique benefits to industries from product design and manufacturing to logistics and sales. The concept allows the real-time monitoring of material flows from raw material acquisition to EOL product recovery by enabling autonomous data exchange and digitalization. One of its most vital components, the IoT, triggers Industry 4.0–related activities with the use of embedded devices and networks such as sensors, actuators, radio frequency identification (RFID) tags, control processing units, and communication devices (Hofmann and Rüsch, 2017). IoT enables users to access embedded systems to read, collect, and store the collected data in a cloud network for further processing. Another important Industry 4.0 concept, CPS, can be defined as a human–machine interface that integrates physical and virtual networks through embedded systems by communicating over the IoT. In this way, the workflow of the system can simply be summarized as CPS, which continuously interchanges collected data into real-time information, that is, big data analytics, via a cloud. These new fully digitalized and automated smart technologies, using the ubiquitous flow of smart data, result in a new degree of control, design, transparency, and resource efficiency in manufacturing operations. Accordingly, traditional production hierarchies evolve into modular and decentralized self-organizations with significant reduction in their organizational hierarchies (Lasi et al., 2014). This simplified organizational structure allows corporations to make faster decisions. Moreover, the new design of manufacturing operations handles sustainability issues in the context of economic, environmental, and social aspects.

Today, products manufactured in smart factories through the stream of smart data supplied by compatible technologies are capable of self-organizing their manufacturing processes in an autonomous manner. These systems are also capable of achieving sustainable material flows for their products throughout their life cycles. These closed-loop product life cycles include the flows from factories to consumers and back for product recovery through smart logistics (Stock and Seliger, 2016). Figure 14.2 depicts a simplified flow of CPS.

Industry 4.0 brings remarkable advantages to the conventional EOL product management, starting from product and process design. The following discusses various aspects of Industry 4.0 in relation to EOL product management. Subsequently, the opportunities for an organization to create and maintain efficient and effective disassembly operations are also detailed.

Disassembly is crucial in product recovery operations, since it allows the selective separation of desired parts and materials (Ilgin and Gupta, 2010a). DTO systems deal with finding optimum levels of disassembly to meet the demand for regained materials and parts. From the reverse logistics systems point of view, a DTO system is of a vital importance, since it constitutes a general form of a product recovery system taking into account different costs and revenues originating from multiple sources. Therefore, the system is charged with the task of determining the optimum number of EOL products to be disassembled to meet the demand for materials and components derived from EOL products. The EOL products can be taken back, collected,

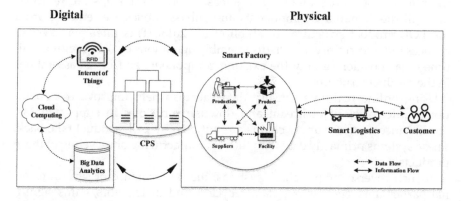

FIGURE 14.2
Cyber physical systems (CPS) in Industry 4.0.

or purchased from end users, landfills, or second-hand sellers. Due to the possible changes in the product structures during and after their useful lives, EOL products are often associated with high levels of uncertainty. The wide variety of returned products adds to this uncertainty, making disassembly yield highly unpredictable. To address this issue, Ilgin and Gupta (2010a) have discussed several questions that contribute to the uncertainty in disassembly yield involving the functionality, existence, and type of each EOL component.

In an Industry 4.0 setting, smart products are designed to be equipped with embedded sensors, actuators, and RFID tags at the production stage to allow manufacturers to store and record product data throughout its life cycle. For instance, sensor-embedded products (SEPs) with RFID tags enable manufacturers to monitor the type and condition of the EOL product and to estimate its remaining useful life without the need for disassembly and inspection, solely based on the data collected prior to product recovery (Joshi et al., 2014; Ondemir and Gupta, 2009). In sensor-embedded designs, environmental conditions such as vibration, shocks, changes in temperature, and component failures can be tracked and recorded. Through RFID tags, valuable disassembly and recycling information can be accessed, including data regarding the bill-of-materials (BOMs), release and sale dates, and disassembly instructions. Therefore, SEPs can significantly reduce the uncertainty in the overall material and component yield while increasing the efficiency of DTO systems.

An example of a similar Industry 4.0 EOL product recovery application can be found in a state-of-the-art autonomous system that facilitates fully automated disassembly operations via a sensory system (Alshibli et al., 2017). The proposed sensory system consists of a robotic manipulator, a digital camera, and an image processing algorithm to identify the depth of the product to be disassembled. In this automated sensory disassembly system, the camera captures the images of components and/or subassemblies accessible at each level and identifies the depth of each available entity. Following the removal of each component or subassembly, these steps are repeated until all the demanded components and subassemblies are removed from the EOL product structure (1Alshibli et al., 2016). This intelligent system reduces the uncertainty of EOL disassembly operations by using online real-time data considering only the existing components and/or subassemblies in the product structure.

Using online real-time sensory data can also help improve the operational efficiencies of upstream and downstream flows in supply chains. For instance, reverse supply chains are initiated by EOL product take-back. These systems primarily deal with the remanufacturing or recycling of these products.

In such reverse supply chain systems, the performance of several external participants, such as out-plant recyclers and distributors, gains significance. This is primarily due to the responsibility of participants regarding the quality, cost, lead time, and delivery conditions of returned products. Through the integration of collected data into the supply chain, manufacturers gain various advantages with regard to careful examination and evaluation of the performance and reliability of suppliers and other service providers.

As an example, SEPs enable manufacturers to monitor the quality levels of returned products, which has a substantial impact on reducing the overall cost and amount of disposal while positively contributing to the quality of remanufactured products and increasing the revenue generated by material sales.

In the following section, a numerical study of a supplier selection problem is presented, in which an Industry 4.0 tool is used for product recovery. The study demonstrates and analyzes the impact of Industry 4.0 on supply chain management and decision-making.

14.3 Supplier Selection Model for End-of-Life Product Recovery of Sensor-Embedded Products in Disassembly-to-Order Systems

Sustainable supply chain management is characterized as the combination of both forward and reverse logistics flows. Forward logistics is the management of downstream material flows starting from suppliers and moving towards consumers. Reverse logistics can be defined as the management of upstream material flows starting from consumers and moving towards manufacturers and/ or raw material suppliers. The primary focus of forward logistics is economic sustainability, whereas reverse logistics mainly focuses on the environmental and social aspects of sustainability without reduction in economic well-being (Ilgin and Gupta, 2010a; Tozanli et al., 2017). A DTO system, similar to reverse logistics, is initiated by EOL product acquisition from a number of suppliers. The primary purpose of a DTO system is to meet the demand for components, subassemblies, and/or materials by making them available via EOL product disassembly through environmentally benign operations. This chapter deals with the supplier selection problem in a DTO system where there is a variety of sensor-embedded EOL products. SEP design provides ease in retrieving components from an EOL product, requiring reconsideration of product recovery strategies (Joshi et al., 2014). As a result of new technologies brought by Industry 4.0, product recovery has moved into a more intelligent platform through the use of combined systems of sensors and RFID tags. With dynamic data collection during, and in some cases, even after, the useful life time of products, the uncertainty surrounding disassembly operations is reduced significantly. Recording dynamic product life cycle data also contributes to the better understanding of the quality and quantity of returned products from each supplier, allowing the central management of product recovery operations.

A DTO facility receives EOL products from multiple suppliers and carries out product recovery operations based on the in-plant capacity as well as through third party service providers such as third party recyclers and distributors. The introduction of SEPs into this flow brings significant changes to the traditional EOL reverse logistics. The ability to read and use life cycle data allows manufacturers to reduce the EOL product procurement cost, since some or all of the previously required operations, such as sorting, inspection, and cleaning, might no longer be needed or might be significantly reduced. This gain originates from the benefits of the information contained in the EOL products regarding their use as well as their release and sales dates, serial numbers, BOMs, make and model, and required disassembly sequence. This embodied information allows manufacturers to use real data on the yield of returned EOL products, which otherwise would be based solely on estimates. This leads to more accurate decisions regarding the appropriate method selection, disassembly path generation, and disassembly line balancing. Similarly, selecting the most appropriate EOL SEP suppliers based on this actual data produces more efficient results, leading to long-term partnerships between the original equipment manufacturers (OEMs) and their suppliers.

14.3.1 A Supply Chain Network Flow for Sensor-Embedded Products

The supplier selection process is investigated from the perspective of OEMs operating in the electronics industry (Figure 14.3). In this network, products equipped with sensors and RFID tags are sent to the manufacturing facility. The accompanying data and information flow is also ensured through an integrated data and information network. In the forward logistics stage, OEMs procure raw materials from multiple suppliers to meet the production line requirements. At this stage, SEPs begin their life cycle following their production in the manufacturing facility. The products are then either transported to wholesalers or sent directly to retailers through distributors to be sold to end-users. As SEPs are purchased by end-users, the product usage phase of the SEPs begins, which concurrently triggers the reverse logistics stage.

In the reverse logistics stage, EOL SEPs discarded by end-users are collected from consumers or second-hand markets by multiple suppliers to be sold to OEMs. Acquired EOL products are warehoused in collection centers by OEMs for the retrieval of the collected data and information regarding their BOMs and use conditions. This process allows OEMs to obtain data regarding the quality levels and the remaining useful lives of SEPs. Using this information, OEMs determine the most appropriate disassembly method for each EOL product. Based on the demand for reusable components, EOL products with high-quality components are sent to a non-destructive disassembly line, preventing further damage to the product structure. EOL products containing low-quality components are sent to a destructive disassembly line, allowing the destructive disassembly of the EOL products. These products, again based on the demand, are disassembled for their material content.

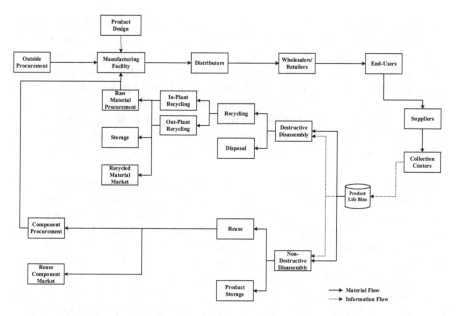

FIGURE 14.3
Disassembly-to-order logistics network of SEPs.

After non-destructive disassembly, the regained components are either sold in second-hand markets or used to fulfill the component demand for in-plant production. If the demand is not sufficient, the remaining components are warehoused for future use. Similarly, after destructive disassembly, materials are either recycled or disposed of. The recycling process is performed either in-plant or by outside recyclers, whereby materials are either sold in the recycled material market, used to fulfill the material demand for in-plant production, or stored for future use. As previously mentioned, OEMs can carry out product recovery operations in-house while also relying on additional external sources such as EOL product suppliers, third party recyclers, and distributors. Therefore, the effective management of the supply chain mainly relies on the performance and the reliability of each player in the network, including manufacturers, suppliers, and outside contractors. In this study, suppliers that procure EOL SEPs to an OEM are evaluated based on the total cost of disassembly, recycling, storage, disposal, component procurement, and product take-back, in addition to the quality of remanufactured products, the material sales revenue, and the total recycling and disposal weights.

14.3.2 Application of Goal Programming Model

Since the majority of real-life problems are multi-objective in nature (Joshi et al., 2014), the supplier selection problem is modeled as a multi-criteria decision making (MCDM) problem. To eliminate the dependency on a single objective function, goal programming (GP) is applied to introduce multiple goals and targets to the model environment. GP, initially reported by Charnes et al., (1955) and Charnes and Cooper (1961) and later extended by Ijiri (1965), Lee (1972), and Ignizio (1976), is an effective tool of MCDM, which is designed to satisfy a number of goals under various technological constraints relevant to the model environment. Using GP, this chapter presents a multiple objective decision model to determine the best supplier based on the goals of minimizing the total cost, maximizing the material sales revenue, minimizing the total disposal weight, and maximizing the quality level of remanufactured components.

When dealing with multiple objectives, GP formulates an objective function and a specific target value for each goal. Target values represent the aspiration levels setting the minimum acceptance level for each goal. GP then aims at minimizing the overall deviation from each aspiration level. The deviation variables can be either positive (ρ_k) or negative (η_k). A positive deviation, ρ_k, represents the quantification of overachievement of the kth goal, whereas a negative deviation, η_k, indicates the underachievement level of the kth goal. Therefore, η is minimized where the goal is to overachieve, ρ is minimized where the goal is to underachieve, and ($\eta + \rho$) is minimized when the goal is to reach an exact value.

GP is categorized into two techniques according to the type of the mathematical programming model: non-preemptive goal programming (NGP) and preemptive goal programming (PGP). NGP assigns a weight to each goal, where the objective is tied to the weighted sum of the deviation. These predetermined weights, which are penalties for goal constraint violations, significantly affect the solution, since modifying them can alter the solutions. Eliminating this shortcoming, PGP, also known as *lexicographic GP*, requires the goals to be defined in a hierarchy based on their priorities, solving each iteratively, starting from the highest priority. The process continues until all priorities are dealt with. In cases where there is no solution before reaching the final priority goal, the model is considered to generate a near optimum solution. In such cases, the current results are then accepted without visiting the remaining priorities. A basic model of PGP (Equation 14.1) can mathematically be described as follows:

Let $1 \leq k \leq n$,

$$lexmin\, u_k = \left\{ u_k \mid u \in P, u_1 = u_1^*,\, u_2 = u_2^*,\, u_3 = u_3^*, \ldots,\, u_{k-1} = u_{k-1}^* \right\}, \quad (14.1)$$

where

   $u \in P$ denotes the set of hard constraints
   $u_1^*, u_2^*, u_3^*, \ldots, u_{k-1}^*$ are the aspiration levels for the goals of the model with
      decreasing priorities

In this study, a product recovery facility is considered where the incoming EOL SEPs are provided by one of two suppliers. The objective of this particular problem is to evaluate these suppliers based on the total cost, the material sales revenue, the total disposal weight, and the quality level of products. Accordingly, the physical conditions of the EOL products and product take-back costs are the two factors that differentiate these two suppliers. The manager of the product recovery facility aims at meeting the demand for components and materials while minimizing the total cost and the total disposal weight and maximizing the material sales revenue and the overall quality level, in that order. The supplier who meets the highest priority goal is selected. If both suppliers meet the highest priority goal, then the subsequent priority goal is considered. The process continues until a decision is reached. In the unlikely event where there is a tie at the end of all iterations, further analysis is conducted to select the best supplier based on additional criteria.

14.3.2.1 Goals

The four goals used to determine the best supplier to select are minimizing the total cost, maximizing the material sales revenue, minimizing the total disposal weight, and maximizing the quality level. The formulated GP model is applied to each supplier. The solutions for both suppliers are compared, and the better supplier is selected. The following assumptions are applied to this problem:

- All SEPs that are taken back are disassembled, and a complete disassembly is applied to each product.
- Components are either reused to fulfill the component demand, recycled to meet the material demand, stored for future use, or disposed of, depending on the condition of each component.
- Recycling is exclusively an in-house operation with retrieved materials being either sold to fulfill the existing market demand or stored for future use.
- SEPs may contain both operable and non-operable components, with non-operable components having zero remaining life time.
- The disassembly cost of each operable component is higher than the disassembly cost of each non-operable component.
- Components to be reused are placed in one of the three life-bins depending on their remaining life time, and the demand is a function of the life-bin of each component.
- Multiple components retrieved from the same EOL product are in identical condition.

The first goal is to minimize the total cost, which is set to be at most TC^*. In the GP, this can be achieved by minimizing the positive deviation (ρ_1) from the predetermined value of TC. Similarly, no restrictions are applied to the negative deviation (η_1). This first goal can be formulated as follows:

$$\min \rho_1$$

$$\text{s.t. } TC + \eta_1 - \rho_1 = TC^*. \tag{14.2}$$

The second goal is related to the material sales revenue. Here, the goal is to achieve a sales revenue of at least MSR^*. Accordingly, the negative deviation (η_2) from the target value (MSR^*) is minimized:

$$\min \eta_2$$

$$\text{s.t. } MSR + \eta_2 - \rho_2 = MSR^*. \tag{14.3}$$

The third goal introduces an environmentally benign behavior to the model and aims at minimizing the number of disposed components. Mathematically, this can be achieved by minimizing the positive deviation (ρ_3) from the predefined value of $WDIS^*$:

$$\min \rho_3$$

$$\text{s.t. } WDIS + \eta_3 - \rho_3 = WDIS^*. \tag{14.4}$$

The fourth goal is to maximize the quality level of components based on the remaining life-bins. Here also, the negative deviation (η_4) from the target value (QL^*) is minimized. This fourth goal can be formulated as follows:

$$\min \eta_4$$

$$\text{s.t. } QL + \eta_4 - \rho_4 = QL^*. \tag{14.5}$$

14.3.2.2 Constraints

The total cost (TC) is the sum of total disassembly cost (TDC), total recycling cost (TRC), total disposal cost ($TDIC$), total outside procurement cost (TPC), total holding cost (THC), and total take-back cost (TB). Therefore, TC can be expressed as follows:

$$TC = TDS + TRR + TDIS + TPC + THS + TB. \tag{14.6}$$

In this model, the total disassembly cost (TDC) increases with each complete SEP disassembly. The model assumes that all SEPs are disassembled and that each SEP contains operable (a_{ij}) and non-operable components (f_{ij}). a_{ij} is a binary variable that takes the value of 1 if the component j in product i is operable and 0 otherwise. Similarly, f_{ij} is a binary variable that takes the value of 1 if the component j in product i is non-operable and 0 if operable. Components with zero remaining life time are accepted as non-operable components. The unit disassembly cost of an operable component (cop_j) and a non-operable component ($cnop_j$) differ, and each component j requires a certain amount of disassembly time (dt_j) regardless of the component life-bin. Therefore, the disassembly cost function can be expressed as

$$TDC = \sum_j \sum_i \left(a_{ij} * cop_j + f_{ij} * cnop_j \right) * dt_j . \qquad (14.7)$$

The total recycling cost (*TRC*) includes the costs of operable and non-operable components from each product i with a unit recycling cost of (crc_j). Hence, the recycling cost function can be shown as

$$TRC = \sum_j crc_j * \left(\sum_i \left(a_{ij} + f_{ij} \right) * w_{ij} \right), \qquad (14.8)$$

where w_{ij} is a binary variable obtaining the value of 1 if the component j in product i is recycled and 0 otherwise.

The total disposal cost (*TDIC*) is defined as the total cost of component disposal. In this study, it is assumed that disposal can only be applied to the components. Materials are either sold or stored for future use. Similarly, each component j is disposed of for a unit disposal cost ($cdis_j$). Therefore,

$$TDIC = \sum_j cdis_j * \left(\sum_i \left(a_{ij} + f_{ij} \right) * z_{ij} \right), \qquad (14.9)$$

where z_{ij} is a binary variable which takes the value of 1 if the component j in product i is disposed of and 0 otherwise.

The total outside procurement cost (*TPC*) is the cost of procured components to fulfill the component demand. Once the component demand is greater than the number of disassembled components for reuse, additional components are supplied through an outside source. The procurement cost can be calculated by multiplying the unit procurement cost of component j, whose remaining life time is within the range of component life-bin b ($cproc_{jb}$), by the number of the component j procured within the range of component life-bin b (l_{jb}). Hence,

$$TPC = \sum_b \sum_j cproc_{jb} * l_{jb} . \qquad (14.10)$$

The total holding cost (*THC*) is the cost of stored components and materials. This function is formulated with the unit holding cost of component j (chc_j), the unit holding cost of material k (chm_k), and the amount of material k (sm_k) stored:

$$THC = \sum_j \sum_i chc_j * s_{ij} + \sum_k chm_k * sm_k , \qquad (14.11)$$

where s_{ij} is a binary variable which takes the value of 1 if the component j in the product i is stored for reuse and 0 otherwise.

The total take-back cost (*TB*) is the cost of SEP procurement. This cost includes the unit take-back cost of each product (*utb*) from the supplier and the unit transportation cost of each product from the supplier to the facility (*utrc*). This total is then multiplied by the total number of SEPs procured (*NSEP*):

$$TB = NSEP * (utb + utrc). \tag{14.12}$$

The material sales revenue (*MSR*) is a function of the amount of materials sold (dm_k), the amount of material stored (sm_k), and the market value of each type of material k (pr_k). Here, it is assumed that all stored materials are sold in the future. *MSR* can be defined as follows:

$$MSR = \sum_k pr_k * (dm_k + sm_k). \tag{14.13}$$

The total disposal weight (*WDIS*) is calculated by multiplying all the components to be disposed of by the corresponding component weight (ω_j):

$$WDIS = \sum_j \omega_j * \left(\sum_i z_{ij} * (a_{ij} + f_{ij}) \right). \tag{14.14}$$

The quality level of the components (*QL*) is calculated as the sum of the differences between the highest life-bin (β_{ij}) that components could be placed in and the life-bin b where they are actually placed:

$$QL = \sum_b \sum_j \sum_i x_{ijb} * (\beta_{ij} + b), \tag{14.15}$$

where x_{ijb} is a binary variable which takes the value of 1 if the component j in the product i is placed in life-bin b for reuse and the value of 0 otherwise.

Assuming that the remaining life time of each component j in product i (rem_{ij}) is known, and three life-bins within the time range of t_1 and t_2 are defined for the system, β_{ij} can be calculated as follows:

$$\beta_{ij} = \begin{cases} 1, & rem_{ij} \leq t_1, \forall i, j \\ 2, & t_1 \leq rem_{ij} \leq t_2, \forall i, j \\ 3, & rem_{ij} \geq t_2, \forall i, j \end{cases} \tag{14.16}$$

The following constraints ensure that each component j in product i is disassembled and either reused (rs_{ij}), recycled (w_{ij}), stored ((s_{ij}), or disposed of (z_{ij}):

$$rs_{ij} + w_{ij} + s_{ij} + z_{ij} = 1, \ \forall i, j. \tag{14.17}$$

Equation 14.18 ensures that each component j retrieved for reuse can only be operable and placed in only one life-bin b after disassembly.

$$\sum_b x_{ijb} = rs_{ij} * a_{ij}, \ \forall i, j. \tag{14.18}$$

Equation 14.19 ensures that each component j stored for reuse can only be operable and placed in only one life-bin b after disassembly.

$$\sum_b s_{jb} = s_{ij} * a_{ij}, \ \forall j. \tag{14.19}$$

The total yield of component j from each remaining life-bin b (δ_{ij}) is calculated by multiplying the total number of components obtained for reuse by the probability of missing component j (pm_j) and the multiplicity factor of component j in product i (ML_{ij}). Additionally, the total yield of component j in life-bin b for each component j must meet the demand for component j in the remaining life-bin b (dc_{jb}). In case of shortage, inventory s_{ijb} and outside procurement l_{jb} can be used to satisfy the remaining demand:

$$\delta_{jb} = \sum_i x_{ijb} * \left(1 - pm_j\right) * ML_{ij}, \ \forall j, b. \tag{14.20}$$

Therefore,

$$\delta_{jb} + s_{jb} + l_{jb} = dm_{jb}, \ \forall j, b. \tag{14.21}$$

Moreover, the total yield of material k recycled from component j (γ_{jk}) is equal to the total number of components sent to recycling multiplied by the weight of component j (ω_j), the recyclable percentage of each component j (per_{jb}), the probability of missing component j (pm_j), and the multiplicity factor of component j in product i (ML_{ij}). Here also, the total yield of material k from component j with the total amount of material k stored must meet the demand for material k (dm_k):

$$\gamma_{jk} = \sum_i w_{ij} * \omega_{ij} * per_{ij} * \left(1 - pm_j\right) * ML_{ij}, \ \forall j, k. \tag{14.22}$$

Therefore,

$$\sum_j \gamma_{jk} + sm_k = dm_k, \ \forall k. \tag{14.23}$$

In addition, a capacity limit (CAP) applies to the materials that will be stored. Hence,

$$\sum_k sm_k = CAP, \ \forall k. \tag{14.24}$$

All variables are restricted to non-negative values. Thus,

$$rs_{ij}, w_{ij}, s_{ij}, z_{ij}, x_{ijb} \in \{0,1\}, \quad \forall i,j,b$$

$$l_{jb} \geq 0 \,\&\, \text{int}, \quad \forall j,b \tag{14.25}$$

$$sm_k \geq 0, \quad \forall k$$

14.3.2.3 Lexicographic Solution Procedure

The lexicographic GP model used in this chapter can be described as follows (Kongar and Gupta, 2002):

Find ($rs_{ij}, w_{ij}, s_{ij}, z_{ij}, x_{ijb}, l_{jb}, sm_k$) so that

$$lexmin\, u = \{\rho_1, \eta_2, \rho_3, \eta_4\}, \tag{14.26}$$

where $\{\eta_k, \rho_k\}$ are defined in Equations 14.2 through 14.5

subject to constraints defined in Equations 14.6 through 14.25 and $\{\eta_k, \rho_k\} \geq 0, k = 1,2,3,4$

As stated in Kongar and Gupta (2002), a step-by-step solution procedure is provided in the following:

Step 0. Read in all the relevant data. Set the first goal as the current goal.

Step 1. Obtain a linear programming (LP) solution with the current goal as the objective function.

Step 2. If the current goal is the final goal in the model, set it equal to the LP objective function value found in Step 1, STOP. Otherwise, go to Step 3.

Step 3. If the current goal is achieved or overachieved, set it equal to its aspiration level and add this equation to the constraint set. Go to Step 4. Otherwise, if the value of the current goal is underachieved, set the aspiration level of the current goal equal to the LP objective function value found in Step 1 and add this equation to the constraint set. Go to Step 4.

Step 4. Set the next goal of importance as the current goal. Go to Step 1.

14.4 Numerical Example

This section demonstrates the applicability of the approach via a numerical example to evaluate two suppliers for the selection of the best performer. Consider two EOL SEP suppliers who can supply 200 units of the same EOL product on a daily basis. Each product contains four operable and non-operable components, where some components are used multiple times in the same product. The remaining useful life of each operable component in each product can be read remotely to be recorded in the database. The quality level of a component is determined by the remaining life-bins it is placed in, where the larger life-bin holds the best-quality components. In this example, three life-bins are considered. In this regard, bin 1 holds the components whose remaining life times are 2 years or less, bin 2 holds the components whose remaining life times are between 2 and 3 years, and bin 3 holds the components whose remaining life times are more than 3 years. The products with zero remaining life time are examined and labeled as non-operable components. Multiple components in the same EOL product are assumed to have identical remaining useful lives. Tables 14.1 and 14.2

TABLE 14.1

Remaining Life Times of Components in
EOL Products from Supplier 1 (in Years)

EOL SEP	Components			
#	1	2	3	4
1	1.22	0.00	2.48	5.04
2	2.53	0.00	3.28	0.79
3	1.92	6.19	2.37	2.58
.	.	.	.	.
.	.	.	.	.
.	.	.	.	.
198	2.53	0.00	3.28	0.79
199	1.92	6.19	2.37	2.58
200	1.05	0.47	0.99	2.08

TABLE 14.2

Remaining Life Times of Components in EOL Products
from Supplier 2 (in years)

EOL SEP	Components			
#	1	2	3	4
1	0.00	1.39	7	2.84
2	0.00	1.47	2.5	0.96
3	2.2	3.47	1.15	6.61
.	.	.	.	.
.	.	.	.	.
.	.	.	.	.
198	1.56	0	4.63	1.82
199	4.61	0.81	0.85	2.22
200	1.81	3.98	7	0.91

TABLE 14.3

Multiplicity, Weight, Recyclable Percentage, Probability of Missing, and Costs of Recycling, Disassembly, and Disposal of Each Component

Components	Multiplicity	Weight	Recyclable (%)	p(m)	Recycling Cost ($/Unit)	Disassembly Cost ($/Unit)		Disposal Cost ($/Unit)
						Operable	Non-operable	
1	2	4.5	0.85	.2	0.56	0.18	0.1	0.23
2	1	10.5	0.6	.1	0.44	0.27	0.12	0.23
3	4	3.75	0.45	.25	2.55	0.58	0.2	0.23
4	1	2.5	0.75	.3	1.34	0.41	0.12	0.23

depict partial data regarding the remaining useful life of each component in each EOL product taken back from supplier 1 and supplier 2, respectively.

The multiplicity, weight, recyclable percentage, probability of missing, unit recycling cost, unit disassembly cost, unit disposal cost, and unit holding cost of each component are presented in Table 14.3.

Two types of material are obtained after the recycling process. The demand, unit holding cost, and unit sales price of each material are provided in Table 14.4. Additionally, the material inventory capacity is 400 units.

The demand and outside procurement cost of components in each life-bin are given in Table 14.5.

The disassembly time for each component varies depending on supplier. Hence, Table 14.6 presents the unit EOL SEPs take-back cost, the unit transportation cost for carrying each product from each supplier, and the disassembly time for each component.

14.4.1 Results

The GP model was solved using LINGO (Lindo Systems Inc, Chicago, IL) v.17.0.74. The results obtained for suppliers 1 and 2 are summarized in Tables 14.7 and 14.8, respectively. The goals are prioritized in the order of total cost, material sales revenue, total disposal weight, and quality level, with total cost minimization being the highest-priority goal.

As can be seen from the tables, the goals of material sales revenue and quality level are underachieved by both supplier 1 and supplier 2. While the goal of total cost is achieved by two suppliers, the goal of total disposal weight is only achieved by supplier 1. Therefore, supplier 1 is chosen over supplier 2.

TABLE 14.4

Demand, Holding Cost, and Sales Price for Each Material

Materials	Demand	Holding Cost ($/Unit)	Sales Price ($/Unit)
1	465	0.95	0.3
2	675	0.95	0.5

TABLE 14.5

Demand and Procurement Cost for Each Component in Each Life-Bin

	Demand			Procurement Cost ($/Unit)		
Components	Bin 1	Bin 2	Bin 3	Bin 1	Bin 2	Bin 3
1	30	24	18	9.98	14.96	19.95
2	18	2	16	14.13	21.19	28.25
3	24	24	9	12.58	18.86	25.15
4	33	22	15	17.22	25.82	34.43

TABLE 14.6

Take-Back Cost, Transportation Cost, and Disassembly Time of Each Component for Each Supplier

Supplier	Take-back Cost ($/unit)	Transportation Cost ($/Unit)	Disassembly Time (min)			
			Component 1	Component 2	Component 3	Component 4
1	13	5	6	6	8	9
2	15	4	5	6	7	10

TABLE 14.7

Results for Goals and Aspiration Levels for Supplier 1

Goal	Aspiration Level	Step 1	Step 2	Step 3	Step 4
Total cost	$1,900	$1,538.76	$1,880.58	$1,888.71	$1,900.00
Material sales revenue	$1,000	$477	$677	$677	$677
Total disposal weight	0	29.25	334.5	0	0
Quality level	250	104	90	142	200

TABLE 14.8

Results for Goals and Aspiration Levels for Supplier 2

Goal	Aspiration Level	Step 1	Step 2	Step 3	Step 4
Total cost	$1,900	$1,547.71	$1,899.31	$1,900	$1,900.00
Material sales revenue	$1,000	$477	$601	$601	$601
Total disposal weight	0	37.5	142.5	56.25	56.25
Quality level	250	114	98	132	174

14.5 Conclusion

This chapter introduced the concept of Industry 4.0 from the sustainable product recovery aspect and examined its integration into existing DTO systems. With this motivation, the chapter presented a network for SEPs as one of the tools of Industry 4.0. Following this, a GP model was created to solve the supplier selection problem. The model was applied to an SEP DTO system designed for product recovery operations. The model produced fast and meaningful results, providing a more realistic approach to the supplier selection problem considering multiple goals with varying priorities.

References

Alshibli, M., El Sayed, A., Kongar, E., Sobh, T. M., and Gupta, S. M. (2016). Disassembly sequencing using tabu search. *Journal of Intelligent & Robotic Systems, 82*(1), 69–79.

Alshibli, M., El Sayed, A., Tozanli, O., Kongar, E., Sobh, T. M., and Gupta, S. M. (2017). A decision maker-centered end-of-life product recovery system for robot task sequencing. *Journal of Intelligent & Robotic Systems*. doi:10.1007/s10846-017-0749-5

Brettel, M., Friederichsen, N., Keller, M., and Rosenberg, M. (2014). How virtualization, decentralization and network building change the manufacturing landscape: An Industry 4.0 perspective. *International Journal of Mechanical, Industrial Science and Engineering, 8*(1), 37–44.

Charnes, A., and Cooper, W. W. (1961). Management models and industrial applications of linear programming. *Management Science, 4*(1), 38–91.

Charnes, A., Cooper, W. W., and Ferguson, R. O. (1955). Optimal estimation of executive compensation by linear programming. *Management Science, 1*(2), 138–151.

Fiksel, J. (2009). *Design for Environment: A Guide to Sustainable Product Development*: McGraw Hill Professional.

Hofmann, E., and Rüsch, M. (2017). Industry 4.0 and the current status as well as future prospects on logistics. *Computers in Industry, 89*, 23–34. doi:https://doi.org/10.1016/j.compind.2017.04.002

Ignizio, J. P. (1976). *Goal Programming and Extensions*: Lexington Books.

Ijiri, Y. (1965). *Management Goals and Accounting for Control* (Vol. 3): North Holland Pub. Co.

Ilgin, M. A., and Gupta, S. M. (2010a). *Disassembly of Sensor Embedded Products with Component Discriminating Demand*. Mechanical and Industrial Engineering Faculty Publications.

Ilgin, M. A., and Gupta, S. M. (2010b). Environmentally conscious manufacturing and product recovery (ECMPRO): A review of the state of the art. *Journal of Environmental Management, 91*(3), 563–591. doi:http://dx.doi.org/10.1016/j.jenvman.2009.09.037

Joshi, A. D., Gupta, S. M., and Yamada, T. (2014). Selection of supplier for end-of-life products based on the optimum profit, quality level, material sales revenue and disposal weight. *Innovation and Supply Chain Management, 8*(4), 134–139.

Kagermann, H., Lukas, W.-D., and Wahlster, W. (2011). Industrie 4.0: Mit dem Internet der Dinge auf dem Weg zur 4. industriellen Revolution. *VDI nachrichten, 13*, 11.

Kagermann, H., Wahlster, W., and Helbig, J. (2012). Im Fokus: Das Zukunftsprojekt Industrie 4.0: Handlungsempfehlungen zur Umsetzung. *Bericht der Promotorengruppe Kommunikation.* Forschungsunion.

Kongar, E., and Gupta, S. M. (2002). A multi-criteria decision making approach for disassembly-to-order systems. *Journal of Electronics Manufacturing, 11*(02), 171–183.

Lasi, H., Kemper, H.-G., Fettke, P., Feld, T., and Hoffmann, M. (2014). Industry 4.0. *Business & Information Systems Engineering, 6*(4), 239–242.

Lee, S. M. (1972). *Goal Programming for Decision Analysis*. Auerbach Publishers Philadelphia.

Ondemir, O., and Gupta, S. M. (2008). Selection of collection centers for reverse logistic networks. In John Affisco (Ed.), *Northeast Decision Sciences Institute Proceedings*, 592–596.

Ondemir, O., and Gupta, S. M. (2009). Cost-benefit analysis of sensor-embedded products based disassembly-to-order system. In Albert E. Avery (Ed.), *Northeast Decision Sciences Institute Proceedings*, 573–578.

Ondemir, O., and Gupta, S. M. (2014). A multi-criteria decision making model for advanced repair-to-order and disassembly-to-order system. *European Journal of Operational Research, 233*(2), 408–419.

Stock, T., and Seliger, G. (2016). Opportunities of sustainable manufacturing in industry 4.0. *Procedia CIRP, 40*, 536–541. doi:https://doi.org/10.1016/j.procir.2016.01.129

Tozanli, O., Duman, G., Kongar, E., and Gupta, S. M. (2017). Environmentally concerned logistics operations in fuzzy environment: A literature survey. *Logistics, 1*(1), 4.

15

Contribution of Sensors to Closed-Loop Supply Chains: A Simulation Study of Sensor-Embedded Washing Machines

Mehmet Talha Dulman and Surendra M. Gupta

CONTENTS

15.1 Introduction

Product recovery has become very important over the course of the last two decades for several reasons, including heightened environmental awareness of consumers, the introduction of environmental regulations that govern the disposal of products, and the diminishing availability of landfill space. Product recovery consists of many processes, including collecting end-of-life (EOL) products and disassembling and reprocessing them based on their EOL condition. Reprocessing can be performed in several ways, such as refurbishing the products, remanufacturing them, or recycling the materials that the products contain.

Recovering products is beneficial for the environment; however, the process by which this is achieved is difficult to plan and implement, because many of the factors associated with this process are uncertain. For example, the condition of the returned products is unknown before they are collected. If the collected products are not in a good enough condition to be reprocessed, the manufacturer will not achieve the potential value. This study proposes embedding sensors into products to track their components during their use phases and thereby, eliminate the uncertainty about the condition of the components contained within them. The sensors can collect information about the use patterns of the products, and this information can be used to determine their condition and that of their components. Thus, effective disassembly and reprocessing decisions can be made before the product recovery phase starts. This can reduce costs and increase the EOL profit that can be gained by reprocessing EOL products.

Embedded sensors are not only beneficial for product recovery. Since they are embedded into the products and collect information during their use phases, the information they collate can also be used to improve maintenance and service efficiency and predict failures, thereby reducing productivity loss and maintenance costs. Thus, proper actions can be taken before failures to reduce productivity loss costs due to failures and the cost of performing service activities during the failure period. In addition, inspection is not required, since the sensors provide data relating to the condition of the components and products.

In this chapter, a closed-loop supply chain system that was specifically built for washing machines is introduced. Within the model assessed in this study, the washing machines were maintained during their useful lives and then collected for EOL processing once their life cycles were complete. The goal of the study was to evaluate the economic impact that the sensors had on this closed-loop supply chain system. To determine this, two systems were developed. One consisted of sensor-embedded washing machines (SEWMs), and the second consisted of regular washing machines (RWMs). These systems were modeled using a discrete event simulation. Several performance measures, including disassembly, inspection, maintenance costs, and sales revenues, were analyzed by performing a design of experiments. The experiments revealed that the sensors had a significant impact on improving the economic performance of the closed-loop supply chain systems.

15.2 Literature Review

This chapter proposes the use of sensors to improve the performance of closed-loop supply chain systems designed for washing machines. Literature about closed-loop supply chain systems and sensor technology was reviewed. Gungor and Gupta (1999) conducted a systematic review of studies about environmentally conscious manufacturing and product recovery (ECMPRO), including closed-loop supply chains, which were published before 1998. Ilgin and Gupta (2010a) added to this research by reviewing the papers that were published between 1998 and 2010. Gupta and Ilgin (2018) have published a book that examined the multi-criteria decision-making techniques used for ECMPRO.

15.2.1 Selection of Used Products

The selection of used EOL products represents a critical decision that directly affects the profitability of a given system. Although some systems are purely designed to reduce environmental degradation, profitability is also a key consideration in most cases. Pochampally and Gupta (2005) proposed a three-phase mathematical programming model that aimed to enhance the efficiency of a reverse supply chain. The first phase of this model focused on the selection of used products, the second phase involved finding the appropriate facilities from the given candidates, and the last phase considered sourcing and deployment plans. In this model, Pochampally and Gupta used a modified version of the cost–benefit function introduced by Veerakamolmal and Gupta (1999). This function identified the difference between the sum of the revenues, total resale revenue, and recycling revenue, and the sum of the costs, total reprocessing cost, and disposal cost. They concluded that optimizing this cost–benefit function could help decision makers to select the products for reprocessing that offer the maximum value gained.

Pochampally and Gupta (2008) modified the cost–benefit function as a fuzzy benefit function and proposed the application of a multi-phase fuzzy logic approach to solve the selection problem. Pochampally et al. (2008) took the probability of breakage and the probability of missing components into consideration while developing the cost–benefit function. Pochampally et al. (2009) used linear physical programming to solve the selection of used products problem. They developed a model that selected the best-used product and identified the best feasible set of components to disassemble from that product. Habibi et al. (2017) proposed an optimization model to solve the disassembly and collection problem in a reverse supply chain.

15.2.2 Remanufacturing

Remanufacturing is at the core of this study. By remanufacturing disassembled components that are in good condition, producers can both enhance the profit they acquire from selling remanufactured products and reduce environmental degradation. Production planning and scheduling are crucial aspects of the remanufacturing operation; as such, a comprehensive literature review of the existing studies that have been published in these areas is presented.

15.2.2.1 Production Planning

The uncertainty and variability that are inherent in remanufacturing systems can undermine the accuracy of production planning. Some studies have sought to provide solutions to the production planning problems associated with remanufacturing. For example, Guide et al. (1999) published a survey paper that reviewed relevant literature related to production planning and control in remanufacturing. They divided remanufacturing into three categories: disassembly, processing, and reassembly. Production planning plays an essential role in determining how much and when to disassemble, reassemble, and order new components or materials. Esmaeilian et al. (2016) examined the future of manufacturing and provided a brief review of the production planning aspect of remanufacturing.

Ferrer and Whybark (2001) proposed a sophisticated material requirements planning model for a remanufacturing plant to effectively manage the demand and supply of material in remanufacturing shops. Souza and Ketzenberg (2002) modeled a system that consisted of both new production and remanufacturing in the same facility. This model aimed to determine a production mix of new and remanufactured products. The product mix was chosen by comparing the profitability of remanufacturing a product with that of producing a new one. This model also considered the uncertainty about the quality of returned products, because this can cause delays in the remanufacturing process if the required components for remanufacturing are not retrieved by disassembling returned products. The idea was modeled by using discrete event simulation, and the proportion of product mixes was assessed based on the results of the experiment. Souza et al. (2002) modified the model presented by Souza and Ketzenberg (2002) by including several allocating dispatching rules. This idea provided an improved solution with reduced flow times and higher service levels for the production mix.

15.2.2.2 Scheduling

Guide et al. (1997a) presented a study that suggests using priority dispatching rules (PDR) such as first come first served (FCFS), shortest processing time (SPT), earliest due date (EDD), and longest processing time (LPT) for remanufacturing scheduling. They proposed the use of an accelerator in addition to these rules. When this method is employed, the materials are checked when they arrive at the reassembly area, and if 50% of them have arrived, the missing parts or materials are determined at the work centers, and their disassembly is accelerated. The goal of this method was to achieve a higher throughput and improved cycle time. This study also included PDRs such as lowest level in bill of materials (BOM), highest level in BOM, and modified due data (MDD). In addition, these rules were combined to break ties. For example, EDD (FCFS) tells us that if the EDD rule is tied, FCFS is preferred to break the tie. With these additional rules, a total of 16 PDRs were used to compare the scheduling performance in the study. Several performance measures were employed in the study. Mean flow time, mean tardiness, root mean square (RMS) tardiness, and percentage tardiness were used. Guide et al. (1997b) considered the impact of product structure complexity on PDR performance. Complexity was considered across three dimensions: reassembly complexity, routing complexity, and depth complexity. The reassembly complexity of a product was measured by comparing the number of units to be reassembled with the total number of units from all products. Depth complexity was measured according to the levels that the BOM product had. Routing complexity was measured by assessing the number of units in a product and the number of operations needed to reassemble it.

15.2.3 Disassembly Line Balancing

Disassembly lines are the preferred method of automating disassembly. Disassembly line balancing helps to ensure that disassembly lines are productive and facilitates the automation of the disassembly system. Gungor and Gupta (2001) developed an algorithm to solve the disassembly line balancing problem that takes the task failures that occur during the disassembly into consideration. Task failures represent a serious problem, because if a task fails, the subsequent operations might not be performed. The algorithm was designed to minimize the negative effects of these failures on the disassembly line. Gungor and Gupta (2002) demonstrated the complications of disassembly lines through presenting a simple disassembly line balancing problem and applied a heuristic procedure to solve this problem. The complications that may occur on the disassembly lines were classified as product considerations, line considerations, part considerations—such as quality and quantities of incoming products—operational considerations, demand considerations, and assignment considerations.

McGovern and Gupta (2006) proposed the use of an ant colony optimization metaheuristic to identify optimal or near-optimal solutions for the disassembly line balancing problem. McGovern and Gupta (2007a) compared several algorithms to solve the disassembly line balancing problem. These algorithms were exhaustive search, genetic algorithm, ant colony optimization metaheuristics, a greedy algorithm, and greedy/hill-climbing and greedy/2-optimal hybrid heuristics. McGovern and Gupta (2007b) developed a formula to quantitatively assess the level of balancing for the disassembly line balancing problem. A genetic algorithm was used to obtain optimal or near-optimal solutions to the problem. The authors also presented a comparison with the exhaustive search method.

Kalayci and Gupta (2013a,b,c,d,e) and Kalayci and Gupta (2014) presented mathematical models for the sequence-dependent disassembly line balancing problem. The aim of the models was to complete the assignment of the disassembly tasks to the workstations under precedence constraints and to provide optimal solutions by using several performance measures. They used different algorithms to obtain optimal solutions to the problem. These algorithms were an ant colony optimization approach, an artificial bee colony algorithm, a particle swarm optimization algorithm with neighborhood-based mutation, a tabu search algorithm, a simulated annealing algorithm, and a river formation dynamics approach. Kalayci et al. (2014) proposed a hybrid genetic algorithm for the sequence-dependent disassembly line balancing problem. Hezer and Kara (2015) investigated a parallel disassembly line balancing problem and developed a network-based shortest route model to solve this problem.

15.2.4 Maintenance

Several maintenance strategies, such as corrective maintenance, preventive maintenance, predictive maintenance, and proactive maintenance, have been used to maintain products. Corrective maintenance involves providing maintenance when products fail. In most cases, a corrective maintenance strategy is employed in the absence of alternative approaches. When preventive maintenance strategies are followed, the components are replaced or reconditioned based on a schedule that is defined by time and use. For predictive maintenance, signal processing tools are used to monitor the products, and proper service can be provided based on their condition. In this chapter, sensors are suggested as predictive maintenance tools. Sensors can monitor the products during their use phases and thereby, ensure that proper maintenance is provided. Proactive maintenance is similar to predictive maintenance. The main difference is that in the case of proactive maintenance, the root causes of the defects are eliminated prior to failures.

Altuger and Chassapis (2009) published a study to demonstrate a multi-criteria decision-making method to determine a preventive maintenance schedule for a bread packaging line. The objective of the study was to select a preventive maintenance schedule that provided the best use, performance, and reliability. To achieve this, the authors used discrete event simulation to model the system. They ran the simulation models for different preventive maintenance schedules and compared the results. Supsomboon and Hongthanapach (2014) conducted a study to develop a preventive maintenance plan under a reliability centered maintenance method for a test machine in a semiconductor factory. They used simulation to model the system and identified the optimal plan through the use of an optimizer. Yang et al. (2015) proposed an inspection maintenance model based on a three-stage failure process with imperfect maintenance. They modeled the system using a Monte Carlo simulation.

15.2.5 Radio-Frequency Identification (RFID) Technology in Supply Chains

The use of RFID systems in supply chains has become common. Blecker (2008) suggested methods of integrating RFID technology into commercial supply chain systems and assessed the steps that should be followed to set up the systems from scratch or update an existing supply chain system with RFID technology. These steps are business analysis, testing, pilot implementation, and full deployment of the system. Coltman et al. (2008) highlighted the importance of RFIDs within supply chains and discussed the implementation challenges that are associated with RFID technology. Ideally, this technology should be integrated throughout the entire supply chain, from raw material supplier to the retailing activities; however, the high implementation and maintenance costs associated with the use of this technology can be prohibitive for small businesses. This might cause delays in the integration of RFIDs into the entire supply chain system. Huang et al. (2011) highlighted the issues that can arise when attempting to use RFID devices: for example, the high initial set-up costs, the high level of technical skills required to run the devices, and the risks involved in using RFID technology. Huang et al. (2009) summarized the contribution RFID devices make to the product life cycle; in the middle of the cycle, they can improve maintenance operations, and at the end of the life cycle, they can assist with the recovery of the product. Kuo et al. (2009) presented brief information about the issues and challenges associated with RFID applications by examining several case studies. Sarma et al. (2009) described RFIDs and explained their use in different industries.

15.2.6 Sensor Embedded Products

Embedded sensors allow producers to monitor products during their life cycles and to gather important information about their condition. This condition information can subsequently be used to determine information about the remaining lives of the components (Vadde et al., 2008). This data is critical in EOL processes such as disassembling products, inspecting the disassembled components, and remanufacturing. The economic contribution of this idea to the systems was discussed in a series of papers (Ilgin and Gupta, 2010b; Ilgin and Gupta 2011a,b,c; Ilgin et al., 2011; Ilgin et al., 2014). In another series of papers (Ondemir and Gupta, 2012; Ondemir et al., 2012; Ondemir and Gupta, 2013a,b; Ondemir and Gupta, 2014a,b), the authors used mathematical modelling to solve the problem of fulfilling remanufactured product demand, refurbished component demand, and material demand by disassembling sensor embedded products.

Embedding sensors can be beneficial not only for EOL processes. They can be used to improve maintenance processes. In a series of papers (Dulman and Gupta, 2015; Dulman and Gupta, 2016; Dulman and Gupta, 2018a,b), their impact on both EOL and maintenance processes was assessed by conducting studies for different use cases, embedding them into different products including cell phones, laptops, and wind turbines.

15.3 Methodology

This study evaluated the performance of two products, a SEWM and a RWM, within a closed-loop supply system. The two systems consisted of two subsystems. The first subsystem involved maintaining the washing machines, while the second subsystem involved the EOL processes of washing machines. These subsystems and the associated operations that were modeled within this study are presented in Figure 15.1.

The first subsystem commences with the production and sales of washing machines and continues until the products complete their useful lives. During that period, it is important to provide proper maintenance and service if the washing machines fail. The second subsystem starts once the used washing machines are collected and sent to the EOL facility. It includes several EOL operations such as refurbishing, remanufacturing, and recycling.

15.3.1 Maintenance of Washing Machines

The washing machines arrive into the system at exponentially distributed interarrival times. The expected life span of a washing machine is 8 years.

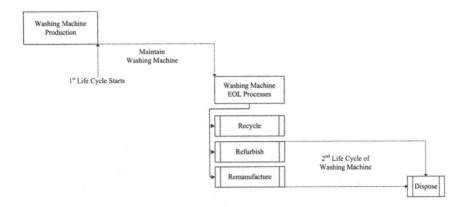

FIGURE 15.1
Maintenance and EOL life cycle scheme of washing machines.

If the machine fails during this 8 year period, a maintenance service is provided based on the corrective maintenance strategy chosen by the manufacturers. Repairing failed washing machines is not an option. The failed components or subassemblies are replaced with new ones. Since the study incorporates a second subsystem, which consists of EOL operations, the goal of the maintenance process is to increase the quality of components or subassemblies by replacing failed components with new ones, so that the return conditions are more promising, and the returned washing machines add more value to the system. On completion of the life cycle, the washing machines are sent to the EOL facility. Figure 15.2 provides an overview of the life cycle of a washing machine.

15.3.1.1 Maintenance of RWM Systems

Within the RWM systems, failed component or components are detected by inspecting the failed washing machines. Service personnel are informed of the failure and subsequently take appropriate actions such as obtaining new components to replace the failed ones. These operations are represented by the recognition of failure and service activation processes outlined in Figure 15.3. Following these processes, the failed washing machines

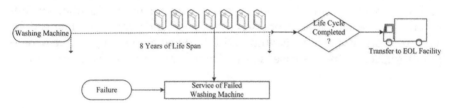

FIGURE 15.2
Life cycle outlook of washing machines.

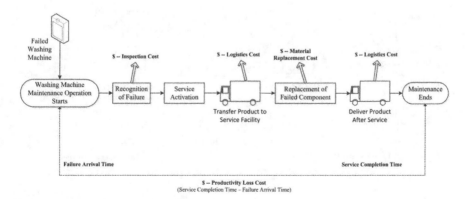

FIGURE 15.3
Maintenance operations of RWM systems.

are transferred to the service facility, if required, or the service team visits the customer's location with the new components. The failed component or components are replaced. If the washing machines are fixed in the service facility, they are then returned to the customer.

The costs associated with the maintenance activities are shown in Figure 15.3. The inspection cost was incurred following the recognition of the failure and the service activation process. The logistics costs included the cost of transporting the washing machines, transporting the service team to the customer location, and delivering the washing machines. In addition, the cost of the materials required to replace the failed components was also included in the maintenance cost. Finally, the productivity loss cost represented an essential part of the maintenance cost. The time between the failure of the washing machine and completion of the service was recorded and multiplied by the price of the washing machine per time unit. Thus, the productivity loss cost due to failures could be identified.

15.3.1.2 Maintenance of SEWM Systems

Sensors can provide real-time tracking information about the washing machines and their components by continually monitoring their performance. This information can then be used to predict failures before the washing machines fail. This removes the need for the recognition of failure and service activation processes. Sensors essentially negate the need for an inspection, and a fault is automatically detected, leading to the activation of servicing. In this case, sensors represent a predictive maintenance

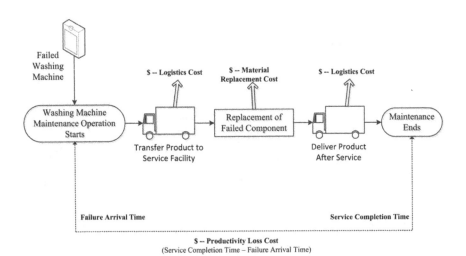

FIGURE 15.4
Maintenance operations of SEWM systems.

strategy for SEWM systems. Figure 15.4 presents an overview of the processes involved in maintaining SEWMs.

Within the SEWM systems, inspection costs can be reduced by eliminating the need for the recognition of failure and service activation process. In addition, productivity loss costs are reduced, because failures and service activities take less time.

15.3.2 Washing Machine EOL Processes

Once the first subsystem is completed, the washing machines are collected and sent to the EOL facility. These washing machines are disassembled via a three-station disassembly line. The disassembly sequence and relevant stations are presented in Figures 15.5 and 15.6.

15.3.2.1 EOL Processes of RWM Systems

The EOL processes of the RWM systems are shown in Figure 15.5. When the washing machines go through stations, the components or subassemblies at

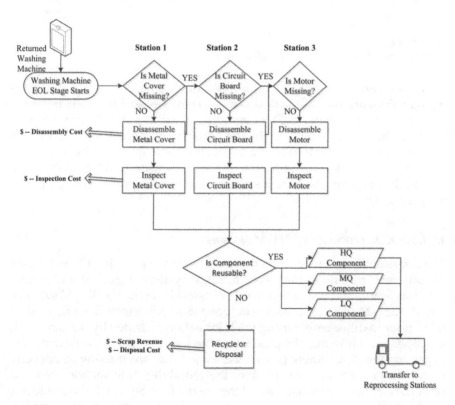

FIGURE 15.5
RWM systems disassembly and inspection processes.

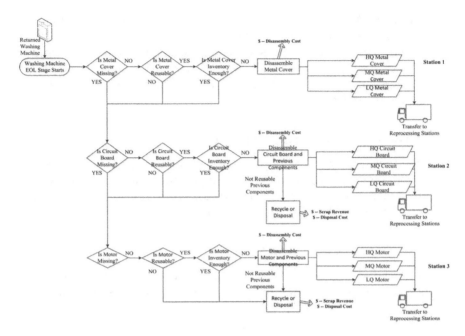

FIGURE 15.6
SEWM systems disassembly and inspection processes.

each station are disassembled, if they are not missing. Otherwise, the washing machines are sent to the next station. The disassembly cost is the function of the labor cost and the time required to disassemble the components. To determine the reusability of the components and subassemblies and their quality levels, the disassembled components are inspected. The inspection cost can be calculated using parameters such as inspection time, labor cost, and machining cost. Once the inspection is complete, proper EOL processes are performed.

15.3.2.2 EOL Processes of SEWM Systems

The disassembly and inspection processes that take place in SEWM systems are different from those that occur in RWM systems. Figure 15.6 illustrates the disassembly and inspection structure associated with the SEWM systems.

In the SEWM systems, missing components or subassemblies will be identified prior to disassembly using the information provided by the sensors. If a component is missing, the product can be sent directly to the next station, bypassing the disassembly process associated with the missing component. If the components are not missing, the reusability information retrieved from the sensors can be used to determine the flow by which the product is processed. If any components are not reusable, they are not disassembled. Instead, they are forwarded to the next station. If the other component in the next station requires disassembly, they are disassembled together. By bypassing the disassembly process for components that are not reusable or disassembling usable components together at the same station, the operator can reduce disassembly costs. If the components are reusable, they are labeled with their quality levels using the information provided by the sensors. The inventory levels of the components are controlled after the quality levels are labeled. If there is demand for components, they are disassembled and sent to the reprocessing area. If there is no demand, they are sent to the next station. If the other component in the next station requires disassembly, they are disassembled together. As is the case with the reusability check, the upfront inventory check can reduce disassembly and inventory costs.

15.3.2.3 Reprocessing of Washing Machines

EOL processing takes place after disassembly and inspection processes. The components in both systems are allocated to one of three categories: high quality (HQ), medium quality (MQ), and low quality (LQ). HQ components can last around 3–4 years. The expected life span of MQ components is between 2 and 3 years, while that of LQ components is between 1 and 2 years. The disassembled and inspected components are transferred to the reprocessing area.

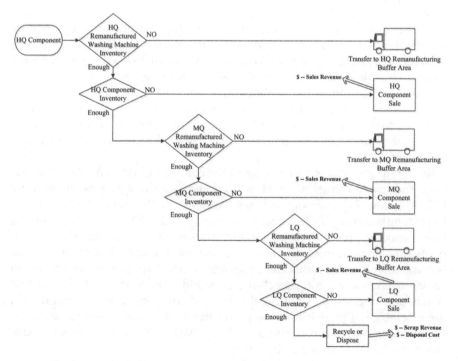

FIGURE 15.7
HQ component flow for recycle, resale, and remanufacturing.

Figure 15.7 shows the HQ component flow. HQ components are transferred to the remanufacturing buffer area if the maximum HQ remanufactured washing machine inventory level is not reached. Otherwise, the maximum HQ component inventory level is checked to sell the components. If the maximum inventory level for the HQ component is also reached, HQ components are sent for use in MQ processes as opposed to being recycled, because these HQ components can increase the quality level of MQ parts and can generate more revenue if they are remanufactured or sold at the MQ level. A similar flow can be observed at the MQ level. If these HQ components are not needed at the MQ level, they are used at the LQ level. If HQ components cannot be used for any of these reprocessing options, they are recycled or disposed of based on the materials they contain.

Revenue and cost measures are associated with the HQ component flow. These include sales revenue, scrap revenue, and disposal costs. If the components are sold, sales revenue increases. If the components are recycled, they generate scrap revenue. Otherwise, they are disposed of, and this increases the disposal costs that are inherent in the system.

The MQ component flow is similar to the HQ component flow. The only difference is that MQ components cannot be used as a replacement for HQ components, because HQ is an upper level, and this replacement reduces the overall quality level of a remanufactured washing machine. LQ component flow considers only LQ components.

The renewal time of the components during maintenance operations is recorded for use in EOL processes. The components can be renewed, in which case the period for which they are in use after the renewal time is recorded. Alternatively, if they are not renewed, the period from the beginning of their life cycle is recorded. This helps to determine the quality levels of the disassembled components. If the components are in use for more than the renewal-time threshold, their condition is worse than that of the other components. The threshold for washing machines is 4 years.

Recycling and resale operations and the contribution they made to the revenue and relevant costs were introduced and explained previously with the HQ, MQ, and LQ component flows. However, if the components are sent to remanufacturing buffer area, as shown in HQ, MQ, and LQ component flows, another process, remanufacturing assembly, is initiated. The components wait in the buffer area until one component from each component type is available. Once the component package is complete, they are assembled to remanufacture a washing machine. This adds cost to the system, and this cost is captured within the assembly cost. In addition, once the components are assembled, if there is no demand for the final product, they are added to the inventory as remanufactured washing machines. Holding costs increase when products are stored as inventory.

For the purpose of this study, it was assumed that demands follow a Poisson distribution. If there is demand, and inventory is available to fulfill

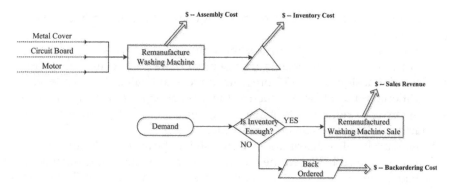

FIGURE 15.8
Remanufacturing and demand flow of washing machines.

the demand, the remanufactured washing machines are sold, and revenue is generated. If the inventory is not available, demand is backordered, and backordering costs are increased in the system. The remanufacturing and demand flow of the washing machines can be seen in Figure 15.8.

15.4 Design of Experiments Study

To assess the economic impact of the benefits of embedded sensors, they were converted into numerical form, and to achieve this, a design of experiments study was used. The goal of the design of experiments approach used in the study was to compare the revenues and costs of both systems. A total of 40 factors on three levels that could impact the outcomes in terms of the revenues and costs of the systems were identified. It was not practical to complete a full factorial design, because these require an excessive number of experiments. The orthogonal arrays method was chosen for the factorial design, because it helps to identify the subset of experiments that need to be carried out. The application of this method reduced the number of required experiments, and the optimally modified factorial design entailed that the results were unbiased. Specifically, an $L_{81}(3^{40})$ orthogonal array was chosen for the factorial design employed in the study (Phadke, 1989). This orthogonal array required 81 experiments for the two systems.

Ilgin and Gupta (2010b) published a paper that described SEWMs. When we were collecting data for our study, Ilgin and Gupta's (2010b) paper was a helpful source of information about the factors that should be taken into consideration in our factorial design. These are described later.

Table 15.1 presents remanufactured washing machine, subassembly, and component prices. HQ and MQ level prices were used for the factorial design.

LQ level prices were not used, because they do not significantly change the performance measures.

Within the context of the disassembly process, the disassembly time for each station and the associated disassembly costs were considered within the factorial design. Table 15.2 presents the relevant values for each level.

Additional relevant factors, such as the inspection times during the subassembly process and the costs of inspecting the components, were included in the factorial design, as can be seen in Table 15.3.

Several probability distributions were used in the factorial design. One distribution was used to determine the chance of retrieving a washing machine that had a component or subassembly missing. Another distribution was used to determine the probability that the components would be reusable. In addition, the conditions of the components and subassembly requirements were determined using a probability distribution. These distributions

TABLE 15.1

Remanufactured Washing Machine, Subassembly and Component Prices

Factor	Level 1	Level 2	Level 3
HQ washing machine ($)	350	325	300
HQ metal cover ($)	30	25	20
HQ circuit board ($)	80	70	60
HQ motor ($)	150	130	110
MQ washing machine ($)	250	225	200
MQ metal cover ($)	15	12	9
MQ circuit board ($)	50	45	40
MQ motor ($)	90	80	70

TABLE 15.2

Disassembly Cost and Time Factors

Factor	Level 1	Level 2	Level 3
Disassembly cost ($/min)	3	2	1
Metal cover disassembly time (min)	0.75	0.5	0.25
Circuit board disassembly time (min)	1.25	1	0.75
Motor disassembly time (min)	1.25	1	0.75

TABLE 15.3

Inspection Cost and Time Factors

Factor	Level 1	Level 2	Level 3
Inspection cost ($/min)	0.6	0.5	0.4
Metal cover inspection time (min)	1.5	1	0.5
Circuit board inspection time (min)	6	5	4
Motor inspection time (min)	12	10	8

can be observed in Table 15.4. The HQ and MQ level condition probabilities were counted in the number of factors; however, LQ level probabilities were excluded from the factorial design, because once HQ and MQ level probabilities were identified, LQ level probabilities could be determined. LQ level probabilities are presented in Table 15.5.

TABLE 15.4

Probability Factors (%)

Factor	Level 1	Level 2	Level 3
Missing metal cover	5	10	15
Missing circuit board	5	10	15
Missing motor	5	10	15
Usable metal cover	90	80	70
Usable circuit board	90	80	70
Usable motor	90	80	70
HQ metal cover return	55	50	45
MQ metal cover return	30	30	30
HQ circuit board return	55	50	45
MQ circuit board return	30	30	30
HQ motor return	55	50	45
MQ motor return	30	30	30

TABLE 15.5

Low Quality Subassembly and Component Probabilities (%)

Factor	Level 1	Level 2	Level 3
LQ metal cover return	15	20	25
LQ circuit board return	15	20	25
LQ motor return	15	20	25

TABLE 15.6

Quality Level Probabilities When Renewal-Time Threshold Is Exceeded (%)

Factor	Level 1	Level 2	Level 3
HQ metal cover return	25	20	15
MQ metal cover return	30	30	30
LQ metal cover return	45	50	55
HQ circuit board return	25	20	15
MQ circuit board return	30	30	30
LQ circuit board return	45	50	55
HQ motor return	25	20	15
MQ motor return	30	30	30
LQ motor return	45	50	55

Table 15.6 presents the probability distributions that were used when the renewal-time threshold of the components or subassemblies was exceeded. The period for which the components or subassemblies were in use was recorded. If this period exceeded the renewal-time threshold, the return quality decreased. For this purpose, the probability distributions detailed later were used to determine the quality levels when the renewal-time threshold was exceeded.

The maintenance aspect of the systems was included in the study, and the factors that had an impact on maintenance were considered in the factorial design. These were recognition of failure and service activation, inspection time of the failure, labor cost, and productivity loss cost. Table 15.7 illustrates these factors and their associated levels. The inspection time of the failure was normally distributed. The mean and standard deviation values for this factor are shown in Table 15.7.

Remanufactured washing machine and component demands were used in the factorial design, because they were deemed to have a significant impact on the revenue of the systems. LQ demand levels were not included in the factorial design. Table 15.8 presents the demand factors and their levels.

Discrete event simulation software Arena 14.7 (Kelton et al., 2007) was used to model the systems. The models were verified by testing the results with extreme input values. Models were also validated by plotting the outputs and

TABLE 15.7

Maintenance Factors

Factor	Level 1	Level 2	Level 3
Recognition of failure and service activation	3 days	2 days	1 day
Inspection time of failure (min)	25	20	15
Labor cost	$30/hour	$25/hour	$20/hour
Productivity loss cost	$2/day	$1.5/day	$1/day

TABLE 15.8

Remanufactured Washing Machine, Subassembly, and Component Demands

(Follows Poisson Distribution)			
Factor	Level 1	Level 2	Level 3
HQ washing machine (/day)	100	90	80
MQ washing machine (/day)	80	70	60
HQ metal cover (/day)	100	90	80
MQ metal cover (/day)	80	70	60
HQ circuit board (/day)	100	90	80
MQ circuit board (/day)	80	70	60
HQ motor (/day)	100	90	80
MQ motor (/day)	80	70	60

observing the behavior of those outputs through the runs. The models were run for 3300 days, which is approximately 9 years. When the 8 year expected life span of the washing machines was taken into consideration, this run period accommodated both the life cycles of the washing machines and the EOL processes. For each system, the models were run 81 times. In addition to the data incorporated into the factorial design, the data set needed to run the experiments is described in Appendix A.

The goal of the experiments was to compare the revenues and costs associated with the SEWM and RWM systems and thereby, determine the economic contribution of the sensors. To carry out this evaluation, several performance measures were used. These measures and their formulas are introduced here.

$$\text{Maintenance Cost} = \text{Labor Cost} + \text{Logistics Cost}$$
$$+ \text{Productivity Loss Cost} \qquad (15.1)$$
$$+ \text{Material Replacement Cost}$$

$$\text{Total Profit} = \text{Total Revenue} - \text{Total Cost} \qquad (15.2)$$

$$\text{Total Revenue} = \text{Sales Revenue} + \text{Scrap Revenue} \qquad (15.3)$$

$$\text{Total Cost} = \text{Collection Cost}$$
$$+ \text{Disassembly Cost} + \text{Inspection Cost}$$
$$+ \text{Remanufacturing Cost} + \text{Holding Cost} \qquad (15.4)$$
$$+ \text{Backordering Cost} + \text{Disposal Cost}$$

$$\text{Sensor Value} = (\text{Maintenance Cost Saving}$$
$$+ \text{Total Profit Improvement}) \qquad (15.5)$$
$$/ \text{Total Number of Sensors}$$

15.5 Results and Analysis

The outcomes for several performance measures, including EOL profit per washing machine, maintenance cost per washing machine, disassembly cost, and inspection cost, are described in this section.

In SEWM systems, the mean EOL profit per washing machine was $87.48, whereas it was $79.88 for the RWM systems. In addition, the maintenance

TABLE 15.9

Experimental Results for SEWM and RWM Systems

Measure	SEWM System ($)	RWM System ($)
EOL profit/washing machine	87.48	79.88
Maintenance cost/washing machine	140.06	146.32
Disassembly cost	35,694.76	40,916.62
Inspection cost	729.52	65,452.26

cost of the SEWM systems was, on average, $140.06, and this value was higher in RWM systems, at $146.32.

The mean value of the disassembly cost of the SEWM systems was $35,694.76, while it was $40,916.62 for the RWM systems. As such, the results indicate that the use of sensors in closed-loop washing machine supply chains reduces disassembly costs. Furthermore, the inspections were also significantly reduced as a result of incorporating sensors into the washing machines. In the RWM systems, the inspection costs were $65,452.26, while these reduced to $729.52 in the SEWM systems. These values are presented in Table 15.9.

The mean values of the performance measures highlight the differences in the performance of the two systems. A pairwise t-test was used to test the significance of this difference. A pairwise test was selected for this purpose, because factorial designs with orthogonal arrays require a subset of certain level combinations for each experiment, and these experiments should be paired for each system. Table 15.10 presents the results of the pairwise t-test.

The SEWM systems were $7.59 more profitable per unit than the RWM machines. The mean difference in the maintenance costs per washing machine was $-6.26. This shows that the maintenance costs of the SEWM system were lower than those of the RWM systems. As shown in Table 15.10, all the p values were less than .0001. As such, it can be concluded that the mean differences between the two systems were statistically significant. The disassembly and inspection cost comparisons and their pairwise t-test results are presented in Table 15.10.

TABLE 15.10

Pairwise t-Test Results for Mean Difference

Measure	Mean Difference (SEWM – RWM) ($)	p Value
Sensor value	13.85	N/A
EOL profit/washing machine	7.59	<.0001
Maintenance cost/washing machine	−6.26	<.0001
Disassembly cost	−5,221.86	<.0001
Inspection cost	−64,722.74	<.0001

TABLE 15.11

95% Confidence Interval of Mean Difference

Measure	95% Confidence Interval of Mean Difference (SEWM – RWM)	
	Lower Limit ($)	Upper Limit ($)
Sensor value	13.18	14.53
EOL profit/washing machine	7.04	8.15
Maintenance cost/washing machine	−6.64	−5.88
Disassembly cost	−5,881.90	−4,561.82
Inspection cost	−67,682.37	−61,763.11

The EOL profit increase and maintenance cost savings associated with the SEWM systems can be interpreted to represent the sensor value. Thus, the value of the sensor incorporated within the washing machines in the SEWM system was calculated to be $13.85. If sensors can be purchased at a value lower than the sensor value identified in this study, SEWM systems are profitable. Additional pairwise *t*-test results are presented in Table 15.11, and these include 95% confidence intervals for the mean difference of the measures.

The design of experiments study covered 63 factors, and failure interarrival time was not included in the factorial design. The inclusion of this variable would have led to high variation, and the experimental results would not have been sufficiently accurate to make comparisons between the systems. However, the impact of failure interarrival time on the performance measures was analyzed through separate runs. Thus, several failure interarrival times were determined for additional runs, and the models were run for each scenario. Figure 15.9 presents the relationship between failure interarrival time and the maintenance costs of the systems. As can be observed in Figure 15.9, when the failure interarrival time increased, the maintenance cost of both systems decreased, and this reduction was exponential. This is reasonable, because the more washing machines fail, the higher the costs of maintaining them.

The maintenance cost difference between SEWM and RWM systems decreases when the failure interarrival time increases. Like the maintenance costs, the differences in maintenance costs between the systems were negatively correlated and exponential. This relationship can be observed in Figure 15.10.

Failure interarrival time not only affected the maintenance cost of the systems but also had an indirect impact on the EOL profit. When washing machines fail, their failed components or subassemblies are replaced with new ones. This was tracked in the system as renewal time and was determined to have an impact on the condition of the returned washing machines and their components. As can be observed in Figure 15.11,

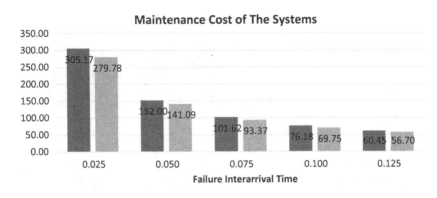

FIGURE 15.9
Maintenance cost of the systems.

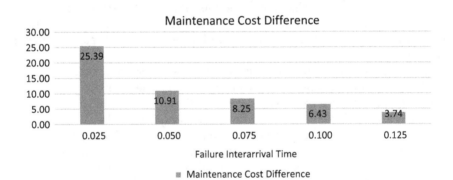

FIGURE 15.10
Maintenance cost difference between the two systems.

EOL profit was at its lowest when the failure interarrival time was at its lowest, 0.025.

An interesting finding from this analysis was that EOL profit of the two cases are close to each other. These cases are the ones that have the failure interarrival rates of 0.050 and 0.125. This can be explained by the replaced components. Once the components are renewed, they are in better condition when they are returned; thus, EOL profit increases. Figure 15.11 illustrates the relationship between the EOL profit values and the change in failure interarrival time.

The relationship between sensor value and failure interarrival time was also evaluated and is shown in Figure 15.12. The sensor value was at its highest when the failure interarrival time was 0.025.

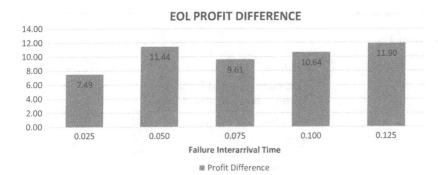

FIGURE 15.11
EOL profit difference between the two systems.

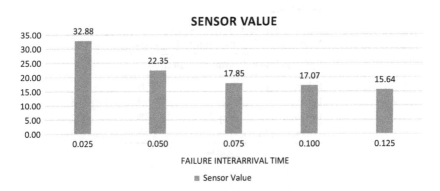

FIGURE 15.12
Sensor value.

15.6 Conclusions

The economic performance of SEWM and RWM systems was analyzed in this study. A comparison of the maintenance costs and EOL profits of the SEWM systems and the RWM systems revealed that the SEWM systems were superior to the RWM systems, because information about the condition of the components and subassemblies can be retrieved from the sensors. Thus, proactive actions can be taken prior to failure, and the disassembly and inspection processes can be improved. The maintenance cost of the systems could be reduced by as much as $6.26 per unit through the implementation of sensors. In addition, EOL profit could be increased by $7.59 by embedding sensors into washing machines. When these economic benefits are combined, the economic contribution of the sensors was determined to be $13.85.

Appendix A

TABLE A1

LQ Remanufactured Washing
Machine and Component Prices

LQ washing machine ($)	100
LQ metal cover ($)	5
LQ circuit board ($)	30
LQ motor ($)	50

TABLE A2

LQ Remanufactured Washing
Machine and Component Demands

(Follows Poisson Distribution)	
LQ washing machine (/day)	50
LQ metal cover (/day)	50
LQ circuit board (/day)	50
LQ motor (/day)	50

TABLE A3

Maintenance Data

Failure interarrival time (days) (exponential)	0.05
Expected lifetime (years)	8
Transportation before service (days)	1
Delivery after service (days) (triangular distribution)	Min (1), Mean (2), Max (3)
Transportation cost ($)	10
Delivery cost ($)	60

TABLE A4

Subassembly and Component Replacement Times
for Maintenance

(Normally Distributed) (Mean, Standard Deviation)	
Metal cover (min)	(1,0.1)
Circuit board (min)	(2,0.3)
Motor (min)	(2,0.3)

TABLE A5

Subassembly and Component Replacement
Costs for Maintenance

Metal cover ($)	40
Circuit board ($)	100
Motor ($)	200

TABLE A6

Subassembly and Component
Failure Probabilities (%)

Metal cover failure	10
Circuit board failure	50
Motor failure	40

TABLE A7

Production and Cost Data

Washing machine interarrival time (min) (exponentially distributed)	3
Scrap revenue ($/lbs.)	0.6
Disposal cost ($/lbs.)	0.4
Holding cost rate	0.2
Backordering cost rate	0.6

TABLE A8

Remanufacturing Assembly Data

Washing machine assembly time (min)	6
Assembly cost ($/min)	4

References

Altuger, G., and Chassapis, C. (2009). Multi criteria preventive maintenance scheduling through arena based simulation modeling. In *Winter Simulation Conference* (pp. 2123–2134). Winter Simulation Conference.

Blecker, T. (Ed.). (2008). *RFID in Operations and Supply Chain Management: Research and Applications* (Vol. 6). Erich Schmidt Verlag GmbH & Co KG.

Coltman, T., Gadh, R., and Michael, K. (2008). RFID and supply chain management: Introduction to the special issue. *Faculty of Informatics—Papers*, 585.

Dulman, M. T., and Gupta, S. M. (2015). Disassembling and remanufacturing end-of-life sensor embedded cell phones. *Innovation and Supply Chain Management*, 9(4), 111–117.

Dulman, M. T., and Gupta, S. M. (2016). Use of sensors for collection of end-of-life products, *Proceedings for the Northeast Region Decision Sciences Institute (NEDSI)*.

Dulman, M. T., and Gupta, S. M. (2018a). Evaluation of maintenance and EOL operation performance of sensor-embedded laptops. *Logistics*, 2(1), 3.

Dulman, M. T., and Gupta, S. M. (2018b, in press). Evaluation of maintenance and EOL operation performance of sensor-embedded laptops. *Journal of Remanufacturing*.

Esmaeilian, B., Behdad, S., and Wang, B. (2016). The evolution and future of manufacturing: A review. *Journal of Manufacturing Systems*, 39, 79–100.

Ferrer, G., and Whybark, D. (2001). Material planning for a remanufacturing facility. *Production and Operations Management*, 10(2), 112–124.

Guide, V. D. R., Kraus, M. E., and Srivastava, R. (1997a). Scheduling policies for remanufacturing. *International Journal of Production Economics*, 48(2), 187–204.

Guide Jr, V. D. R., Srivastava, R., and Kraus, M. E. (1997b). Product structure complexity and scheduling of operations in recoverable manufacturing. *International Journal of Production Research*, 35(11), 3179–3200.

Guide, V. D. R., Jayaraman, V., and Srivastava, R. (1999). Production planning and control for remanufacturing: A state-of-the-art survey. *Robotics and Computer-Integrated Manufacturing*, 15(3), 221–230.

Gungor, A., and Gupta, S. M. (1999). Issues in environmentally conscious manufacturing and product recovery: A survey. *Computers & Industrial Engineering*, 36(4), 811–853.

Gungor, A., and Gupta, S. M. (2001). A solution approach to the disassembly line balancing problem in the presence of task failures. *International Journal of Production Research*, 39(7), 1427–1467.

Gungor, A., and Gupta, S. M. (2002). Disassembly line in product recovery. *International Journal of Production Research*, 40(11), 2569–2589.

Gupta, S. M. and Ilgin, M. A. (2018). *Multiple Criteria Decision Making Applications in Environmentally Conscious Manufacturing and Product Recovery*. CRC Press, Boca Raton, Florida.

Habibi, M. K., Battaïa, O., Cung, V. D., and Dolgui, A. (2017). Collection-disassembly problem in reverse supply chain. *International Journal of Production Economics*, 183, 334–344.

Hezer, S., and Kara, Y. (2015). A network-based shortest route model for parallel disassembly line balancing problem. *International Journal of Production Research*, 53(6), 1849–1865.

Huang, G. Q., Wright, P. K., and Newman, S. T. (2009). Wireless manufacturing: A literature review, recent developments, and case studies. *International Journal of Computer Integrated Manufacturing*, 22(7), 579–594.

Huang, G. Q., Qu, T., Fang, M. J., and Bramley, A. N. (2011). RFID-enabled gateway product service system for collaborative manufacturing alliances. *CIRP Annals—Manufacturing Technology*, 60(1), 465–468.

Ilgin, M. A., and Gupta, S. M. (2010a). Environmentally conscious manufacturing and product recovery (ECMPRO): A review of the state of the art. *Journal of Environmental Management*, 91(3), 563–591.

Ilgin, M. A., and Gupta, S. M. (2010b). Comparison of economic benefits of sensor embedded products and conventional products in a multi-product disassembly line. *Computers & Industrial Engineering*, 59(4), 748–763.

Ilgin, M. A., and Gupta, S. M. (2011a). Evaluating the impact of sensor-embedded products on the performance of an air conditioner disassembly line. *The International Journal of Advanced Manufacturing Technology*, 53(9–12), 1199–1216.

Ilgin, M. A., and Gupta, S. M. (2011b). Performance improvement potential of sensor embedded products in environmental supply chains. *Resources, Conservation and Recycling*, 55(6), 580–592.

Ilgin, M. A., and Gupta, S. M. (2011c). Recovery of sensor embedded washing machines using a multi-kanban controlled disassembly line. *Robotics and Computer-Integrated Manufacturing*, 27(2), 318–334.

Ilgin, M. A., Gupta, S. M., and Nakashima, K. (2011). Coping with disassembly yield uncertainty in remanufacturing using sensor embedded products. *Journal of Remanufacturing*, 1(1), 1–14.

Ilgin, M. A., Ondemir, O., and Gupta, S. M. (2014). An approach to quantify the financial benefit of embedding sensors into products for end-of-life management: A case study. *Production Planning & Control*, 25(1), 26–43.

Kalayci, C. B., and Gupta, S. M. (2013a). Ant colony optimization for sequence-dependent disassembly line balancing problem. *Journal of Manufacturing Technology Management*, 24(3), 413–427.

Kalayci, C. B., and Gupta, S. M. (2013b). Artificial bee colony algorithm for solving sequence-dependent disassembly line balancing problem. *Expert Systems with Applications*, 40(18), 7231–7241.

Kalayci, C. B., and Gupta, S. M. (2013c). A particle swarm optimization algorithm with neighborhood-based mutation for sequence-dependent disassembly line balancing problem. *The International Journal of Advanced Manufacturing Technology*, 69(1–4), 197–209.

Kalayci, C. B., and Gupta, S. M. (2013d). Balancing a sequence-dependent disassembly line using simulated annealing algorithm. *Applications of Management Science (Applications of Management Science, Volume 16) Emerald Group Publishing Limited*, 16, 81–103.

Kalayci, C. B., and Gupta, S. M. (2013e). River Formation Dynamics Approach for Sequence-dependent Disassembly Line Balancing Problem. In *Reverse Supply Chains: Issues and Analysis*, edited by S. M. Gupta, 289–312. CRC Press, Boca Raton, FL. ISBN 978-1439899021, Chapter 12.

Kalayci, C. B., and Gupta, S. M. (2014). A tabu search algorithm for balancing a sequence-dependent disassembly line. *Production Planning & Control*, 25(2), 149–160.

Kalayci, C. B., Polat, O., and Gupta, S. M. (2014). A hybrid genetic algorithm for sequence-dependent disassembly line balancing problem. *Annals of Operations Research*, 1–34.

Kelton, D. W., Sadowski R. P., and Sadowski, D. A., (2007). *Simulation with Arena*. (4th ed.). McGraw-Hill, New York.

Kuo, S. Y., Yang, C. F., Chou, S. Y., and Chen, J. L. (2009). Editorial for special issue on RFID network technologies and innovative applications. *International Journal of Internet Protocol Technology*, 4, 219–220.

McGovern, S. M., and Gupta, S. M. (2006). Ant colony optimization for disassembly sequencing with multiple objectives. *The International Journal of Advanced Manufacturing Technology*, 30(5–6), 481–496.

McGovern, S. M., and Gupta, S. M. (2007a). Combinatorial optimization analysis of the unary NP-complete disassembly line balancing problem. *International Journal of Production Research*, 45(18–19), 4485–4511.

McGovern, S. M., and Gupta, S. M. (2007b). A balancing method and genetic algorithm for disassembly line balancing. *European Journal of Operational Research*, 179(3), 692–708.

Ondemir, O., and Gupta, S. M. (2012). Optimal management of reverse supply chains with sensor-embedded end-of-life products. In Lawrence K. D. and Kleinman G., eds. *Applications of Management Science*. Emerald Group Publishing Limited, 109–129.

Ondemir, O., and Gupta, S. M. (2013a). Advanced remanufacturing-to-order and disassembly-to-order system under demand/decision uncertainty. In Gupta, S. M. eds. *Reverse Supply Chains: Issues and Analysis*. CRC Press, 203–228.

Ondemir, O., and Gupta, S. M. (2013b). Quality assurance in remanufacturing with sensor embedded products. In Nikolaidis Y. eds. *Quality Management in Reverse Logistics*. Springer-Verlag, London, 95–112.

Ondemir, O., and Gupta, S. M. (2013a). A multi-criteria decision making model for advanced repair-to-order and disassembly-to-order system. *European Journal of Operational Research*, 233(2), 408–419.

Ondemir, O., and Gupta, S. M. (2014b). Quality management in product recovery using the Internet of Things: An optimization approach. *Computers in Industry*, 65(3), 491–504.

Ondemir, O., Ilgin, M. A., and Gupta, S. M. (2012). Optimal end-of-life management in closed-loop supply chains using RFID and sensors. *Industrial Informatics, IEEE Transactions on*, 8(3), 719–728.

Phadke, M. S. (1989). *Quality Engineering Robust Design*. Prentice Hall, New Jersey.

Pochampally, K. K., and Gupta, S. M. (2005). Strategic planning of a reverse supply chain network. *International Journal of Integrated Supply Management*, 1(4), 421–441.

Pochampally, K. K., and Gupta, S. M. (2008). A multiphase fuzzy logic approach to strategic planning of a reverse supply chain network. *Electronics Packaging Manufacturing, IEEE Transactions on*, 31(1), 72–82.

Pochampally, K. K., Nukala, S., and Gupta, S. M. (2008). Eco-procurement strategies for environmentally conscious manufacturers. *International Journal of Logistics Systems and Management*, 5(1–2), 106–122.

Pochampally, K. K., Nukala, S., and Gupta, S. M. (2009). *Strategic Planning Models for Reverse and Closed-loop Supply Chains*. CRC Press, Boca Raton, Florida.

Sarma, S., Mickle, M. H., McFarlane, D., Cole, P., and Engels, D. W. (2009). Guest editorial. *IEEE Transactions on Automation Science and Engineering*, 6, 1–3.

Souza, G. C., and Ketzenberg, M. E. (2002). Two-stage make-to-order remanufacturing with service-level constraints. *International Journal of Production Research*, 40(2), 477–493.

Souza, G. C., Ketzenberg, M. E., and Guide, V. D. R. (2002). Capacitated remanufacturing with service level constraints. *Production and Operations Management*, 11(2), 231–248.

Supsomboon, S., and Hongthanapach, K. (2014). A simulation model for machine efficiency improvement using reliability centered maintenance: Case study of semiconductor factory. *Modelling and Simulation in Engineering*, 2014, 45.

Vadde, S., Kamarthi, S., Gupta, S. M., and Zeid, I. (2008). Product life cycle monitoring via embedded sensors. In Enviroment conscious manufacturing. Edited by: Gupta S. M., Lambert A. J. D. Boca Raton, FL: CRC Press; 91–103.

Veerakamolmal, P., and Gupta, S. M. (1999). Analysis of design efficiency for the disassembly of modular electronic products. *Journal of Electronics Manufacturing,* 9(01), 79–95.

Yang, R., Yan, Z., and Kang, J. (2015). An inspection maintenance model based on a three-stage failure process with imperfect maintenance via Monte Carlo simulation. *International Journal of System Assurance Engineering and Management,* 6(3), 231–237.

16

Prediction of the Efficiency of a Collection Center in a Reverse Supply Chain, Using Logistic Regression

Kishore K. Pochampally and Surendra M. Gupta

CONTENTS

16.1 Introduction

Today, there is much emphasis on the reprocessing (recycle/remanufacture) of end-of-use products due to growing population, finite resources, and limited disposal capacities (Gungor and Gupta, 1999). Hence, reverse supply chains are designed and implemented to collect end-of-use products from consumers, reprocess them at recovery facilities, and then sell recycled goods and remanufactured products on the market (Alkhayyal and Gupta, 2018). An important driver for companies engaged in a reverse supply chain is that many end-of-use products represent a resource for recoverable value (Ilgin and Gupta, 2010). Furthermore, the increasing environmental consciousness of consumers and government regulations offer the possibility of satisfying customer demand with remanufactured products instead of exclusively producing new products. This mode of demand satisfaction may offer a cost advantage over the production of new products (Gupta, 2013). Another advantage is that remanufacturing lead times may be much shorter than production lead times (Gupta and Ilgin, 2018).

The implementation of a reverse supply chain requires at least three parties: collection centers, where consumers return end-of-use products; recovery facilities, where reprocessing (remanufacturing or recycling) is performed; and demand centers, where customers buy reprocessed products (Pochampally et al., 2009).

The timely delivery of proper end-of-use products by collection centers to recovery facilities is critical to meet the ever-increasing demand for recycled goods and remanufactured products. To this end, this chapter demonstrates with two illustrative examples how to predict the efficiency of a collection center using logistic regression (Pochampally and Gupta, 2014). In the first example, a model is built to predict the probability of on-time delivery based on the number of trucks owned by the collection center. In the second example, the probability of a collecting center meeting specifications is estimated based on the age of the sorting equipment used by the collection center.

Section 16.2 gives a brief introduction to logistic regression. Sections 16.3 and 16.4 illustrate the first and second examples, respectively. Finally, Section 16.5 gives some conclusions.

16.2 Logistic Regression

A logistic regression equation to predict the probability (p) of an event, based on the value of one explanatory (independent) variable x, can be written as follows in Equation 16.1:

$$p = \frac{e^{a+bx}}{1+e^{a+bx}} \tag{16.1}$$

where
  e is Euler's number (2.71828)
  a and b are constants (Groebner et al., 2017)

A scatter plot between p and x, for given values of a and b, looks like an "S-curve," as shown in Figure 16.1.

The best values of a and b are those that best fit the existing data, that is, the actual values of (x, p) pairs. Equation 16.1 can be transformed into Equation 16.2, which then can be used to apply the least squares estimation method as in a linear regression problem.

$$Log\left(\frac{p}{1-p}\right) = a + bx \tag{16.2}$$

Since $(p/1 - p)$ represents the "odds" of the event of interest, we can also write Equation 16.2 as Equation 16.3:

$$Log(odds) = a + bx \tag{16.3}$$

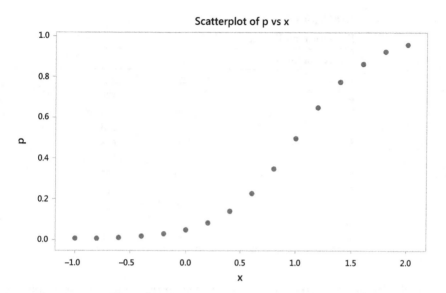

FIGURE 16.1
Scatter plot of p and x in Equation 16.1.

An estimate of log(odds) for a given x, and for given a and b, is called the *fitted* log(odds) for that x and can be calculated using the right-hand side of Equation 16.2.

The actual log(odds) for a given (x, p) pair can be calculated using the left-hand side of Equation 16.2.

A residual for a given x can be defined as the difference between the actual log(odds) and the fitted log(odds), as shown in Equation 16.4. The example in the next section will clarify this.

$$\text{Residual} = \text{Actual} \log(\text{odds}) - \text{Fitted} \log(\text{odds}) \qquad (16.4)$$

The best values of a and b are the ones that minimize the sum of squares of all the residuals.

16.3 First Example

In this example, the following data, as shown in Table 16.1, are collected for 11 collection centers: number of trucks owned (x) and proportion of on-time deliveries (p).

A scatter plot, shown in Figure 16.2, is plotted for the data in Table 16.1. Evidently, the plot shows an "S-curve," which motivates us to fit a logistic regression model as in Equation 16.1.

TABLE 16.1

Data for First Example

Collection Center	x	p
1	20	.225
2	40	.236
3	60	.398
4	80	.628
5	100	.678
6	120	.795
7	140	.853
8	160	.86
9	180	.921
10	200	.94
11	240	.968

To obtain the best fit (best values of *a* and *b*) for the data in this example, we must start with some random initial values of *a* and *b*. Let the initial values be $a = 1$ and $b = 2$.

Then, for each collection center, the actual log(odds), fitted log(odds), and residuals are calculated and shown in Table 16.2. For example, for collection center 1, the calculations are illustrated here:

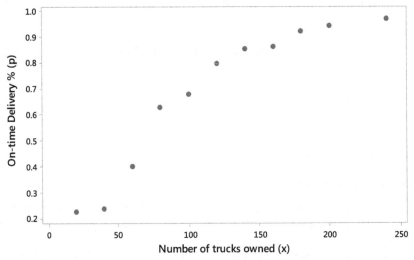

Scatterplot of On-time Delivery % (p) vs Number of trucks owned (x)

FIGURE 16.2
Scatter plot for data in first example.

TABLE 16.2

Residuals for First Example

Collection Center	Actual Log(Odds)	Fitted Log(Odds)	Residual
1	−1.24	41	−42.24
2	−1.17	81	−82.17
3	−0.41	121	−121.4
4	0.524	161	−160.5
5	0.745	201	−200.3
6	1.355	241	−239.6
7	1.758	281	−279.2
8	1.815	321	−319.2
9	2.456	361	−358.5
10	2.752	401	−398.2
11	3.409	481	−477.6

$$\text{Actual log(odds)} = \log(p/(1-p)) = \log(0.225/(1-0.225))$$

$$= \log(0.29) = -1.24$$

$$\text{Fitted log(odds)} = a + bx = 1 + 2 * 20 = 41$$

$$\text{Residual} = \text{Actual log(odds)} - \text{Fitted log(odds)}$$

$$= -1.24 - 41 = -42.24$$

The sum of squares of all of the residuals is then calculated as

$$(-42.24)^2 + (-82.17)^2 + ...(-477.6)^2 = 841,666$$

The Solver tool in Excel® can then be used as shown in the screenshot in Figure 16.3 to obtain the best values of a and b (J1 and J2 cells, respectively, in the screenshot), which minimize the sum of squares of residuals (G13 cell in the screenshot).

The best values of a and b, as given by the Solver tool, are −1.603 and 0.022, respectively, and the corresponding sum of squares of residuals is 0.655. Hence, the logistic regression model for this example is as shown in Equation 16.5:

$$p = \frac{e^{-1.603+0.022x}}{1+e^{-1.603+0.022x}} \tag{16.5}$$

Equation 16.5 can be used to predict the on-time delivery performance (p) of a collection center for a given number of trucks (x) owned by the collection center. For example, if $x = 90$ trucks, $p = 0.60$.

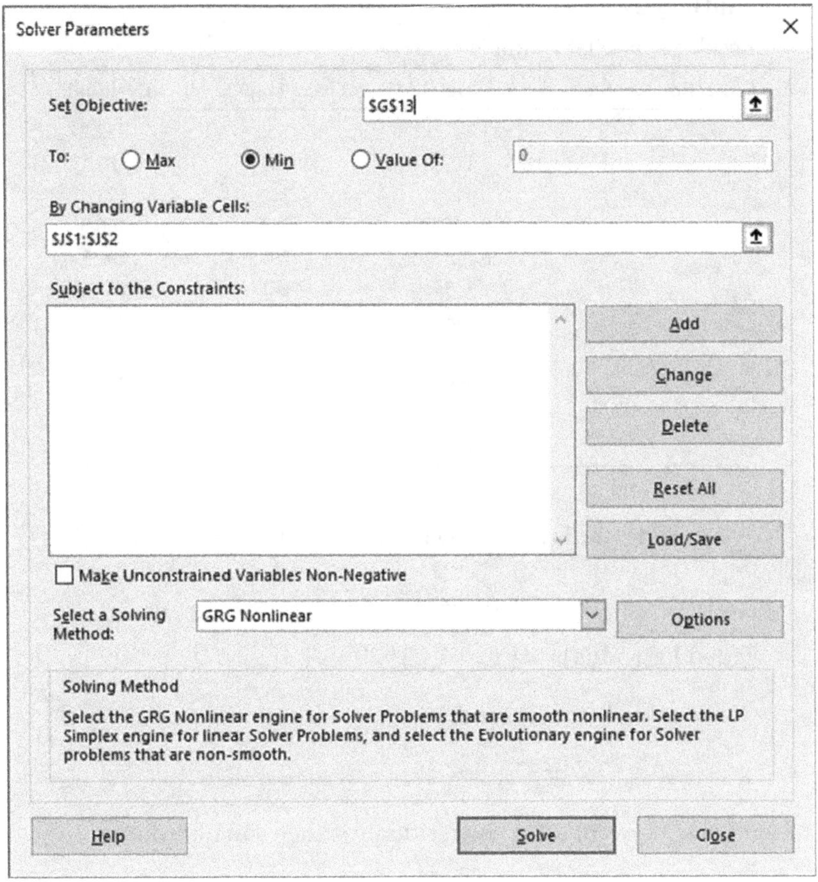

FIGURE 16.3
Solver tool in Excel® for first example.

Minitab® can be used to reproduce the above result in just a few steps, as follows:

i. Arrange the worksheet as in Table 16.3. Notice that the word "Actual" is removed from "Actual log(odds)," because otherwise, Minitab® would use the same label in the output, which is a regression equation for fitted log(odds).

ii. Stat -> Regression -> Fitted Line Plot (this opens the dialog box shown in Figure 16.4).

iii. Click on OK. This results in the graph and equation shown in Figure 16.5 (the minor difference from the Excel output is due to rounding error). A *p* value of .000 for *Regression* is also produced in the session window. Since this value is less than the standard level

TABLE 16.3

Minitab® Worksheet for First Example

Collection Center	x	Log(Odds)
1	20	−1.24
2	40	−1.17
3	60	−0.41
4	80	0.524
5	100	0.745
6	120	1.355
7	140	1.758
8	160	1.815
9	180	2.456
10	200	2.752
11	240	3.409

of significance (.05), it means that the logistic regression model is statistically significant.

16.4 Second Example

In this example, the following data, as shown in Table 16.4, are collected for 12 collection centers: age x (in years) of the machine used and whether the collection center met specifications in all of the last 50 orders. Notice that unlike in the first example, the dependent variable here is not a probability

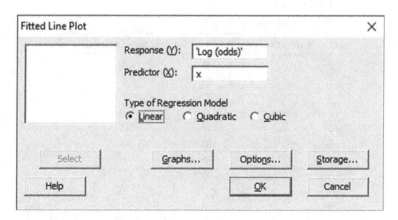

FIGURE 16.4
Minitab® dialog box for first example.

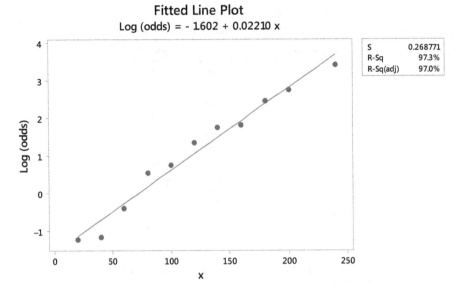

FIGURE 16.5
Minitab® output for first example.

but a binary variable (1 if specifications were met and 0 if not). Hence, the solution approach is slightly different from the one in the first example.

A scatter plot, shown in Figure 16.6, is plotted for the data in Table 16.4. Evidently, the plot shows (a mirror image of) an "S-curve," which motivates us to fit a logistic regression model as in Equation 16.1.

TABLE 16.4

Data for Second Example

Collection Center	x	Met Specifications?
1	57	1
2	73	0
3	22	1
4	59	0
5	15	1
6	36	1
7	68	0
8	49	0
9	27	0
10	59	0
11	10	1
12	78	0

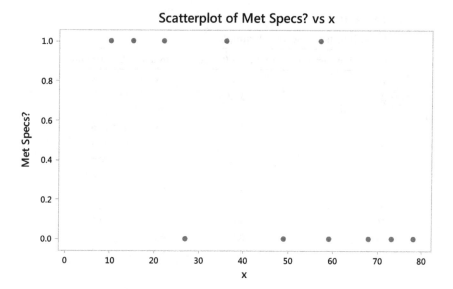

FIGURE 16.6
Scatter plot for data in second example.

To obtain the best fit (best values of *a* and *b*) for the data in this example, we must start with some random initial values of *a* and *b*. Let the initial values be $a = 0.03$ and $b = 0.05$.

Then, for each collection center, the fitted log(odds), the fitted probability (*p*) of meeting specifications, and the "likelihood" that we wish to maximize are calculated and shown in Table 16.5. For example, for collection center 1, the calculations are illustrated here:

$$\text{Fitted } \log(\text{odds}) = a + bx = 0.03 + 0.05 * 73 = 2.88$$

$$\text{Fitted } p = \frac{e^{\text{fitted(log(odds))}}}{1 + e^{\text{fitted(log(odds))}}} = \frac{e^{2.88}}{1 + e^{2.88}} = 0.95$$

Since collection center 1 did indeed meet specifications all the time, we wish to maximize the fitted *p* for this collection center. Another way of saying this is that we wish to maximize the "likelihood" of fitted *p* (.95) for this collection center. Let's look at another example (collection center 2):

$$\text{Fitted } \log(\text{odds}) = a + bx = 0.03 + 0.05 * 57 = 3.68.$$

$$\text{Fitted } p = \frac{e^{\text{fitted(log(odds))}}}{1 + e^{\text{fitted(log(odds))}}} = \frac{e^{3.68}}{1 + e^{3.68}} = 0.98$$

Since collection center 2 did not meet specifications all the time, we wish to minimize the fitted *p* (.98) for this collection center. Another way of saying

TABLE 16.5

Likelihoods for Second Example

Collection Center	Fitted Log(Odds)	Fitted p	Likelihood
1	2.88	.95	0.95
2	3.68	.98	0.02
3	1.13	.76	0.76
4	2.98	.95	0.05
5	0.78	.69	0.69
6	1.83	.86	0.86
7	3.43	.97	0.03
8	2.48	.92	0.08
9	1.38	.8	0.2
10	2.98	.95	0.05
11	0.53	.63	0.63
12	3.93	.98	0.02

this is that we wish to maximize the likelihood of $1 -$ fitted $p = 1 - 0.98 = 0.02$ for this collection center.

The best values of a and b are the ones that maximize the *product* of all of the likelihood values, that is, 0.95*0.02*0.76*………*0.02. Since it is mathematically difficult to maximize the *product* of all of these likelihoods, we calculate log(likelihood) for each collection center, as shown in Table 16.6, and then maximize the *sum* of all the log(likelihood) values. For example, for collection center 1, the calculations are illustrated here:

$$\text{Log}\left(\text{likelihood}\right) = \log\left(0.95\right) = -0.05$$

TABLE 16.6

Log(Likelihoods) for Second Example

Collection Center	Likelihood	Log(Likelihood)
1	0.95	−0.05
2	0.02	−3.7
3	0.76	−0.28
4	0.05	−3.03
5	0.69	−0.38
6	0.86	−0.15
7	0.03	−3.46
8	0.08	−2.56
9	0.2	−1.6
10	0.05	−3.03
11	0.63	−0.46
12	0.02	−3.95

The Solver tool in Excel® can then be used as shown in the screenshot in Figure 16.7 to obtain the best values of a and b (R1 and R2 cells, respectively, in the screenshot), which maximize the *sum* of log(likelihood) values (O15 cell in the screenshot).

The best values of a and b, as given by the Solver tool, are 3.49 and −0.09, respectively, and the corresponding *sum* of log(likelihood) values is −4.9. Hence, the logistic regression model for this example is as shown in Equation 16.6:

$$p = \frac{e^{3.49-0.09x}}{1+e^{3.49-0.09x}} \tag{16.6}$$

Equation 16.6 can be used to predict the probability (p) of a collection center meeting specifications all the time for a given age (x) of the machine used. For example, if $x = 45$ months, $p = .36$.

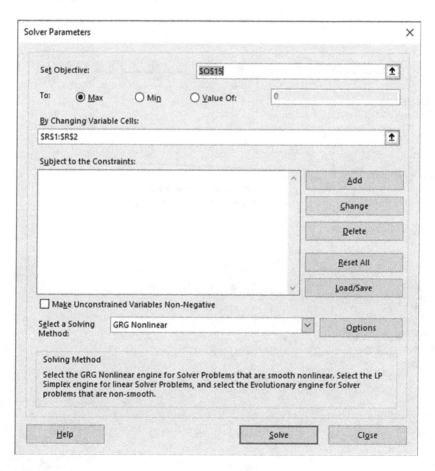

FIGURE 16.7
Solver tool in Excel® for second example.

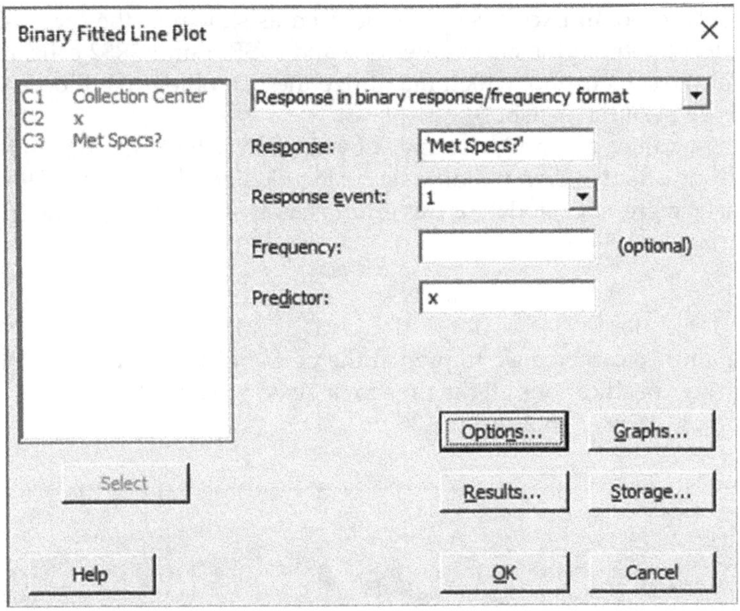

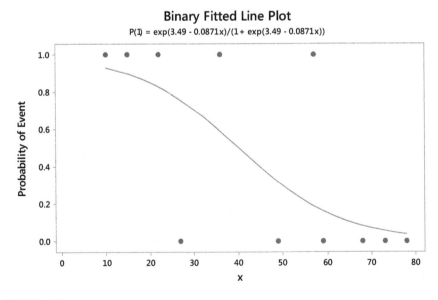

FIGURE 16.8
Minitab® dialog for second example.

Binary Fitted Line Plot

P(1) = exp(3.49 - 0.0871x)/(1 + exp(3.49 - 0.0871x))

FIGURE 16.9
Minitab® output for second example.

Minitab® can be used to reproduce this result in just a few steps, as follows:

i. Arrange the worksheet as in Table 16.4.
ii. Stat -> Regression -> Binary Fitted Line Plot (this opens the dialog box shown in Figure 16.8).
iii. Click on OK. This results in the graph and equation shown in Figure 16.9 (the minor difference from the Excel output is due to rounding error). A *p* value of .011 for *Regression* is also produced in the session window. Since this value is less than the standard level of significance (.05), it means that the logistic regression model is statistically significant.

16.5 Conclusions

This chapter demonstrated with two illustrative examples how to perform logistic regression to predict the efficiency of a collection center in a reverse supply chain.

References

Alkhayyal, B. A. and Gupta, S. M., *"A Linear Physical Programming Approach for Evaluating Collection Centers for End-Of-Life Products"*, Applications of Management Science, Emerald Publishing Limited, United Kingdom, Vol. 19, 65–79, 2018.

Groebner, D., Shannon, P. and Fry, P., *"Business Statistics: A Decision-Making Approach"*, Pearson, United States of America, 10th edition, ISBN: 978-0134496498, 2017.

Gungor, A. and Gupta, S. M., "Issues in environmentally conscious manufacturing and product recovery: A survey", *Computers and Industrial Engineering*, Vol. 36, No. 4, 811–853, 1999.

Gupta, S. M., *"Reverse Supply Chains: Issues and Analysis"*, CRC Press, Boca Raton, Florida, ISBN: 978-1439899021, 2013.

Gupta, S. M. and Ilgin, M. A., *"Multiple Criteria Decision Making Applications in Environmentally Conscious Manufacturing and Product Recovery"*, CRC Press, Boca Raton, Florida, ISBN: 978-1498700658, 2018.

Ilgin, M. A. and Gupta, S. M., "Environmentally conscious manufacturing and product recovery (ECMPRO): A review of the state of the art", *Journal of Environmental Management*, Vol. 91, No. 3, 563–591, 2010.

Pochampally, K. K. and Gupta, S. M., *"Six Sigma Case Studies with Minitab®"*, CRC Press, Boca Raton, Florida, ISBN: 978-1482205572, 2014.

Pochampally, K. K., Nukala, S. and Gupta, S. M., *"Strategic Planning Models for Reverse and Closed-loop Supply Chains"*, CRC Press, Boca Raton, Florida, ISBN: 9781420054781, 2009.

Author Index

Subject Index

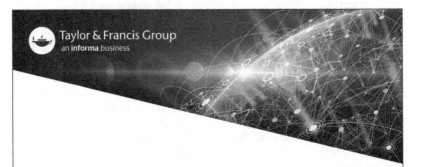